THE BRIDGE

THE ERNEST POOLES

THE BRIDGE
My Own Story

by
ERNEST POOLE

NEW YORK
THE MACMILLAN COMPANY
1940

Reprinted with the permission of the Original Publishers

JOHNSON REPRINT CORPORATION
New York • London

1971

SERIES IN AMERICAN STUDIES

Editor-in-Chief: Joseph J. Kwiat

PROGRAM OF AMERICAN STUDIES

UNIVERSITY OF MINNESOTA

FIRST PRINTING.

Library of Congress Catalog Card Number: 78-156934

First reprinting 1971, Johnson Reprint Corporation

Johnson Reprint Corporation
111 Fifth Avenue
New York, N.Y. 10003, U.S.A.

Johnson Reprint Company Ltd.
Berkeley Square House
London, W1X6BA, England

Printed in the U.S.A.

To M. A.

ILLUSTRATIONS

THE BRIDGE

I

WITH A GRAND WARM GLOW OF EXCITEMENT, WHEN I WAS A fat little five-year-old boy, I sat watching my mother with new eyes, as I listened to the story she told. Like our big brick house in Chicago, ever since I could remember (and let me tell you that can feel like a mighty long time when you're five years old) my mother had always meant for me absolute security—but now I heard a friend of hers draw out of her the dramatic account of how, nearly ten years before I was born, when she'd been slim and delicate, she had fought for the life of her baby, my sister, in the Chicago Fire of 1871. Years later, for her children, she wrote her story of that time. My mother was a quiet woman and her story was quietly told. Just as she told it, here it is:

"On Sunday night, October 8, 1871, your father and I went over on the West Side to the Third Church to service. As we were returning, we stopped on the Rush Street bridge, attracted by a light in the sky from a distant fire, but thought nothing of it. About midnight, however, back at home, we were awakened from a sound sleep by an unusual noise on the streets. We had just gone to housekeeping and were living on the North Side, near here, in a block of frame houses not far from the lake. I called to your father to get up and see the cause of such a stir at that hour of the night, and his exclamation from the window—'The sparks are raining on us!' was the first intimation I had of disaster.

"Your father went at once on the roof with the men from the adjoining houses to fight the burning brands with buckets

1

of water. I began packing. In blanket shawls I put all the silver and a change of clothing for each, instructing the two maids to pack what they most valued in the same manner. This done, I began filling trunks. The gas house had burned and our only light was the lurid glare of the fire on all sides of us and from the flying sparks, which, when the front door was opened, blew in showers clear back to the dining room. Your father came down from the roof and said:

"'Mary, you have lost your head. We are not going to burn.'

"But we were—for the words were hardly out of his mouth when the waterworks back of us caught and the water supply was cut off. We left the house. As I stepped out the door holding Marion, then but eight months old, followed by the two maids, the fire literally surrounded us and there was no choice of way to go. To the beach at the foot of Superior Street was the only opening. Fences, even trees were blazing and the wind blowing the red-hot sand like a sandstorm. I had on a blue and white flannel wrapper covered by a purple coat. My hat was soon lost. Marion was in her night clothes, with a coat wrapped around her. While the maids helped your father carry some of our things from the house to the sands and he found a wagon to bring the trunks, Baby and I mounted guard over our bundles. Looking back I could see all over the city great blasts of fire a hundred feet high.

"It was dawn, and still the fire raged. Your grandfather Howe then found us and suggested that on the baby's account we had better join a company of women and children going out on the lake in a tugboat leaving the lower pier near the river. So leaving your father and the servants with the household goods, I followed along the beach past crowds of hurrying refugees, with the red-hot sand driving in our faces. Suddenly, your grandfather—who carried in a great cloth bag the heavy silver communion cups of the Fourth Church—fell on the sand, gasping he could go no farther, but urging me on for the sake of the child. I almost ran—at intervals wading out into the water, holding the baby above the waves to try and cool her and help her to catch her breath as she struggled choking in my arms. Fortunately I met your uncle Charley, and he said:

" 'I'll leave my things and go with you.'

"When we reached the lumberyard we met a sea of fire. The piles upon piles of lumber were blazing and we were driven to the lake. As a gentleman by us remarked:

" 'We now have our choice, fire or water.'

"And so it was. My strength was almost gone, and had not Fredericka, the German nurse maid, been sent by your father to join me then, I fear I would have given out; but she took Baby and we turned out on a pier of stone, jumping from rock to rock, to reach the tugboat at the end. But it was so crowded, the captain refused to take another soul on board. Desperate people stood by begging to be carried away, and I saw one man take out a pistol and cry:

" 'I'll shoot you if you don't take me on!'

"But the tugboat steamed away. We hailed a man in a rowboat. He paid no attention to us until I held out money, and then he agreed to row us to the lighthouse at the mouth of the river. The lighthouse pier, as we disembarked there, caught on fire. Hastily the women and children were huddled inside, while the men with axes and water fought the flames. Fortunately a cow had wandered for safety out to the lighthouse, and Fredericka caught and milked her and fed Marion, who was by this time exhausted and starved, for it was now nearly noon. I collapsed and went up in the lighthouse to rest. Fredericka came to me and said:

" 'They are giving out the last provisions and you must come and get something.' Grudgingly they gave coffee and handed me a raw potato, saying: 'Don't eat it until you have to.' While I was drinking my coffee, your father appeared. He had a towel bound around his head and a bottle of brandy in his hand, and called: 'Are Mrs. Poole and family here?' and then fell flat on the floor in a faint.

"The excitement was so great, nobody felt sad or downhearted. People were all in the same box and excitedly told of their experiences, and greeted each new arrival, often friends and neighbors.

"It was by this time four o'clock of Monday afternoon, and your father decided to try for passage on a tug plying the river from the lighthouse to the West Side. We went on the second load. How awful was that trip through the city! The dense smoke—the flying, burning brands! As I bent over the gasping baby, blowing through a wet shawl into her mouth to give her air, a man touched me on my arm and said:

" 'My God, Madam! Is it a baby? No baby can get through this alive!'

"But he was wrong, for I kept working and so we came through the smoke and flames. We were landed at the North Western Station and, hurrying on board a train, told the conductor to take us to the first place where we could get a decent hotel, and so found ourselves at nightfall in Elgin. The people there couldn't do enough for us. We were the first refugees and fire curiosities, as well we may have been with our bedraggled clothing and smoke-blackened faces. To our kind new friends your father said:

" 'Already people are starving back there. I've got to have a few hours' sleep but at daybreak I'll be ready to lead your young men back into the city. Cook all the food and coffee you can.'

"All night the good people of Elgin cooked and worked; and in the morning the young men, led by your father, carried great bags and baskets and cans of food and coffee by train back into the city, which was half smoking ruins now, and so fed the starving people on the sands where we had left them. Your grandfather had been badly burned, but had gone to the West Side to stay with friends. He had saved nothing.

The Bridge 5

His trunks on the beach had been rifled by thieves. Our own things, however, were found intact, so in a few days we had our trunks and comparative comfort. Your father opened an office in a stable that same week, and so we began life again, living at first on the West Side. Many years later it came about that your father was able to build, on the ruins of Grandfather Howe's old home, the house which is our home today, at 89 Pine Street (which is North Michigan Avenue now)."

All this had happened long ago. But the story of my mother's battle for her baby's life was often told among her friends and, at a dinner of businessmen given to celebrate the swift rebuilding of the city, it was made the climax of the principal speaker's address. He rose to such emotional heights that my father, deeply moved, wiped his eyes and said to the speaker:

"Judge, I think we should be told the name of this heroic young woman." The disgusted judge replied:

"Why, Poole, you damned fool, she's your own wife!"

And when I heard the story first, that day when I was so very small, it moved me as it had my dad. My mother! My own mother—so safe and quiet—like our house! And she'd gone through those roaring flames! With a hot swelling in my throat, I stared at her, struck speechless. What was the world coming to, if things could happen to *her* like that? It was long before I could sleep that night. I little dreamed of what the world would really come to in my time or of how, from the safety I had known, I was to be driven by winds of change over the long bridge of years into the vast fury raging in the world today. I was only a fat little boy, who'd been so thrilled by the story he'd heard that he could almost see his mother fighting her way through smoke and flames. For though it was twelve years or more before I even began to think of writing stories all my life, the fascination they had for me goes so far back I can't even remember when I heard the first one told.

More were told to me now by our new nurse, who came that year to my young brother Abram and me. Irish American, young and gay, her stories were of Irish fairies—leprechauns, she called them—perfectly gorgeous little yarns. And the greatest thrill about them was that in nearly every one the bad little fairy came out on top! She was always ready to play games and she had two new ones, all her own, games of which we must not speak even to our mother, she said; they were secrets between herself and us. One we called The Magic Trunk. In our big nursery closet she had a huge trunk which she kept locked but, when she came home from her afternoons out, she would first blindfold the two of us, then enter the closet and open the trunk. Breathless we'd wait till she clapped her hands. Then tearing off our bandages we'd see that the trunk was locked again and our young nurse stood smiling there, with a gift for each of us. Another game she called Magic Hands. She was a clever seamstress and, with the family mending piled on a low table, she'd sit on one side while we sat on the other. This was our most exciting game, for her object was to get us so absorbed in the fairy story she told that neither one of us would see her snatch something from the low table between. As she reached the climax of her tale, try as we would to keep our eyes glued to the sewing in her lap, up they would go to follow the flight of some bad little leprechaun into the sky. In that instant out would flash a hand and, before we could see it, she would laugh and gaily cry that she had won and show us the small garment she'd snatched from the table right under our eyes!

Oh, what a wonderful nurse for two boys! She stayed for about six months in our house. Then one night we were aroused in our beds by a loud commotion in the hall. Our mother came in, with two big rough men. Quickly they searched the room and the closet and then ran off to search the whole house. Badly scared by their roughness, we begged for our nurse but were told she was gone. It was not until years later I learned she had slipped out the back door that night and that she had been one of the cleverest shoplifters in the Middle West! Our gifts had come from Marshall Field's. Regretfully we gave them back and wondered where our nurse had gone?

As a good safe place from which to work, she had picked our house because it was one of the most respectable in town. For we were what our mother called "dyed in the blue Presbyterians." Our Grandfather Howe had been deeply religious. The old North Church had held its first meeting right in his house and, when it combined with another to form the Fourth Church, the communion cups and salvers were kept by Grandmother Howe, and she always baked and cut the communion bread with her own hands. When on that night of the Great Fire our grandfather was overcome on the beach by the weight of the heavy cups, he buried them there in the sand. When he came back next day they were gone. Somebody had stolen them. But then came a touch of that irony which the life of this graceless world does sometimes turn on righteous men. For Grandfather Howe had stood rigidly against any church creed but his own; and so it was a hard pill to swallow when, about a year after the Fire, a large cloth bag was left at his door, with the communion silver intact and a note by the thief explaining that in confessional his priest had sternly ordered him to return these sanctified articles to their home. Such a proof of generous power from the detested Church of Rome cut into Grandfather Howe like a knife!

Grandmother lived with us after he died. Though strong in her religion and morals, she was a woman with hosts of friends. On New Year's Day they came to our house, where from ten in the morning till night she served her famous fruit cake and eggnog. But she was forever helping the poor and visiting some of the worst of our slums. Not far from our house down toward the lake, then only a few hundred feet away, was a notorious district of shanties known to the police as The Patch. Her many generous visits there left such an impression that, when she died, the Patch turned out for her funeral and their main saloon was closed for the day.

After Grandmother was gone, our mother faithfully carried on the religious tradition. Though she often gave parties and made social calls, she not only brought up seven children but still found time for charity work and for church activities. Every Sunday we children went first to church and after that to Sunday school. In the infant class so righteous was I that I looked with holy horror on the rude boy next to me, who whispered profanity into my ear. When he saw how I felt, he would chuckle and say:

"You think I'll go to hell for this!"

And I couldn't deny it. I thought he would. Joe Patterson was his name. He became a good friend of mine later on. He now controls the New York Daily News.

But religion brought no gloom in our home. With seven children, four girls and three boys, the big house hummed from morning to night. Around one side of it was a yard, with a red brick stable at the rear. Here we lived and worked and played in absolute security. I look back now and wonder how Mother ever managed us all? Our father couldn't help her much for, though a kindly generous man, he often came home to us at night with nerves strained to the breaking point by his day on the Board of Trade. Whenever anyone mentioned the Wheat Pit, I learned to glance quickly at my mother to see the dark shadow that came in her eyes. In the daytime she had not only her children but the whole household on her hands. Dresses, shirts, underclothes, bed linen, nearly all were made in the house. Twice a year our "sewing woman" arrived and our mother worked at her side. She taught her daughters to do it, too. Their underclothes were all tucked by hand and trimmed with ruffles of embroidery. Much of this they did themselves. Our mother used to say to them:

"It's not enough to be good or pretty. You've got to be something much more than that to meet this new day!" For even in that safe world of ours, my mother felt the breath of change.

Until one by one they went East to school, the girls worked with a governess in our long schoolroom downstairs. We worked there, too, when we were small. In that same room, for the girls and their friends, an afternoon dancing class was held. Their teacher at first was old Mr. Bournique, who taught dancing to "all Chicago," those days. He danced holding the skirts of his long frock coat, for that was considered elegant. Later one of his sons took our class, and now we boys were forced to attend; and scowling at my partner, I learned my polka, galop, military schottische and waltz.

Except for my four sisters and my cousin, Blossom Cook, I had no use whatever for girls. But Bloss was almost as good as a boy. From Evanston on Saturdays she came with other cousins to play in our big attic through glorious noisy afternoons, with express wagons racing up and down, fire engines going to fires, armies charging on forts made of trunks. We had a carpenter's bench up there and I let my imagination run wild over the wonderful things I would make. Excitedly I whispered to Bloss Cook one afternoon that by next Saturday, when she came, I would have a flying machine and with it we'd jump off the roof and go a flying up the street! I remember her disappointment next week when she arrived, in a freshly starched white dress and pink sash, all agog for our flight, and I had to tell of my shattered dream!

Though we had our own tree on Christmas Day, I liked still better Christmas Eve, when we went out to Evanston. I remember the dark snowy streets and the fine crunch of our steps up the walk to Aunt Mattie Walcott's frame house, the

Christmas tree with gifts for us all and the songs that we sang
after supper, with aunts and uncles and cousins of all ages
around the piano. My father did not come on these trips. Instead, he gathered a dozen working boys from the city
streets, bought for each one a new outfit of clothes and then,
after a jolly restaurant dinner, took them all to the theater.
On nights before the holiday he read to us The Christmas
Carol, and this was how he lived up to its creed. Sometimes,
in these modern days of what an Irish poet called "Organized
charity measured and iced, in the name of a cautious statis-
tical Christ," I think of Dad's parties on Christmas Eve. Sentimental, extravagant, random charity? Call them all the names
you like. But they must have been warm genial times. My
father loved Dickens. So did I.

Christmas joys were by no means all the fun we had in
wintertime. With cousins and friends we made snow men
and forts for snow fights in our yard and drove in our two-
horse sleigh, which had red tassels and tinkling bells and two
tall red plumes at the front. Fast cutters would go madly by.
We were not allowed to hitch with our sleds and, with black
envy in my heart, as I watched the jolly ragged boys, whose
mothers let them do as they liked, dash by on sleds tied to
wagons or sleighs, I thought:

"Gosh, but it's tough not to be poor!"

It was equally tough to be too small to play with the Cyrus
McCormick boys, whose great handsome brownstone house
rose only a block away from our own. With one of them,
Harold, my oldest sister had once run a lemonade stand on
our corner, giving a stick of candy to everyone who would
buy five cups. Though their family was close to ours, Harold
and Stanley were much too big to care to play with little kids
like my brother Abram and me. Down the street would come
their stout pony with six or eight sleds in a long string behind,
the pony galloping like mad to "crack the whip" around our
corner and sending half of them head over heels. I saw one

boy nearly bust his head! When would I be old enough to have a real good time like that?

We had three horses in our barn and often we went there on rainy days to take long exciting dives through the hay chutes to the stables below. In bed at night, I used to love to listen to carriages, jingling harness, thuds of hoofs on wooden pavements. The streets were paved with cedar blocks and, when they were torn up for repair, we used to build block houses there. In place of the modern street lights were gas lampposts at that time, and at nightfall I would wait for my friend, Joe the lamplighter, who sometimes let me carry his long flaring kerosene torch. Fire engines thundered by, with gong clanging, horses tearing and the fire-station dog racing and barking just ahead! Where was the fire? we would ask. If only just once it could be in our house!

No such luck ever came our way, but I did get a little thrill out of my friend the junkman who, croaking "Rags and iron," slowly drove his old wagon down the alley behind our barn. To him for a few pennies I sold what iron and rags I could find in our house. But the pennies were not the attraction. For me his fascination lay in his harsh guttural croaking voice, his dirty face with ragged beard and his strange deep tragic eyes. For he came from a world I knew nothing about, and even then I loved to explore into all that was strange in this queer big human adventure of ours.

When I was still only six years old, I was given my first bike. It had a big wheel with a small one behind, and you had to look out or you would "take a header" right over the handle bars. I took one myself one afternoon, headfirst into the garbage can, and was given a terrible bath that night! Spring came and elm trees budded all along our quiet street, which is Michigan Avenue today. No rush and roar of traffic then. In the evenings, rugs were spread on front stoops and neighbors came to sit with us, or an old man across the street called to our mother:

"Mary, bring over those monkeys of yours. I've got some lemonade for them."

Our father flew kites with us boys on the street and on other evenings we played with children in the neighborhood. Often in the afternoons our sisters took us out with them. My legs were short and I was fat; and so, as those girls raced me along in their favorite game of I Spy, with my Neapolitan cap nearly slipping off my head, I would shout protests at such speed. But my indignation could always be stopped by the promise of ice cream after the game, or candy at Madam Marie's little shop. The photographic studio of old Max Platz was not far from there, and he once took a picture of Abram and me dressed up as Mr. and Mrs. Tom Thumb. In these costumes, for the reward of a stick of candy for each, at home we would come solemnly in and sing at Mother's supper parties. On one such night, I heard some most respectable ladies, stiffly dressed in gowns with huge bustles billowing up in the back of their chairs, discuss how shocking and disgusting was this thing called "dress reform," introduced by the early suffragists. And it must have been soon after this, as one of my sisters has told me since, that when I was going "over town" with her on a shopping trip, suddenly I spied on a wall a huge glamorous poster depicting young Lillian Russell in tights. I stopped with a jerk, off came my cap and unconsciously I stroked my smooth shining bang of hair, a habit I had when thinking hard.

"Who's that lady?"

"An actress."

"What's that?"

"Nothing you need to know about." And my sister tried to drag me on. But still I balked, with my questioning eyes glued to that fascinating dame. Then suddenly my expression cleared.

"I see!" I said. "It's dress reform!"

We often shopped at Marshall Field's, then called Field and

Leiter's and occupying at that time only a quarter of a block. The show windows were in charge of young Harry Selfridge, the floorwalker, who soon became the manager. He was a stocky man with chop whiskers; in his tight-fitting frock coat, I often saw him bustling about or standing at the entrance door on the corner of State and Washington streets. My father said of him one night:

"There's a young man who will go far. He's offering their employees a dollar apiece for all good ideas for the improvement of the store."

He was married in Central Music Hall and, during the wedding service, the Lord's Prayer was chanted by the twelve bridesmaids from their seats in the orchestra in the front row. Years later he went to London to start his own great enterprise, which is now so widely known all over the English-speaking world.

Marshall Field himself in those early days was often to be seen in his store, inspecting every department each week. Born and bred in Massachusetts and now an elderly handsome man with iron-gray mustache and hair, I remember his bright smiling eyes, low voice and air of elegance. My two older sisters went to dancing school with his son. Many years later one of them, who had married and gone East, came back for a time and, shopping at Field's one afternoon, she came out to the roar of motor traffic. While she stood looking for a taxi, suddenly a resonant voice behind her bellowed:

"Miss Poole's carriage!" She turned with a start and discovered the beaming old doorman of early days.

"Do you remember," he asked her, "how I took a cinder out of your eye here one afternoon?"

In the great modern city, she told me, it was good to feel one's self for a moment back in the old neighborly town. I had the same kind of a welcome myself years later, at the recent World's Fair. I had motored from Cleveland that day and I was dog-tired. It was a hot night. As I swung into the boulevard on the lake front to the south, I stopped by a spruce young traffic cop and leaning out I said to him:

"I was born in this city; it's home to me still—and I'm so damned sick of the traffic rules in New York, where I've had to live ever since, that I want to know how fast I can go in Chicago, now that I'm back." He reached promptly into my little car and, with his hand on my shoulder, said:

"Boy, open her up to forty-five!"

And so I did. It was good to be home!

II

Just before I was seven years old, with my older brother Ralph I went to the University School for boys. There seemed to be hundreds of them at first, nearly all much older than myself, but nobody bothered me and I soon felt quite at home. On our first declamation day, up to the high platform I marched with never a thought of being scared; but then I turned to speak my piece, and one look at the ocean of faces below brought my heart into my throat. In vain for a moment I struggled to speak. My voice a weak croak, I swallowed and glared, burst into tears and ran to my desk, and there, to a roar of laughter that came from all around the room, I buried my hot head in my hands. School was utterly spoiled for me now! But on that same afternoon, an older boy of about fourteen came to me out in the yard and, with a wonderful kindly smile, asked me what I was so scared about.

"It's easy enough to speak a piece. You just have to get used to it," he said.

I can't remember anything he said or did for me after that, except to smile at me now and then. But his position in the school put a stop to the jeers at my expense. For he was Jack Lincoln, grandson of the President, and all Chicago was talking then of the Saint Gaudens statue just unveiled in Lincoln Park. I had been up there myself with my mother, to stare at that bronze figure of the gaunt lean man from Illinois. And now his grandson Jack was my friend! I adored him, and in my worship I swore I would show him I was no 'fraidy cat. On the next declamation day his turn came just before my own. From the platform he looked down with a smile and began in a slow reverent tone:

"Fourscore and seven years ago our fathers brought forth upon this continent a new nation, dedicated to the proposition that all men are created equal." I did not know what piece he was speaking. Only bits of it reached my ears: "We are met on a great battle field. . . . The brave men, living and dead . . . that this nation under God may have a new birth of freedom, and that government of the people, by the people and for the people, shall not perish from the earth!"

All my life I was to remember those words as the creed of a grand religion I found. But then I was only a fat little boy who stared up at that boy whom he adored; and the light I saw shining in Jack's eyes so lifted me out of my blind fears that, when my turn came a few minutes later, I hurried up to the platform and—stammering, stopping to swallow hard, but fiercely struggling on and on—I got through my short piece to the end. And then with a tingling glow I saw Jack Lincoln leading the applause. When I got back to my desk, I was so happy I wanted to cry! I looked at that wonderful boy and thought:

"You'll be President yourself someday!"

But Jack Lincoln couldn't be—for only a little after that he fell suddenly ill and died.

At home were other reminders of the great war President. As a young girl, my mother had gone, in a dress of white tarleton trimmed with black velvet, to Lincoln's first inaugural ball. My father, when only a boy of eighteen, had been in Sherman's army marching through Georgia to the sea. In a corner house opposite ours lived old Sam Johnson, whose friend General Sheridan often came to stay with him there; and on Sundays an endless procession of buggies or sleighs drove slowly by, with the occupants craning their necks for a glimpse of the famous cavalryman. And in a house just up the street lived old Isaac Arnold, who still wore an imposing black stock and whose big keen eagle eyes looked out from under heavy white brows. As one of Lincoln's right-hand men in the Congress of war days, he had introduced the resolution to abolish slavery.

But if the Negroes had been freed, there were still in this country men who felt that their condition was only another kind of slavery. Already in the great new grimy factories and mills, in which the machine age had been born, such men were stirring up the workers to another civil war that was to last all the rest of my life and which I was to see and write about. I had no inkling of it then but, through another close neighbor of ours, in that same year of 1886, I caught my first glimpse of a darker and more dangerous life outside. In a house only a block away lived Judge Gary, an elderly man who often passed with his little dog and, in a house just up the street, read Shakespeare aloud on Sunday nights. And now suddenly this old man became the central figure in an uproar nation-wide.

In Chicago and through the Middle West, a depression had started two years before and, as conditions grew steadily worse, hundreds of thousands lost their jobs and in riots and demonstrations fought bloody street battles against the police and the hated "Pinks," as the Pinkerton detectives were called. Among the more radical leaders was a small group of anarchists, nearly all of them foreign born, who in their speeches spoke of dynamite as a symbol of the people's rights. When in April 1885 an inaugural banquet of businessmen, my father among them, was held one night in the newly erected building of the Board of Trade, crowds of workingmen gathered outside, booing and waving red and black flags—black for starvation, red for the blood of humanity. From a wagon Albert Parsons, a fiery young editor born in Alabama, who had come from Texas to Chicago a few years before, urged the crowd to march on "this Board of Thieves" roar-

ing out the Marseillaise. And a German anarchist, Samuel
Fielding, bitterly shouted to the mob:

"How long will you sit down to your fifteen-cent meals
while those fellows inside are sitting down to a banquet at
twenty dollars a plate?"

Police reserves dispersed the crowd and there was no violence that night, but other such demonstrations occurred and
there was talk of a general strike. All that next year the tension grew and on May 3, 1886, in a riot outside the McCormick plant, one striker was killed and six badly wounded by
the police. August Spies, a German anarchist editor who had
been a speaker there, issued next day a circular with the title
—"Workingmen, to Arms!" It attacked employers and police
and concluded:

"If you are men, if you are sons of your grandsires who
have shed their blood to free you, then you will rise in your
might, Hercules, and destroy the hideous monster that seeks
to destroy you! To arms we call you, to arms!"

As the feeling in the city rapidly grew more ominous still,
a few days later, at a mass meeting addressed by Fielding,
Parsons and Spies on the West Side in Haymarket Square, the
speeches were not so violent and, as a drizzling rain set in,
the leaders, to keep the crowd together, were planning to
move the meeting into some hall in the neighborhood, when
from the adjoining streets some two hundred police marched
in and ordered the mob to disperse. And in that next minute,
with a blinding flash and roar, the first bomb ever thrown in
America exploded in the dense ranks of police, killing one and
wounding seventy-three. The rest opened fire on the crowd
and shot some sixty of them down.

Scare headlines in the papers next day, in Chicago and all
over the land:

"Now It Is Blood! . . . Work of Death Begins! . . . Howling
Assassins Rush to Hiding!"

In Chicago all radical centers were raided by the police,

who made wholesale arrests. Eight anarchist leaders were brought to trial and, although it was never proved that any one of them threw the bomb, as accessories to the crime and because they had publicly incited to violence for years, Parsons, Spies, Engel, Lingg and Fischer were condemned to death and the others to imprisonment. Young Lingg killed himself in his cell, but Parsons, Spies, Engel and Fischer, in November of that year, were hanged in the Cook County jail. Young Parsons had not been arrested but had come out of hiding to give himself up and stand trial with the rest. On the gallows, before the trap was sprung, he cried:

"Let the voice of the people be heard!"

Nearly twenty years later I met his wife, an elderly Spanish-Indian woman who had big dark poignant eyes. With a quiet smile she told me:

"In the war they freed the Negroes. My husband died to free the whites."

I knew nothing of all this at the time. From my safe little world looking eagerly out, this is what I saw and heard. 'Way over on the West Side, I was told, some terrible men called anarchists had thrown bombs and killed many brave police and had been put in jail for it, to be tried for murder and hanged, so that decent people could be safe. But for me the greatest thrill of all was the fact that our old neighbor, Judge Gary, was to be their judge, and that both the court and the jail were only a few blocks from our house! Already the judge was getting letters that threatened to kill the brave old man if he dared to hang those murderers! And so close was our house to his, who could tell but what we'd be blown up, too, by a howling mob some night with bombs?

"They'll surely kill him!" the women cried. "Bombs will be thrown! We're none of us safe!"

Even our mother grew so stirred up that she wanted my brother Ralph and me to be taken to school by the coachman. Our father cried—"Rubbish!"—and refused. But next morning on our way to school, I looked back and saw him following far behind. When school was over we moved to the country for the summer and missed the trial. But next autumn on our return to town, as the day of the executions drew near, we went and stared up at the high barred windows of the jail, where the murderers were, and with pity and horror I grew icy cold, as I pictured them with ropes 'round their necks swinging and kicking in mid-air! When it was all over, one afternoon back in our quiet neighborhood, safe for decent people once more, from her house across the street an old lady rushed over and rang our doorbell and, when our mother came, cried:

"For God's sake, Mary, get your child! He's hanging out of the attic window!"

Racing up, she found me there, leaning out of the open window holding the hands of my brother Abram, aged five, and swinging him slowly to and fro. After the rescue, she scolded me well, but in an injured tone I said:

"I wasn't doing anything—only just showing Abe how it feels to be hanged by the neck until you are dead."

Though I had no use for anarchists, I knew they were trying to help the poor; and my sympathies were with them there, for my mother was always doing that. To the Presbyterian Hospital, the Half Orphan Asylum and the homes of poor families she often went, and sometimes she took us along. We went often with her to the West Side to see old Miss Parsons—Parsy, we called her—who had been our sewing woman and still came to help at our house. What horror poor Parsy must have felt when a man whose name was the same as hers was hanged for inciting to violence! For Parsy was no revolutionist. She lived with her sister, Mrs. Dyke, whose husband had once owned a farm over there but had sold it for a song, before the boisterous city came rushing out onto the prairie to bring a boom. And now, right where their farm had been, with large sooty factories and tenements all around them, the two old women lived in a crazy little frame house in a back yard.

They had come from England when they were small. They made for us plum pudding for Christmas and at Eastertime hot cross buns and, when we went to see them, they feasted us with tea, cookies and cake. I remember the welcoming smile on Parsy's wrinkled face, the black crocheted cap and apron she wore and the bag of pink and white peppermints tucked in her black reticule for us, when she came to our house. She had many stories to tell of her life in England as a small girl; and she sang a song called "The Poor Little Sweep," which brought delicious tears in my eyes. It was grand to feel so sad and nice and yet know that in a minute or two we would come to the happy ending I'd heard so many times before. I loved that old woman and for many years I wrote to her nearly every week. Often I thought how tough it was that, just because of the one mistake made in selling that farm too soon, she couldn't be rich and had to be poor. And when I read shining accounts of the thrift, the industry, the patience and all the other virtues by which our early pioneers grew to be great millionaires, I thought of Parsy and wondered why *her* virtues had not been rewarded like that? And yet upon the other hand, I loved her rickety little house. And this feeling she had stirred may have had a good deal to do with my work as a writer later on. For not only did I hotly rebel against the hard conditions of life among people in the tenements, but I honestly liked being with them. And Parsy had started me feeling like that.

But in the years when I was small, my sympathy for this old friend brought a mighty awkward moment to my mother in our house. For Parsy was nearly seventy then and she had been weak and ailing that spring and I had heard my mother say:

"I'm afraid poor Parsy won't last through the summer."

Soon after that she came to our house and, while she sat with us at lunch, my pity and curiosity grew to a point where I felt I must speak.

"Parsy, do you think you'll last through the summer?" I abruptly asked. The poor old creature turned with a start.

"Why, yes, my dear, of course I will."

"Mother doesn't think so," I said. And it made me pretty doggoned sore when, with a quick embarrassed laugh, my mother cried:

"Ernest, you terrible boy, I think nothing of the kind!"

Gloomily I looked down at my plate. So my mother was a liar, eh?

Parsy did live, and for several years she still came to stay with us, when Mother went away on trips to rest cures with my father, or to see my sisters at school. One after the other, with sobs and tears, my three older sisters, when I was still small, departed East to boarding school. The oldest went when she was fourteen. For weeks before she started, Mother and our sewing woman made piles and piles of blue and white frocks and petticoats and other such things. In vain my sister begged for bustles.

"Absurd at your age!" our mother replied.

She wanted a Lillie Langtry bang but this also was denied. Off she went at last from home, with a gold watch from Father and from Mother a blue locket inclosing samples of hair of each of us. Mother went with her and took me along, for the first big trip I'd ever made. By train to Philadelphia we went and from there by hack out to Ogontz, which was then at the height of its fame as a stylish but respectable and religious finishing school. It stood in lovely spacious grounds given by its wealthy supporter, Jay Cooke, the powerful banker who had acted for our government to finance the Civil War. I had a glimpse of him that day, a tall white-haired imposing old man walking beneath the chestnut trees. Fifty young lady pupils arrived, each one with credentials from the minister of her church at home. My sister had a dozen

such letters to prove our strength with divinity men, and our
mother gave them all to the little Lady Principal, who received
us in a black silk dress and black lace cap with a purple bow.

Nearly every spring while the girls were at school, Mother
took my young brother and me to Atlantic City, so that our
sisters could join us for Easter vacation there. The two principal hotels were the Brighton and the Traymore. Of the
Brighton we did not approve. It was full of Episcopalians
and fashionable women, and even some "fast women," too.
With interest I used to watch the big-bustled ladies who came
out, to see just how fast they could go. If that was fast, I
asked myself, how on earth did a lady walk to be slow?

The Traymore was respectable and Presbyterian, right in
our line. In that immense frame building, on stormy nights I
used to lie listening from my bed to the winds that howled
and shook it so, and thinking of the sailors all over the ocean
in the storm, trying to get into good safe harbors. My lifelong feeling for harbors and ships was planted deep in me,
those nights. In the afternoons my small brother and I loved
to go to the beach, build heaps of sand and pretend they were
islands and we were marooned. Each on his island, we'd stay
until dark, when the incoming tide all around us grew so
deep we had to wade ashore. Our greatest excitement came
in fights with a gang of small boys at the hotel. There were
five of them and two of us but, when they downed us, I
wouldn't give in.

"Wait till our sisters get here," I said. "They'll help us
fight you. They're both big. Each one of 'em weighs twice
as much as you do."

They were interested. We all weighed ourselves and, when
my two sisters arrived from school a little before supper one
night, in the stylish new Easter suits that Mother had bought
them in Philadelphia, a line of keenly expectant small boys
stood eying them closely at the door, to try to judge how
heavy they were. Deep was our disappointment when those
girls refused to fight!

III

For us the best time in all the year came at our summer home in Lake Forest, north of Chicago on the lake shore. School over and a whole summer ahead! We went by train and were met by jolly old Sam Dent, the colored man who owned the livery out there. A slave down South before the war, deep notches had been cut in his ears so that he'd be marked if he ran away. He was prosperous now, and so jolly and kind that we boys fought for places beside him on the front seat of his livery rig. Some years later when he died, so loved was he by his summer friends that on the day of his funeral most of the men stayed home from business and, with their sons big and little, on foot, followed the kindly old man to his grave.

For Lake Forest in those early years was no large region of handsome estates but a personal lovable place, a simple village, with only two score of summer homes. No telephones, no electric lights, and not even a telegram was delivered unless the local agent could find some boy in the village to ride down to our house on his bike. Our house was an ample frame affair with covered porches around three sides. It stood upon a shadowed lawn, with dozens and scores of lovely trees of all sizes and kinds for us to climb, along the edge of an eighty-foot bluff rising from the lake below. A deep ravine was at either end, and inland over across the road were our pastures, gardens and greenhouse. There was a barn, with horses and cows, and a chicken house, which we managed,

24

close by. And we had many secret places down in the deep cool ravines.

In vain we begged our mother to let us go out on the lake, in a small leaky scow that we had made. It was much too dangerous, she said. But we had a small pier, where we fished for perch and thought of the Indians in canoes who had come by this way to Chicago, only fifty years before. We built rickety rafts and poled them about. Forbidden to go in swimming or even to wade, for the water was cold, we could not disobey our mother, so we went in hopping instead. And all this time her warnings of danger out on that great windy lake seemed silly to us, till one awful night, when a boy our older brother knew rode up on his pony with the news that a friend of theirs had been drowned. Did Mother say: I told you so? She did not. She sat perfectly still. One by one we kissed her and crept silently up to bed. Long after my brothers had gone asleep I lay there, chilled by some great darkness pressing down. I had liked that boy. I could hear still his jolly laugh, see his bright gay challenging eyes. All ended now, sunk deep in water black and cold! They were dragging for his body tonight! . . . At last I heard Mother. Swish, swish, swish—her long dress came up the stairs. Softly she opened our door and came in, as she always did at night. I lay without stirring, without breathing. She noticed it and whispered:

"Are you asleep?"

I reached out sharply and gripped her hand. She sat down and slowly her other hand stroked mine till at last my hold relaxed and, with that strange and dark and horrible heavy feeling lifted from me, I fell asleep.

But shocks like that were soon forgotten in our busy summer life. I remember a secret tunnel we found under one end of a bridge extending across a ravine. The tunnel was some thirty feet long and so small that even little boys had to wriggle and crawl to get through. My older brother tried it first. When he came out at the other end, I asked him how it was in there. Grimly he told me it was fine. So I tried it. Halfway through I poked my head into the wasps' nest he had met. They were pretty angry now and, crawl and wriggle fast as I could, I came out with stings all over me. Quickly concealing all signs of pain, I told my trusting innocent five-year-old little brother that it was perfectly swell in there. Poor kid! I can still remember his howls and the mud with which we plastered him!

Our gardener was old Tim Howe. Tim knew about all kinds of things and liked to tell us about them. Our mother had small use for him; she said he told things all day long. But Tim was so human and Irish and nice. Though good-natured with us as a rule, what a rage he would fly into when we robbed or trampled his gardens—hurling stones or shaking a stick as he chased us out of his domain. He knew such wonderful cuss words, too. Once, when a lucky throw of mine with a stone hit him on his hand, not even the terror of my flight, with old Tim thundering close behind, could quite spoil my hot delight in the terrible things he was calling me!

And Tim was not only human but wise. As local justice of the peace, he sometimes heard cases right in our garden; and at such times I would stand near, watching and listening, thrilled by the angry voices and eyes of these people who brought to Tim their disputes. For these disputes were often almost as good as regular stories, and stories were a passion of mine. Slowly and patiently chewing his quid and generously giving his time—not his but ours, my mother said—Tim would hear them out to the end and then, in a shrewd and sensible tone, would talk until they quieted down. And when at last they went away with all their troubles settled by Tim, he would look at his big silver watch and discover it was time for lunch.

A great event for us each year was the coming of some three hundred children from the Half Orphan Asylum in the city out to our home. In hayracks they arrived from the train, shouting and cheering. All day we helped our parents and sisters lead them in games and picnic with them on our lawn. Soon making friends among the boys, we took them down to the beach and ravines. One year I liked one of them so well that I stuck to him all day long. Every time that I showed him some treasured secret place of mine or my fishhooks, bow and arrows or air gun, promptly he would reply by talk of secret places of his own in the large asylum in town, or by bringing from his pockets marbles and a spinning top and a broken little knife. Bravely he boasted of his life—but when at last the time came for him to go back to that dreary home in the city, suddenly his courage failed and he startled me by the change in his face.

"Golly, but it must be fine to live here!" he said huskily. I caught the wretchedness in his eyes.

"Sure it is, but you said it was fine in your place, too," I answered. Sharply he turned his back on me and, as he stood with hands clenched tight, suddenly I knew this kid was trying hard as he could try to keep from busting right out crying! A big lump rose in my throat! I swallowed. It was hard to speak.

"Want this air gun?"

"Hell, no!" His voice was a fierce choking whisper. "Jesus Christ, but it's hell to be poor!" And he turned and ran stumbling to the hayrack waiting to take him to the train. I went straight down into the ravine to a secret tree of mine and, quivering with pity still, I stayed till the orphans were all gone. Faintly I heard them cheering and singing but, beneath the noise they made, I could still hear that low fierce cry: "Jesus Christ, but it's hell to be poor!"

With my emotions so quick to be stirred, I had an attack of religion out there, one of two such experiences that came about this time in my life. The other one had been back in Chicago, where I was so profoundly moved by a preacher who came to our church and declared that we'd all go to hell unless we gave all we had to Christ that, when the collection was passed, I quickly made my estimate of how much money our family had, then wrote upon a pledge card—"I give ten thousand dollars"—and signed it with my mother's name. A smiling elder later on returned the card to Mother and so prevented my saving us all from "the hail that shall eternally lash the howling millions of the damned!"

My second attempt took place in Lake Forest. There every Sunday we walked to church. It was well over a mile from our house but our mother could not bring herself to work horses on the Sabbath day, and so, in Sunday dress and bonnet with her black lace parasol, she led the procession of children and guests. I picked up a grasshopper once and in church gently dropped him down the neck of a stout dame seated in front of me. I can still hear her startled snort! Our regular preacher, a lovable man called Jimmy McClure by most of his flock and widely known in the Middle West, never tormented me by his talk. But one Sunday in his place I heard an evangelist, who grew so fervent in his claim that nobody could be a real Christian unless he tried to bring souls to Christ that in the afternoon I went out and perched on our high board pasture fence. An enormous Irish cook I knew soon came lumbering along, dressed up in her Sunday clothes.

"Don't you want to come to Jesus?" awkwardly I asked her. But in my embarrassment my voice was scarcely more than a whisper; she didn't hear me and passed by. Much relieved, I began to feel that this was not so hard, after all. But then a lean gardener came along and, when I softly asked him if he didn't want to come to Jesus, sharply he retorted:

"What the hell is that to you?"

For a moment he looked at me, small and fat, perched high upon that wooden fence. Then he spat tobacco juice and chuckling loudly passed on. And my face grew hot as fire, for I could hear him chuckling still.

"Well," I decided as I climbed down, "that's enough of this Jesus business for me!"

To a peaceful cow in our pasture under an apple tree I flew, climbed the tree and leaped on her back and with whacks of a stick I galloped her around till her milk was spoiled for a week! But it helped to cool my feelings down. And when that Sunday evening, in a long row of seats on the bluff, I sat with our family and guests singing Moody and Sankey hymns and watching a round silvery moon rise over the waters of the lake, with relief I told myself that this was the kind of religion I liked.

Our father had two trotting horses so fast that, hitched to a light surrey, they made in three minutes the mile to the train. Each morning at seven in our house, roused by the loud ringing of the "rising bell" below, we boys would dress and breakfast with Dad—his watch on the table, the team outside —and then with him we would make the dash for the depot (we didn't say "station" then), arriving just as "the business-man's train" for Chicago was about to pull out. The Chicago and North Western Railroad gave us fine service, for those days. Old Marvin Hewitt, the President, had a summer home not far from ours. When he was young he had begun as a telegraph operator on the line. One of his three sons-in-law, who knew the Morse code as well as he, once told us a story of a time when the train that carried their private car was held in a lonely little station up in the forests of Wisconsin by a serious wreck ahead. After some hours of delay, old Mr. Hewitt fussed and fumed and ordered the station master to try for more news of the wreck. Listening with his son-in-law, he heard this message clicked down the line:

"How much longer to clear that wreck? This damned old war horse Hewitt is raising merry hell up here."

Silence. Then came the reply:

"Easy on that language, boy. President Marvin Hewitt knew the Morse code before you were born."

"Oh, my God!" As the scared young station master turned, he was met by chuckles from his chief. For Mr. Hewitt, like most of our pioneers, was proud of the humble beginning he'd made.

Often before supper at night, in our large family phaeton, we drove with our mother to the depot to meet Dad at the evening train. The depot was gay with color then. No automobiles but all kinds of rigs, from buggies and small phaetons to high brightly colored drags and dogcarts with tandem teams and huge low victorias; ladies with parasols everywhere, and gossip and visiting all about.

In those first years every summer our father, with half a dozen men friends, went in a private car to Minnesota to shoot prairie chickens. We loved to go to the depot to see them off on their night train, with their pack of hunting dogs. But these trips brought trouble for me. For one of the men had a plump little daughter, and my father and he announced that I was to marry her later on. Dad even bought a ring for me and made me put it on her finger. I didn't mind so much at first, for she was a pretty little thing; but when she came to see me, I soon grew bored to death with the kid. She was not like my cousin Bloss Cook, who could get so excited about my wonderful flying machine. Neither my schemes nor my ideas nor my secret places nor my games interested her in the least. All she wanted to do was to sit and smile and dimple at me. It made me doggoned sore. Just because our fathers loved to shoot prairie chickens together, they had given me this little dimple to play with for the rest of my life! No, by gosh, I wouldn't stand it! Grasping her firmly by the hand, I led her down into the ravine, well out of my mother's ken, and climbed a tree and gloomily sat there without speaking till she went home. My mother scolded me well for this and said next time she came we must play in the house. And I did as I was told, even though Mother went out that day. But the game that I invented—called "mountain"—was for me to climb on top of our large pantry icebox and sit there deaf and dumb, till at last the pretty little thing got sick of dimpling up at me and departed for her home. So ended my first love affair.

My father seldom went to church but on Sundays he took us boys for walks on the beach in the afternoons, and on Saturdays we took long drives in the light surrey with his team, far out onto the open prairie. I remember him with the reins in his hands, quietly puffing a cigar and resting his eyes on the great lovely rolling fields of wheat and corn. With his nerves all strained by the Board of Trade, he needed such rest. It was home to him, for he had been raised on a Wisconsin farm. One day he pointed to a low hill and told how only a few years ago he had seen a flock of tens of thousands of pigeons, so thick they darkened the sky, come by that way. They flew so low that with clubs and boards the farmers could knock hundreds down.

From the time when I was seven years old, he took us boys on camping trips up into Wisconsin, hunting deer in the virgin pine forest and fishing from boats on chains of lakes, where there was still not a house to be seen.

We saw many Indians on those trips. I remember my disappointment when one of them, who was a chief, refused to sell us the little canoe that he had made for his small son. We caught bass, pike and muskellunge. Game as salmon, the muskellunge were still enormous in those days. I hooked one that weighed twenty-four pounds and would have jerked me out of the boat, if the guide hadn't snatched the line from my hands.

After long days on lake or in woods, we came back to camp for enormous suppers of fish, potatoes, bacon and flapjacks. From eating so much fried food, I once got such a case of cramps that our father in alarm started us all for the nearest town. It was twenty miles away and, as the springless wagon jolted over those corduroy roads, my pain steadily increased.

But suddenly we came to a log schoolhouse in a clearing and, when the little teacher there learned of the trouble I was in, from a bottle of blackberry brandy she gave me two or three long swigs. And my agony died and I grew so gay that my relieved father, with twinkling eyes, said:

"Look out for that grand medicine, boy. You'll find it everywhere you go. And you've got to learn to know when to stop." I beamed upon him and, with a sigh, gave back the bottle and said:

"Gosh!"

For many years our summers all centered on those camping trips; and there, as I grew older, I learned to know my father better, through the campfire stories that he told about his life.

Born on a farm near Johnstown, New York, where his grandfather had changed the family name from Vanderpoel to Poole, as a boy he had seen the last survivors of the Mohawk Indians. One of them, an old half-wit who went by the name of Indian John, came often to my grandmother Poole in the farmhouse kitchen and, to show that he wished to be fed, said: "Haw!" and put his hand to his mouth. One spring when my father was still a small boy, the family moved by the Erie Canal, lake boat, train and covered wagon to their new home, a Wisconsin farm. All summer they worked with ax and plow to get food and shelter for the next winter. One day in the early fall, by some mysterious instinct having been able to follow their trail, a man suddenly appeared at my grandmother's kitchen door, said "Haw!" and, with his hand to his mouth, asked her to feed him. Indian John!

When not helping on the farm, my father went to a country school and later worked his way half through Beloit College, coming home each Saturday for a fresh hamper of cooked food to last him through the following week. He found time to fiddle at barn dances which often lasted all night long. In his junior year, in the Civil War, he enlisted and went

South and was in Sherman's army marching through Georgia
to the sea. But the stories he told were not of the glory but
of the horrors and pillage of war, as our foraging troopers
took the last food from starving old rebels in the hills. He told
of one old couple he'd seen standing silent and grim by their
door, while the hated Yanks tramped through their house,
smashing tables and chairs in room after room, taking all
food supplies from the storehouse and all livestock from the
barn. My father was a farmer's son, and it made him "so all
fired mad" that, from our commissary that night, he filled a
huge sack with that same food and carried it back to the old
people who had been robbed.

He caught typhoid on that march and, not caring to take
a chance in the field-hospital hells down there, he got a railroad ticket and pinned it to his uniform and, most of the
time in delirium, made the long trip to Wisconsin, home.
There my grandmother nursed him back to health. When at
last his mind cleared and he saw his mother sitting sewing
near his bed, she told him:

"Abram, all these weeks while you've been crazy as a loon,
you've kept under your pillow those filthy old army pants
of yours. You've waked right out of your sleep and got wild,
every time that I tried to take them away. For Heaven's sake,
let me burn them now."

"Wait a minute," he whispered. "Let me think!" As he
tried to, he fainted, for he was so weak; but when he came
back to consciousness, he tried again and again and again.
"There's something I've got to remember!" he said. At last
the memory came. He told her: "Mother, bring your scissors
here." And when she did, he gave her the pants and said:
"Now cut carefully, just where I say." She obeyed and found
a roll of bills, all the money he had in the world, sewed into
them—his army pay!

With this meager capital, he followed the tide of young
men into the cities from the farms and in Chicago made his

start as bookkeeper in a Board of Trade office, keeping one set of books in the daytime and another one at night. But he was so fond of music and plays that, whenever he could get nights off, he ushered at the theater and concerts and the opera and, when the great Patti came to town, was one of the wildly cheering lads who after the performance unharnessed the team from her carriage and themselves dragged it to her hotel.

Anxious to save every dollar he could, he lived in a cheap boardinghouse, where he shared a small top-floor room with a lean young inventor, who went to bed at nine each night. When my father came in late, in order not to make a noise, he took off his shoes and in the dark came cautiously up three flights of stairs. But on opening the door to his room, often in his stocking feet he would stumble over the iron contraption protruding from under his roommate's bed. Down he would crash and, his roommate aroused, there'd be a devil of a time! It never entered my father's head that the thing he had stumbled on was to save untold thousands of lives on American railroads, preventing smashups and the deaths of brakemen on the icy tops of freight cars upon winter's nights. He knew only that he'd stubbed his toes and so he swore fervently at his friend. His roommate was George Westinghouse, who had not sold his air brake yet and knew enough about the ways of our first great corporations so that he thought it safer to sleep with his invention right under his bed!

Saving and working, my father soon went into business for himself and bought a seat on the Board of Trade; and there he did so well that he was able to marry at twenty-five. He had about twelve thousand dollars then and he spent more than half of it on a wedding trip with my mother down the Mississippi on one of the great glamorous river boats to New Orleans, where in old French shops they bought furnishings for their new home. Only a year or two after that, back in Chicago they lost them all in the Fire of 1871. All the next day he spent feeding the starving and, on the day after that, in an unburnt section of the town, rented a table in a barn. At tables all around him were many business friends of his, whose records had been burned like his own. Relying on their memories and trusting each other because they must, they cleaned up trades as best they could and, in the new temporary quarters of the Board of Trade, went on with their business in wheat and corn.

Still bringing his lunch each morning from home to his office in a tin box, as was the custom at the time, my father in the next few years did some trading on his own account. But only a little after this, he was caught in a corner in wheat, run by two big operators who were out to "squeeze the shorts." For nearly a month, with everything he had in danger, he endured that sleepless strain; but then, one stifling August morning, he fainted on his office floor. When he came to, he figured that, by using every dollar he had, he could cover his shorts and get out and be ready to start life again. So down into the Pit he went and bought wheat enough to meet his trades. But when he came out to the hall, he had another spell of faintness and he leaned against a wall. Just at that moment a famous old trader, who knew him and liked him, came hurrying by and, catching sight of him white-faced there, rushed over and asked him what was his trouble. And on learning what he had done, the big man whispered:

"You're wrong, boy, wrong!" Already he had him by the arms and was rushing him back into the Pit. "Sell wheat!" he whispered. "Sell it, sell it—all you can and quick as you can!"

Barely knowing what he was doing, my father followed that tip from his friend. A half-hour later, the corner broke and prices went plunging down so fast that, by the end of that wild day, he could cover his trades and get out, with just about the money he'd had a month before, when the corner began. It was broken, he learned later on, because one of the two men running it took to drinking so hard under the strain that he was on the verge of d. t.'s and, to save him, some of his friends, on the night before the corner broke, kidnaped him and locked him up in a house in the country. His partner then, who was the weak sister of the firm, acted on his clairvoyant's advice, lost his nerve, stopped buying wheat and began to sell, and so started prices crashing down. When he told me the story, my father said:

"It taught me two big lessons. First, never sell America short, for this country is going on to big things. And second, quit trading for yourself. It ruins your judgment. Leave it alone."

To recover his health, he went for six weeks out to his brother's cattle ranch and, when he came back, he did a commission business only. This he was able to build so fast that, by the time he was thirty-five, he had offices in Chicago, Milwaukee, St. Louis, New Orleans and New York. During a big depression he failed and had to start all over again, about the time that I was born; but though he built up a good business once more, he confined it to his office in Chicago from that time on.

We children seldom saw him there, for Mother did not like the Board. But she did take us now and then and, from the visitors' gallery looking down into the hall and its shallow arena called the Pit, where several hundred brokers stood shooting up their hands in bids and filling the air with a frenzied roar, we would catch a glimpse of our father standing quietly just outside. When he saw us, he'd wave his hand and send up a boy with red apples from the huge wicker basket of old Anny the Apple Woman down there. And that was all we saw or heard, nor had we then the faintest idea of how the lives of millions of farmers and peasants all over the face of the earth, and of all people who ate bread or starved because the price was too high, were governed by this roaring Pit, the main wheat market of the world. We knew nothing of that when we were small. But many years later, from a man who had since become a millionaire, I was told this story of what he had seen of our father one day on the floor:

"I was only a boy of sixteen, working for P. D. Armour then, and he sent me in from the Stockyards with a message for your Dad, who was running a corner in wheat for him. It was a big day and the Pit had gone wild and, from that screaming crazy mob, a dozen young floor brokers kept dashing out to take orders from your father, then dive into it once more. Quiet as though he were out in the country, he stood watching and smoking a cigar. Your father was short and stocky, and the glimpse I had of him that day made me think of pictures I'd seen of General Grant in the Civil War."

IV

WHEN I WAS ABOUT ELEVEN YEARS OLD, ON THE STREET NOT far from our house I was held up by a gang of "Micks," about a dozen ragged small boys. For we had "public enemies" even then. Two of them jumped on me from behind and the gang soon had me down. While I struggled and squirmed, they took my watch and, when at last they let me go, they told me from that time on the whole gang would be "after me"! For weeks, on my way home from school, I lived in fear that they would grab the safety bike on which I rode. And at first for my protection but soon for the sheer joy of it, I joined another gang of boys, most of them from public school, who ranged all through our part of town.

Our leader was proud of the fact that his older brother had fought in the Ring. With an ex-prize fighter as our coach, we were fully equal to the Micks and, with fists and clubs and slingshots, we had some glorious fights with them. I soon found out that these ragged boys were no strange terrible creatures but just as human as myself, and this discovery helped me in my work as a writer later on, for some of my memories of that time went into the opening chapters of my book, The Harbor. Our main battlefield was The Patch, near the lake, where Grandmother Howe had once helped the poor. The shanties since then had been torn down to make way for the region of new land made by the city dumps. With its hillocks of rock and dirt and its stretches of high rank grass and weeds, it was a fascinating section for our gang of small boys to explore. In a little shack out close to the lake lived old Cap Streeter and his wife. For years he had been a squatter there, with rifle and shotgun resisting all attempts to put him off. Later, when the land was valued at many millions of dollars, "the Streeter claim" became for years a famous case fought through many courts. We knew him as a shaggy old man, who had boats and fishing tackle for rent and told us stories about his life as a sailor on the Great Lakes.

Our other favorite hunting ground, in our battles with the Micks, was the neighboring region of lumberyards reaching close to the mouth of the river, where we had secret strongholds among the towering stacks of boards. Farther inland, near the river, were unpaved streets, which on rainy days were sloughs of mud; and their wooden sidewalks were built so high that often, exploring there after dark, we would see the shadowy forms of hobos sleeping underneath. As I peered in alone one afternoon, one of them growled:

"Who the hell are you?" I thrilled with scared excitement.

"Just a kid," I answered.

"Yeah?" Suddenly he smiled at me. "Thinkin' of tryin' life on the road?"

"What road?"

"It ain't one road, it's a million, all the way from here to the Coast." Then, with his big dark dirty face softened and his voice dropping low, he went on to picture life on the road and, when he saw how thrilled I was, he told me that if I'd bring him twenty dollars he'd take me along. But something in his voice and eyes had deepened my fear of this strange man, so I left him and ran off to join our gang, over on Rush Street bridge near by. We often went there to jump on the bridge as it swung out for some ship to steam through. One of our gang once missed his jump and fell some thirty or forty feet down into the greasy water below. With the bridge tender's rope we hauled him out and built a fire to dry his clothes, so he wouldn't be caught when he went home.

In our own house—since I always obeyed, when my mother

forbade me anything, and yet on the other hand felt I was free to do anything she did not taboo—to keep her from women's worries, I never spoke of my new friends; nor did I speak of them even to Dad. But now through him I had with my gang an exciting unforgettable night. A staunch free trader all his life, in 1892 my father was strong for Grover Cleveland and, when the great President came to Chicago on his campaign, Dad took my brothers and me to lunch at the Grand Pacific Hotel over town, to see the President drive by. With him was his lovely young wife. Our mother had no use for her. A parade was no place for a lady, she said. But for me the real excitement came that night, when Dad agreed to let me march in a torchlight procession being formed in our neighborhood. I joined my gang some blocks from our house, on a street which far as eye could see was filled with men and boys in line. With thousands of kerosene torches held high and flaring up into the night, the boom of bands, the songs and cheers, that street was a roaring river of life! Our little gang was already in line, but we were few and our leader's brother, a ward politician, angrily asked him why in hell he hadn't got hold of more recruits? Instantly I saw a chance to bring in a good friend of mine, who was hopefully hovering near. For months all my efforts to get him into our gang had been in vain, just because he was a Jew. But when now I asked if he could march, promptly our anxious chief replied:

"You bet he can! There ain't no Jews! We're all Democrats tonight!"

In that same year, when I was twelve, I had one of the ugliest nights of my life. Among my new companions I'd learned so much and yet so little. Because I had no use for girls, certain allusions had passed me by. But now at night-fall one of the gang took me down a dark muddy street close by the river to a house, where from a lighted window a naked fat woman beckoned and smiled. While I stared at her, he gripped my arm; and tighter and tighter grew his grip, as he snickered and poured into my ears things he said I ought to know. Shocked and disgusted, I came home. My disgust even turned on my mother that night, as I looked at her with furtive eyes and thought of the way in which I had been born. When she came to my bed, I turned my face, for I didn't want her to kiss me good night. In the days that followed, she must have noticed and learned enough to guess my trouble, for she gave me a book one night and asked me to read it carefully. It was only a little book, written by a doctor who was a leader in the Y. M. C. A. Young people today would laugh at its tone. But it did give me facts that cleared away the disgust that had come with the torrent of mud poured into my soul by that boy that night. Few boys were given books like that then. My mother was far in advance of her times.

Those times were reticent, and they were hard as adamant against divorce. In our church was a man who had forced his wife to divorce him so he could marry another. That other came with him each Sunday to church. I remember how lovely and stylish she was and the desperately friendly look in her eyes as they walked up the aisle. For she longed to get into the social life of the North Side through our church, and yet nobody ever spoke to her. My mother didn't hound such people, she simply left them strictly alone. And though she went so often to church, she never brought Grandfather Howe's rigid creed into our home, nor did she have any use for religion of the vivid emotional kind. When a rich young woman, whom we knew, was converted by Dwight Moody and her fervor rose so high that she wanted our Sunday-school class, in which she had a little son, to march down Rush Street from our church with a huge red satin banner on which "Resist the Devil" should be inscribed in letters of gold, my mother put a stop to it, for my sister taught the class. And when the fervent rich young dame came to our house and asked Mother if she couldn't kneel in prayer with her and beg Jesus to forgive her sin, Mother dryly answered:

"No, you cannot. My dear young woman, I loved Jesus before you were born."

She never wasted time in worry over her immortal soul. Mother was always too busy for that. I remember her saying once:

"I simply can't imagine not going to Heaven when you die."

When I read modern novels that speak of the gloom in the Presbyterian Church, I think of my mother and of the "Cleric," a group of twelve clergymen who dined one night a year at our house. With my brothers I used to stand in the pantry, peeking into the dining room at that genial group of men and listening to the funny stories they told over their cigars and port.

My mother was a temperance woman. As we boys grew older, there was a decanter of wine on our dinner table at night. It was poured once for us, never twice. She seldom spoke of temperance but I remember her saying how disgusting she thought it was for anyone to drink too much.

Several years before this time, our house had been built larger, to be ready for the "coming out" of my sisters, home from boarding school, and to give us all plenty of room as we grew. We three boys had two bedrooms and a study, on the third floor. In the study a huge green-shaded lamp hung over the square table, where we did our schoolwork at night; and around the room were bookshelves, a small workbench with carving tools, a magic lantern, a printing press and electric batteries. There was great excitement downstairs when the telephone was first put in and we crowded close around it, while our father from his office spoke to each of us in turn. Gosh, but it was wonderful!

"And they say the time for miracles has passed!" cried
our mother. "I wonder what next?"

Our dining room was some thirty feet square. At the large
round table we seldom had less than ten at meals, and "the
big top" for twenty was constantly being put on for dinners
for my sisters and their friends. I remember the damask table-
cloth and the silver and crystal on such nights. The first of
these many parties had come when I was about ten. My two
older sisters then, on finishing school, had spent nine laborious
months with a governess abroad, and they were radiant to be
home with clothes from Paris, ready to dance. Subscription
balls in public halls were scarcely ever heard of then; everyone
still entertained in their homes, with the help of caterers.
Kinsley was the best known of these. And when our girls
"came out," at a dinner dance and cotillion of a hundred in
our house, I remember our excitement as the Kinsley colored
cooks and waiters poured into our basement, unpacked huge
boxes and hampers of food and set up long serving tables.
At the dinner Mr. Kinsley himself stood behind our mother's
chair. His daughter later married one of the leading bankers
in town, a close friend of our family. So the whole town, or
our part at least, was all bound together by personal ties.

I can still hear the music that night softly playing under
the stairs and see Mother, in her blue silk dress with a bustle,
standing with the girls in the hall to receive the guests. There
was a fine old-fashioned style about my mother at such times,
and fervently I told myself that she was a lady and no mistake! I remember the cotillion with its gaily colored "favors"
to be given to your partner in each of the many figures
through which the dancers romped that night. How much
more colorful it was than the monotonous drone and throb
of the eternal jazz today! Johnny Hand and his orchestra
supplied the music for our dance. He was a jolly little old man
and, sawing on his 'cello like mad, he grew jollier and jollier

after the punch began to be served. Johnny brought out "all Chicago" and fathered the girls as he had their mothers. He played at their weddings, too. From the years of the Virginia reel, quadrille and waltz and polka, to Sousa's two-steps, the lame duck and the beginnings of ragtime, Johnny came often to our house.

But life was not all sparkle and gaiety for those sisters of ours. I can still hear their groans and sighs over the calls that had to be made. They called after all parties to which they had gone and even those to which they had been asked. They called after weddings and funerals. All dressed up, with our mother off they would go in the family brougham. The North Side received on Mondays, and on Wednesdays they had to drive to the South Side, a full hour away. And all these calls my sisters made had to be returned at our house!

To two of the wealthiest homes in the city our girls were not allowed to go. In one, the young wife had "sold herself for money" to an old millionaire; in the other, the wife was suspected of having a secret love affair with one of the leading magnates in town. But though our house stood like the Rock of Gibraltar for morality, religion was warmed by humanity there. Our family hymns on Sunday nights soon grew to be big genial times, with young men coming to supper first and later a crowd around the piano.

On spring evenings with their beaux our girls rode off on safety bikes, single or tandem, with tinkling bells and twinkling lanterns, up to join the thousands of other such riders in Lincoln Park. Bicycling came into style for girls in about 1894. Our sisters felt themselves dashing indeed in their jaunty modern costumes, short tweed skirts over good thick bloomers, stiff shirtwaists and Fedora hats. Dashing? Yes, but still secure. For them their safeties meant safety first. I remember the righteous wrath in our house when my oldest sister's young man brought her home a bit *after* eleven o'clock!

All summer long, young men, with their luggage packed on the handle bars of their bikes, rode out to Lake Forest and joined the girls who had come by train, for week-end parties at our house. When twenty or thirty of them came, cots were put up in all the spare rooms; and on Saturday evenings, till midnight but not one minute later, there would be a supper dance, with Negro fiddlers from the village. On Saturday afternoons they played croquet and tennis on our lawn, the girls in skirts that reached to the ankles. As I picture them now they remind me of how, not very long ago, a gracious old man in London answered a modern pert young maid, who asked him what he thought of her "shorts":

"My dear, I'm afraid I am no fair judge—because, you see, in my day an ankle was an ecstasy."

At those week-end parties, our guests played no games on the Sabbath Day. In the mornings they all went to church, they took long walks in the afternoons and gathered with the family for supper at small tables on the veranda on Sunday nights. The veranda had many convenient nooks where there were rocking chairs built for two. Known to us as "encouragers," those chairs made many a match in their time.

Our golf club was started when I was still in my early teens. One of the first such clubs in the country, it grew so fast that in a few years we had a large clubhouse and parties galore, with the men in white flannels and pink coats, and a golf team whose captain was the national amateur champion. Later my young brother played on the team, and I remember our father's anger when he learned how a man at the club had told the boy, just before a big match, he had five hundred dollars on his game.

So life was rapidly changing out there. Fashionable and even "fast" women began to be seen at the club, in their gaily colored dogcarts, watching the game on the polo field. And the first of the motorcars, "horseless carriages," appeared. We had one, a high two-seated affair with small wheels and narrow tires. In this my younger brother and I had a puncture while driving out from town. We had never had one before. We pulled out the nail and stuck on a patch but in Evanston the patch blew off. Then we had a bright idea. It was only a nail hole, so if we tried something thicker than air it might plug the hole and we'd be all right. At a grocery store near by we bought a gallon of molasses and into the tire we pumped it all and then proceeded on our way. To my brother who was driving I said:

"Speed her up to twenty, Abe, we're late!" And at that terrible speed we tore along for nearly a mile. Then with a bang the molasses blew out a great jagged gap where the nail hole had been and, for the next twenty miles, each time that damned wheel turned around, it sprayed us with the thick hot stuff, as we drove to Lake Forest on the rim!

V

LONG BEFORE THIS THERE HAD COME TO ME A PASSION SO CON-suming it nearly led to a life career. My father loved music and, when I was twelve, he tried to start my younger brother with a teacher on the violin. But Abram at ten was already absorbed in sketching and painting and had no time for music. Eagerly I took his place. When he saw how I worked, Dad promptly encouraged me to keep on; he gave me a better teacher soon; and with Mother I went to concerts of the Chicago Orchestra. It was called the Thomas Orchestra then, for Theodore Thomas was still conducting the great orchestra he had made. A grand old drillmaster he was, not only for his orchestra but for humble beginners like me. Never sentimental or cheap, he gave me a first exciting sense of the tornadoes that can rise on that immense mysterious sea that we call the soul of humanity.

I heard other fine conductors and famous violinists from abroad. I put photographs of them on my desk and even began to wonder if I couldn't ever play like that? I grew so intense in my new dream that I practiced often till late at night. On those evenings my father would come up to our study with his cigar and watch and listen for a while, while my young brother sketched and painted and I worked on my violin. At one such time, when our mother came up to see if our schoolwork had been done, I heard Dad in a low voice say:

"Damn the schoolwork. Leave 'em alone."

Then suddenly Chicago, our big windy smoky home town, helped us two kids on our way with a vision of such beauty as we had never dreamed could be.

In the rhythm of the city's growth there have been some mighty beats. One of them our mother had felt in the Fire of 1871 and the amazing energy with which our fathers as young men built a new city and made a fresh start. Since then, in an astounding spread for miles along the edge of the lake and inland onto the open prairie, its houses and apartment buildings (flats, we called them in those days), its sweatshops and big factories, its stores and business offices, its barrooms and its brothels and gambling joints had pushed their way and, towering over all of these, from the steel mills gorgeous columns of flame poured up into the grimy night. In ugliness, disorder and haste, in the smoke of its mills and the sweat of its builders, the giant new city had been born.

But now in 1893 we came to another climax in the disorderly drama of its growth. For out of this sprawling energy rose a vision of pure loveliness that is before me still as I write. Never have I seen a world's fair in all this country or abroad that could compare with the White City that appeared on the edge of our lake. I went there often by day and by night. Drawn first like most kids to the Midway Plaisance, with its side shows and barkers and Zulu bands, forerunners of the jazz of today, later I began to feel the grip of the greater show down there, to sense the stately majesty of those immense white columned buildings set in spacious gardens, parkways and lagoons, with little lights by thousands twinkling in the summer nights. For the first time in my life, I had a sense of being lifted—lifted up by something grand. Just what I felt I did not know. I do know now. It was that wistful instinct deep hidden not only in one small boy but in all the hungry soul of our land. It was America saying:

"Look. Someday we shall come to this. Someday we'll have finished with all our grime and disorder and haste. Someday we'll have time for a world of beauty and leisure—far ahead."

Far ahead. Will it ever be? For beside this voice was another one, deep and strident, crudely strong and real as all reality. In long exhibition halls crowded with all sorts and kinds of new inventions and machines from laboratories, mines and mills and factories all over the land, this second voice could there be heard by those with ears for the meanings of things, speaking of forces already at work to sweep America on her road. For these machines were the mothers of change that have rushed our young people into the cities to factories, mills and labor strife, opened world markets that brought on wars, hurled millions of little people like me over the bridge from yesterday to the vast confusion of today.

Two voices. I heard only the first. The second I heard in later years in gathering crescendo, not only here but all over the earth, and later we shall come to that. But then I was only a small boy who fervently longed to become a violinist and who, on those nights in the White City, stared with his small painter brother at the loveliness of it all until he felt something deep inside lifting him up into the sky.

I worked hard at my music in those next years. I found plenty of time for it, for my other work at school had come easy from the start. I was even able to crowd in a good many other activities there, on the school paper, in the "gym" and in football and baseball in the Park. In the winters the boys of our neighborhood had a little skating club, only about a block from our house, in the yard of one of Mother's friends. Though our hostess invited both sexes there, we did all we could to discourage the girls from coming. Rudely we called them The Chips. One, more courageous than the rest, used to shout her derision through the fence. She was Margaret Ayer. Years later one of her fine Chicago novels took the Pulitzer Prize. We were glad to be rid of such female pests, but there was one woman for whom we would always stop playing hockey when she came. Her son was a goal guard in our games. Clever, good-natured, red-headed and fat, his name was Leslie Carter and he lived with his father near by.

His mother had left them to go on the stage, and there so glamorous was her career that we'd stop playing and stare with a thrill, when she drove up in a hansom cab and, leaning out in her gorgeous clothes, called, "Leslie darling!" and took him off to supper and the theater.

From the years when I was small, our mother had often taken us boys to what she called plays of the better class, at Hooley's and McVickar's, the two best theaters over town. She had no use for such wild dramas as Camille and Sapho, and not until I was sixteen did I go to see Sapho, all by myself. From the front row of the peanut gallery, I watched and listened spellbound, until we came to the big scene where Sapho gripped her departing lover by his knees in wild despair and, as in the effort to shake her off he dragged her 'round and 'round on the floor, she screamed:

"It's the grip of a drowning woman!"

Then the stout coachman at my side, whose sympathies were all with the man, leaned far out over the gallery rail and yelled:

"Bite the bitch, bite her! Bite her hands!"

The scene collapsed in a roar of laughter.

About this time, the boys in our skating club were asked to join a dancing class for twenty subscription dances that year. Girls again! In solemn conclave we met and debated. At last I gloomily declared:

"We've got to come to it someday, so let's go and get it over with."

Next week we bought tuxedos and went to a large stone house on the Lake Shore Drive. In the dressing room a boy we knew, Joe Ryerson, said in a casual tone:

"I suppose all you fellows know how to dance like the rest of us here." We answered: "Good God, no!"—and in alarm stared at the thirty strange girls in the ballroom seated in a long line by the wall. But one by one we were pushed in and, in the weeks that followed, on Friday nights from eight till

ten-thirty, so well did those girls employ their charms that
very soon, completely enthralled, we were fighting for cotillion partners at Christmas dances and through the year. That
winter we skated with them, too, played tennis with them in
the spring and in summer went on hilarious house parties up
along the shore. They were grand girls and among them I
made friendships that were to last for years. I remember, all
through Lent one spring, how I lurked each afternoon near
the doors of St. James Church (St. Jimmy's we used to call it
then), just to catch a glimpse of a girl who came with her
mother to vesper service.

But my music came first for me still; and with deepening
interest in my work, my father gave me a lovely violin made
in Cremona by Albani, one of the best known fiddlemakers
of Stradivarius' time. He had bought it at the world-famous
shop of Hill's in London, a place where he was liked so well
that years later, when I went to the shop, they took me to a
little back room and from a steel safe brought out four
"Strads" priced at thousands of dollars apiece, and left me
alone to play them.

Meanwhile, back in Chicago, when at seventeen I was ready
for Princeton with all examinations passed, my parents agreed
that I stay home and have a whole year for my music first.
And that was a crowded year for me. Though practicing on
my fiddle still, I spent now nearly half my time on harmony
and composition with one of the best teachers in town, whose
own compositions had been played by the Thomas Orchestra.
Listening to that orchestra and the great music of the world,
humbly I began to hope that I could write music myself someday. Such an idea was no novelty in our family, for my mother
as a girl had often stayed in Pittsburgh in the home of her
cousins the Nevins, who had brought the first piano over the
Alleghenies in a wagon long ago. And while I was still a
small boy, their descendant, Ethelbert Nevin, already on the
crest of his fame as a popular composer, had come to visit us

and give a recital at our house. But though we had thought his Rosary and Narcissus lovely music then, now I was instinctively listening for more rugged stuff.

Through one of my older sisters, whose friend was night superintendent at the Illinois Steel Works, I went down there a number of nights and almost heard the kind of music that I had been listening for. Gripped by the fascination of those immense dark sooty buildings, the thunder and crash of mighty machines, the roar of the furnaces, flares of flame, I came one night to a high platform on which stood a lean young man, with his hand on one of three levers before him and his hard tense straining eyes fixed on three monstrous tanks called "converters" about a hundred feet away. From their huge round funnel tops rose torrents of flame of many hues. By their color judging the exact moment when the boiling steel inside had reached just the proper heat—for a mistake of a minute, he shouted, would mean thousands of dollars lost—suddenly he yanked that lever. Slowly one of those huge tanks swung forward and, with a deafening roar and a dazzling burst of light, poured its hellish molten mass down into receptacles below, while tiny human shadows skurried like demons all around!

I stood on the platform for hours that night with eyes and ears straining to take it all in. Oh, God, if I could make music of this! The thought haunted me in those next weeks, for I was a youngster terribly intense about himself at that time. Often the music almost came. To help it come, I sat down one day and tried to put the whole monstrous spectacle into words. Still no music. But to my surprise, as again and again I tried to find words for what I had seen and heard, I found this new search so absorbing that the question began to rise: Music or words, which shall it be?

The question was not new to me, for in those years I'd spent hundreds of nights reading with Father in his study long after the family were in bed. Never since have I found

a man who knew Dickens and Thackerary so well. He had
an intimate lawyer friend who knew them nearly as well as
he. Even from their offices they would call up one another,
speaking not as themselves but as characters in Pendennis or
Oliver Twist. And they carried on long dialogues, for they
knew those characters like brothers. With his Dickens or
Thackeray, Smollett or Sterne, Dad would sit buried in one
huge chair while I would sit in another close by, both of us
silent, till something he read would remind him of some real
life he had seen, and then he would stop to spin me a yarn. A
wonderful storyteller was Dad, a living proof of my belief
that in our country in those days the best stories were not
written but told, tossed off on the side by busy men, the main
power of whose creative instincts went into the business of
building up America.

Listening to the tales he told, more than once I had wished
that someday I could write down stories like that, just as people told them. The same idea took fresh hold on me now. So
it was that I began to turn from music to this job of writing
which has held me ever since. And yet those early years of
music have always kept such a grip on me still that, in nearly
every story I write, it is by their voices and not by their faces
that my characters grow real—so real, in those rare hours
when at last I can feel I am writing my best, that I sit like a
stenographer, listening to people speak and racing my pencil
to jot it all down.

Next year I left Chicago. But I was to go back many times,
for Chicago will never let me go. My father once said:

"You're a lucky boy. You'll live to see Chicago finished."

I never have. I never will. Changing, changing, all the time,
like our whole country, it never stops. And it is of that ever-
restless heaving human sea of change and growth, in Chicago
and all over the world, that I have written ever since, as a
little reporter of vast things seen, a pygmy in a giant show.

VI

PRINCETON IN 1898 WAS NO GREAT UNIVERSITY BUT A COLLEGE of twelve hundred, rooted in traditions still, a warmly deeply personal world, where boys from all over the country mixed together and made friends. And this business of making friends became so absorbing to me at the start that for a time I dropped my music and wrote only of college life.

At first I felt like nothing at all but a little freshman worm. On my walk with a suitcase from the train, on the night when I arrived, I met a brass band and behind it a roaring "peerade" of sophs, in huge "horse hats" of orange and black. Fearfully I skurried by. In my room in Upper Pyne, I found my trunk and began to unpack. Soon other freshmen looked cautiously in and talked for a while, then went back to their rooms, for this was a big hazing night. Into my room came a group of sophs led by Colonel Coulter from Tennessee, full of Bourbon and looking for freshmen Yanks. Of me they at once demanded the names of all other freshmen in the dorm and, when I was obstinate about that, they started in to haze me well. Suddenly one of them spied a large bottle of "neutralizing cordial," a villainous cure for indigestion, much in use in our family. My mother had slipped it into my trunk. It looked like whisky. He started to drink and drank nearly half before he could stop. Then he asked me what in hell I meant by keeping such liquor in my room; and the hazing tuned up to a point where, stripped nearly naked, I asked to know if a freshman who'd had all he could stand wouldn't be allowed

to fight? This apparently made quite a hit with the Colonel
from Tennessee, for he promptly answered:

"All right, son, you've had enough."

They left me but others came that night, and all that week
the hazing continued, both indoors and out on the streets.
Through those first chaotic days I began to learn my way
about. I soon found a group I liked and we formed an eating
club, and together we went to the freshman reception given
in the president's house. Because President Patten had been
my grandfather's close friend, I was on the reception committee, and a Lawrenceville boy from our club asked me to
introduce him to Mrs. Grover Cleveland, who lived with her
husband at Princeton then and had come to meet our freshman class. He had heard of her wonderful memory and
wanted to test it out, he said. When I took him up to the
large group around her, she turned and, with a quick welcoming smile, said:

"Why, how do you do, Mr. Mount!"

"Doesn't that beat the devil?" he asked me, when we had
moved away. "The only time she ever saw me was last spring
at Lawrenceville, when our whole class of ninety-two seniors
passed her in line to shake her hand! And yet she still remem-
bers my name!"

Curfew bell on Old Nassau tolled at nine o'clock each night
and custom forbade us freshman worms to go outdoors after
that. But skurrying by dark back streets through the forbidden
hours, our getting together went on so fast that, in two weeks
after we came, one warm early autumn night, we marched
singing and cheering down Nassau Street to meet the sophs
in the Cannon Rush, around the famous old cannon from the
Battle of Princeton, planted behind Old Nassau. Coming onto
the campus, with our football men in front, we all broke into
a run. In front of us rockets shot into the sky and on both
sides burned colored lights. Just before we dived into the
sophs, one of our junior coaches shouted as he passed me:

"Throw up your arms!"

I raised mine high and, in the wild scrimmage that followed, as all around me boys stumbled and fell and others piled on top of them, with arms on the shoulders of my neighbors, I rode through and was not sucked down. Thank God for that junior! An arm was broken and several ribs were cracked that night. Little I dreamed of how, years later, in the Russian Revolution, I was to use that lesson I'd learned.

In that exciting college fall I had no time to look ahead. The classroom work came easy and it took no hold on me; it seemed all regular prep-school stuff; so I did just enough to get by and gave my time to the life outside, spending four or five hours a day getting news for our daily paper, "The Prince." All over Princeton I rode on my bike to cover the stories assigned to me. Athletics, music and dramatics, class politics, meetings large and small, into them all I burrowed for news and came back to the little "Prince" office to write. No chance for any fine writing there— "The Prince" wanted facts and facts alone and a style strictly conventional. It helped me little to learn my craft and I failed of election to the board. But it was worth while all the same, for that fall it took me into every corner of college life. And though as a figure in that life I made such a poor showing that four years later I was voted "the most useless man" in my class, I made many close warm friends, who played in it leading parts, and saw Princeton not only through my own but their more closely observing eyes. It was not the Princeton of today but a gripping endearing little place, where everything centered on your friends and Princeton spirit and a life where many queer customs persisted still. Here is a glimpse of one of them, from a letter I wrote to my mother in the spring of freshman year:

"Yesterday was our first spring day. All the seniors were tearing around rolling hoops while the juniors were busy playing marbles. The idea goes way back for years. They can do these things. Underclassmen can't. I met the leader of the glee club and the managing editor of 'The Prince' both racing along Nassau Street with their big hoops rolling ahead. The president of the Athletic Association was absorbed in spinning a little red top, while down the street a crowd of juniors were engaged in a game of marbles. It all strikes a fellow as funny at first but these are old traditions here."

Another custom was called "fresh fire." On the nights before exams, when hundreds of students worked late in their rooms, about every hour someone would throw his window open wide and lean out and yell "Fresh fire!" Instantly would come replies—"Fresh fire!"—shouted far and near. Hundreds of windows would be raised and, with lungs, tin pans and pistols, for some five minutes a thousand students would blow off steam, until the cry—"All over"—came. Then the desperate cramming for exams would go on for another hour or more, until the next yell was heard. And this would continue half the night.

Arthur Poe was our great football star. I saw the two games that he won against Yale—the first by a run the length of the field for a touchdown, just at the end of the game; and the second by kicking a goal from the forty-five-yard line in the last half minute of play. It was cold that night on the old Yale field and already nearly dark—cold and dark for Princeton— only time for one last play. Suddenly we saw our team go into a huddle and then little Poe, who played end, dropped back and held out his hands for the ball. Poe! A breathless silence fell. The ball was passed back to him and, as Yale came crashing through our line, it rose just above their heads and we saw it sail and soar to go between the dim dark goal posts nearly fifty yards away! I remember the wild tornado of cheers and after it thousands of bared heads, as voices all around me, voices of men young and old from every part of the country, joined in the singing of Old Nassau, our hymn in victory or defeat. That song never lost its thrill for me, for it gave me a sense of belonging to something bigger than my little self, a feeling which in a larger way was later to mean so much in my life.

We sang at Princeton and sang in parts. Close harmony was our second name. We sang at games and in the grillroom of the earlier Princeton Inn, and in the reunion tents of the grads through Commencement Week in June. One hot June night in sophomore year, I came in late to the old rooms that I shared with two of my closest friends, rooms well known to many grads. Booth Tarkington in his Princeton days had so often come there that we had a sofa called "Tark's corner" still. That night I found our three beds filled and many grads sleeping on the floor. Soon after I had lain down with the rest, a most God-awful bedlam broke from a brass band on the street below. Then a low Southern voice beside me drawled:

"For Christ's sake, brother, let's you and me go on down and collect that band and start it on, so we can sleep."

We did so and it took some time, for the big band marching down the street had suddenly strayed like a flock of lost sheep, quite inebriated lost sheep, scattering up into side streets but each one playing determinedly still. When at last they had been sent on their way, my Southern friend confided that he felt like some good music now. So did I, and until dawn we wandered about Princeton, from crowds in big alumni tents to little groups under bushes and trees, joining in close harmony. Songs of the North and more of the South, from the negro spirituals to that weird old folk song, "Franky and Johnny." My companion of the night knew fifty-one verses of that song, for he had traced it back, he said, to the place where it started, New Orleans, nearly a hundred years ago, with American words set to the music that had come from the south of France. Between singing we smoked and had long talks. Since leaving college he had become a police magistrate in Louisville and he told me numberless little stories about his life.

"If you aim to go writin' about the world that I reckon

we're comin' into," he told me, "take along a bottle of Bourbon, son. You may need it."

Oh, Louisville, you were right!

"The big thing Princeton can do for you Yanks," he said to me at the end of our night, "is to make you acquainted with us Rebs and so help bring North and South together."

And for me it did work out that way, for in my years at Princeton, in stories and songs and long long talks on walks off through the country with my many Southern friends, I came so close to the Old South that I learned a dozen dialects and many old ways and habits they had of thinking and feeling about things. Most of those habits are gone today. They were fast going even then, but still some trace of them was left. I went with a Virginia friend one night to the grillroom at the Inn for the singing. It was only nine o'clock and the evening had just begun. We took seats at one of the long bare tables, down which the colored waiters were shoving steins of beer like sleds and, as we raised our steins to drink, I asked my Virginia friend about some girl that we both knew. With a friendly smile, he answered:

"Sorry, old man. I never talk about a girl I know when I'm drinking."

He meant girls only of one kind. There were plenty of another kind in Trenton, only ten miles away. Hundreds of students knew them well and some of them came over at times into Princeton by back streets. But one day on the front campus I found a crowd of several hundred angry jeering Princeton boys around two hysterical sobbing girls, booing and shoving them off the campus! They were all very well in back streets but they had no place near Nassau Hall!

Except for an occasional night at the Haymarket dance hall in New York and a few talks and drinks with a girl who was called "Martini" there, I left such women and girls alone and kept to those of the other kind that I met at college proms and at week-end dances in homes of friends up on the Hudson, in Philadelphia and New York. My Philadelphia roommate lived in a quaint brick house on Spruce Street with a great-uncle and two great-aunts, one of whom weighed three hundred pounds. The great-uncle was a Voltairian and hadn't any use for church, but the two great-aunts were deeply religious; and they were such friendly lovable souls that, no matter how late we had danced at some party on the night before, we cheerfully rose in time for church. I can still see those dear huge old ladies beamingly conducting a half dozen Princeton sophomores down the aisle to their family pew.

I met many girls on those week-end trips, among them a Creole from New Orleans. I can't remember the talks we had but they must have been pretty lively affairs, for among some old letters the other day I found a little note from her in which she declared to me:

"All my life I have loathed Platonic friendship. Now, thank Heaven, I've found a man with an equal horror of it!"

In another old letter, one from my mother, I found this interesting side light on the dances of those days:

"One thing I want you to make up your mind *not to do,* when you come home for Christmas—and that is *not to smoke at private dances.* It is bad form, inconsiderate to your hostess and displeasing to your girl partners!"

What about the girl partners of today, with their vermilion fingernails flipping the ash off Luckies and Camels, which they fondly designate Humps?

Christmas time in Chicago brought a rush of cotillions, with elaborate figures and favors to lend spice and color and variety to the night. Our summers in Lake Forest, too, were gay with golf and tennis and house parties. Many college friends of ours from East and South came to visit us there. When my Philadelphia roommate came, we went to a dance on the first night but, right at the start of that party, I met a girl so completely different from any I had met before that I took her out in the garden, and there I grew so interested I quite forgot my stranded roommate until it was time to go home. I met her again next Christmas in town. She had many other swains and an outrageous habit of refusing to dance with anyone till he had danced with a wallflower first. I took her to the opera and went to tea at her house one day, and there before an open fire I stayed so long that I missed a dinner to which I had been asked that night. And this sort of thing, with that same girl, has happened thousands of times to me since.

But all thought of girls, even that one, was lost in what happened to me now. Back at Princeton the business of making friends had been organized even in my time, with the "right" freshman and sophomore groups, if you were lucky enough to get in them, leading you on into one of the upper-class clubs. There were only seven of these in my day. I was headed for one of the four at the top, for my older brother Ralph was there. But when elections came, I learned that one junior blackball had kept me out! The news came like a thunderbolt. With a cold sick feeling, the bottom dropped out of my college life. But my Philadelphia roommate then, who had been elected and was much wanted in the club, refused to join without me. For weeks he slaved and maneuvered and schemed against that junior to get me in, and at last, one lovely evening in April, when with hundreds of others I lay on the dark front campus listening to the seniors singing on the steps of Nassau Hall, he came to me and said:
"You're in!"
All the conventional business of social life at Princeton then seemed small to me compared with the loyalty of that one friend. I had been known as Two Beers Poole. My nickname was utterly shattered that night!
After it came two joyous weeks, and then a tragedy so black that I remember it vividly still.

In our group were three roommates, known to us as Runt, Chris and Phil. Runt was small but he had a wonderful build. Later on, in senior year, he was captain of the gym team and after college he went West and joined the Canadian Mounted Police. Chris, a big handsome lovable lad, was a mathematical shark and meant to be an engineer. Phil was an athlete, lean and hard with sloping shoulders and a slow appealing smile. He spoke little. I liked him. Phil and I had often canoed together down on Stony Brook that spring; and now one Saturday afternoon with Chris he tried to shoot the dam. The canoe capsized and, though both swam well, they were caught in the whirlpool beneath the dam and in spite of their struggles were sucked down.

I remember our sophomore club that night. All year it had been a place where, in jerseys with our hats on at meals, we had shouted and sung and hurled plates. It was completely silent now. Some of us did not eat at all and the rest sat eating with heads bent down. At last in a low awkward voice a lad active in the Y.M.C.A. asked if we wouldn't come to his room and see what God could do for us. Abruptly up came some of the heads, eyes glaring at him. Again they bent down.

"Bull!" someone muttered at my side. And though we all went to the funeral, our real good-by to our two friends came later in the room of their grim strong little roommate, Runt. He had filled a silver loving cup that Phil and he had won at prep school. We stood in a circle and passed it around in utter silence till at last it came to Runt. He raised it quickly, said— "Here's to two men!"—drank deep, then talked of other things. And so did we all, but it was a strain. We left him soon. As we went out, I turned and looked back and saw him with his head in his clenched quivering hands!

That tragedy made me realize how my religion had been slipping away. It was not for lack of church, for in Princeton at that time we still had compulsory morning chapel through

the week, and on Sundays we all had to go to two longer
services. The vesper service with singing we liked, but through
the long tedious morning sermons we read books or drowsed
and dreamed. At one such time old President Patten, who
for some time had been droning along, abruptly threw back
his great white head and glared out over the chapel and
said:

"I was asked if we have freethinkers at Princeton? No, I
replied! For it takes almost as much thinking for a man to become a freethinker as it does to believe in God!"

But I did some hard thinking now. What was it all about?
I asked. Was there really any God above, and down here
what was this show called life, and what was I doing to make it
worth while? Religion going, my music gone. What was left?
My writing. And for that, what had I done since I came to
college? Damned little! I had tried to write for "The Prince"
but had failed. With some friends I had started a small literary club that met several evenings a month to smoke and talk
in somebody's room about Kipling and other writers we liked.
But that was about all I had to my credit. Now I decided to
start in.

So I did work hard in those last two years, and presently
we shall come to that. But most of it was not for the classroom; for, although I did enough to get fairly high marks each
term, with only a few exceptions I found little or no stimulus
there. All that has been changed since my time, but the classrooms of my day were mainly places of genial ease or utter
boredom, until exams, when the desperate cramming came.
We had the Honor System then. Nobody spied on you during exams, you could even go out now and then if you liked.
But at the end of your paper you wrote:

"I pledge my honor as a gentleman that during this ex-
amination I have neither given nor received assistance."

Only once did I see a man break that pledge. Sitting just
in front of me, furtively he kept looking at notes. Beside me

the president of our class leaned forward and touched his arm and said:

"Tear up your paper and flunk this." He did.

But sometimes there were liberal interpretations of the pledge. On the night before an exam in European general history, for which the prof gave generous credits if on your paper you could pledge that you had read five volumes of collateral reading he had advised, I found in his room a football man, a sophomore, sitting smoking his pipe and listening to five freshmen whom he had ordered to read aloud the five volumes recommended. One was a life of Napoleon, another was a life of Bismarck and a third was a short volume on the Hanseatic League. I can still see the face of my friend as he sat in perfect bedlam and took all that history in!

I remember another football friend in an exam on philosophy. I saw him writing rapidly on and on until he filled some thirty or forty pages. Then he turned in his paper and went out. Later on the campus I asked:

"Bill, what in hell were you writing in there? You know nothing about philosophy."

"Not a damn thing," was his cheerful reply, "except for the first question. I knew just enough about that so I could fill the first page with it. Then I turned over and began writing all the verses of Old Nassau. I wrote that song a dozen times and turned in a good thick paper to old Jerry [our prof] on the chance that, with two hundred papers to read, he'll never get time to read 'em all. I think I've a damned good chance of passing." And two weeks later he told me he had!

As for me, in those last two years, I was able to find a few courses with some of the best profs in college, men who did help me a lot. One of them was old Andy West, one of the greatest Latin scholars in our country at that time. On the score of seniors, who had elected his course that fall, he smiled and said in a genial tone:

"Gentlemen, thank God they're gone—all the boneheads—

only you are left. I think I may safely assume that every man before me reads Latin as easily as English, so we are about to enjoy ourselves. I can best introduce to you this course by saying: Once upon a time there was a civilization called pagan. We are now about to enter it."

And the revealing looks he gave us into the life of Imperial Rome left in me memories so strong that, many years later in that old town, one of the things I held against Mussolini was the way in which his noisy Fascisti kept rising up between me and the Rome of Andy West.

But it was in English that I did my hardest work. I not only read but wrote stories and plays. I wrote two librettos for the Princeton Triangle Club. Both were rejected, and only one of my stories was published in our magazine, "The Lit." But still I kept on. I was looking ahead, and now I was learning to dig for myself for material to write about and for ways of writing it. From the night discussions of our small literary club, I had Kipling as my favorite still and took as my slogan that verse of his:

> But each for the joy of the working, and each
> in his separate star,
> Shall draw the Thing as he sees It for the God
> of Things as They are.

I read Tolstoy and Turgeniev, too, and was excited and stirred to the depths by their realist pictures in fiction of the surging forces at work in the Russia of their time. But what about my country, my time? What were the forces working here and how could I get close to them and see them in terms of human life? With my Philadelphia roommate, who was as hungry as I in the search, nearly every evening I spent in the old college library, reading all the books we could find on the new social trends of our day. Woodrow Wilson helped us there. He was our favorite prof and our friend. Since his coming to Princeton two years before, his courses on political science had drawn the students to him in crowds. Homely and plain, with a rugged style, there was magnetism in that man and often a quaint humor, too. In a lecture one day on marriage as related to the common law, he smiled down from the platform on some three hundred of us and said:

"I never get over being amazed at the men who somehow do succeed in persuading girls to marry them."

Chuckles from all over the hall, with everyone glancing at some friend who was the homeliest man he knew, while up there on the platform the very homeliest one of us all stood smiling at the lot of us!

Wilson came several times to our rooms in the evenings to smoke and talk with a group as interested as ourselves in what he had to tell us about America, old and new. He recommended books to read and they gave me an exciting sense of new life stirring in our land. Theodore Roosevelt was President and was busy settling the great coal strike of that time. Only a few years before, as police commissioner in New York, he had begun the long slow job of cleaning up the city slums, with the help of his journalist friend, Jacob Riis. Hungrily I read Riis' book upon How the Other Half Lives, and his descriptions of tenement life on the Lower East Side of New York took my thoughts far back to my old friend Parsy in Chicago, in her rickety little back-yard house among the crowded tenements. More and more that tenement life appealed to me as a tremendous new field, scarcely touched by American writers yet. How could I see it at firsthand and dig into it deep for pictures and stories? Toward the end of senior year, I made several trips to New York and, passed on from one man to another, finally I landed at the University Settlement in the heart of the Lower East Side. They agreed to take me in as a resident the following year. So, when college was over, I went there early the next fall.

VII

I CAME ABRUPTLY INTO A WORLD DARK AND HARSH AND GUT-tural—but fascinating, wonderful! The Lower East Side in 1902 was not at all as it is today. Already so packed with immigrants that upon our block alone nearly four thousand men, women and children were jammed into huge tenement hives, with fresh thousands constantly pouring into the region from abroad, it was in those exciting years a seething furnace of hopes and dreams, age-old hatreds, fears, religions, radical new philosophies, brought by people from many lands, all hurled together to start new lives and become "Americans." In its deep narrow streets at night, roaring with humanity, between long lines of peddlers' carts with flaring kerosene torches over-head, poured dense deafening torrents of people in outland-ish costumes, from gaudy shawls and kerchiefs to the long black gowns of bewildered old Polish Jews. Their shrill harsh voices spoke in tongues that were completely strange to me, and strange their faces, strange their eyes! They excited me; they baffled me! How ever get close to such people as these, to write about them? Where begin?

Battered by this avalanche of impressions strange and new, I remember, after dark one day, climbing into the high seat of a bootblack stand for a shine and, with memories of Chi-cago, my big home city of neighborhoods, watching desper-ately for some sign of any neighborhood here in New York. If only the same faces would pass me twice, or friends would meet and gossip a while! But still the crowds came roaring by—new ones, new ones, all the time!

"Hell! It's hopeless!" I told myself. "I might as well quit and go on back home!"

But in the Settlement where I lived, a large brick building six floors high with residents' quarters at the top, the new head worker, young Bob Hunter, had already gathered a remarkable group of men, over half of them in their twenties still and some of them like me learning to write. A genial crowd, they took me in, and made me feel I was not alone in tackling this baffling life. Finding that I liked small boys, Hunter at once put me in charge of their basketball games up on the roof. I soon felt myself at home with these kids and, when he saw how well I got on, Hunter then suggested that I work up a report on newsboys, bootblacks and messenger boys for the New York Child Labor Committee, which was then helping to launch the crusade against child labor all over the land.

I agreed and for weeks I ranged the crowded quarters of the city, talking to wise tough little guys, liking them and making friends by giving them suppers and cigarettes and by taking some of them to the big top gallery of the old Academy of Music to see the wild melodramas there. By such bribes I got the facts and stories I wanted about their jobs and lives. In true reformer fashion then I centered on the worst ones, the toughest and the wildest, the hundreds down by City Hall near what was then still Newspaper Row. For these were the real street Arabs who slept at night in doorways or under Brooklyn Bridge close by. Toward midnight in roaring crowds they'd gather around the shipping-room doors of the World, Herald, American, Tribune, Globe and Sun, to get the early first editions. With these they'd race off through the streets; then back they'd come, some for more papers, others to spend the money they'd earned on late suppers and at crap games in sheltered nooks. I found one game going strong about nine o'clock one night and they were still at it when I passed again toward dawn. And many of these were little boys, only six and seven years old. I remember one who

said he was five and who drank three huge cups of coffee at
supper with me in a lunchroom at three a.m.

Finding that quite a few of the boys worked in Chinatown
close by, I got in touch with an undertaker, who did a thriving business there, and persuaded him to take me into the real
opium dives. Into a laundry we would go and, in a rear room
kicking aside a pile of dirty linen, my guide would lift up a
trap door and by a ladder we would climb down into stifling
little rooms where in bunks lay white women and girls. For
errands up to the world outside they used tough little messenger boys, like the street Arabs I already knew. Many were
already hitting the pipe. I tried one myself with one small
boy, who grinned when he saw how that sweet smoke made
me sick to my stomach. Nor was it only the opium habit that
these small kids were getting there, for most of them by the
age of fourteen had venereal disease.

In such stuffy chambers of horrors I reached the climax of
facts and color for the report I was to write. Now for reform!
At the Settlement I wrote a report crammed with little yarns
so lurid that the Child Labor Committee begged me at once
to rewrite it in form for publication in some magazine.
Thrilled by the chance, I started in. Soon I was completely
swamped. But one of my new Settlement friends, Leroy Scott,
who had worked on a paper two years and was later to reach
such success as a fiction writer for magazines, generously spent
a whole day of his time showing me how to shape that mass
in a way to give it form and life. For two weeks more I wrote
day and night, then took it to old Mr. Gilder of the Century
Magazine. He liked my article, he said, but he could not run
it soon and he knew our Committee wanted quick action. So
I took it to S. S. McClure, whose new muckraking magazine,
with Lincoln Steffens, Ida Tarbell, Ray Baker and others on
the staff, was already the best seller of any magazine of its
kind. I went to Chicago for Christmas then and, three days
after I arrived, a letter and a telegram came—the telegram,

from Gilder to say he had found he could publish my article soon; the letter, from McClure, accepting it and inclosing a check. Jubilant over this double success, I had a grand Christmas and so did my father. Dad was quite as pleased as I. But next week on my return to New York, I found that in my article McClure had cut all mention of venereal disease in small boys. I protested that we needed this; it was one of our most effective points to use in our child labor campaign.

"All right," McClure answered. "Now I'll tell you what I'll do. Imagine yourself in a room with six grown-ups and six little girls. Tell this part of your story so that the grown-ups will get it but the six little girls will not—and then I'll print it." And he did.

Puffed up now by foolish pride and thinking I was ready for fiction, I wrote in quick succession three short stories and sent them to magazines. Very promptly back they came, and back I went to articles. I wrote some more about street boys. One was published by Collier's and two others by the New York Evening Post. So I did my part in picturing the city street life that helped to breed the gangs, pimps, gamblers, petty thieves and public enemies of today.

Meanwhile at the Settlement I had been making lifelong friends—Walter Weyl and English Walling, Arthur Bullard and Fred King, Howard Brubaker, Leroy Scott, Bob Hunter, Phelps Stokes and several more. All still young men, from Harvard, Yale and colleges in the West, they mingled here with older men from universities abroad, and they made what education I'd had look mighty thin and picayune.

Walter Weyl at twenty-eight had behind him seven years of hard postgraduate work in Europe and, to get closer to actual life, he had just spent months in helping the American miners prepare their case for the settlement of the big coal strike. Not only an economist but a philosopher as well, friendly, kindly, deeply observing, with an interest ever fresh

for other people's points of view, he proceeded to draw me
out on mine, then very nicely punctured them and led me to
wider deeper views of the fast-changing world of our time.

Walling's approach was an onslaught. He glanced at the
books I'd brought from college and then tossed them on the
floor.

"Come in and look at mine," he said. In his small room
across the hall, on shelves and tables and the floor, were stacks
of radical modern books on economics, piles of government
reports. He chuckled at my look of dismay. "I'm not asking
you to read all this. You seem to have the makings of a
damned good story writer," he said. "So don't spoil it. Read
just enough to bring you out of ancient fogs to some real
view of these modern times, then get the rest of it hot out of
life. Make friends with these tenement people and listen, listen
all the time. They've got a lot to teach us boys, so for the
love of Jesus Christ don't let's be uplifters here!"

But he himself was tainted with the uplift fragrance soon—
for, owing to the prominence of his family in the West, a
Hearst sob sister tracked him down and, when he refused an
interview, she wrote out of her own fluffy head a story in
which she quoted him thus:

"It shall be my aim all my life to live among the lowly and
bring a little sunshine to those whose lives are full of clouds."

On the night when the story appeared, with a double quar-
tet composed of ourselves and several East Side boys we knew
to supply a humming accompaniment, softly from the Evening Journal Walling chanted those noble lines. Ribald
laughter at the end, and then with our lowly young tenement
friends we went to Little Hungary Café to get some sunshine
out of wine from Budapest.

So we began our lives down there, not uplifters but mixers
and explorers. In our large settlement building, humming with
activities from early morning till late at night, we lived on
the two floors at the top and helped with the clubs and classes

downstairs and there made friends who brought us in touch
with the tenement life outside. But much of the club and
classwork was done by people who came from uptown,
among them a small group of girls who called themselves The
Junior League. From their group was born the chain of powerful organizations now so well known all over the land.

Almost every evening we had visitors for dinner; at our
long table often some forty people would sit down. I remember Jane Addams and Lillian Wald, Clarence Darrow, H. G.
Wells, John Burns, Keir Hardie, Ramsay MacDonald and
many more. French and Germans and Russians came. The discussions in our living room over coffee and cigarettes covered
nearly every phase of the new social movements here and
abroad. And feeling the whole world astir with big new
dreams and new ideas, hungrily I drank them in. My whole
outlook was changing fast. I was for the people now, the
driven masses everywhere, and anything to better the hard
conditions in which they lived. But what took hold on me
from the start was not so much reforms and reformers as the
untouched life around me. How to picture it? That was my
job, and in that, too, I got help from some of our visitors.
Lincoln Steffens came one night. He'd liked my stories of
street-boy life and he told me:

"Stories are your line. You'll come to fiction soon enough.
Don't try to hurry it. First dig hard for hunks of life just as it
is, and write 'em down just as they come. And in anything
you write, for God's sake don't put it on ice by trying to see
both sides of it. That leaves both writer and reader cold.
Choose your side, your personal angle, and then warm up to
it! Don't just see it—feel it, feel it hot and strong!"

Ray Baker came one night and he said:

"Remember, Poole, in writing of the life down here, you're
writing to Americans, people in small Western towns and on
ranches and on farms, who know nothing of this life at all.
To make it real to them you might try a plan that I have

found worth while. When I'm at work I keep in mind a dozen Americans I've known, men and women of different kinds who seem to me to represent my million readers everywhere; and never for a minute do I forget 'em while I write. To bring your stories close to them, get used to picking out of life not only dramatic incidents but all kinds of significant little details about faces, voices and tricks of speech. Don't be afraid of taking notes. You won't use many but they'll help to soak you in this life you picture, so that it's all real to you—and only then can you make it real to your readers everywhere."

So I did in those next years. So did Leroy Scott, Howard Brubaker, Arthur Bullard and others who came there to write. For our settlement, like Hull House in Chicago and other such places all over the land, was a new school for writers about life in the tenements. Many were economists who wrote surveys and reports, but other youngsters like myself, who were to write fiction later on, kept to the more colorful side and into that vast human gold mine, all so new and strange to us then, we dug for stories hot out of life and burned the candle at both ends.

With our friend Henry Moskowitz as guide, we went to countless cafés, large and small, Russian, Polish and German cafés, Socialist, Anarchist, free love, freethinker and actor and poet cafés, where, coming from the oppression of Europe into the sudden freedom here to argue and shout and write as they pleased, young Jews were burning up their lives in this great furnace of ideas. Over black coffee and cigarettes they would talk fervently half the night and then, after three or four hours' sleep, go to the sweatshops where they worked from dawn till late evening, when again they'd rush for those midnight cafés to plunge into the ferment of new dreams!

I watched their faces, scowls and smiles, the flashes in their quick black eyes. I heard their bursts of laughter or loud excited argument. I was learning Yiddish now and caught fragments of their talk, dramatic little tales they told of jealous husbands, wives and lovers, poverty and bitter rebellion, wild ambitions, hopes and dreams for themselves and the whole human race. And all these little stories, with tricks of gesture and of speech and details about faces and eyes, I'd jot down at the Settlement, working often half the night. I had no time to bother with plots or to round out my stories then. Chunks of life intensely real, I took them all just as they came. But as I soaked myself in notes, more and more I learned to pick the dramatic and the significant out of the mass I gathered down there and to make them real to readers outside, in articles filled with such little yarns. There was nothing uncommon about it at all. Thousands of others, I've no doubt, have learned to write in some such way. But few have had material like that immense new field of life, the Lower East Side in those early years when the great pot seethed and boiled and new Americans were made.

In that first year I met Abraham Cahan, the first real revolutionist and writer from Russia I'd ever seen. Quickly he became my friend and opened up a Russian world of revolution, books and plays, that stirred me deep, as Tolstoy and Turgeniev had in my last year of college. I read Cahan's big Socialist paper, *Der Vorwärts*, and, from the Bunch of Letters from East Side readers that he ran in it each day, I culled more intensities, bits of stories, raw and hot, right out of that Ghetto life. With Cahan I went to theaters on Grand Street and the Bowery and there saw Yiddish problem plays that pictured in vivid realist terms the dramas of this melting pot, in which young people threw off the ways of their parents and all anchors of old Jewish life, launched blindly into the new world here and called New York America.

But much of their background overseas was still to be seen and heard and felt among the bewildered old people here. Long before this, in the Week of Atonement, I'd squeezed my way into dark and stifling little synagogues, where men with white shawls over their heads in wailing frenzy of entreaty prayed all day and all night long to Jehovah to forgive their sins. They at least still believed in their God. But on the night of Yom Kippur, last day of that dramatic week, into my room at the Settlement burst three small Jewish friends of mine, boys of eight and nine and ten, and brought to me their argument. For two of them were orthodox still and looked with horror on one small boy with bright black eyes and a huge shock of hair who shouted at them:

"Dere ees no Gott! All lies, all lies, my brudder say! No Gott! Only people—poor people like us! And all must be brudders and rise for our rights!"

My little living room was the scene of countless other dramas and problems of that seething life. For I shared it with Fred King, the hardest worker of us all. Tall, rugged and lean, with a deep low voice, slow smile, strong steady piercing gray eyes, Fred had been born up in Maine, had gone to Yale and there read Tolstoy and decided to spend his life working for the underdogs. Attached to the police force, he was one of the very first probation officers in New York. Convicted criminals, freed from prison before they had served their terms, were put on probation in his charge. He slaved for them; he got them jobs. So into our room in the evenings came young ex-pickpockets or "dips," hobos, panhandlers, thieves of all kinds; wife beaters, drunkards and dope fiends came. Their old mothers or wives or mistresses, gaudy young prostitutes even, came to intercede in their behalf with sobs and tears and torrents of talk. Some of them fell on their knees. Wives came to get husbands sent back to jail, then came to get them out again. And often this little court in our room continued far into the night.

From such intensities we turned on quieter nights to poker games—and a strange assortment gathered then. I remember a young White Slaver with a glass eye, who was often there, and a middle-aged ex-burglar who had been lamed for life,

he said, by a charge of shot fired into his leg as he entered by
a window a bedroom in a house uptown. From Newspaper
Row Frank Simonds came. He was studying war maps even
then, for he had a crazy notion that there would be a big war
in Europe someday. Arthur Bullard, too, often sat in our
game, for he was one of our residents now. A prison worker
intense as King, in his spare time he read hungrily radical
Russian papers and books, for he hoped to go to Russia soon
and write about the ferment there. So did I, and we became
close friends.

With Bullard and King I went to police courts. In one of
them a wise and shrewd old magistrate let me sit beside him
listening to the quarrels, crimes and problems that poured into
his court. With Bullard I went out to the Island to the immense grim prison there to see various friends of his, and with
King I visited others in their cells down in the Tombs. And
with an old pickpocket I knew I went late at night to cafés
of the underworld. I remember Eddy Doyle's in Chinatown
on a Saturday night, when from midnight on it was packed
with crooks and their gorgeously dressed young mistresses,
who had put on all their jewels, for this was a gala night.
Young pickpockets in evening clothes came straight from
Weber and Fields' big music show on Broadway and here
openly showed to friends the watches, pins and pocketbooks
they had taken on that night.

With all these varied and hungry explorations into the life
down there, writing, writing all the time, for months I
crowded days and nights. At twenty-two it is easy to live on
one's nerves for a time, and so did I then. But late in March I
took the grippe and was sick in bed for two weeks. It left me
feeling weak as a cat and, to get back my strength again,
gladly I accepted the generous invitation of some wealthy
friends uptown to go with them in a private car on a two
weeks' trip to the Grand Canyon in Arizona. What a swift
prodigious leap back into the life of safety and ease that I

had once known so well! No problems and no tragedies. Congenial people young and old, all friendly, quickly taking me in. Over the prairies and across the empty silent desert beyond we went to the Canyon. There we had Western ponies to ride and I kept in the saddle from morning to night. Down into that stupendous gorge we rode to the winding valley beneath, lovely with the flowers of spring and inclosed by cliffs rising miles to the sky. And vast deep stillness, utter peace.

But after a few days of this, back we rushed East to New York. And then came an experience that left its mark on me for life. For in the close and fetid air of rotten old tenements packed with people, I had an awful close-up view of the death that comes from poverty.

VIII

THE CRUSADE TO HALT THE GREAT WHITE PLAGUE WAS THEN just starting in New York. To prove that "consumption" was spread by infection, the committee had chosen a tenement block where the Plague had left deadlier records than in any other block in town. And now I was asked to take those records to the spot, trace down the stories behind them and so give a picture in human terms that could be featured in the press. I agreed and went to work, with little or no conception of how black that picture was to be.

The Lung Block, as I named it then, was far down on the East Side near the river. In early years, when that quarter was a center of fashion in the town, many of the buildings had been great handsome private homes, but long ago they had been turned into grimy rookeries, the spacious rooms divided into little cell-like chambers, many only stifling closets with no outer light or air. I can still smell the odors there. In what had been large yards behind, cheap rear tenements had been built, leaving between front and rear buildings only deep dank filthy courts. Nearly four thousand people lived on the block and, in rooms, in halls, on stairways, in courts and out on fire escapes, were scattered some four hundred babies. Homes and people, good and bad, had only thin partitions between them. A thousand families struggled on, while many sank and polluted the others. For dissipation came easy here. The Lung Block had eight thriving barrooms and five houses of ill fame. And with drunkenness, foul air, darkness and filth to feed upon, the living germs of the Great White Plague, coughed up

78

and spat on floors and walls, had done a thriving business for years.

There was one building called The Inkpot. It was dark as night inside. In its front and rear tenements, five floors high, lived a hundred and forty people. Among them I found three sick with the Plague. Rooms here had held death ready and waiting for each new family that moved in. Up on the third floor was a room with two little closets behind it. In one of these a blind Scotchman slept and took the Plague in '94. His wife and his fifteen-year-old son both drank, and the home grew squalid as the big house. He died in the hospital. Only a few months later his little daughter caught the disease and lay coughing through long sleepless nights. She died, and the mother and son moved away. But behind them the germs lived on. One year later, in October, a Jew rented this same room. He was taken sick and died in the summer. The room was rented again in the autumn by a German and his wife. She died of the Plague in the following spring. Then an Irish family came in. The father was a hard steady worker and loved his children. His wife kept things neat and clean. The home this time was winning the fight. But six months later he took the Plague. He died in 1901. And this was the record of only one room in seven years!

I found so many rooms like that! For weeks day and night I worked through the block. With health inspectors, doctors and visiting nurses I made my rounds, and later by myself I posed as a settlement visitor one week and as a "fresh-air man" the next. As the records kept piling in on me from the living present as from the past, and I met so many men, women and kids who appealed to me, yet were doomed to die, the strain grew so unbearable that, in an effort to save a few lives, I took people to hospital clinics uptown and, through the help of Lillian Wald, had others sent away to the country. For a few there was hope; for most there was none. I remember one we were able to save, a winsome little Italian boy. He was only five years old and his name was Yutzi Romeo. I can still see his beguiling smile. But even more clearly I recall the look in the face of a girl of sixteen. Though she worked all day in a factory to support her family, she had gone to night school, too, for she "meant to be somebody," she said. But the long strain had worn her down and now she was coughing day and night. I took her to a clinic uptown. As the doctor bent over his stethoscope, she stared straight in front of her and I caught the trapped hunted look in her eyes. As the doctor slowly raised his head, in his look I could read the sentence of death. So could she. She was silent all the way home.

From such scenes in those dark weeks I turned for relief to the life outside—to the barrooms and the sailors there, jokes they cracked, smutty stories they told. I watched a couple of gun fights, too, and heard the pistol shots of the Bulls as they chased a young killer over the roofs. I helped the Sporting Parson, in his boys' club not far away. A Baptist preacher thirty years old, all through his twenties he had tramped each winter from the Dakotas to Maine, preaching in the lumber camps. He was a genial husky thoroughly out-of-doors sort of man, just the sort I needed then. One evening he gave me a pipeful of a smoking tobacco he used, called Canal Driver's Delight, and it nearly knocked me down. In his two bare little rooms, for the Irish and Italian boys who came crowding in each night, he chalked a ring on the board floor and set them to boxing, in the hope that, when they learned to use their fists, they'd give up their habit of fighting with knives. Boys often came in with bloody shirts from stabs that they had just received. One of them was Dago Joe, a squat young bull of about sixteen with a swarthy pockmarked face and dull smoldering black eyes. He climbed into the club through a window one night and at two a.m. I heard him still there at the piano, in the dark. And I stood at the window for some time, gripped by the tension and poignant depths in the crude strong music that he made.

There was a huge Danish woman, too, on the Lung Block, who became my friend. Sailors came and stayed with her, "deep-water" sailors, by which I mean that they shipped on voyages 'round the Horn to Singapore and Shanghai and other fascinating ports. As gifts or loans when they sailed away, they had left a lively marmoset, a scarlet parrot, heathen idols, painted shells and other things that pulled my thoughts out of the stinking rooms near by and sent them careering far off over the Seven Seas. I sometimes felt the Wanderlust and, in those lovely days of spring, wandered along East River piers where lay the last of the ships with sails, listening to the "chanteys" of their crews as they heaved on the ropes and slowly, slowly the big ships moved out on the river, bound for the sea.

But from such whiffs of the ocean world back I would dive into the Lung Block, all the more bitter that human beings should be choked to death in such foul holes, when there was so much fresh air and health and sunlight so close by. Why must people live like this, work like this and die like this? The whisper in Yiddish I heard one night I've never forgotten, I hear it still.

"*Luft—luft—giebt mir luft!*" Back in a rear tenement, a young Rumanian Jew lay dying of consumption. I had come with a doctor into a room only ten feet square, where six people lay on the floor packed close, rubbing heavy sleep from tired eyes. Four children slept in a closet close by.

"Breath—breath—give me breath!" For two long weeks he had lain there dying. From his soiled bed he could touch and infect the table where the two families ate; the cooking stove was but six feet from him; the cupboard, just above his pillow; he could even reach one of the cradles, where his baby girl lay staring frightened at his strange position. For his wasted body was too feeble to rise and too choked and tortured to lie down. While his young wife held him up in her arms, again and again that whisper came, but with a new meaning soon, for he begged us to kill him that night, begged until I thought I'd go mad! With the doctor I went out and sat on the stairs and there I begged for a stronger shot of morphine to ease the poor devil's pain:

"He can't live but a week! You've told me so! He's infecting everyone with him in there! Why keep him in agony day and night?" My friend the doctor answered:

"I'll make him sleep, brother; I'll make him sleep." So merciful morphine did its work.

"The struggle is ended," I wrote the next night, "the smothered whisper forever hushed."

While I still sat at my desk writing this grim story down, my big quiet roommate, Fred King, came back from an evening he'd spent with a boy called Dopey Ed, in a cell in the Tombs. When I gave vent to my bitterness, King asked me with a tired smile:

"Why don't you quit writing and take a real job that will do something for people like that?"

"Writing will do this job!" I replied.

"Yeah? Pen's mightier than the sword? What the Lung Block needs is the ax."

"We propose to get it!" I said. "We mean to raise hell with the politicians till they get busy and tear the whole stinking damned block down!"

Next month, when I finished my report, I called it The Plague in Its Stronghold, and in it I wrote, with all the fervor of twenty-three:

"This Plague Consumption must be stamped out! It has hung on the earth for thousands of years! It has killed not millions but billions of men, women and children; more than all wars and plagues the world over! And now of the seventy millions in our country, seven millions must die of this scourge unless the present damnable ratio be brought down!"

My report was featured in the press. Reporters came to write up the block. I took them around, with photographers.

The Bridge 83

Hearings were held up at Albany. I gave my testimony there. So we raised hell with the politicians, and at twenty-three I thought that our campaign would succeed. I was wrong. For the landlords on the Lung Block had many influential friends. So came delays, delays, delays, until in the papers the story grew cold. It took thirty-two years to bring the ax. It came at last, under the New Deal. The rotten old block was razed to the ground and in its place you may see today the airy sunny apartment houses of Knickerbocker Village.

All through the hectic weeks of my work in the infected rooms down there, a young East Side medical student I knew, Harry Lorber, often came along. He is a noted surgeon today, known to countless thousands as a lifesaver and friend, generous with courage and cash, and such a storyteller that I could fill a volume if only I had space for them here. All through my weeks in the Lung Block, he made me drink a quart of milk and swallow six raw eggs a day. In spite of that, he found at the end I was running a little fever each night, so early in June I went home to Lake Forest for two months of outdoor rest. I was glad to be back in that old life, so clean and comfortable, pleasant and safe, with friends and people that I loved. And yet it seemed so different now, for I couldn't forget what I had seen. Fred King came out to join me there and we played tennis and took long walks. My family liked him. He loved the life. But he, too, had his memories. From our rooms at the Settlement in New York, we had looked across deep crowded courts to the shabby back of a red-light house, where men bought ten-visit tickets, which were punched each time they came. Fifty cents a visit was the price. It was a cheap vile old house and at the back looked viler still, for through the lighted windows we'd seen naked women and heard yells and screams of laughter, often right on through the night. These memories were in us still and, one bright morning in Lake Forest, at breakfast together Fred muttered to me:

"Seems tough in a lovely place like this to dream of whore-houses and prisons at night."

"Same here. The Lung Block," I replied.

Soon after that he returned to New York and, rested and aired, my fever gone, late in July I followed him. But back on the Lower East Side, I kept clear of the Lung Block now. A journalist and story writer then, as I have been ever since, I jumped from one story to the next. No more disease and death for me! I'd come to the East Side to write of its life and, for contrast from what I had seen, I turned to its more genial parts.

At the Settlement lived Howard Brubaker. Just a few months younger than I, Howard was a little man with a chuckle that nobody ever forgot and a smile that went from ear to ear. With that lovely sense of humor which has given him such a place on the staff of the New Yorker since, already he was on intimate terms with countless young East Siders who gladly welcomed him into their lives. And he took me with him now. On summer evenings we ranged together "East Side, West Side, all about town." We knew all the street songs of those friendly Al Smith days and with two other lads we made a quartette and supplied close harmony at beach picnics and East Side balls. Through Howard I made some grand girl friends, took them out to Coney Island, had supper there, did all the shows and did not bring them home till dawn. Then back to the Settlement we would come, to pull mattresses out on our fire escapes for little Sunday-morning naps. Upon many stifling nights we dragged our mattresses up to the roof, and we found a dim weird world up there, with the great hot glow of the city striking up into the sky but all around us dark shadowy roofs packed thick with acres of men and women and children, sleepers like ourselves. And as I wrote about such scenes and all these new young friends of mine, more and more human and close they grew and my liking for them grew warmer still. Thank God for Howard Brubaker and the doors he opened for me into the laughter of that life! Often, too, on summer nights we went to the Henry Street Settlement. Compared with our own huge institution, here was a deeply personal house, the home of Lillian Wald and her hard-working Visiting Nurses. No matter how hard they worked by day, the younger ones could be gay at night. We danced with them; and on her little back veranda, I had long talks with Lillian Wald. Later she meant more to me than any woman in social service and her home became for me "the house with open windows" which she was to write about. Indeed, that title came from me, for there I had found windows opening out on a whole new world of service and of brotherhood.

Meanwhile with English Walling I was having a look into Tammany Hall. Over on the Bowery on a hot roaring August night, we sat by a desk on a platform at one end of a long crowded poolroom, headquarters of Little Tim Sullivan, who was the local Tammany chief. In his thirties slender and handsome still, well dressed and affable, Little Tim had just come back from an afternoon at the races and, as he sat chatting there, he was opening his enormous mail. Into one pile he tossed invitations to summer picnics and balls, with some four hundred dollars' worth of tickets that he was expected to buy. And this was his mail for only one day!

"This political game costs money," he smiled. "Here's two for the Hesper Club. I'm buying 'em—five dollars each—but I want you two boys to go in my place. How about it?"

We promptly agreed, for the Hesper Club, whose members were bookmakers at the great tracks, had a reputation for style and dash. Their picnic was something I'll never forget. Sunday morning, on an East River pier, at the gangway of their picnic ship stood two smiling pretty girls, who pinned red carnations to our coats and gave us each a small box of cigars.

Though the Seth Low reform administration had clamped down the lid on the city tight, as we steamed up the river that day I found roulette and faro going strong all over the decks, with thousands of dollars being raked in; and in their ball game later up river at the picnic grounds, the lightweight champion Terry McGovern and other celebrities gaily played, while from the side lines bets were shouted:

"Five hundred Terry don't make first!"

But best I remember a talk we had with an old state senator. When he learned that I was a Princeton boy, he said: "Then you belong in Tammany Hall." And when I asked him why, he explained that one of our most famous early Princetonians, Aaron Burr, when Alexander Hamilton helped organize the officers of the American Revolution into the Society of the Cincinnati, had promptly countered by declaring: "The privates are good enough for me," and for them Burr had helped to form the Tammany Society, known in New York as Tammany Hall.

"And started of and by and for the common people," the senator said, "we have stood for them ever since. How many gentlemen reform politicians do you see here today? Not one. They are home with their families or in their dressy country clubs. That's why reform may come and go, but always Tammany comes back—because we mean democracy—always, the whole year around."

He told an amusing little tale of how Boss Platt, the Republican chief, after elections one autumn sent down to the East Side to learn what in hell had become of four hundred Yiddish votes for which he had paid. But in Yiddish you read from right to left, and so those voters, having been told to make their marks in the "first column" on the ballot, had marked the first column *from the right* and cast their votes for Prohibition, the smallest party at that time! The joyous Prohibitionists had got drunk on ginger ale that night!

As the friendly old senator rambled on about city politics

and the genial humorous human kindly side of Tammany Hall—friends of the people all the time, in both their troubles and their joys, getting them jobs and paying the rents of widows about to be dispossessed, giving them food and shoes and clothing, helping poor mothers get boys out of prisons, working for them the whole year 'round—he said nothing of the tribute they levied on the underworld, on crooks and pimps and prostitutes and gambling joints, nor did he speak of the strong-arm gangs that Tammany used on election day nor of the crowds of repeaters carted about from poll to poll to cast their votes all over town.

But that autumn I saw them for myself. Howard Brubaker and I had a young Jewish lawyer friend, Emil Fuchs, who said that to get an inside view of an election we ought to take jobs as police deputies at the polls, and he offered to arrange for that. On election day at six a.m. we met him at headquarters, where his chief, after a pleasant chat, swore us in as deputies. Then instantly his manner changed. To a big cop standing near he said, in tones ominous and deep:

"Officer, take these two men back to the reserve room and give 'em each a badge and a gun."

As we went out we heard chuckles from Fuchs, and very quickly we grew grim. Back in the reserve room, filled with huge burly deputies, we were supplied with badge and gun and sat down to wait for our call. Howard was sent to Staten Island, I to a place on the Bowery. I took one look at the crowd in that place and quickly put my gun away in a drawer in a corner—and just in time! For into the poll reeled a huge drunken hobo and, when asked where he came from, roared:

"From Niagara Falls but I don't *give* a damn! I'm go'n' to vote! Who'll stop me?"

"I will!" piped the Republican watcher. He was a dapper little lad, an Episcopal clergyman from uptown. Plucky as a bantam, he yelled: "Officer, arrest that man!"

But I was arresting nobody, nor were the two regular cops

in the room, for into it from the street outside poured a howling mob of Bowery bums and, in that wild free-for-all, from
the window ledge to which I had leaped, I saw the little
clergyman tossed about like a leaf in a storm! Me a policeman?
No! I cried. When the scrimmage was over and our two cops
looked for the hobo, he'd disappeared. There were many
other fights that day and in not one did I use my gun. But if
completely failing in my sworn duty as a cop, I did see an
election from the inside. And when the long day was over
at last and doors were locked and our two cops brought in a
supper of sandwiches and foaming pails of delectable beer, I
stayed on with the watchers to watch the count and make
notes for the story I would write.

   That winter I turned to labor and labor unions on the East
Side. I had seen how the people lived and died. How did they
work? I asked myself. My friend Leroy Scott was already
writing his novel, The Walking Delegate, as union leaders
were called then; and through him I met some of them and so
got into the clothing trades. I had come there just in time to
see the change from old to new—from the boss who worked
in his little shop and knew everyone he employed to the great
impersonal clothing factory risen out of our new machine
age. I went through many where floor after floor was crowded
with workers at machines in rooms well lighted, airy and
clean, where they worked only eight hours a day. In the old
sweatshops, on the other hand—foul dark little rooms, I visited scores—the day was often sixteen hours, from before daylight till long after dark. And yet many preferred them to the
new, for the constant drive and speed and strain in the great
new clothing mills took all the life out of them, they said,
while in the old sweatshop they worked as they pleased, talked
and sang when they pleased, sent out for beer and drank with
the boss, who worked right with them and was their friend.
Many of them were Socialists and in Cahan's Socialist paper,
Der Vorwärts, I found this letter written by one:

"What's the matter with me?" he asked. "I am a Socialist. I believe that all bosses are my enemies and all fellow workers are my friends. But next to me in our shop sits a man who is one of the meanest rats I know! He steals my things; he tries to sneak the shirts I've made away from me! I hate that man! And this is wrong! For it is my boss that I should hate—yet he's jolly and kind and I like him! What is the matter? I'm all mixed up!" When Abe Cahan read me that letter one night, I remember how he chuckled and smiled till there were wrinkles all 'round his eyes. "Even Socialism is funny!" he said.

But Socialism was gaining fast in the sweatshops and factories of those days, and no such perplexities entered the heads of the fervid young Socialists I knew. I went to their meetings large and small and, out on the streets at night, heard their impassioned harangues to the crowds. I even carried soapboxes for some. I argued with them in little cafés, often till three and four a.m. For the Lung Block and the sweatshops had made of me a rebel, too. I found some of them such appealing lads, in their fervor and faith in this great dream for which they were slaving day and night, that more than once I was tempted to join them. And yet I did not; I still held back. For intense though I was myself at that time, I told myself I'd got free from one church and I didn't propose to get into this other and write propaganda all my life, instead of the truth as I saw and felt it. For Kipling's slogan held me still.

That spring, as on the year before in the Lung Block I had sought relief in the harbor life close by, so from the sweatshops I turned to it now. With another attack of the Wanderlust, I spent long spring days on East River docks, then drifted down to the Battery to watch the immigrants from Ellis Island pour into the city toward night. And I went out to write them up for the best editor friend I had, Jack Cosgrave, then running Everybody's. Out on the Island I spent two weeks. It was not the half-empty place it is now; it was packed with frenzied herds of people. Over a million came in that year and, one lovely day in May, with Walter Weyl from morning to night I watched ten thousand of them pour through that roaring citizen mill in the gateway to America. In barges from ships every hour they came, to be herded in and out of various government buildings and so into a great lofty hall. From a high platform at the front, with the Stars and Stripes overhead, we looked down on a score of long narrow pens divided by stout iron bars, twenty lanes all packed with people, men, women and children, Irish, Germans, Swedes, Italians, Greeks, Bohemians, Slovaks, Croats, Poles and Galician and Russian Jews. In bright-colored costumes, kerchiefs and shawls, with luggage in huge bags on their backs or dragged along, with smells from their tense sweating limbs and the deep guttural hum of their voices making a vibrant roar, they pressed forward with wild anxious eyes fixed on the doctors waiting there, for inspections which they had still to pass before they could enter the promised land. Most were admitted but some were shut out, and we could hear the frantic shrieks of friends and families torn apart!

How would they like it, those who got in? These people had gambled their old-country homes, their last dollars, their very lives on this move! Gripped by the vast intensity of poignant passions, hopes and dreams, our thoughts flew on to what they would find, to farms and railroads, mines and mills, to factories and sweatshops and dark crowded tenement hives. Success or failure, life or death, for them which was it lay ahead?

Late that day, in a narrow hallway leading to the baggage rooms, I watched them rush for bags and trunks. Directing them all where to go, a little official was standing there. A swarthy, doughty little man, who told me he'd been born in France, he spoke a dozen languages and to the torrent of questions they asked he shouted back in their mother tongues. Now shoving them on, now holding them back, when they pressed him too fast he would laugh and shout "Boo!"

"Look at them—peasants—cattle!" he cried, as one herd went thundering down the hall. "Look at their faces; look at their eyes! What do they think about? What do they know? To their villages ship agents came, for there is fat profit in immigrant trade! So the ship agent told them of big fine farms —land free, land rich, where they shall be! Shall they find those farms? Ha ha! My God! The ones that are left are so damned poor that farmer boys all run to towns! But did the ship agent tell them that? And did he tell what they shall find in Chicago and Pittsburgh and New York? Did he tell what it costs, the living there, or how fast they must work and in tenements die? Ha ha? My God! He spoke only of wages— wages to make them rich as kings! And their peasant eyes jumped out of their heads! So they sold all they had and bought tickets and came! And now they shall go to be happy and free and rich as kings! They think like that! But how shall they like what they shall find, how shall they work, how shall they live and what shall their children grow to be? What shall they do to America? Boo!" he shouted with both arms raised, as another wildly excited herd came rushing at him down the hall. They shouted and he shouted back. And in that roar of many tongues, myself excited as the rest, I thought again of the mines and mills and crowded tenements ahead. What would America do to their lives? With a feeling that gripped me by the throat, I thought only of that and never stopped to face the last question he had asked:

"What shall they do to America?"

IX

WHAT SHALL THEY DO? AS I'D WATCHED THE JEWS AND ITALIANS struggling for a start in New York, so now I saw other races in my home city in the West; for in that summer of 1904 I was sent by the Outlook to Chicago, to live for six weeks in Packingtown and write of the big Stockyards' strike. Never have I seen a setting more dramatic for a strike. From the open prairie close by in the west—it was still open in those days—the setting sun threw gorgeous colors on the billowy clouds of smoke belched from the huge chimneys of slaughterhouses in the Yards, a region about one mile square, the buildings set among open pens for thousands of cattle, sheep and hogs. Dealers and cowboys on Western ponies were constantly riding about in there, and the bellows of panicky steers, the bleating of sheep and the squeals of hogs, the heavy odors of the beasts and of their offal and their blood, poured out upon us day and night, while more stench came from Bubbly Creek, a little river through whose foul waters gases bubbled from beneath.

At the University Settlement there I got a warm welcome from Mary McDowell, one of the grandest human beings it has ever been my luck to know. She knew and loved these people and gave me access to their homes. Into cheap frame houses all around us, far and near, were crowded thousands of families. In the evenings I came into rooms where snoring men lay thick on the floors. These men were unskilled laborers, with pay that averaged through the year only about eight dollars a week. They were striking for a raise and against the system of paying by checks, which on Saturday nights could be cashed only in barrooms on Whisky Row. There were twenty-eight on one block in the Row and I came to know some of them well, for nearly every evening in one or another I sat in a corner, with my pipe and a glass of beer, smoking, watching, listening. Irish, Germans, Slovaks, Poles, Lithuanians, Czechs and many more, for each race there were saloons where each could speak in his mother tongue. Many could speak no English yet. When I tried it on one big Lithuanian, he kept dumbly shaking his head, till at last I ventured the one word:

"Strike?" It worked like magic. Out shot his fist.

"Yo' bet yo'!" this new American cried.

As negro strikebreakers were brought to the Yards, it grew hard to keep order outside. In early morning and at night, Mike Donnelly and his fellow strike leaders went along the picket lines urging against violence. To keep the people quiet, picnics were planned and mass meetings held, and there again did Donnelly urge his strikers:

"Leave the scabs alone! Obey the law! Keep out the militia and we'll win!"

From labor unions all over the country and other sources money poured in. A commissary was organized and, to the fast-increasing number of families in need, food rations were dealt out each day. But the rations were scant and the tension grew, for more thousands of negroes came into the Yards, most of them brought up from the South. Just how many there were we could not tell, for now the Packers kept them inside, fed them there and slept them there, while along the high stockade surrounding the whole region stood twelve hundred armed deputies, day and night.

Yet in spite of them I was able to make a little exploring trip inside with Professor John Commons one night. From the University of Wisconsin he had come down to watch the strike. Slim and delicate though he was, never had I met such a prof for getting right to the stuff of life. "Some economist!" I told myself. In a dark secluded spot we climbed the high fence around the Yards, dropped down inside and made our way through narrow lanes and in and out of buildings. Down long passages pitch-dark Commons went just ahead of me, tapping his way with the stick in his hand. We came into large rooms dimly lighted. In one we found many long board tables and the air was stuffy still with odors of food and cigarettes. Other rooms were crowded with cots. But all were empty. Where were the strikebreakers tonight?

At last at the end of one dark hall we could see a glow of light and, as we drew nearer, we heard a roar of voices outside. We came out into a big square court on a tumultuous scene that night. Around an open ring in the center, sitting and standing, packed close together, and from roofs of sheds all about, with whoops and cheers some five thousand negroes were watching two big naked black bucks fighting fast and hard in the ring. Bets were shouted by the black men as they urged their champions on. And it gave me a thrill when I recognized the tall powerful referee.

"My God, what a story!" I whispered to Commons. "Inspector Nick Hunt of the police!"

So this was how the Packers kept amused their strike-breakers at night!

From this and other scenes and stories gathered out of the life of the strike, I wrote my Outlook article—or rather, as had been arranged, I wrote half and the other half was written by a new friend I'd made, a brilliant witty dark little man who was later to win such a name as a writer, Bill Hard, then on the Chicago Tribune. Bill gave the Packers' side of the struggle and I the side of the employees. For I could feel none other now. Talking with the men in their homes and at the Settlement dancing with girls and singing close harmony with the boys, I'd been so quickly making friends. And listening to all they told me of their lives and jobs in the Yards, my sympathies were so hotly stirred that, when my Outlook work was done, I went on to put the whole case for the strikers into one brief narrative of a Lithuanian, who with his wife and five children had come from the oppression of Russia to be free in this new land, and here for years had struggled in vain to feed and clothe his family on his pay of eight dollars a week. Two of his small children had died and his wife was threatened with t.b. Two weeks later my story appeared, and it must have been read by the man in the White House, for only a few days later an agent from Washington came and said:

"The President has sent me here to check up on that Lithuanian story of yours and get the facts. Where's your man?" I smiled back and answered:

"He's not one man; he's forty thousand. You'll find him all around the Yards."

I volunteered my services then as press agent for the union and, in the last weeks of the strike, my new job gave me a chance to sit in strike-committee meetings and see the whole struggle from inside. We met each night at the Transit House, an immense old-fashioned frame hotel with rambling porches at front and sides and scores of Western ponies at the rows of hitching posts. The big barroom was crowded with ranchmen, cattle dealers and cowboys at night. There, too, came the newspapermen, some of them hostile and suspicious of any information I gave, but with others I succeeded so well in feeding them the stories they wanted that they soon became good friends. Into our headquarters one day breezed a lad in a wide-brimmed hat, with loose-flowing tie and a wonderful warm expansive smile.

"Hello! I'm Upton Sinclair!" he said. "And I've come here to write the Uncle Tom's Cabin of the Labor Movement!"

He already had a man digging for "the inside dope" on conditions in the Yards, and I gave him some tips on where to get more, and the color that he wanted. Then he dived into the life of the strike and I lost track of him for two weeks.

"Well?" I asked when we met again. "Have you made a good start on your job?"

"Start? I've finished!" he replied. "I've got all that I need to get on the spot and now I'm going home to write!" And so he wrote The Jungle, the Uncle Tom's Cabin of the machine age.

Soon after that, one Saturday night, Mike Donnelly took me off along the shadowy porch of the Transit House to a quiet spot and there he said:

"Well, Ernest my boy, you've done grand work without any pay and been a real friend and we've liked you here. But I think you'd better be leaving us now."

"Why? What's the trouble?"

"We've come to a point where I'd like to have you out of this."

"Why?"

"We've got no money," he replied. "Contributions from unions and other friends all over the country have dropped so low that now we've only got enough to feed our people for three days and, to get money and get it in time, we've got to make news that will bring the militia and line up organized labor behind us."

"But my God, Mike, that's just what you've been talking against!"

"I know I have; I didn't want it!" bitterly he answered. "So help me God, I don't want it now!"

"If the troops come in, you'll lose your strike!"

"Maybe so and maybe not. As it is, we haven't got a chance, unless the newspapers put this strike back again on the front page."

"What news will you make?"

"It's Saturday night. Hundreds of black scabs in the Yards have sneaked out to go on a drunk up the Levee. Later tonight they'll be coming back by the bridges over Bubbly Creek and quite a few of 'em will fall in."

"Thrown in! Drowned!"

"So the Packers will claim."

Excited and tense, I was thinking hard.

"Look here, Mike, how much do you need to feed your crowd?"

"A thousand a day."

"Just as I thought. If I get five thousand dollars tomorrow, will you hold off for another week?"

We argued a little and he agreed. Early next day I went to see Jane Addams at Hull House, told her our troubles and asked for her aid. All Sunday long that strong delicate woman, lover of social justice and peace, went about the city to various sympathetic rich friends. She had the five thousand dollars by night. And so no strikebreakers were drowned and the struggle went on as before. But just as Donnelly had feared, since the story had grown cold in the news, contributions again dropped off and, with no food for their families, more and more strikers began to break ranks, sneak into the Yards and beg for their jobs. And though the strike was settled at last in what Donnelly claimed as a compromise, it was a virtual defeat. I wonder how it would have turned out if troops had come to Packingtown and made the story hot again?

Through those last weeks I had lived on my nerves and on little strychnine pills given me by a doctor down there. And so, when the long struggle was over, I went home to Lake Forest to rest. Though my mother and father all these weeks had known of my activities and had read what I wrote about the strike, though some of the Packers were their friends and my father had worked on the Board of Trade for old Mr. Armour in earlier days, not once had he tried to interfere with my work for the strikers. And now his only comment was—

"This never would have happened if Old Man Armour had been alive." I glanced at him in quick surprise.

"That's what I was told by a striker," I said, and I gave him a story I had heard from an old Irishman one night.

"This niver would have happened if Old Man Armour had been here," he said. "Ah, there was a grand shrewd old divil, who knew how to get on with the boys! We struck against him now and then but what good did it do us in the end? Like a dog he could make you work for him and yet keep you liking him all the time! Every morning he'd get out to the Yards by seven, when the whistle blew, and all day long he'd make trips through the plant, where he knew every one of us by name—for we were not so many then. I remember one day, when I was a lad at work on the cattle-slaughter floor, I was whistling at the job. He heard me and called me and up I came.

" 'Do I pay you to whistle?' he asked. Work stopped and the boys all listened.

" 'No, sir,' I said, 'I throw that in.' But the laugh that I started he stopped with a grin.

" 'I pay for what I get,' he said. 'You come to my office to-morrow at seven and by God I'll pay you to whistle till night!'

"So he did. It was August. The day was hot. Quite a crowd of the lads who were then out of jobs had gathered to see what he would do. His office was on the second floor. Out of his window the old divil leaned with a face full of love for me and said:

" 'I want you close to me, me boy. Climb this hitching post.'

"I did. Ten feet it was but up I went. When he had me roosting at the top, he told me to whistle. I started in. The heat grew worse and so did the remarks of the crowd of the

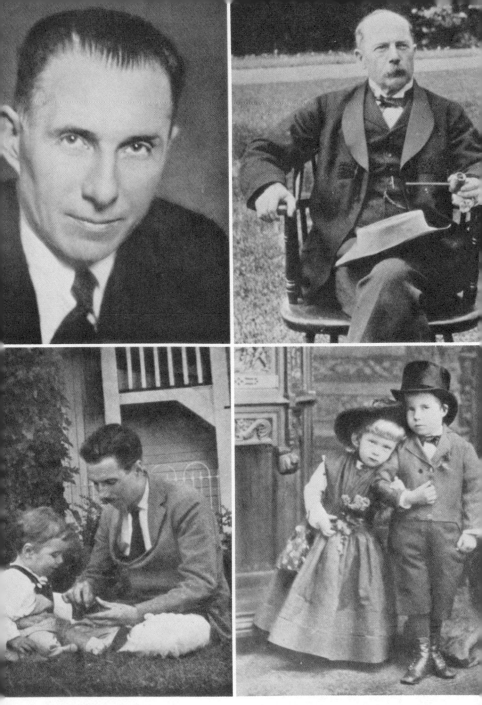

ERNEST POOLE
WITH ONE OF HIS SONS

HIS FATHER
WITH HIS SMALL BROTHER
AS MR. AND MRS. TOM THUMB

lads below. I sweated like a pig on me roost, and oh God, how dry I got! But every time I stopped me tunes, out of the window he'd stick his great head and shake his chop whiskers. " 'Heigh, you young divil, whistle!' he'd roar. And the laugh that I got from the lads below set me wild to be down with me fists in the crowd! But at noon he sent me up a dry lunch and kept me whistling on till night. Niver again in all me life have I whistled either at work or at play! That was how the Old Man got on with his boys. And so he would have, even today. He'd have found some way to head off this strike."

But those had been the old personal days. Going, going, almost gone. Already in New York I had watched the change from little sweatshops, where the boss worked, joked and ate with his men, to the factory where the only sound was the buzz and hum of machines. And now out here in the West, in this new era of great corporations with tens of thousands of workers employed, I had seen one of the first big battles fought between them and their men—men they never talked with, joked with; men they did not even know by their outlandish foreign names.

Even the life in Lake Forest had changed. From a simple village of homes it had grown into a region of handsome estates. And though our own house was still as before, two of my sisters had married and left and the youngest was soon going abroad with my brother Abram, who had finished Princeton and was going to Munich to paint. And my mother was an invalid. On days when she felt well enough, we took long drives together. I read to her one of her favorite novels, Pendennis; and glancing up from my reading at times, I caught her watching me in a way that made me feel she realized she'd never live to read what I wrote or to follow my life through the years ahead. She said nothing about the Stockyards' strike and little about my work in New York, for she could feel it pulling me away from her, and she wanted me

close to her now. So we drifted back on memories to trips that
we had made together and to the years when I was small.

But at twenty-four so gripped was I by the world of humanity I'd found that, after several weeks at home, I began
making trips to Chicago and saw the city with new eyes. I met
a secret-service man, who was making for Roosevelt a study
of hobos and their use in politics. Dressed in ragged clothes as
tramps, we went one night to the big saloon of Hinky Dink,
one of the most sinister powers in city politics at that time. In
his long dirty barroom packed with hobos and city bums, I
found a half-soused giant with shaggy gray hair, huge dark
face and wide-set burning eyes. And when I begged him to
put me wise on how to make my start on the road, he grabbed
me and shoved me against a wall, pinned me there with both
huge arms and roared:
"Jesus! What don't I know of the road? I'm here, I'm there,
I'm Christ knows where! I'm blacksmith to all America, bo!"
With his hot breath in my face and his great eyes burning
down, in a wild rich lingo that I couldn't give now if I tried,
with stops for drinks, with jerks and shoves and lurches back
to our place at the wall, all incoherent his story poured out. A
blacksmith's son in a town in Ohio, he had hit the road at sixteen and for nearly forty years, stopping for a week or a
month when he felt like it to work at the forge, he'd shod
horses on cattle ranches in Texas and in lumber camps in the
North. He'd worked on railroad bridges, too, in steel mills
and in mining camps, and then again had hit the road and slept
in the open in hobo camps, around huge fires where they'd
cooked half a steer in one night for their supper, he claimed.
And had he voted? Jesus Christ! He'd voted on election days
from 'Frisco to Denver, Chicago to Pittsburgh and down the
Big River to New Orleans! And how did he vote? What the
Hell did he care? Jesus! He'd got big pay for it, too!
From that quick glimpse of the hobo world I turned to

other regions of life in the teeming tenement quarters of town. Down in the Bohemian district I spent a long exciting night in a little Czech café, to which Kubelik, after playing with the Chicago Orchestra, came at eleven with his violin and played for his countrymen till they carried him on their shoulders out to his taxi just at dawn. I met Clarence Darrow one night, in the little West Side flat of some friends; and after supper he held us for hours in the spell of the stories he told about the labor and criminal worlds. With deep feeling he read aloud a little Tolstoy story about a Russian cobbler who had tried to live like Christ. And after that I walked with Darrow through the dark tenement districts home.

"I liked your Stockyards story," he said. "Do you mean to keep on writing about the underdogs in life?"

"Yes."

"That's good. They're worth it. Only one thing. Don't be afraid of showing up all their so-called crimes and sins. They're human. Show 'em as they are."

I had another little talk about my work with my father one day. I had lunched in the Loop with a woman who knew the tenement life so well that she was a gold mine of stories for me. After lunch she was still telling me one, as we started to walk to the West Side. As we passed the Board of Trade, suddenly we met my father. At sight of us he stopped in his tracks and the smile on his face went from ear to ear! Stung by this insult to my companion, I left her and ran back and cried:

"What do you mean by insulting my friend?"

"But Ernest! Good God!"

"Never mind how she looks! That's my business and not yours! She's a gold mine of stories right in my line!"

"All right, all right, I'm sorry!" My father wiped the tears from his eyes. "Thank the kind God for you, my boy, you've furnished me with amusement from the day when you were born. And I'm proud of your writing; I hope you'll keep on.

Only don't pass the Board of Trade with a woman tall and thin as a beanstalk, wearing a brown derby hat and puffing a big black cigar!"

In spite of that little incident, we were close to each other still. On evenings when I stayed at home we read together as before. And behind all his amusement over my young intensity, I could feel his eagerness to see my young brother Abram and me make good starts in the jobs we had chosen. Soon after that, he saw us both off one evening on our train for New York. My brother was going to seven years' work in the studios of Munich and Paris, and I was often to see him there. For the present, this country held me still, so I went back to New York to write and live on the Lower East Side as before.

But then from Chicago came the news that my mother was dying. I went home and stayed there till the end; and as I felt her slip away, it seemed to me that with her was going all the old safe settled little world I had once known. But both my mother and her world would always be a part of me. Long after she lost consciousness she kept a tight grip on my hand.

.

X

AFTER SHE DIED I CAME BACK TO NEW YORK, BUT THE SHOCK
of her death had changed me so that the life there had lost its
grip, and desperately I wanted something new to work for
now. I found it in Russia. Not in a creed. For the doctrines
and the programs of the radical factions over there and the
wrangling between them, I had very little use. What took
hold of me so hard was the common purpose behind it all, to
set a great people free from the tyranny that bound them
down. How naïve this sounds today! For it is hard to realize
now how little we knew about Russia then or of what a part
it was to play in jolting us out of our world into the chaos of
modern times. It seemed to have nothing to do with us then, a
vast dark country far away. But we had read George Ken-
nan's accounts of the tragic heroic lives of the early revolutionists. In New York I had met some of them, and now
through them I was to meet the most humanly appealing and
dramatic one of them all.

I came into a tenement room one day and stopped short,
with a tingling little shock. A gray old woman was standing
there. Her hair, cut in prison long ago, had grown again; in a
great wavy mass it framed a face broad, heavy and lined, with
eyes deep under high arched brows. She was Katharine Breshkovsky, or Babushka (Little Grandmother), for so she was
called by the thousands of young people whom she had
brought to work for her cause. She knew well the appeal she
had for us and so, in the tenement room that day, she stood
quietly, her big powerful eyes smiling warmly straight into

mine. When I asked her to tell me her story, she answered in a deep low voice:

"I will tell you the story of Russia, too."

We sat down. I had brought a stenographer, and an interpreter was there. For eight long hours without a break—except for the questions I threw in and her stops to light a fresh cigarette—Babushka talked on and on. And here is the story that she told:

"More than fifty years ago, when I was still a little girl, my whole country lay asleep. The starving peasants were bowed low. So deep was their subservience that when, on our large estate, I used to tell how I hated the bad flogging government, my old peasant nurse would beg me to whisper. My mother was religious and spoke to me of the teachings of Christ, but I was soon bewildered by the incongruity between those teachings and our life. She told me to treat all people as brothers, yet when she found me chatting in the great kitchen with our household serfs, she sternly said that I must not forget my place as a nobleman's daughter. She taught me Christ's command to give away all that I had; but when the next morning I went out and gave my handsome little cloak to a shivering peasant child, again she sharply reproved me. I had long spells of thinking. My father helped me think. He was a man of broad liberal ideas. We read together many books of science and travel. By sixteen I had read much of Voltaire, Rousseau and Diderot, and I knew by heart the French Revolution.

"Fired by what I had read, I saw the poor degraded serfs around me and longed to see them free. At first I believed that freedom could be reached through the government. The abolition of serfdom, trial by jury and other reforms had been promised by the Czar, and these promises sent a new social impulse sweeping through the land. I read of thousands like myself going to help the peasants as doctors and schoolteachers, so I opened a little school for peasants upon our estate. I found the peasant an abject creature, who could think only of his hut and his little plot of soil. The new rumors had rekindled his old heart-deep hope of freedom and, since for ages the serf or 'soul' and the plot of soil had gone together, so the peasant thought that his soul and his land would be now together freed. But when his promised emancipation at last was put into effect, being no longer bound to the land, his landlord promptly ordered him off to a strip of the very poorest soil. In dull but growing rage he refused to leave his good plot for the wretched little strip.

"'Masters, how can I feed my children through a Russian winter here? Such land means death to us!' he cried.

"Then troops were quartered in their huts, old people were beaten and daughters raped. The peasants grew more wild than before, and then began the flogging. In a village like ours, where they refused to leave their plots, they were driven into line on the street, every tenth man was called out and flogged with the knout, and some of them died. Two weeks later, as they held out, every fifth man of them was flogged. And when they still held desperately to what they felt to be their rights, again the line, and now every man was dragged to the flogging. This process lasted until at last, bleeding and exhausted, all over Russia the peasants gave in.

"Three years later I married a liberal young landowner, who took deep interest in reforms. In order to teach the peasants better tillage of their land, we started an agricultural school. Some of the younger landowners grew interested in our work and we met together frequently. We searched the laws and edicts, found certain scant and long-neglected peasants' rights of local suffrage and taught the peasants to use them. They crowded to the local elections and began to elect as officials liberals who honestly held their interests at heart. But when the more despotic landowners were ousted, their leader soon denounced us as a band of conspirators. My husband and I were put at once under police surveillance, my father was deposed from office and some of the others in our group were exiled to Siberia. Punished so as criminals for teaching the peasant his legal rights, we saw the government as it was and the spirit of revolution was kindled. This was in 1871 and I was twenty-six years old. My husband, like me, had a whole life before him and therefore I thought it only fair to speak frankly. I asked him if he were willing to suffer exile or death in our cause. He said that he was not. Then I left him.

"I joined a revolutionist group and traveled from village to village for years, everywhere urging the peasants to rise. In order both to elude the police and to break down the peasants' cringing distrust, like my comrades I dressed in enormous bark shoes, coarse skirt and drawers and heavy cloak, and used acid to roughen my face and hands. So I worked and ate with the peasants; I learned their speech; I traveled on foot, forging passports to show to the local police. By night I did my organizing. Into a peasant's hut I would come. The little low room, with a dirt floor and rafters just above my head, would be packed with men and women and children. When I recalled their floggings and pointed to those who were crippled for life, they would cry out so fiercely that the cow in the next room would bellow and have to be quieted. Then I told them that, to be free and live, the people must own the land that they needed. From a little book of fables written to teach our principles, I read to them far into the night, while the firelight showed a circle of great hairy faces, dilated eyes, staring with all the reverence every Russian peasant has for that mysterious thing, a book.

"These books, more effective than oral work, were printed in secrecy at high cost. But many of us still had jewels, costly gowns and furs to sell; and new recruits added to our fund. We had no personal expenses. Weary work for us, you say, traveling each alone like that. Yes, when the peasants were slow and dull and the spirit of freedom seemed an illusion.

But when that spirit grew real, one felt far from weary! Then, too, we had occasional grippings of hands with comrades and stout words of cheer were sent from one group to another. An underground system was started, a correspondence code invented, the movement spread through thirty-six great provinces of Russia and became better organized. So the People's Party was formed. The government, alarmed by their spies, now began to make wholesale arrests. I was under a peasant's name in Podolia. In my wallet was our manifesto and with it maps showing the places that had been already reached and those next to be organized. A servant girl spied them and told the servant of the police agent there. He came rushing to me then, jerked out our manifesto and, eyes popping with excitement, read it in a loud hoarse tone. As that simple but stirring proclamation of freedom, equality and love was read, the poor peasants thought it the longed-for proclamation from the Czar. The news spread. Men, women and children rushed up. Soon the district attorney came, and he, too, read the paper aloud. Then suddenly came the chief of police. He glanced at the wild joyous faces around and seized upon the document. " 'What is this?' he asked me roughly. 'Propaganda,' I replied, 'with which the gendarme and the attorney are viciously inciting the people.'

"In jail I was led down to the 'Black Hole.' I was pushed in; the heavy door slammed and bolts rattled in total darkness. At once I was sickened by the odor. I took a step forward and slipped, for the floor was soft with filth. I stood still until, deadly sick, I sank down on a pile of straw and rags. A minute later I was stung sharply back to consciousness and sprang up covered with vermin. I leaned on the wall and found it damp, and so all night I stood there in the middle of the hole. And this was the beginning for me of prison and Siberia.

"I was taken to St. Petersburg and there awaited trial in the fortress of St. Peter and St. Paul. My cell was clean and a hole above gave air. My bed was an iron bracket, with a mattress and pillow of straw, rough blanket, sheet and pillowcase. Food was shoved beneath my door and there I stayed for forty months. In solitary confinement? No, I joined a social club. For on that first night, as I lay in the dark, suddenly I sat up and listened. I could hear nothing but, as I lay down, my ear approached again the iron pipe supporting my cot. Tick, tick, tickity, tick, tick! I felt along the pipe and found that it went through to the next cell. Again I listened. Tick, tick, tick! I had once heard a code like that planned at a meeting in Moscow, but I could not recall it now. At last, however, I had an idea. There are thirty-five letters in the Russian alphabet, so on the pipe I began to rap—once, then twice, then three times, then four, and so on until for the last letter I rapped thirty-five. No response. Slowly and distinctly again I rapped the alphabet. My heart was beating quickly now. Steps came down the corridor, the guard approached and passed my door. Slowly his steps died away. Suddenly—Tick! . . . Tick, tick! . . . Tick, tick, tick!—and so through to thirty-five! Somebody had answered me! Then very slowly we spelled out words, and by this so clumsy code the swifter code was taught me. After that, for three years, the pipe was almost always talking. How fast we talked! It sounded so!"

In the New York tenement room where we sat, her great gray head bent over the table, her face was flushed, her eyes flashed back through thirty-five years of danger and prison, and her strong subtle fingers rolled out the ticks at lightning speed. Then she continued her narrative.

"Our club had nearly three hundred members in solitary confinement," she said, "some in cells on either side of mine, some below and some above. Did we tell stories? Yes, and good ones! Young students, keen wits, high spirits!" And old Babushka chuckled deep. "How some of those youngsters did make love! A mere boy, two cells to my right, vowed he adored the young girl of nineteen, five cells to my left on the floor above, whom he had never laid eyes on. I helped tick his gallant speeches along to the cell just below hers, and from there they were ticked up the pipe by a sad little woman who grieved for her babies. Our club was not all a club of pleasure. The pipe raved at times, or spoke dark good-bys. By the time that we were brought to trial in 1878, a hundred had died or gone insane. The hundred and ninety-three of us left were packed into a little hall, and I had a strange shock as I now looked at these clubmates with whom I had daily talked. White, thin, but still the same stout hearts! Our trial was a farce and, when I protested against this brutal mockery, my sentence was lengthened to six years at hard labor in the mines and life exile in Siberia.

"Secretly at night, to avoid a demonstration, ten of us were led out of our prison. In the street below were ten *telegas*, heavy hooded vehicles with a *troika* [three horses] each. Into one I was placed, a stout gendarme squeezed in on either side, and just before my knees sat the driver. We went off at a gallop and so our five-thousand-mile journey began. The Great Siberian Road was rough, five thousand miles of bumps of all sizes, and our springless *telegas* jolted and bounced as our horses galloped along. We were all dressed in convict clothes. The men had also heavy chains on feet and wrists; their heads were shaved. For sleep we were placed in the *étapes* [wayside prisons], reeking, crawling, infected with consumption and typhoid. We slept on bare benches in close foul air. Through the log walls we could hear all night the jangling of fetters, the moaning of women, the cries of sick babies.

"You keep asking for scenes and stories, my boy. Never have I told of my life in the way you are making me tell it now. For you see we were thinking of our dream, and did not much notice the life outside. On reaching the Kara mines at last, I found that the hard-labor year was reckoned as eight months instead of twelve and that my forty months in prison had been taken from my six-year term, so I had but eight months more to serve. After that I was taken to Barguzin, a bleak little group of huts far up in the ice near the Arctic Circle. There I began to look for work. Seeing a few forlorn little children, I proposed to open a school, but the police agent forbade me and showed his rules from St. Petersburg, which forbid an exiled teacher to teach, an exiled doctor to heal the sick or an exiled priest to comfort the dying. With three young student exiles there I decided to escape and make our way a thousand miles to the Pacific. With a bent old peasant as guide, we set out one Arctic night, leading our pack horses for weeks over snow and ice down into a region of forests, rocky crags and deep ravines. We had only hardtack to eat, and some pressed tea and a little tobacco. So we walked for about six hundred miles. Then they found us and brought us back. The three young students were sent again up to the Arctic wilderness, while I was brought back to Kara and sentenced to another four years.

"In the prison I rejoiced to find seventeen women politicals, with whom I lived in four large cells, while we worked in the shops of the mine. Here at first we had books and writing materials and were quite comfortable. But a few weeks later, eight of the men politicals escaped and for this we were all punished. One morning the Cossack guards entered our cells, seized us, tore off our clothes and dressed us in convict suits alive with vermin. Then in an old prison close by we were thrown into foul little stalls off a low grimy hall which contained two big stoves and only two little windows. For three months we did not use our bunks, but fought with pails of scalding water till at last all the vermin were killed. We had been put on the 'Black Hole diet' of black bread and water. For three years we never breathed outside air and we struggled constantly against the outrages inflicted upon us. After one vile outrage, we lay like a row of dead women for nine days, refusing to touch any food, until certain promises were exacted from the warden.

"When my prison term was over at last, I was taken to

Selenzensk, a little Buriat hamlet on the frontier of China. The seven years that followed were the hardest of my exile, for in all that time I spoke to but three Russian politicals, who stopped there only a few weeks. In winter, when outside my hut it was fifty below zero at night, I used to climb with a little stool up on top of the big brick stove. I grew almost frantic with loneliness and, to keep my sanity, I would run out on the snow, shouting passionate orations, or even playing the prima donna and singing grand-opera arias to the bleak landscape, which never applauded!

"The seven years over, I was allowed to travel all through Siberia. In September, 1896, pardoned at last by the government, I was allowed to return to Russia, and three hours later I was on the train."

Her long exile at an end, in Russia for eight years since then, traveling as before in disguise, she had met with small secret groups in rooms of city tenements and on river boats at night, in peasant huts and in the forests. She'd had many narrow escapes from arrest.

"Once in Odessa," she told me, "the police came into the house where I was. Their suspicions had been aroused and they searched from cellar to roof. I at once became an old peasant woman." In a twinkling she had changed. Her shawl had come up over her head, her hands were clasped in her lap, her head nodded. A bent, decrepit old peasant looked from under the shawl with a vacant grin. "My ruse succeeded. That same night, friends dressed me in silks as a grand lady and I drove to the railway station in style!

"So it has been all through these last years," she said, as she ended her story that night. "I find friends and fellow workers ready to help me wherever I go. For our movement has grown so fast, in these terrible months of the war with Japan, that now we are four hundred thousand strong. Day and night we work, my boy! In place of sleep and food and drink—the dream of freedom! Freedom to think and speak, justice to all!

This dream is old in American breasts. For this cause I have
the honor of making to free Americans our appeal."

The appeal she made had such success that she spoke to
crowded halls all over the country and generous contributions
poured in. I had other talks with her and in each one my excitement grew. For the same powerful influence she'd had on
young people in other lands to bring them to work for her
cause, she now exerted here so well that she set many of us
wild to go to Russia. How many thousands have gone since
then! I was one of the first of them.

XI

FOR NOW I FOUND A WAY TO GO. IN JANUARY, 1905, TOWARD
the end of the Russo-Japanese War, which had cost hundreds
of thousands of lives and had brought on the Russian people
even heavier taxes than before, a priest, Father Gapon, led an
immense procession of workingmen, women and children to
the Winter Palace to beg their little Father, the Czar, to end
it all and give them peace. His Cossacks rode into the crowd;
in the panic a few shots were fired and then with their car-
bines the Cossacks mowed the people down. An insurrection
followed that, with rioting all over the town. When the news
came to New York, I went to the Outlook and begged them
to send me. They thought it over and gave me a contract.
Could I be ready to start that same week? Day and night I
rushed about to Russians of all sorts and kinds, getting letters and advice—and money, which I was told to deliver to
revolutionists over there. A clever attractive young Polish
girl, with whom I had often danced at night and who was a
stenographer, got free from her regular job for two days and
went with me on my rounds taking shorthand notes on my
interviews. She gave them to me neatly typed. Pay? Not at all,
she was doing her bit for the cause of Free Poland and Russia, she said. When at last I was ready to go, I spent half the
last night with my Settlement friends at Little Hungary Café,
drinking and singing the Marseillaise. In the cold gray dawn
I reached my boat, where a man from the Outlook brought
letter of credit and passport just before we sailed. Then exhausted I tumbled into my bunk and slept deep for a day and

a night. On the voyage I made friends with an enormous English-woman of about sixty, who looked like a man; and as we neared England, in her deep bass voice she said:

"I don't know what you are up to, young man, for you have been very secretive this trip, but I think it's something likely to get you into serious trouble. No need to answer. I'll say just this. My home is on the Isle of Wight. Come there and I'll take care of you."

In Paris I had been told to see a famous Russian exile. Like so many of the leaders I met, he was a liberal, one of those who were to be shot as reactionaries years later by the Soviet. But my manner of meeting him was revolutionary enough, even for a lad of my age. Warned to be careful in my approach, I followed directions and went first to a sad-looking little French painter, an anarchist who, in his studio in the old *Quartier Latin*, had been living for years in what he still tried to believe was free love with a huge bullying brunette. Like any henpecked husband, he was glad of the chance to slip away. We went to a public library.

"Now do just as I do," he said. From the shelves we brought books to a table and began busily making notes. Across the table a woman in black sat apparently as absorbed as ourselves but, while they both kept their eyes on their work, my companion spoke softly with her in French; and very soon I heard her voice, in English barely above a whisper, say to me:

"Do not look up. In this room sits a spy of the Czar who follows wherever I go. You are an American?"

"Yes."

"Going at once to Russia?"

"Yes."

"You wish to meet my husband here?"

"Yes."

Then of my companion she asked:

"You have seen his credentials?"

"Yes."

"Very well. Tonight at twelve. Café Odéon. Cabinet Five." And she went on writing as before.

At midnight in the *Quartier Latin*—in that same little café from which Camille Desmoulins at my age had been torn from his lovely young bride to be taken to the guillotine—in Cabinet Five, a tiny room on the low-ceilinged second floor, I met a tall lean bearded man, who looked to me like a German professor. We talked for two hours. He gave me more leads and letters and several thousand rubles, too, to deliver to friends in St. Petersburg. Next morning I took a train to Berlin. The Associated Press man there advised me to get a fur overcoat and took me to a friend who had one; he was a German correspondent just returned from the Russo-Japanese front. As we bargained over the price of the coat, I tried it on and in one pocket my fingers closed upon brass knuckles.

"All right. I like this coat. I'll take it," I decided. Later I gave the knuckles to a revolutionist. I wonder if he ever used them in the tumultuous years ahead?

Alone on my train for Russia, as we drew near the frontier, with deepening suspense I thought of all those secret letters and notes and all that money concealed in my clothes. Would they by any chance search me? No, thank God! Safe across the line, in a slow lumbering Russian train, with sparks from the wood-burning locomotive showering out on the white snow, in my second-class compartment I sat smoking cigarettes and drinking tea from a samovar, with my excited hungry eyes upon the darkening landscape of snowy fields and forests of birch and pine. Through the thin partition at my back, in the next compartment, a woman's voice, deep, rich and low, was singing Russian love songs. It is good to be twenty-four. I could scarcely sleep that night.

I found St. Petersburg dull and cold. As I drove from the station in a small sleigh through the poorer parts of the town, the streets were deep covered with grimy snow and crowded with little low sledges. Men and women with old coats or shawls, rough caps and broad coarse faces, were trudging wearily along. Most of them paused at every gilt ikon to bow and make the sign of the cross. One woman carefully fished out a coin from a tiny bag under her shawl and dropped it into the ikon box, while her ragged little girl stood shivering behind her. A funeral group of five came by—two working-men bearing between them a small box covered with fancy white paper, three dull-eyed women walking behind. From the church domes deep rich bells were booming. There were no street cries, no shrill little newsboys darting about, hardly a newspaper in sight—but uniforms by hundreds, uniforms of soldiers and other servants of the Czar. Uniforms, ikons, poverty. How grim and dreary and quiet it was! No sign of revolution there. At my hotel I found S. S. McClure, the man who had first put me in print. His nervous hands shook as he packed to go home, for he had been talking with Russians from early morning till late at night.

"Don't believe what the Reds will tell you!" he said. "This whole situation is quieting down! To bring off this revolution of theirs is going to take ten years at least!"

This was in 1905, and he timed it nearly right; but in the exciting weeks that followed, I couldn't believe it would take so long. St. Petersburg quiet? Yes, indeed, but with what human dynamite beneath!

That same morning, as I had been told, I delivered the money I'd brought to a dark slender Englishman, Harold Williams, correspondent of the Manchester Guardian, who had lived in Russia for years and knew liberals and Socialists well. He was a kindly friendly man. When I gave him the money, he smiled and said:

"I'll see that it goes where it belongs. Now let me help you get your start."

He took me first to a bank to draw money.

"Quiet? Yes, and so it has been," said a bank official there. "The foreign correspondents told the most ridiculous lies about the Father Gapon affair. I was here in this room at the time and I did not even notice that anything was going on."

"Strange," smiled Williams as we came out. "The troops charged up and down the street right beneath his window! Let's try the chap in that jewelry shop." So we entered a shop across the street and talked with the proprietor. When I told him I had come from New York to see a revolution, he smiled.

"The truth is," he answered in French, "that very little has happened. To show you what lies can be told in this town, I was here during the so-called riots, and knew nothing about them till night."

"Strange," said Williams in the street, "I was here that morning, too, and saw all his shopwindows barred!" I smiled back.

"What a quiet town. Let's have a little truth for a change."

"All right," he agreed, and took me next to the office of a liberal paper. We found it far from quiet there. A score of men and women and girls were writing and talking rapidly over steaming glasses of tea and little Russian cigarettes. We went back and saw the editor, a tall man with huge shoulders, pointed beard, deep brown eyes and a jolly smile.

"Each day we speak out more boldly," he said, "and our boldness is only a sign of the powers rising all around us. As these other powers rise, deep and different enough to make ten revolutions instead of one but all groping in the dark, we, by suddenly speaking out and spreading opinions of all groups, are beginning to clear away darkness and let the new forces come face to face. So many opinions are bound to clash. The question is: Can this wild deep-burning soul called a Slav be patient enough to fight only on paper? Probably not, but we can do much to clear away the needless quarrels. We are growing every day. Six weeks ago we had twenty subscribers, today we have twenty-five thousand!"

"But don't you expect to be suppressed soon?"

"Undoubtedly. We have been before—three times, in fact,

in this last year. A few of us go to prison of course but the rest of us simply take a new name for the paper and start again. Nothing now can keep us down!"

With Williams I went later that day to see a cartoonist friend of his who was working for the underground press. He had just spent six weeks in jail. Now he sat by an open stove at work on a caricature of the Czar. He had tossed one into the stove as soon as he heard our knock on his door, but he drew another while we talked. He spoke in broken English.

"Always the stove," he told me. "I keep my drawings all in my head. Now I show how the people raigard their Little Father since he have killed them." He bent over and drew rapidly. "Before now always the people think: 'The police are bad—priests all bad—and government ministers also bad. But the Little Father, if we could only come to him, he would save us and cure all our wrongs!' But when they come, he say only, 'Kill!' So now he look to them like this!"

As he held up his monstrous caricature, we heard quick raps upon his door—one, then five, then two. He smiled.

"I shall not burn it now," he said. He called; the door opened. A girl came in. She was richly dressed in furs, her dark face was flushed from fast walking and her black eyes sparkled as she told some bit of news. While talking she glanced over at me, the man nodded, and from under her cloak she slipped a package of newspapers, took from him his caricature and several others he quickly drew, and with these she went away. The newspapers that she left had been printed in Paris and Geneva by the revolutionist press and sent by a dozen different routes to addresses that were constantly shifted to elude the censors and spies. They had been two weeks on their way, passed on by many different hands. Ten thousand packages like this were constantly dodging through Russia, to be opened in well-to-do homes, city tenements and peasant huts and even in army barracks, I learned. So worked the underground mail in Russia, daringly but quietly. "St. Petersburg Is Quiet," I thought. "Good title. Keep it in your head."

Late that day I went to the Nevsky, street of shops and fashions, for a look at the rich and the Old Regime. Between the grim old palaces and the lighted windows of handsome shops on either side, poured the imperial city's gay life. What costumes and what uniforms of warm rich colors or of white! Officers on horseback passed and troops of Cossacks from the plains, mountain chiefs, Caucasian princes, merchants from Persia and Turkestan, and women in costly furs in sleighs behind sleek black Arabian horses. In that Russian winter, night began at three o'clock, and over a canal close by were strings of colored lanterns and beneath them crowds of skaters on the gleaming dark blue ice. Eagerly I drank it in, the color and glamour of Old Russia. A few hours later, waiting for Williams, I sat in a sleigh on a snowy side street. Through a gate I looked into a moonlit court, and Russian voices singing came faintly from a room above. Down the street glided a tiny low sledge. A huge driver towered silent in front, and behind sat a little woman with dark face and shining eyes. Her head nestled back in her soft fur collar, she drew on a long Russian cigarette and gazed dreamily up at the moon. Tingling, I watched her go. "St. Petersburg is quiet," I thought.

With Williams that evening I went to the home of a well-known Socialist leader. He greeted us with a shrug of his shoulders.

"Well, I shall be arrested," he said. "Three nights ago I went with a friend to a meeting of forty workingmen leaders. Spies were there and so followed arrests. Early this morning they took my friend and now it will be my turn soon. So I am waiting. But come in."

As he talked in Russian with my companion, I recalled what I'd heard of this man. Long ago, on a night like this, he had been arrested and sent for eleven years to Siberia; but now in the next room I could hear his family talking and laughing, at intervals a contralto voice sang snatches of some little song, and he himself looked unconcerned. He had a strong blunt face, black beard and big quiet piercing eyes. He turned to me and spoke in English.

"The French Revolution was nothing," he said. "When I think of sights that must here be seen and of sounds that must be heard, I am wretched. We must have not one but three revolutions burst at once. It is like there were three mighty rivers rising forty years ago—rising, swelling, rushing on—I mean trying to rush on, but dammed up and now the dam must give 'way. What are these three rivers? The peasant's longing to live and not starve, the workingman's longing to live like a man, the longing of the man who thinks to speak out freely what he thinks, to write what he thinks and to vote as he thinks and elect a people's government. These rivers they have dammed with spies, prisons and Siberia. So now, as the bursting time draws near, these three powers work in darkness, each apart, none pull together. God only knows what will happen here. How stupid and how pitiful and blind is such a government! But the people are not pitiful. The people who even in poverty and oppression could create such literature, such music, these people feel something is spoiled in their souls, and so they will rise in darkness and this blind government will crash down!"

There come so many memories from those glamorous days and nights, when the whole struggle was new to me! Often I felt revolution was near; then again, with the hot impatience of twenty-four, I rebelled against what I felt to be deep abject submission there; but from that I would dive again into the regions of revolt.

On an evening cold and sparkling, about ten o'clock I left my lodgings in a quarter across the river, picked out a little horse and sledge, showed the *izvostchik* with a map where it was I wished to go, and off we galloped down the street. I eyed with approval the vodka bottle which he drew out from under his seat, for I knew that by this our speed would be doubled. Faster and faster the little sledge darted under noses of horses; it swung against three stout old men, upsetting one and making all three teach me Russian furiously! Skidding around corners, we shot out on a broad stone bridge. Below us to the right and left lay the Neva's cold blue ice, spanned by other low-arched bridges studded with frosty twinkling lights. The moon above and behind us shone clear on the city ahead, on long lines of government buildings, palaces and lofty columns, on Byzantine spires and the gold dome of St. Isaac's towering over all. Soon we were slipping along by the edge of an immense snow-covered square, with rows of trees and blue arc lights and, upon the river side, a great long building with yellow columns, sculptured frieze and row on row of lighted windows—the Winter Palace of the Czar, scene of the Gapon Massacre only a few weeks ago! No charging troops of Cossacks now, no screams, no guns, no sheets of fire—only sleigh bells, merry voices. But as I sat watching there, soon a different voice was heard. All alone across the square, reeling, falling, rising, came a huge bareheaded man with long coarse hair tumbling down over his face to his shoulders, a ragged brown coat belted with rope, old red and gray cloths wrapped 'round his legs. Through the hair his eyes glared out, he shook his beard from side to side, threw back his head and roared defiance at the palace of the Czar! "Grand!" I thought. When he had gone, I punched my *izvostchik* to start on, for again his vodka bottle was tilted from his mouth to the moon!

A few minutes later I walked up two flights of low stone steps, with soft carpets underfoot, and was shown into a spacious room with open fires and rich rugs and deep wide lounges. Some thirty people sat at tea around a giant samovar. Our hostess, a well-known novelist, seated me next to her son, who spoke English. He was only a boy of sixteen, slim and straight, in school uniform; but his face was flushed, his high forehead was wet and he was deeply excited. He had just come from a meeting of a secret society, which he said had spread in two years to schools all over Russia. Some of his friends had been sent to jail, but still the society grew and grew, and now a secret summons had gone out all over the country to strike! They would strike because the bureaucracy had squeezed out all the studies that could make a boy want a free country, he cried; they would strike against this system of spies who followed them even to their homes!

I lunched with his older brother next day at the Mechanical Engineers. The dining hall was a cloud of smoke from two hundred or more cigarettes. Students all in their twenties were there, some of them with heavy beards, long hair and rounded shoulders, but most of them younger, spruce and trim, and my young host was one of these. He had a little short mustache and gay sparkling black eyes. As the talking rose to a roar at the tables all about, he pointed to a long full line of bulletins tacked to the wall.

"The only free press in Russia!" he said. "They tear down some—we put up others—news from all the colleges—of revolution everywhere!"

In the Gapon insurrection hundreds of these students had been beaten on the streets, some had been killed and others jailed; but a week ago three thousand of them, meeting in a hall, had dragged the Czar's picture from the wall and torn it to shreds. They wanted him down!

Late one afternoon that week I drove out through factory suburbs and there I saw thousands of men on strike, standing gloomy in the sooty snow. They had struck for higher wages. Their pay was forty cents a day and, when I saw the places they lived in, my hot sympathies were stirred. A "corner" in that district was a spot on a tenement floor, for which a laborer payed a rent of two rubles (one dollar) a month. Their food was black bread, cabbage and soup, and on holidays vodka to get drunk on. They had asked for shorter hours, too, only twelve instead of fourteen, so that they could learn to read and write. In the dull little shops and stalls on the streets I saw few shop *signs* but only shop *pictures* of the wares to be bought within. For these men were so ignorant still. As they stood gloomy in the snow, only now and then I heard a voice raised angrily. Then silence fell, for down the street came a Cossack patrol, a dozen strong lean creatures splendid as the beasts they rode, with thick mustaches curling up and hard jaws and flashing eyes. Talking and laughing, they rode by. Inside those factory walls, I learned, were soldiers armed with Gatling guns. So the workingmen stood in silent groups. St. Petersburg was quiet still.

Soon after this, with a Russian friend, I went to a secret night school in a working-class part of the town. We turned into a dark archway under a six-story tenement and came into a courtyard. In the rear was an old brick house, which we entered. The stone stairs were wet. A stout little boy, who sat on a step with a four-year-old girl, told us where to go. We swung back a heavy iron door and my friend gave a series of secret raps upon a smaller wooden door. It opened and we entered upon a scene I shall never forget.

It was a long narrow room, lighted only by two lamps which hung from the low ceiling. Their light shone down on two hundred faces, all intent and motionless. From the front of the room came a woman's voice—low, restrained, only now and then trembling slightly.

"This is a lecture in history," whispered my companion. And a few moments later—"She is describing the French Revolution of 1848."

Half of the two hundred men sat on benches; the others stood up. The one aisle was packed to the front. Most wore heavy overcoats. Nearly all of them were young.

"She is describing how Socialism grew in France," whispered my friend.

I was watching a thickset lad to my left. He had black hair, close-cut mustache and heavy eyebrows. His blunt face was lean and brown, the cheekbones prominent. He sat with a hand on each knee, leaning forward. Now and then he turned aside and breathed deeply, thinking hard, and then again bent forward.

"She explains now why the French workingmen decided they must rise for political freedom," came the whisper at my side.

To my right stood a man of middle age. He had been standing for a long time in his heavy sheepskin coat; his shoulders slouched in a weary way; his hands in front of him held his cap. His bearded face was frowning, with dark intensity in his eyes. Behind him sat a pretty young girl dressed in a fur hat and jacket. She sat with one arm thrown 'round the girl next her, who wore only two ragged shawls. I turned back to the older man. His face had suddenly lightened! So had all the faces around me, eyes all gleaming in the dark! The young girl and her companion were now holding each other close! The young man to my left had risen! From in front the woman's voice was still low.

"She is telling how they built the barricades in Paris!" whispered my friend.

I had enough for my story now. Back in my room I began it at once and wrote all through that winter's night. I remember toward daybreak the room grew cold and for a moment I realized that my tense hands were icy, too. I used large sheets of thin paper and, to get them by the censor, I put my story in the form of a business letter to my friend Walling in New York. At the start I wrote like a Yankee shoe salesman reporting to his chief at home. The first two pages I filled with complaints about the market for shoes in Russia. But after writing enough of this to make any censor yawn, I broke a long sentence and went on:

"Article begins from here. Title—St. Petersburg Is Quiet. Quote. This city is a silent chaos!"

And then in some six thousand words I gave the pictures I had seen and those tense voices I had heard, in the quiet that comes before a storm.

XII

AFTER THIS I SETTLED DOWN A BIT AND LIFE WAS NOT SO HECTIC now. I lived with a Russian family in a middle-class quarter of the town. I had a comfortable room, with a table to write on, a stout tile stove, the slow tick-tick of a tall brown clock and a view on a quiet street below. Down there the corner grocer had two big open barrels of caviar out in front on the snow. So cheap it was in Russia then! I was working hard to learn the language. I heard the family speak it at meals, and again at ten in the evening the blithesome little mother would knock softly at my door. "Meester Poole. Pleass—some tea?" And then at her samovar she would serve me tea and simple Russian words. Like hundreds of others in Russia, those days, she earned a living by translating books; and she was doing Booker T. Washington's Up from Slavery at that time.

"How different your Negroes are from our poor silent peasants!" she said.

Her three-year-old boy had an old peasant nurse. With coarse black hair drawn tight back, she had a face like an Indian squaw and small black eyes that twinkled and stared. All her wrinkles would double into smiles when the three of us sat on the floor and I asked the tiny boy the names of his toy dogs and houses. She told him old old legends and crooned drowsy peasant sleep tunes as she rocked his cradle at night. She grew very sad when a letter came from her village, written by the priest. It was so cold there now, she said, that her people huddled on top of their stoves; and everyone was starving to death, because the strong young men and boys had all been taken a long way off and killed in some war they knew nothing about.

The husband of the family became my Russian teacher soon, for he had just spent a year in London and he spoke quite fluently a broken English all his own. For hours each evening we sat at a table, on which he had placed a small pack of blank cards and a heap of cigarettes. We read a story by Turgeniev. Every word I did not know I wrote upon one side of a card; on the other side I wrote it in English. I kept the cards in a pack in my pocket and, on my journeys about the city, whenever I had a few minutes to spare, I studied those cards till I knew all the words. In two weeks I'd learned five hundred, and in a month I knew enough Russian to catch the gist of what I heard. In the meantime my interest in my new teacher had increased, for when visitors came he had such a way of drawing stories out of them.

In his late twenties still, Tarasov was a queer-looking man, tall and powerful, big-boned, stoop-shouldered, with a strong round face and quickly observing genial eyes. He was a chemist. Early one morning I found him studying a row of thin little slabs of wood. Each slab he had treated with a different kind of varnish, he said, in his search for the lost recipe for the varnish used centuries ago in Italy on Cremona violins. When I told him of the passion I'd had for my fiddle and music, as a boy, he took me to the shadowy little shop of a friend of his, who repaired violins for the Imperial Orchestra. And we went there many times, for it was a place where men of all factions in St. Petersburg at that time, conservative, radical, rich and poor, but all fiddle lovers, met as friends. There I met a young brunette—slim, with lovely big dark eyes and glossy hair wound in coils on her head. In her artist lover's studio I played to her on her violin. With Tarasov I went to the annual Salon, to watch the jury, his father among them, decide which paintings to hang on the line. As a painter his father had won his fame by portraits of peasants all over north Russia and even down in the Ukraine. The son had often gone along with his father on those painting trips. He knew the peasants, loved the life in the country, and he urged me to see it now.

"Come to the villages," he would say. "Our government is shockingly bad and we need deep revolution here, but all these plans of people in cities are nothing but nice little paper things. The Russia outside is more deep than the paper and you will find the real Russia out there. Revolutions in towns will come and will go, but always the life of peasants flows on, so slow, so deep, so silent as Volga. Like that great river it makes no noise, but in the end it will decide the future of Russia. Come and see."

To this I agreed and we planned a trip. By train we went to a small town about halfway to Moscow, and from there on a zero day we drove in a sleigh with a *troika* team of three horses over the sparkling snow some twenty miles to a country school, built by a liberal friend of his, where we were to stay for a week and visit the villages near by.

"Oh, you brutes, you lovely brutes, you devils!" shouted our stout driver through his thick and grizzly beard. He leaned far out and cracked his whip and off we galloped out of town. Good-by to towns and railroads and the twentieth century! I was looking for peasants now!

"How about the driver?" I asked. "Let's see how he feels about the war." Tarasov climbed up on the driver's seat and I drew deep breaths of the cold dry air. It was good to be in the country! The horses still went on a run, one trotting under a great arched yoke, the other two galloping at the sides. My seat was low and soft with furs, and the smell of the pines was a bracing change from the smoke of cigarettes. "This is going to be slow work," said Tarasov, looking down. "He thinks we may be government spies. He is laughing at us. This

laugh is so little that you cannot hear it at all, but it is an enormous thing in our way. Please—hand me up two cigarettes."
  "Leave the war alone and try him on wolves. Are there
many around here?"
  "He says there are not many big wolves but millions of little
ones."
  "What does he mean?"
  "You will quickly find out if ever we have to sleep in any
peasant's hut. But look—here come your first peasants now."
Four of them, they trudged behind rough flat sledges loaded
with fagots, drawn by shaggy little ponies. Brown fur caps
and sheepskin coats and enormous gray felt boots; broad
stolid faces, curious stares from twinkling eyes. "The little
laugh again," said Tarasov.
  For twenty miles we sped along, now through forests of
birch and pine and again out over great fields of snow. Everywhere dead silence. Even in the three-foot drifts we plunged
through without a sound. Only now and then came sledges,
trudging ponies, stolid faces. As we dashed through villages,
lonely clusters of log huts, our jingling bells brought faces to
the small and deepcut windows; but nobody came outside.
To shake off the strange dead silence, once I jumped out for
a run, but at this the driver laughed and lashed his team to
such a pace that, as I seized the edge of the sleigh, I found
myself flying through the air about nine minutes out of ten!
Then in I climbed and on we went and silence settled as before. The pine forests darkened soon but out on the fields the
sun still hung radiant on the edge of the snow, which took on
shades of pink and rose. The light struck the driver's old
brown face and turned it a dull copper red. But he seemed to
notice nothing.
  So we came in the evening dusk to the little log schoolhouse
where we were to stay, and then at last the long silence was
broken by voices that I hear still as I write.

"Quick! Look here, Ivan! I think there is a devil here!" A peasant boy bent over my shoulder, delightedly watching my fountain pen. It was the next afternoon. On my bed were two more husky boys with a huge white St. Bernard pup, and Tarasov sat back in an old straw chair, getting stories out of them, after distributing cigarettes. In a corner was part of a big brick stove built into the walls of roughhewn logs in order to warm three rooms at once. From one of them came a babel of voices, for ours was the one spare room of the schoolhouse. All afternoon a constant stream of children large and small poured in. Even the St. Bernard pup brought in his mother and two mongrel friends.

That evening we watched ten little girls at supper in the kitchen. They were boarders at seventy kopecks (about forty cents) a month, for in their villages were no schools. They were very little girls, with bright-colored kerchiefs upon heads which kept bobbing up and down over porringers of soup, while small hands clutched wooden spoons or thick slices of dark rye bread. The reddish glow from the deep brick oven showed smiles, white teeth and laughing eyes. Low giggles for the visitors. As later we sat at supper ourselves, we could hear them at high jinks in the hall, and every few minutes they trooped to the door with a chorus of "Thank yous" and "Good nights," the only English words they knew. Later we went up to their bedroom. A pillow fight ended and they sat up, a demurely blanketed row all together in one enormous wide bed. Over each pillow on a nail in the log hung a limp bag of clothes; at the foot of the bed stood twenty felt boots. The teacher set the candle down and slowly it grew lighter. Eyes twinkled over blankets, and they all listened eagerly while I spoke to them in English.

"What fun it is!" cried one wee girl. "Such talk is coming out of his mouth but it means nothing to us at all!" And they all dived back into pillows in a perfect gale of mirth. Then

I distributed cakes of chocolate with a paper doll tied to each. It took a long time to say good night.

Later, in the teacher's small study, the copper samovar steamed and hummed as the charcoal embers glowed beneath, and we sat drinking tea until midnight. The teacher was one of old Babushka's girls, and she belonged to the moderate wing of the Social Revolutionists. In New York Babushka had told me about her. She was dark, slim and delicate and looked feverish from overwork; she had eaten nothing at supper that night. But her eyes shook off their weariness and kindled as she told the story of her four years' struggle to break the dead silence here:

"When I came, I found them dull and cross and gloomy little people. Why? Was it by nature? Please just listen to them now! No, their natures were all right; it was only this dead dull life and the fact that they had no lunch. With all its heavy taxes, the government could not spare the money to establish a single school in all these six villages; so in this little private school we took in children from all six, over a hundred of them in all, and most of them spent between two and three hours walking to school and back through the snow. They had breakfast at six and supper at six, and they had not a bite between. Of course they were cross and stupid! So I tried to give them all lunch. I found we could give a pot of coarse soup and a piece of black bread for one kopeck a day. But when I told this to the mothers, they laughed, for the peasants have no midday meal. They have lived so for centuries, and this starvation is only a part of the rigid system of poverty here. So I had to give up my plan and try to teach the children unfed. But it was hard to leave them at noon, eat lunch myself and then come back and find a hundred faces dull and cross from lack of food, and to know that these were only a hundred among millions of peasant children starting life half starved like this! At last I flatly refused to teach till the mothers would give the one kopeck a day. The mothers did some slow hard thinking. Eager to educate their children, one by one at last they gave in and so the children had their lunch. But still a few last protests came. One withered old mother of forty appeared and stood staring in the doorway and, when I asked what she wanted, she said:

" 'I gave you twenty kopecks for soup. My boy had soup once—yesterday. That leaves nineteen kopecks. I want nineteen kopecks back.'

" 'But why?'

" 'Why? Don't you think we need other things besides this foolishness?' she cried. 'We need oil for our lamp and we still owe the *fist* (village usurer) for the money he loaned us to give to the tax man last year. I tell you we want those kopecks back! We think it is a foolish thing for the boy to eat here from a bowl of his own. When he ate with us last night, he said: "Today in school I had my own bowl!" Soon he will be too proud to eat out of our one big bowl with us!'

" 'But that big bowl is dangerous!' I told her. Then I made her think about the village next to ours, where syphilis had spread so fast that nearly half the people already had that vile disease. And I tried to make her see it was spread not by devils and evil eyes but by infection in just such places as the common soup bowl. At this her face grew tight with fear, for she dreaded that disease for her boy. 'Well,' she said to me at last, 'I will try your way; you may be right. My man may beat me for it at first, but you can keep the nineteen kopecks.' And she walked slowly out on the snow.

"As time went on the mothers were pleased because their children now learned so fast and talked at home of all they had learned. I myself began to see how bright these children really are. And not only bright. They taught me many other things. One afternoon I was tired and, when they were making too much noise, I cried out: 'Silence!' very crossly. Then at once I felt my mistake and begged their pardons for shouting so. Complete silence fell and we looked at each other. Their faces were so solemn, I couldn't help smiling.

" 'I think I frightened you,' I said.

" 'Oh, no,' said softly one little girl. 'But it is so fine for us to have some one beg our pardons!'

"So they taught me not to be cross. And they taught me how to teach them, too. Slowly I left the rigid system laid down by the government for its schools and, instead of cramming children's heads with things that they must learn by heart, no matter how little they understand, I try to vary from the book to fit the teaching to each child. Why not? Are all children alike? Shall they be treated like so many stones of exactly the same weight and size? No, you must closely watch each one and talk with him and get to know him. Only then can you help him learn his best.

"But there are so many things for them to learn beside what is in books, if ever they are to better their lives. Such forces for evil are working here. Vodka is one. The government has the monopoly and so encourages drunkenness. One of our drunkards had a small son, who for years had seen his father reel into the hut nearly every night and beat his mother, calling her all kinds of vile names. The little boy watched from the top of the stove. When he came here, he seemed to be all made of nerves; he had sudden fits of crying in the middle of a class. But slowly he began to change. You see, before he came to us, he had always been alone with his parents. The children in his village had laughed at him and pointed at his father lying drunk in the street. But finding the children here kind and jolly, he soon began to learn how to make friends. Of course I came to know him, too, and he told his parents about me. One morning the father came to the door—sober, though still a little unsteady. He was a good-hearted man—only the drink habit in him was bad. I liked him at once and we had a long talk. Later he changed and, in this last year, he has stopped four other fathers who I told him were drinking too much.

"I can feel a deep deep power hidden in these peasants. Slowly it is rising; every year I grow more sure that they are moving slowly upward. But because in this they are helped by liberal schools like this one, the government is against us still. The other day four girl teachers from schools in the next district drove over fifteen miles to consult me about my new methods of teaching. They stayed with me till four o'clock. At six the police agent burst in. Why had those teachers come, he asked. I told him.

" 'It makes no difference! This was a meeting, and meetings without permission are forbidden!' he angrily cried. So now he is watching me closer than ever. They always pay most attention to schoolteachers."

So she finished her tale. In the village close below, the church bell began striking midnight. I went out and looked down the dark prairie slope. Here and there a few clumps of fir; along the horizon a dreary pine forest; below me some twenty snow-covered huts huddled together around a small church. Again came the feeling of desolate silence, and with this feeling the bell was in tune.

Tarasov and I talked long after that, then slept until ten o'clock the next morning. I was awakened by children singing, and later in the sunny schoolroom I sat on the window sill with three boys, while a crowd of children stood around the old cracked piano singing with might and main. The voices sounded very sweet. This was a holiday; all had gone to confessional—because they must, and were now here—because they wished. Every few minutes more trooped in. The girls soon started various games, one like Hide the Handkerchief. The air was crowded with laughs of all sizes. Suddenly there was a shout at the door and two boys appeared with the priest's old fiddle. Tarasov had told them that I played. It was a sadly battered violin. The E string collapsed at once and a

moment later the D string gave up. But on the two strings that
were left I began to do things which were greeted with storms
of applause; and then, to cap the climax, I played Down the
Mother Volga—"just by looking at the book!" they cried.
All joined in the singing now and, as I watched their laughing
faces, I recalled the anxious words of their little teacher about
the police agent's visit:

"He is watching me closer than ever. They pay most attention to schoolteachers."

Why?

"Oh, Zenaida, don't be so bashful! Come out or I'll come
and pull you out!" So cried the jolly peasant boy who had
brought us to call on Zenaida, the village belle. We sat on a
bench in a small low room with brown log walls and rafters
just above our heads. The room was hot and stuffy, for the
two little windows were kept sealed tight all winter long.
Before us was a great oven stove of gray brick cut into the
rear wall, and beside it was a curtained doorway, through
which peeped the giggling beauty.

"She has such muscles," said the boy, "she can throw the
St. Bernard pup from the stove to the door!" I looked at the
pup—weight two hundred pounds. Protesting whispers from
back of the curtain. "Yes, you can, I saw you do it last night!"
He turned to us. "You ought to see her work in the field!"
Beseeching whispers and frowns from the door. "Well, if you
don't like what I say, come on out and do your own talking!
Come out!" Complete hysteria. "All right, then, I'm coming
in!" He dived through the curtain. Giggles and scuffles,
tumbling chairs! Then through the door he dragged the panting village belle and seated her on a stool by the stove. "Now
look at her! Didn't I tell you?"

We looked, and he had told us right. Zenaida was a beauty.
Crimson lips and blushing cheeks, black hair and big dark
sparkling eyes. Soon Tarasov had her talking, while her sis-

ter, the small housewife, smiled over the humming samovar and served us tea and *barankee* (big soft pretzels), jam and white butter. She could, for her husband ran the gristmill of the landowner near by. Zenaida was soon to be married, she said, so we asked to see the happy man.

"Oh, I don't know who he is," she laughed. "I only know it from the blacksmith, the old sorcerer in the next village. I went there and told him I wanted a lover. He frowned and pulled his beard and said: 'Well, girl, pay me three kopecks and I will make you very happy.' I payed and then he cooked for me grass soup in a big bowl. He said: 'Drink this and you will soon have a lover. The soup will cast a spell as far as five villages from here.' So I drank it. Bah! How bitter it was! When I began to spit it out, his old beard shook and he grabbed my arm and shouted: 'Girl, be careful! Don't spit out charms or you'll die an old maid!' He scared me so that I drank it all! And last week from that village a young man came to see me and he stayed two hours here! Perhaps he is the one—but I don't know!"

"If he is not," Tarasov smiled, "the right one will soon come, my dear." And to me in English he said: "On the day when she goes to church to be married, she will wear either a white or red flower—a white one if she is still a virgin—but like nearly half of our peasants girls, Zenaida will probably proudly wear red."

Soon we thought we were all friendly enough to try some deeper talking, so we asked about the war with Japan.

"It's a funny thing," laughed the boy. "The newspaper that comes to the priest always says: 'No losses.' But in our letters from the fellows off at the war we hear things like this: 'Fat Ivan had his head shot off. Old Alexiev is shot through the stomach.' And still the newspaper says: 'No losses!' I think Ivan and Alexiev must be fighting without heads or stomachs!"

"Don't laugh about it. It is sad," said the little housewife.

"In his last letter Alexiev said: 'We cannot fight the Japanese because they have such clever schemes and good maps and telephones. Why have not our officers these things? We are fighting as blind as if we had handkerchiefs tied over our eyes!' Poor old man! And now he is dead. And what good does it do us? What do we care for land and forests 'way off by Japan? And yet for this Ivan lost his head and old Alexiev lost his stomach! It is bad that only one man can say: 'War.' And then hundreds of thousands of others must die!"

I wonder what such women are saying about Stalin today?

The next morning Tarasov's friend, the *barin* who had built the school, drove over in his sledge to take us to see his small estate. He was a kindly man in his thirties, with a brown beard and appealing eyes. The morning was cloudless. Above the small schoolhouse the sky was fresh deep blue, all around us were fields of dazzling white. We climbed with the *barin* into his sledge, buried our feet in sheepskins and straw and pulled our thick fur collars up high. Before us, on a narrow bar, sat a peasant boy of sixteen, who sang and joked and shouted as he urged the horse along. I soon climbed up on the bar at his side and sang for him the gay old song The Man Who Broke the Bank at Monte Carlo. He was greatly delighted at that and whipped the horse into a gallop. Over the rolling fields we went, tipping and sliding, plunging through drifts, while the St. Bernard pup and his mother dashed up little snow clouds on either side. Then we drove through a forest and up a low hill and swung into the yard of the *barin's* estate, behind his old white-pillared frame house. In a long log stable on one side were a hundred cattle munching in stalls; and across the yard was a gristmill, run by a steam engine, which was puffing and panting now, while a dozen peasant men and women stood about watching it grind their rye. Their rude pole sledges were outside. To raise the rye, have it ground in the mill, bake it into huge loaves of black bread, eat this bread, with tea, cabbage, potatoes, and then again to raise more rye—this was the circle of their lives.

"A monotonous circle? You are right," the *barin* said. "Around us are twelve villages, with about a thousand peasants, and my grandfather owned them all. Then came the emancipation of serfs in 1861, but still their condition seems little changed. This circle you speak of has been their life for ages, and so it may be for ages to come. And yet I cannot believe that it will. Come indoors and I will tell you why."

We went with him, not to his frame house, for he had closed it long ago, but into a small cozy cabin among the huts of his field hands near by.

"When I leave all the turmoil of Petersburg and come back to this bear den," he said, throwing himself on an old blue lounge and lighting a cigarette, "all life seems to me to slow down but also to grow more real and sure. There are no great brilliant schemes here to reform the world in a moment; only a slow hard struggle upward. Yes, I mean it, always upward. Slowly but surely the ignorance of a thousand years is being lit up by education. Schools are desperately scarce, but there are many other ways of teaching the peasants to better their lives, and in all these ways the liberal *zemstvo* [legislature] of this district struggles ceaselessly on." He told of *zemstvo* warehouses for modern plows and grain seeds and fertilizers, sold to the peasants at cost; of agricultural teachers moving about from village to village, of wood lots cleared and marshes drained to give the peasants more tillable soil. "All this is slow and sounds dull enough; but it is sure and it means food; it means escape from land famine," he said.

"But clogging even this slow advance, the Imperial Government, mistrusting liberals everywhere, blocks our work at every turn, and at the same time taxes the peasants more and more heavily each year. They are taxed till they have to sell horses and cows and even borrow from the *fist*. When the tax time comes around they break out in desperate riots, where even the women rush out in a frenzy and beat the tax collectors, and are then flogged by police. Every autumn a score of women, bruised and cut, are lodged with the men in the village jail, and a few are taken to town to prison. So quiet settles down again. Quiet once more, but how long will it be till all over Russia, if this goes on, the peasants will rise in such a way that even liberals like myself dread to think of it? For God knows what may happen then!"

Later in the afternoon we went down to see the *fist* in his tiny village store. In cahoots with the district police, I'd been told, he charged the peasants thirty per cent for the money he lent. At his door a cur dog snapped at our legs. We pushed the door open and went in. The *fist* was a short gnarled shaggy old man and his square face set like rock, as he answered Tarasov's smiles by scowls.

"Well? Well? Well?" he snapped and snarled. Who were we both, he wanted to know, and what had we come for? Where were we staying? What business had this young American here? As Tarasov tried to reply, I looked about at the low log walls, where crowded upon hooks and shelves was his wretched stock in trade, including articles left in pawn, from a clock and a samovar and felt boots to one lone and dusty little bottle of perfume. "Well? Well? Well?" the *fist* kept snarling. Not even Tarasov could break through. So we gave up and left him. In the *barin's* small sledge, with a great radiant setting sun throwing its glory on the snow, we drove over the rolling fields back to the schoolhouse some miles away.

What a contrast! What a welcome there! Among the visitors gathered to see us were a young peasant and his wife, who wanted us to come to their hut and stay with them for a week. Delighted, we accepted at once. And as later that evening we sat with the teacher in her room, sipping tea and listening to the jolly laughter of the small girl boarders in the room just over our heads, we wondered how we should ever be able to leave these people we liked so well. We were very soon to find out!

A loud knocking on the outside door. We listened and heard the cook go and unbolt it. After that came a deep hoarse voice which made the teacher catch her breath; and then, with heavy marching steps, the police agent strode into the room. His friend the *fist* had probably told him of our visit that afternoon. My first feeling was an inward chuckle. His face was so pompous, his thick black beard so aggressive and his stupid eyes so filled with dignity and power. He stopped short and clicked his heels.

"To my ear comes the news that two foreigners have come to this schoolhouse," he began. "By what right are you here? Have you permission from the governor of the province? . . . No? Then this is serious! Did you come to make riots or, if not, for what? I say if not, then for what?" he asked triumphantly. "You!" to me. "How do you earn your living? . . . A writer? Ha! This is very bad! Show me your passports! You must! At once! . . . H'm— H'm— H'm! How do I know this American fellow is the person described? I repeat the question! . . . No, fellow, I cannot believe you. . . . Viséd by our Consul in Berlin? Ha! Berlin!" He carefully filed this fact in his book. "Now, the next question to you is: What was he doing in Berlin? . . . H'm— H'm! Well, I shall report all this—I shall leave nothing unreported! And I insist that you leave this place at once—tomorrow! I bid you good night!"

But Tarasov stopped him with a coaxing hand on his arm; and his smiling friendly talk and my gift of a large cigar had such effect that the great man before leaving came to our room and, standing stiff with dignity but just a little gracious now, let us take a flashlight picture of him holding my brief bag—which was stuffed with notes on talks I'd had with city revolutionists!

When the outer door had closed, we came back to the

teacher's room, ready to laugh long and hard. But we did nothing of the sort. For the little teacher, lying pale and weak on the lounge, begged us now to go away, to leave all her villages alone and not to bring her any more into trouble with the police! Deeply repentant, we promised at once to do as she asked. And early next morning we said good-by.

XIII

"Goot-by! howdooyoudo! thenk you!" Katya and Na-
diejda, peasant girls of eight and nine, stood excitedly at the
schoolhouse door, stamping their clumsy felt boots in the
snow and laughing and shouting while we waved back, till
our sledge went over the prairie roll and the log schoolhouse
sank out of sight.

Then only jingling bells. Behind a white horse with a huge
blue wooden yoke over his neck, we sat in the bottom of the
low sledge with the driver, a young giant with splendid shoulders, face lean and brown, jaws firmly set and a smile that
made me like him at once. He liked us, too, for our trouble
with the police had made him feel that we were both of his
kind. He was the leading spirit among the young peasant
radicals.

"We have to keep quiet now," he said, "but wait till we
have time to get together with lads like ourselves all over
Russia! Then you will see what we will do!"

I waited twelve years and then I saw, in 1917.

Through his help our drive to town was prolonged to an
all-day visit with peasants along the road. Best I remember a
talk I heard in a village *tracter*, a cabin of logs and sod, where
tea and vodka could be had. We came into a low square room
and sat down on a bench by a deep little window. This bench
ran around three sides of the room and before it were narrow
tables with stools. The low log walls were patched with newspapers and lithographs, most of them tattered and old. In one
corner was a yellow brick stove and in another hung an ikon,

Madonna and Child staring blindly out of a gilt frame, with the eternal little wick lamp flickering into their faces. Around us sat a dozen peasants and an old pilgrim tramp in brown rags. He stared at us and so did the peasants. An old clock ticked. A speckled cur dog sneaked out and sniffed. Still silence. But our young driver, by winks and nods and whispers about us, broke the ice and the talk began.

"America!" A short burly peasant with sandy beard turned abruptly and looked at me with little hard suspicious eyes. Then he turned to Tarasov and asked: "Why did you bring him here? Why did *you* come here?"

"Why not?" smiled Tarasov. "This American is a jolly good fellow. We drive and eat and smoke and drink. Why not?"

"But where is your business?"

"Gone. Killed by the war. My business is smashed and I am poor. But what's the use of being blue?"

"Oh, this devil's war!" The peasant banged the bench with his fist.

"Why devil's war?"

"Why? Hu! If you were here in our boots, you would see quick enough!"

"See what?"

"Oh, my good fellow, I am not a fat little baby and neither are you! I say it is a devil's war! Just wait a few weeks and you will see them bring poor young Matvei home! You will hear him cuss and roar!"

"But who is he?"

"He got caught in the wheel of a big gun. My cousin wrote me all about it. His right leg was cut off by the wheel, all but a bone sticking out from his thigh. And his left arm was torn off by a shell, and for all this trouble what do they give him? How he will roar! Three rubles a month! A fine life he will have, with a wife and five children. His wife now goes from hut to hut. She shouts: 'What can I do with three rubles a month? Can I feed my five little brats and my man who has lost his leg and his arm?' Then she puts her head in her dress and boohoos like a baby! I tell you, *barin*, all my soul gets sick when I think of this war. Why was it started—why—why? What do we care for Manchuria? Are we pigs like the Japanese? Do we want all the land in the world? No! We want to keep our own lives! Don't even our lives belong to us?" The short man was now shouting. The other peasants all bent closer. Fingers ran through long coarse hair. Eyes showed how gloomy ran the thinking.

"Oh, my dear fellow," said Tarasov, laying his hand on the peasant's arm. "You and I must get handsome young wives and raise many sons in place of those killed."

"Don't joke!" he shook off Tarasov's hand. "I see your game. You try to make me talk of something funny, but I won't. Now what do you think about this war? What will be the finish?"

"God knows."

"God! It's always God—God! That won't do, I tell you! This is our job! We must help ourselves!"

"But how? You and I are simple men. We know only that one ruble is only half as good as two and that you cannot drink at once twenty bottles of vodka. But to think out these big ideas—"

"Hold on, my good drunkard! The peasant is gray [uneducated]—but let me tell you that no wolf has eaten his brain!"

"Well, what do you wise, wise peasants want?"

"Not this!" With his knuckles he mimicked the roll of a drum. "Flags, bands, bright breeches—bah!"

"Then tell me why it is that they can make us all be soldiers when none of us want to be?" At this the peasant scratched his head.

"It's like the seventeen sheep I had before they grabbed them for the war. Even if my shed were on fire, if just one of my sheep had run in the others would have followed him. But

PICTURES TAKEN IN A RUSSIAN SCHOOLHOUSE AND VILLAGE VISITED
IN 1905

look here—I'm sure of this—if only a few peasants begin to refuse to go off to be killed for nothing but three rubles a month, then all the others will start refusing and the whole army will melt like snow. It will! Because who can force us to fight except other soliders? Don't you see? They must have us to make us! Hold on!" he cried as he jumped up. He went to a window. "Look out here! Some more of our fellows have just been taken off in the train to be butchered!"

We all looked out. Along the road a procession of sledges was coming slowly back from the railroad station ten miles away. On each sledge sat a peasant woman muffled in shawls and staring ahead. One of the youngest stared in a way that seemed utterly blind. She had under her shawl a baby. It was dressed in its Sunday clothes. Silently we came back and sat down.

"Well, my wise peasant," asked Tarasov, speaking low, "how can you make things better? What do you think about your share in this government?"

"I? Oh, I think quite easily."

"But what?"

"That nobody can do more than he can."

"That is no answer. What do you mean?"

"What do I mean? If you can't understand so simple a thing, how can I talk to you?"

"But try."

"No use, I tell you. You can't understand till you yourself have tried to squeeze life out of a little field and then have this squeezed from you in taxes, while your children starve. When you have a life like ours, you often get to thinking hard."

"But what do you think at such times, my old plow philosopher?"

"That nobody can do more than he can and that, if all our plows should stop, then even the big men in the towns would all have to stop eating our bread!"

"Well, but you must plow, you know."

"Oh, you can't stop me up like that! I say they are now eating *our* bread! All our village money they take and spend, not for our roads and things we need but for themselves! We are just cattle! But even their cattle—us, I mean—they would treat better if they had sense. We peasants, when we want our cow to give good milk, we give her water and hay and grass; and we know that her calf will be no good unless we let it feed from the mother. Now try and catch me. By the milk I mean my crops. By the calves I mean my children. And I say that my crops must be used to feed my children. I say that all the tax money we pay must be used, not in the towns but right here around the village. We want barns full of plows and new machines and everything to make the land better. We must, because it is worse every year. And besides this, we want a fine school. One school peasant is worth two gray ones."

"Oh, look here, my friend," said Tarasov, "I'm not so sure that school instruction does not do more harm than good."

"Maybe it does, if it's only in books, but what I want in a school is much bigger. I want it to teach us all that we need in our work and our lives to be happy here. I will tell you what I mean by that. This winter I had the luck to find an old red Holy Book, and there I learned about Stepan of Perm. Do you know who he was?"

"I don't," said Tarasov. The name was about as familiar in Russia as that of George Washington at home.

"Ha! You don't. Then I, the gray peasant, will tell you. Stepan of Perm was a rich man's son—but he left all his riches and got right down deep into our poverty—and so he became a Holy Man—not by preaching and fasting but by helping peasants to work. He worked right with them, gave them his life. He was not at all like our village pope. Our pope always prays and prays: 'My God, *give* me this and this.' But never: 'My God, *take* something.'" At this sally the whole crowd laughed, but quickly he held up his hand. "Let's not stop for jokes," he told them. "I say Stepan was not like that. His praying was working—he worked hard—and I think his sweat was more sweet to God than all this holy oil in the lamps. When Stepan helped a sick peasant to plow, or when he got together a crowd and dug big ditches to dry off swamps and so give us more tillable soil, I say this digging and plowing was like praying—only better—because it gave bread to our brats. All the peasants who saw him soon began to help each other in work like that. And this help was just the beginning of a heaven right down in the village instead of 'way up above the clouds! We can't see through the clouds anyway; we don't know if there is any heaven up there!"

He gulped down a last glass of tea, and rose stiffly to his feet.

"Well, now I must go and mend my sledge. My boy Alexei broke it by throwing a log on it too hard. Alexei has a fine strong arm—such muscle! And besides, he's smart. But don't you fellows tell him this, I don't want Alexei spoiled."

Then he went out. We, too, were soon on the road once more, and for an hour Tarasov filled in what I had missed in the peasant's talk. Later we stopped again and again at other teahouses along the way. At last in the dusk we drove into the town that we had left the week before, and went to Moscow by a night train.

In Moscow we spent an enthralling two weeks. When now I read what modern Americans write about Soviet Russia, I often wish they could have been with me that winter in 1905, in the brewing of the storm. For so much that some of them attribute to the Soviet, both good and bad, weak and strong, is not Bolshevist but just Slav; and all the elements in the Slav were centered and intensified in the Moscow of old days. A race half Oriental but with the strength of the cold still North; a people slow-moving, violent, deep, ruthless in its cruelties, lovable in its friendliness and ways of welcoming strangers in; impractical and disorderly, too absorbed in its living and dreaming to throw any vigor or zest into the dull labor of each day—the "deep burning soul of the Slav" was here, in this strangely personal town which warm-heartedly laid its grip upon me, almost from the start.

But at first how grim it looked to me! A dreary sad old city with the dirty snow and ice of late winter on its narrow winding streets. Yet a city of violent contrasts, between the cold dark tenements and stinking hovels of its slums and the gorgeous palaces of merchant and industrial magnates, Moscow's *nouveaux riches.* One of them had begun life as a peasant; Tarasov's father had painted his portrait; and for that reason his house steward asked us in and allowed us to wander around. Vaguely I remember the corridors and banquet hall, ballroom and picture gallery, where genuine treasures of breathless beauty were surrounded by the most terrible stuff, in a setting of savage abundance and of arrogant display. Hotly I rebelled against it, after the poverty I'd seen, and back we came to the life outside. I saw churches, churches everywhere, with their shining gilded spires, cupolas and rounded domes, pink or green or vivid blue, coloring the town's whole life. Always I kept hearing bells, some of them harsh and jangling but others deep sepulchral booms. In the Kremlin high over all, Tarasov told me bloody tales of ancient violence done by Czars. At night in hilarious little cafés, filled with army officers, merchants and war profiteers, we listened to Gypsies singing and were served by Tartar waiters. And near the Kremlin were long arcades with hundreds of shops that were piled with goods from the East, shops in which at every turn you met faces from the Orient. Yes, East and West were mingled here!

But beneath the old color of it all, eagerly I hunted out the stirring drama of new days. With letters from St. Petersburg, we were warmly welcomed by students in their cold little rooms, in cellars crowded with workers on strike and even in army barracks by small groups of mutinous men. Again I heard tense voices like those in St. Petersburg, so tense with forces long pent up, I felt sure this human dynamite must burst into action soon! But Tarasov insisted still:

"Only one little part of Russia is here. Revolution must depend in the end on the people in the villages."

In this he was supported by a lithe blond girl we met one night, a girl of birth and breeding who spoke English easily; she had intelligent quick blue eyes. A follower of Babushka and a Social Revolutionist, she kept a little bookshop filled with books and newspapers all approved by the censor, a most respectable little shop. But after one glance at the letter I'd brought from old Babushka in New York, she led us into a small back room and there, as she read the letter through, she smiled and shook her head.

"Oh, Babushka, you naughty old dear, why will you take such chances?" she said. "We never use any letters here."

And yet this girl in her small back room was a postmistress all the same, a clearing house for messages from hundreds of revolutionists working through the villages and coming at times to leave information for comrades with Masha in her shop. And Masha had trained her memory to keep all such messages in her head! She talked to me of their work that night.

"We are not like the Marxian Socialists who wish all Russia industrialized; we love the country and the life in villages," she said. "We work for a Russia all, all free—free in thinking, speaking, writing, free to live and work as it likes and to own in common the land and other things it needs for life. But we don't care to see ugly factory towns spread over this beautiful country we love; we work for a Russia of open fields and forests and of villages still. I am glad you have had a glimpse of our work in schools and villages here in the North. Now go to those in the Ukraine and in the grand and lovely Caucasian Mountains to the south—for you will find real action there."

Tarasov gave her his quiet smile. "We have some business

there," he said, and in Russian he told her of a plan he'd
brought from friends in England to help the Caucasians in
their revolt. We shall come to it later on. As Masha listened I
could see excitement kindle in her eyes. And she promised to
send word of our mission ahead of us by the underground
mail.

We went first down to the Ukraine. From snow and ice we
came in March to slush and mud in two sprawling factory
cities. From them we had planned to drive at once out to the
villages, but in both cities we were delayed; for when we showed
my credentials to the authorities, as we must, a lavish hospi-
tality was forced on us and kept us there. I remember one
governor of a province, old and fat, with sly small eyes, who
held us long with his welcoming talk and insisted that we do
the town with a young aide of his that night. A spruce handsome lad in uniform, again and again the aide asked me in
French:

"Why do you only talk with these girls? I assure you the
whole Regime of the Czar guarantees the immunity of each
one." When at last we got rid of him, I asked:

"Good God, Tarasov, why in hell do these people enter-
tain us like this?" He smiled and answered:

"It is my fault, a little joke that I play on the Czar. From
Chicago you brought a letter from Mr. Harold McCormick,
your friend; and his name is now widely known over here,
both because McCormick reapers are already sold in our land
and still more because he has married the daughter of your
Mr. Rockefeller, who owns great oil fields near Baku. And
since these officials cannot read a word of the English in this
letter, I have told them that you yourself are Mr. Harold
McCormick."

"Damn! And so we've wasted three good days!"

I tore up the letter and, traveling on, we did visit some villages after that, but I shall not try to picture them now, for to

do so would be to repeat my descriptions of villages in the North, except that here the poverty, disease and ignorance and despair made me feel there was little chance of any real action in the Ukraine. But we went on down to the Caucasus and we found action in plenty there—the Middle Ages suddenly plunged into a modern revolution, in the rockiest most romantic of all the dominions of the Czar!

XIV

I SAT WITH TARASOV UP IN THE BOW OF A BLACK SEA STEAMER. The air was balmy, the stars hung low and from the horizon ahead the great planet Venus threw a little path of light to meet us, up across the sea. Down in the steerage close behind lay a mass of Armenians, Russians and Turks, sleeping, gambling, smoking, drinking. Packed around us were a score of gay Caucasian students homeward bound from a Russian university, and with them a Circassian prince and his young Caucasian bride, whose dark beauty made me ready at once to believe what I had heard: "The Georgian girls are the diamonds of Russia." The students, too, were strikingly handsome in their brilliant uniforms. They were all rushing home to fight.

"All classes," cried one, "are rising! Our beautiful mountains will soon be free!"

The mountains, dark and silent, towered up out of the sea; we caught glimpses of turreted castles above and quaint fishing hamlets below. The students told us stories of oppression and revolt and sang wild old mountain ballads, the music quick and throbbing with the hot blood of the South. The Georgian princess loved those songs, and under her black mantilla you could see her big eyes sparkle like the diamonds in her ears.

"Is this all real?" I asked the American consul, when we reached Batum. I told him the stories I had heard.

"Well," he answered grimly, "here we've had one general strike, a massacre of men, women and children by Cossacks only two weeks ago, five thousand Cossacks camped around us, the province under martial law—but beneath it all a secret committee of revolutionists running the town. They are of all classes, rich and poor; they give orders, they try criminals, they punish for every kind of offense. Five spies have been shot in the last week; one of them was killed last night right here below my window. Oh, you'll see enough!"

That afternoon, with the prince and his wife and two students, we drove twenty miles through soft green valleys white with blossoms. We saw Kurds and Caucasians there, little Greek churches, Mohammedan mosques. Through the students we talked with some of the peasants, in cabins dark and bare inside, where cattle, pigs and people all slept together on the dirt floor.

"And still the Russians raise their taxes!" one of the young students said. "Do you wonder they are ready to fight?"

They were ready. You could feel it in their low harsh voices as they told of Cossack outrage. At dinner back in our hotel, in whispers our gigantic waiter told how his own little niece had been raped. We heard more that night down on the docks, in the crooked narrow streets of the port, in long low drinking rooms filled with men in Russian blouses or in kilts or flowing robes with knives in their belts. Asia and Europe all mixed in together, boiling!

Still later, to our hotel room came a tall black-bearded man with a low voice and clear steady gray eyes. Our friend Masha in Moscow had done as she promised and sent word about us ahead, and to this man Tarasov explained the plan he'd brought from England. A group of English liberals, among them a young officer in a munitions company, offered to ship by a roundabout route five thousand rifles, free of cost, with a thousand rounds of ammunition, to be landed secretly on the Caucasian coast at night. The tall man took it quietly.

"Our central committee in Tiflis must learn of this from you," he said. Tarasov smiled.

"And we must learn, direct from the people everywhere, whether they are ripe for these guns." The Caucasian looked calmly back.

"You will find them ready," he said. Then he talked on into the night, telling us just where to go and promising to have word sent ahead by the revolutionist mail. Long after midnight I lay in bed in the dark, unable to sleep. Gunrunning in wartime is not a soporific sport. Suddenly I opened my eyes. A shadowy giant stood by my bed. A dark arm came out and I felt in my hand the cold steel of a revolver. I rolled out of bed, on the other side.

"Tarasov! Ask this man what he wants!" With exasperating slowness Tarasov woke up and questioned.

"He was our waiter at supper," he said. "He bought this pistol from a French boat and he wants you to take it up inland and kill a few Cossacks like those who raped his niece."

"Tell him to do his killing himself—and now let's have a little sleep!"

Two days later we sat in a diner on the *train de luxe* for Tiflis. At one long table down the center were gathered some forty or fifty men, with beards black and gray and white. Sons of the clan chieftains of half a century ago, they were revolutionists now. Their brothers and sons had been killed in the war; their beloved free country had been enslaved sixty years back by the Russian Czar and had been taxed into famines and riots—till now the richest spot in Europe was choked in its struggle toward civilization, mines undeveloped and vineyards untended. "We are beggars sitting on bags of gold!" one old graybeard bitterly cried. So now they were going to Tiflis, to meet with others and demand a constitution of the Czar. They looked like clan chieftains still. Hairy faces, sunburnt, glowing; rough deep voices talking fast in harsh mountain dialects; coarse woolen gowns, red, orange, or gray, with a poniard at the waist and across the chest a cartridge belt; flowing sleeves and big fur caps or hoods or turbans, heavy capes of black goatskin thrown back over chairs. And with them were frock suits, silk hats! For some of these gay mountaineers had been in Paris when news came of this struggle to be free. Hats tipped back, faces flushed with wine, eyes gleaming under thick black brows, their big hands gestured as they talked. The Middle Ages dashed into a modern revolution!

Tarasov was soon boon companions with a chief whose wide gray beard flowed over an enormous chest, whose fists showed big and hairy in his loose red sleeves.

"Only three weeks ago," he said, "one of my workmen came to me bloody and blue from Cossack whips—knouts with iron nails for lashes. I galloped to the railroad crossing where he had been beaten, and found four mounted Cossacks there. 'Why did you beat my man?' I asked. 'Do you call that a beating?' asked one. 'Why, we only swung our knouts a little!' I took their names and wrote to their colonel. No answer. I went to him. He laughed. 'What harm is there in beating these stupid mountain cattle?' he asked. In the Batum riot next week, I saw a little boy five years old imitating the men and shouting: 'Down with, down with—' he didn't know what. I saw six Cossacks rush on him; I seized him and took him to their colonel, showed the child's face bleeding, told of scores of women and children I had seen flogged by his men. 'Ha!' cried the old colonel, himself still wild from the sight of blood. 'Using women and children, eh, to rouse sympathy for their cause! Well, we will kill all their brats till the parents learn their lesson!' I took the child home to his mother. Half dead with terror, she fell on her knees and kissed my hands and then my boots. The child had been out with his nurse and had gone too near the riot, and the nurse had been killed, she said. So now the boy's father and two uncles all are revolutionists!"

In the rich gay streets of Tiflis we saw hundreds of chiefs and nobles—with such women! Radiant beauties, Georgians,

Persians, some in the latest Paris gowns, others in gorgeous old-time costumes, laughing from carriages by day, and by night tripping up the broad carpeted stairs at the opera. Dreams again! But then we wandered through crooked slum streets and saw revolting poverty. We met with the central committee of revolutionists one night and to them Tarasov told again of the offer of English aid. The guns were to be shipped in a Norwegian vessel, he said, in two hundred and fifty cases of twenty rifles each—small cases of only two hundred pounds, to be landed in small boats at night by the revolutionists. Till daybreak we discussed details of how that landing might be made and to what points the guns might go. The committee was ready. Tarasov was not.

"First," he insisted, "we must see that your people are ready for these guns. It is hard to believe these atrocity tales."

"We ask you to believe nothing," they said. "Go and see for yourselves." And they mapped out a trip through the mountains. "We shall send news of you ahead. Go and see and then come back. We shall be waiting for you here with a full plan for your English friends."

To get the needed passes for the trouble zone we wished to see, we took train to Koutais and went to the Russian governor there. We entered the anteroom, showed my credentials and stood while two attachés ran light but careful fingers over us in search of bombs. After that we were ushered in. Two gigantic Cossack guards kept close behind us and in the room were several more. The governor, with soft white beard flowing over his richly embroidered blue gown, sat back in a reclining chair puffing slowly at the stem of a Turk pipe five feet long, while a kneeling servant tended the bowl. He beamed on us with his little blue eyes and said he was glad we had not come sooner, for then Koutais was dangerous; but now his Cossacks had made it all peaceful; we would find it a charming old town. Tarasov asked him if he had any objection to the trip to mountain villages we had planned.

"None at all," smiled the governor. "My only concern is for your safety. These mountaineers have a habit of plunging a wide-bladed knife far into your vitals and twisting it there, in a way that produces, I am told, excruciating agony. Having once been young myself, I suspect that you will not heed my warning. But if you do go, please let me know where, that I may take precautions for you through my Cossacks and police."

So kind was the courteous old prince that again I doubted the stories I'd heard. I wandered through steep narrow streets and saw picturesque peasants chatting in markets, I peered into quaint dark smithies and booths of tailors, carpenters, shoemakers. Buds, flowers and blossoms everywhere. Stolid peasants came trudging by under enormous pigskins of wine. And such girls! They leaned from tiny balconies and laughed low rippling laughter from behind high garden walls. In our hotel we found again the Circassian prince and his bride. Even lovelier than herself was her sister, who had joined them there. She spoke French and in long absorbing talks I almost forgot the work I had come for. For though at first she made me feel that she was all on fire to help set her mountains free, she went on to speak only of herself, of her life as it had been and of what she meant it to be. Then she wanted to know all about me. With her relatives we drove at sunset out onto a mountainside and picnicked in an orchard all pink with blossoms, where a gray old mountaineer served us with delicious wine. Frogs croaked in the darkening valley below, but high above the great snowy peaks shone flaming in the afterglow. The young sister sat at my side, and so fast did our little affair get on that, back in our hotel that night, I wrote to my father in Chicago:

"These Caucasian mountains are the loveliest I've ever seen and a mine of wonderful stories, too! I may even marry and settle down and stay here for the rest of my life!"

Sheer romance—how fantastic it seems, looking back from

the glare of this modern age! But susceptible though I was in those days, what was even a girl like that, compared to five thousand rifles and the chance of getting more from our country through the stories I sent home? I had come to these mountains to see revolution. In Koutais I found signs of it soon. Again and again on the streets a score of Cossacks would ride clattering by, and then from these same people, whom I had seen so gay before, came angry scowls and flashes of eyes and murmurs that rose to cries of defiance.

Next day I lay after luncheon in a meadow looking up at the snowy peaks. How quiet it was! Only tiny sounds of life in the grass and a tinkle from the brook that slipped under a ledge of rock and red roses close by. But then, with a deep-rolling clatter of hoofs, around a sharp curve in the road swept a hundred Cossacks, huge splendid brutes sitting straight in their saddles, laughing, whooping and lashing at oxen of the carts that they passed by. I heard quick breaths, and a little girl came running with a baby in her arms. Close by me she stumbled, pitched into a hollow. A loud sob of terror! When I ran over and stooped to lift her, she gave a shaking breath of relief; but she stared at the Cossacks as at devils. I led her off to the inn close by, where Tarasov sat talking still, and with him we climbed to her father's cabin. In the middle was a smoldering fire; a black iron pot hung over it. Along one wall ran a wide low bench covered with bedding for the whole family. The little girl went to one end of the bench and stared at a huddled white figure there. It was her fifteen-year-old sister. Raped by a whole band of Cossacks, she lay moaning, shivering, shaking. A midwife had come and had said she would die. We found her father, tall and deep-chested, with black beard, red turban, brown cloak and a poniard in his belt.

"When I rushed to the Cossack barracks," he cried, "the colonel only grinned and said: 'Point out the men who did it! I can't punish a whole regiment!' When I came home and told

PICTURES TAKEN IN THE CAUCASUS ON MY FIRST RUSSIAN TRIP IN 1905

this, my little girl who brought you here, her eyes got big, she took me out and whispered: 'Can't I go? I saw them do it! Can't I point to the men who did it?' I took her; but the big colonel got red and gave her a shove that made her fall with her head on the floor! What right has the Russian Czar to turn loose such wolves among us? But their time will come! In a gorge not far from here last week, a crowd of us waited for a train! On it were two hundred Cossacks! Every peasant of us knew of some young girl raped like mine! The train came rushing through the gorge! The track was gone! Soon two hundred wolves were dead!"

Low moans from the cabin. The little sister came out for a dipper of cold water. As she carried it in, her hand shook; her eyes seemed watching something still.

Not so peaceful after all. What a discreet old governor! But his Cossack officers were not. On a train that we took from Koutais that night, we joined a genial group of them and, draining quarts of vodka, they laughed till the tears rolled down their swarthy cheeks, as they told us the same stories we had heard from the mountaineers. We laughed with them and I spun such yarns of cowboys, dance halls, gambling hells, that one young major clapped me on the back and swore he was my friend for life! But when they had all dropped to sleep, I wrote in my notebook the stories they'd told, until slowly the light from the smoky swaying lamp overhead was blurred in the first gray of dawn. Then the train stopped, we got off and the long train rumbled on.

Cold drizzle and a small station surrounded by deep forest of pine. Beside us paced a sentry and another stood guard by a freight car where Russian soldiers lay asleep. In the station we drank steaming tea and ate eggs and hunks of cheese and blue bread, and in this we were joined by our Cossack major, who had jumped off the train behind us. He was bound for the same place as we were, a village twelve miles back in the mountains. "The most dangerous place you could pick out!"

our friend the governor had said. The major proposed to drive with us there. Under his tall white-plumed cap was a dark glowing face with black mustache, gleaming teeth and deep sparkling eyes. As we galloped down hills and through forests, he swore at the local police and spies.

"Eternal bribes and blackmail!" he cried. "When they see two soused peasants together, they shout: 'A revolution!' So it is in this village ahead. Five months ago the peasants refused to work the fields of the nobles. 'A revolution against our Czar!' screamed the spies, who are paid for such talk. So from our barracks a hundred miles over the mountains we rode hard, all night and all day, to reach this spot. And what did we find here? Nothing at all! Not an ounce of excitement to warm us up! These mountain peasants are quiet as curs! All we can do is to drink and eat and sleep and have our fun with the women! You will soon see for yourselves!"

First we saw only poverty. The children all were weak and thin; no jolly shouts, only dreary silence. The bare cabins looked bleak in fast-thickening rain.

"Well," I said to Tarasov, "I hope the governor learns of this and has us fired out of here. For of all the cold wet holes on earth—"

"Right, stranger," said a sad-eyed peasant on crutches, who stood close by. "It's a damned dead place for sure."

"Where in hell did you learn English?"

"Four years with Buffalo Bill," he replied. "He make me a Cossack in rough rider troop and we have one hell of a good time. But I broke my leg bad. So here I am home." He spat sadly into the mud. But when I told him why I had come, he brightened. "Good. Write it in all your most big papers—how we are poor and why we strike! I will show!" And he took us to peasant huts where all morning we heard their stories of woes.

"Poorer and poorer every year!" one stooping white-headed old peasant declared. "Ever since I was a boy we have been slaves to the landowners here! Always they kept raising the rents; and besides, the judges and priests and police made us pay and pay in bribes, or they would beat us or curse our souls! And we could do nothing, for we were unarmed! But so at last we decided to strike. We stopped work in their fields and the owners grew angry. They took our cattle! We took them back! And the police and judges shouted: 'This is revolution!'"

"We cannot revolt without any guns," the little village doctor said, "so we outlaw our oppressors instead. We say to the landowners: 'Keep your fields.' And to the governor: 'Stay in your town. We will pay you all your taxes; we will pay for your judges, priests and police. But let the judge sit alone in his court, the priest in his church and the policeman in his jail. We ourselves will settle our disputes, punish our criminals, marry our lovers and bury our dead.' And so we have done. But now this outlawed government in fury has brought the Cossacks here to drive us on to violence, and God only knows how soon it will be till our young hotheads rise with only knives and clubs! For as a doctor night after night I am called to young girls bleeding from rape. Twenty Cossacks had a girl one afternoon a week ago! I could do little! She died last night! They are not men but devils!"

To hear of all this from the devils themselves, we dined in the regimental mess of the jovial major and his friends. When we told of the governor's warning about the dangerous peasants here, they laughed and cried: "Pigs! Lambs! Quiet as mules!" These stupid peasant devils would give them no excitement, so they took it out on the girls. "The girls are beauties!" was the cry as the vodka went around. The only woman at the table was the colonel's enormous wife, a swarthy dame with black down on her lip, bass voice and a chuckle that seemed to come from far down in her abdomen.

"You should have seen her when she was a wench," her lean brown husband proudly said. "When she pranced around a ballroom you could feel her shake the floor!"

After dinner their two small sons played a little Cossack game. With bare feet planted firm on the ground, hands rubbed in wet sand to make tighter their grip, each grabbed the other by the nose, and so began a tug of war. To roars of cheers from the officers, they tugged till their faces grew fiery red and their eyes glared through tears that came from the blinding torture of that pain. But still neither boy let go. If he did, he would be thrashed, I learned. So on and on and on they tugged—glaring, panting, snarling—little savages trained from their birth to violence, as police of the Czar.

Soon after this the whole atmosphere changed. We were summoned to the guard tent and told of a telegram just received. The governor had learned we were here and insisted that we leave at once. What a discreet old governor!

In spite of him, in that next week, we made a hasty trip through the hills, avoiding the Cossacks and guided on from village to village by peasants belonging to secret committees who'd learned of us through their underground mail. Fast workers, scarcely sleeping at night, in notebook and on kodak films we gathered the evidence we had come for. Then from a small railroad town we took train for Tiflis, to meet once more with the central committee and talk guns.

"God, but I'm tired!" I said on the train. "Now for a good long all day sleep!"

But I did not sleep so long.

"They have killed the engineer! The bandits shot him!" somebody cried. Our train had stopped in a steep high valley with bare black mountains on either side and in front a rocky gorge, where the locomotive engineer had been killed in the train ahead of ours. Our own engineer refused to go on. Hour by hour we waited and by nightfall our impatience warmed.

"Well," said Tarasov quietly, "let us run the engine ourselves." He took me into the roundhouse, climbed into the locomotive cab and showed exactly how every lever, throttle and valve did its work. "I ran one for two weeks once in Poland," he explained. It struck me as funny. "Why can't we?" he urged. "They only run fifteen miles an hour, and all *you* will have to do is to throw wood into the furnace."

At last I agreed. We offered our services and were at once surrounded by admiring passengers. But soon I noticed scowls and sneers and growls from the railroad workingmen. I grew uneasy and said to my friend:

"I don't believe in this bandit story. This looks to me like a railroad strike. Ask these men if we are scabs?"

He asked and learned that I'd guessed right. We went to the stationmaster and Tarasov ruefully told him:

"We shall not drive your engine now. The young American hero has decided to resign."

We found the strike leaders and showed our credentials; and then, returning to our compartment, we pulled down the shades on the station side, took the leaders in from the other side and talked with them till late that night.

"This strike is only a test," said one. "The central committee has ordered it to find out how strong we are. Someday we will strike every railroad in Russia. Your *zemstvo* men and your students can talk and the peasants can burn estates and get slaughtered. But we can cut all Russia in pieces—and we mean to do it soon!"

It was not soon. It took twelve years. Then they did it, in 1917.

Later that night we walked down the track. Russian soldiers were singing there, fifty of them in a circle, in their long gray coats and capes. High above the deeper voices a clear sweet tenor soared to the moon. Behind rose an ugly water tank, machine shop, roundhouse, telegraph poles and a long stone tenement; and before it were the shadowy forms of some two hundred men and women. No music there but only a hum, broken by a passionate rise in a speaker's voice or a roar of applause.

For two nights we heard sentinels pacing by our window; their sharp challenges rang out; from the distance came sounds of sudden fights and by day the soldiers encircled the train. How could we get to Tiflis and finish up our business there before the old governor in Koutais heard of our trip and put spies on our trail? When they learned of our trouble, the strike leaders found a wagon and team, with which we could make the eighty-mile journey; but just as we were ready to start, a train crept out of the mouth of the gorge. The locomotive was run by soldiers; five more with leveled rifles stood along the sides and at front; and so the train moved in through silent scowling crowds of men. It started back for Tiflis at noon. Just before that, I took a snapshot of the soldiers on the engine. For this we were promptly put under arrest and made the trip to Tiflis with a sour-faced old cop in our compartment on the train. Slowly we crept up the gorge, stopping while men ran ahead to examine every bridge. At a station farther on we saw a soldier carried in, his head still bleeding from a gash; and once we heard a rifle crack and saw a peasant in a field fall back over a stone wall.

At Tiflis we were taken to the chief of police of the Caucasus. It was only a big bare room, and the chief at his desk was only a plain modern man in uniform. But the room for sixty years had been like a gate to Siberia, the prison feeling was in the air, and this was helped by the two big cops who stood close behind us. Beside them were our traveling bags, and in my small brief case were all my revolutionist notes! Would the chief search the luggage of an American? If he did, could he read English? As I weighed the chances, I glanced at my companion. Me they could only send out of Russia, but to him they could do what they liked. And yet he chuckled and smiled and joked all through that painful hour. This we had arranged on the train. I was to be the in-dignant young tourist, and Tarasov, my courier, was to joke with the chief at the ridiculous fuss I made over so small an annoyance as this. So I protested loud and long in English against our arrest, and Tarasov translated and smiled. I pro-tested still more hotly against having my luggage searched; again Tarasov translated and smiled. He even smiled when the chief decided to waive my protest, and he joked while the chief began slowly to go through my notes. The minutes wore on. I could feel those cops closely watching both our faces. But Tarasov chuckled still. Then I grew pleasantly warm all over—from the feet up! We were released! The chief could not read English!

We had to go slow in meeting our revolutionist friends that day, for now we were constantly watched by spies. But after hours of dodging about, we met the leaders late at night and talked again till nearly dawn about the details of their plan for landing those rifles on the coast. One of them would go later to England, there to see Tarasov's friends with a letter from him and so arrange for the delivery of the guns. It was only one of many such plans attempted in Rus-sia at that time and, like so many others, it failed. But it sounded grand to me that night! I remember how excited I was, as in parting I gripped hands with those men—journalists, landowners, workingmen, princes, doctors, lawyers and mountaineers. A few of them were young as I—Caucasian students—like Stalin. I wonder if he was there that night?

We left Tiflis the next day. On account of railroad strikes, the trains could not be trusted, so we hired a low rude open carriage and started at sunrise over the mountains north to Vladikavkaz, a town from which I meant to go to London, there to write. For that glorious mountain run, we had thirty-two horses in eight relays, and covered the hundred and sixty miles in thirty-four hours. What a ride! Tiflis had been hot and sultry but by midnight, high above the clouds, we drove between snowbanks ten feet high, over the famous mountain pass through which Asia had once poured her hordes to sweep Europe into the Dark Ages. As we drove under towering cliffs and through roaring gorges, it was not hard to picture those wild hordes of long ago—their campfires, horses and rough carts, their battles with owners of the pass, their shouts and screams and hairy faces! Easy to picture, for the past had left many traces there. Forts and ruined castles rose in every narrow spot; and Tarasov, who had traveled once for eight months through those mountains, told me what he had learned of the people, Tartars, Armenians, Turks and a score of Caucasian tribes, all mingling and clashing in this caldron of the world!

At midnight we stopped for five hours' sleep in a cold stone inn above the clouds, and there a silent little man climbed down from his seat by our driver, where all the way from Tiflis he had listened to our talk; and at dawn, when we went on, another listener took his place. All this kept the present in our minds. But when at nightfall we emerged from a last deep gorge and galloped straight out onto a desolate steppe of South Russia, we looked back at the mountains —huge and dim and silent, towering over the present as they had towered over the past—and asked what would the future be? I wonder if we had met young Stalin?

XV

By the time I reached London later that week, I had used up my Outlook letter of credit and had only seven dollars in cash, so I sent to my father an S.O.S. By a little ironical trick of fate, the letter I'd written him some weeks before, with its startling news that I might stay in the Caucasus all my life and possibly get married there, had wandered out through the slow Russian mails, over Europe and across the sea, and did not reach his office in Chicago near the Board of Trade until the day of my London arrival. While he read it in alarm, suddenly my cable came:

"Out of Russia completely broke please cable money London Morgan."

And then he leaned back and chuckled deep. My grand old father was still amused!

He cabled me funds and I settled down in a wonderful furnished room in a little house on Duke Street, which with breakfast and lunch included cost me only eight shillings a day. The room was a glamorous place to me because of the heathen idols and other reminders of the Far East, left by British officers from India on furlough home. Back flew my thoughts to Kipling and his slogan for young writers like me, that we draw the thing as we see it for the God of things as they are. Well, the thing was Russia now and I had much writing still to do. Early each morning my kindly old landlord brought into the room a shallow tin tub and filled it with water for my cold sponge, then brought my breakfast and after that left me to work there all day long. For nearly a month I was alone. In the evenings I went to theaters, or more often, perched by the jovial driver up on the top of a horse-drawn bus, I rode for hours looking down on the teeming rich night life of the town. Then back to my room, to find my slippers and night clothes laid out on an easy chair before a glowing fire of coals. To my father on one such night I wrote:

"Here I am on my first big writing job—in the grand exciting old city of your beloved Dickens, Dad!"

For me the whole trip had been like that. I had seen the first act of a drama which was later to rock the world; and talking with radicals of all kinds, I had thought myself radical as the rest. But beneath all that, in the heart of me, I was a story writer and in my early twenties still; and so for me my trip had been a glamorous writing adventure into a Russia wild, strange and deep, to write stories of its struggle for freedom and so get American aid, and then to come back to my own safe home. A World War and revolutions spreading all over the face of the earth? America torn deep by it all and hurled still farther over the bridge from the yesterday we knew so well into the vast fury of today? No thought of that ever entered my head as in London I wrote busily on.

Then English Walling arrived from New York and took me to Parliament to meet the Labor Party leaders, Keir Hardie and John Burns; and one afternoon at a Fabian meeting we had a talk with Bernard Shaw. But I can remember now nothing of those interviews, for they seemed tame to me compared with the exciting Russia I'd seen. Much more clearly I recall an amazing performance of Magda by Eleanora Duse one night. Later we went over to Paris and had long absorbing talks with the Socialist leaders, Jean Longuet, Marcel Cachin (turned Communist since) and with Russian exiles. Then out into the Paris nights, for we were in our twenties still. But my few night adventures were but the mildest of affairs, for all the energy I possessed still went into my Russian work. Writing, writing, writing—I had to make the most of this! In the *Quartier Latin*, at the old Hotel Corneille I had the same octagonal room where Little Billee of Trilby fame had once lived and loved and painted and dreamed—at least my landlord told me so. There I wrote on rainy days but, in the sunny weather of that fresh lovely *mois de Mai*, each morning on the top of a bus I lumbered far out to the *Bois*, sat down at one of the tables in the empty garden of a café, ordered a tall cool glass of absinthe and then, after a sip or two, often forgot it in my work. For so deep did my writing bury me that I would be startled when at last I heard French voices breaking in on the Russian voices heard in my head, and looked up and found tables all around me filled with gay Parisians at lunch!

At last my Russian work was done. From our Settlement group in New York my good friends Bullard, Brubaker and King came over to Paris, and from there we went up to the Alps to tramp. With us went Walling and Struthers Burt, whom I had known in Princeton days. From Chamonix to Martigny and thence to the Matterhorn, up the Rhone valley and over the Grimsel—the pass where even still we could see the cliff-clinging little road by which Napoleon long ago had poured his army down toward Rome—on we went through Interlaken to the Jungfrau and later Lucerne. Up each morning with the sun for a hearty breakfast of chocolate, eggs and rolls and honey, with our rucksacks off we started on our thirty-mile tramp of the day. How good that cold clear sun-filled air and the mountain springs at which we stopped to drink and light our pipes and talk! Bullard was hungry for all I could tell him, for he was going to Russia soon to stay there for two years or more. Walking together we talked of that and of the plans and dreams we shared for the freedom of the whole human race from tyranny of every kind, from

poverty and sweated toil. Like the snowy mountains towering high above our heads, so were our dreams! It is grand to
be young!

From the Alps I went with Struthers Burt to Munich to
join my brother Abram, who for nearly a year had been
working hard at his easel there. With him and his Princeton
roommates we argued and sang till late at night in the old
Simplicissimus Café. More dreams, quite different from my
own, for my brother was already immersed in a world of
color and line and form that I knew little or nothing about.
But in place of Hitler and his creed, Munich in those free joyous days was filled with students not only of painting but of
music. This I knew, and in concert halls and student cafés and
great beer halls that rocked with songs, I filled my thirsty
spirit deep.

Then in August our father came abroad, with the old Chicago lawyer friend who had played with him those dialogue
games, in which each spoke a character part in the Dickens
and Thackeray novels they loved. We joined them in Carls-
bad, Abram and I, for we felt very close to our father still,
all the closer since our mother was gone. From his long dark
loneliness he was hungry for his sons and proud as Punch of
the good starts we had both made in our careers. I remember
his broad welcoming smile and his first greeting:

"Hello, boys. Here's a box of real good Havana cigars."

It was good to have such a father still—to cross the Atlantic
and work and explore and adventure into strange new fields,
with always a sense of that father behind us, that strong safe
father, that strong safe home in that strong safe America!

Back in Chicago again that fall, on silent evenings my
father and I often read together as before. I'd begun writing
immigrant stories for Lorimer of the Saturday Evening Post,
and Dad warmly approved of that.

"Good editor. Fine writer, too," he said of Lorimer one

night. "His Letters of a Self-made Merchant will stand as the realest picture of a businessman in my time."

More silent reading. I smoked a pipe and my father a cigar. When I drank a little ale, he'd look grimly over the tops of his glasses. "Worst stuff you can put in your stomach," he'd growl. But once he looked up abruptly and said: "When I read your first Russian article here, I was so happy I damned near cried."

When I returned to New York after Christmas, I found our old Settlement group breaking up. Walling had gone with Bullard to Russia; and Fred King, with some forty boys taken from jails and reformatories, was starting a Junior Republic in a farmhouse in the Connecticut hills. Brubaker and I spent a week end there, and later went to live with some friends in a roomy old house on Fifth Avenue close to Washington Square. We were known as the A Club. Brubaker, Walter Weyl and I, Leroy Scott and Miriam his wife, Mary Heaton and Burt Vorse, Bob and Martha Bruere, Charlotte Teller and several others were there. With most of us writing books, stories or plays and all of us dreaming of reforms and revolutions of divers kinds, life in that house was a quick succession of intensities, large and small, from tremendous discussions about the world to hot little personal feuds and disputes; but through it all ran a broad fresh river of genial humor and relish in life. On warm spring evenings some of us sat out on the stoop on Fifth Avenue, sipping mint juleps brought from the old Brevoort Café. So many memories crowd in, I can only pick a few from them. Charlotte Teller was a good friend of Mark Twain and, from his house around the corner, often he'd stroll over, in his white suit with his great shock of snowy hair, sit down by the fireplace, light a cigar and drawl stories to our admiring group. Why did we admire him? Because beneath his good-humored jibes at all radical theories and creeds we could feel him a rebel like ourselves, and because he was a giant, and because he could tell stories as we'd never heard them told before. Here is one that I've never seen in print. If only I could tell it in that slow drawling voice of his! Some one had mentioned Hadley of Yale.

"President Hadley," drawled Mark Twain. "Now there's a very remarkable man. I'll never forget what he said about me, the day when I was invited by Yale to come up and be given a degree. The great platform was filled with men to be honored. Our writer group was put somewhat upstage. Quite a few of the boys were there, Howells, Cable and other writers I knew; and as each was called down to receive his degree, President Hadley in a few words gave a most wonderful summing up of the character and achievements of each. As each came back, he'd whisper to me: 'Sam, what will Hadley say about you and your dark and checkered career?' They made me so nervous I couldn't sit still. At last my turn came. Downstage I walked. When an official called the name of Samuel Clemens, the New Haven boys all rose to their feet and made quite a noise. When at last it was over, Hadley declared: 'After this demonstration, anything I could say would be useless.' Hooded and honored I came back without knowing what Hadley had meant to say. I was disappointed and so were the boys. But one of them told me, at the end of the ceremonies that day: 'Sam, every speech that Hadley made was written ahead in a little book, which is in the hands of his secretary, that young woman over there.' Eagerly I went to her and never have I flattered a female as I did that young woman that day. At last she let me see the book. As I turned the pages, every speech exactly as it had been spoken was there. Faster I turned them with feverish hands! And on the last page I read these lines: 'Samuel Clemens. After this demonstration anything I could say would be useless.' "

Other well-known writers came to the A Club in that year but the most dramatic of them all was the great Russian, Maxim Gorky. Over in Russia, Walling and Bullard had helped him plan out a campaign to raise a million dollars here for the cause of Russian freedom. On account of his world-wide fame, we had been able to organize a committee of such men as Mark Twain, William Dean Howells, S. S. McClure, Arthur Brisbane and many more. They met him at dinner at our house, the newspapers all featured him and his mission started well. But then came a disaster which threw a revealing glare upon the last remaining Puritanism in New York. For Gorky had brought with him a lady with whom he had lived for many years and who was to share all the rest of his life. She was a princess and a star in the Moscow Art Theater. He could not marry her because the Russian Church refused to grant him a divorce from his first wife, who meanwhile had happily mated again and had a good home and children now. Although the New York papers all knew of his companion, they agreed to suppress the story on account of his mission here. But then Gordon Bennett, we were told, cabled from Paris to his paper, the Herald, to run the story. They did. That forced the others to do the same. And so fast did the scandal grow that, when Gorky and his lady came at midnight from a meeting back to their small hotel near our house, where she had been known as his wife, they found all their luggage piled out on Fifth Avenue in the rain!

Shocked and outraged, he brought her to our house and there they stayed for nearly a week. One by one our committee resigned. Not even old Mark Twain had the courage to face that Puritanical storm. With his mission utterly defeated, Gorky was terribly bitter against America those nights; but all the more grateful was he to the friends who had stood by him through the crisis. While he was staying with his companion out on Staten Island in a liberal Englishman's home, we had a beach party one night; and I can see him clearly still, a giant figure, tall and lean, kneeling by the fire, with slouch hat over his great blunt face and dark burning cavernous eyes, reciting for us in Russian in his deep dramatic voice

Poe's Raven. I can still hear that "Never more"—which in Russian is "*Neekogda.*"

That spring another Russian came, sent to us by Walling and Bullard on a smaller speaking campaign. A young liberal revolutionist imprisoned in St. Petersburg, he'd escaped from the grim fortress of St. Peter and St. Paul and on a little fishing boat had come through the breaking ice of the Baltic and reached London with just money enough to take steerage passage to New York. Young and slim, though starved and pale from his long months in prison, he had a gay appealing laugh and nothing could quench his faith in his dream. It shone in his quick radiant smile and in his dark gleaming eyes. But he still wore the battered straw hat and seedy clothes in which he'd been arrested the summer before. In his broken English he said:

"On ship I could not understand why captain up on bridge look down and laugh at me so many times. When ladies come he point to me below in steerage. They also laugh. Why am I so funny like that?"

"It isn't you; it's your name," I replied.

"But what is the matter with my name? I come to your country without any money, so I think that to help me come in I must have a rich American name, and I choose the most rich name I know."

"But that's just it!" I told him. "When the captain pointed you out, he said: 'That's John D. Rockefeller down there!' "

He used his real name after that and fervently he started in to perfect his English for a public-speaking tour. And so impatient was he with the progress that he made that in utter exasperation he exclaimed to me one night:

"Three weeks have I been in your country and not even yet do I speak fluently the English!"

But he soon did. Meanwhile I had written his dramatic life story for the Post. On the strength of this publicity, he spoke at meetings all over the East and raised some fifteen thousand dollars. Now to buy rifles! I brought to him at the A Club one night a young Yale man whom I knew, whose firm manu-factured arms and had long experience with South American revolutions.

"How will you get your guns into Russia?" he demanded at the start. The Russian hadn't thought of that. "I'll tell you," said my Yale friend. "You'll ship 'em in piano crates from here to Brazil, from there to Naples and then to the Baltic, where they'll arrive with their pedigrees lost. Your agent will be there ahead; he'll have found a revenue man he can fix; and when those fifty pianos are landed, the said official will open the crate marked twenty-two. It will take him a long time, for the boards will be nailed so damnably tight. And he'll find a real piano inside. Then he'll look at the other forty-nine crates and say: 'Oh, hell!' in Russian. So they'll get through and you and your friends will be all set to revolute."

"Fine! Wonderful!" the Russian cried.

"Now for the rifles. You can buy some good old Mausers this year in Vienna at about three dollars apiece. They come a lot higher over here but the cause of Russian freedom is mighty popular, these days, so I think I could get the trade to give you some fairly good guns at that price." The Russian quickly figured.

"Fine! Then with fifteen thousand dollars I can buy five thousand guns!" But the Yale boy's smile was grim.

"Don't you want to shoot 'em off? Because if you do, you'll need ammunition. You see, when you shoot off a gun at an army you want to have plenty of cartridges or else be ready to run like hell. You should have at least a thousand rounds, which will cost you three times the price of the guns."

My Russian friend grew very sad.

"Then I cannot buy guns; I must buy grenades."

"We're not in that business," Yale replied. But others were, and our Russian friend must have managed somehow to reach them, for in May mysterious strangers came to him at night in our house, and his small bedroom next to mine was soon stacked with heavy boxes marked soap. On the hot June day when he left us to go back to Russia, an express wagon came to our door; and the Irish driver, carrying box after box down four long steep flights of stairs and out to the street, grew so infernally hot and sore that he'd slam each box into his wagon—while from the open windows above, we drew quickly back, expecting a roar! But none came and, gaily waving good-by from his seat by the grim driver, our Russian started for his boat. We lost track of him after that. What he did with those boxes we never knew.

XVI

AND NOW I WAS READY FOR ANOTHER TRIP ABROAD. NOTHING
exciting this time, just a tramp again in the Alps. And yet that
trip was to bring me the greatest happiness in my life, and in
a way so intimate that I shall not care to go into too many
details here.

It began among a group of friends, Walter Weyl and I,
Paul Kennaday, Howard Brubaker and several more, who
used to meet on spring evenings in a cozy little alehouse, The
Old Grapevine, in our neighborhood. The Lieber Augustines
we were called. Most of us were single and swore we'd remain
so and, to strengthen our resolve, we made for ourselves such
mottoes as these: "One kind word may lead to a wedding
march"—and "Better a lion alone in the desert than live with
a wildcat in your room." But deep beneath our stout defiance
three of us were weakening even then, for Paul Kennaday,
Walter Weyl and I planned to go to Switzerland and, as
tramping companions, each one suggested his future wife!
Walter Weyl had my sister Bertha in mind and Paul Kennaday and I two young women who were then together in
the Dolomites. Mine was the girl with whom six years ago
I'd spent that evening in a garden at a small Lake Forest dance.
Though we had seldom met since then, the thought of her
had kept popping up through all my various trips and adventures. It was a thought which I found hard ever to keep long
out of my head. So I wrote to her now. There was no reply.
The plans of the other two also fell through and so, with my
sister and Kennaday only, I went over late in June. In Switz-

erland, joined by my brother from Munich and later by Arthur Bullard from Russia, we tramped for some three hundred miles. And in August, at a small inn where we had stopped on Lake Lucerne, word came to me from my girl of the garden that my letter, long delayed, had finally reached her in Lucerne and that she'd be glad to join us now.

She came that week. There followed long rows upon the lake and long, long talks about ourselves; and in those talks my interest grew into suspense unbearable. Meanwhile with our companions we tramped from Lucerne to Interlaken, over the Gemmi Pass to Martigny and thence across the Great Saint Bernard. As we neared the top of that bleak pass in the early afternoon, a light snow began to fall on the wet dark rocks and it grew cold, so we dropped in for tea at a low stone inn. There we found three young Alpine guides with rope and picks, just down from a climb, drinking a fiery liqueur and singing a lighthearted song of challenge "to our glacier bride, the lady with the icy kiss and the everlasting arms!" Soon a huge old monk came into the room. In deference at once they rose. He sat down with them and talked for a while and, when they left, we joined him, for by this time we had learned he had once been a famous Alpine guide. When we asked him why he'd become a monk, he told us this story:

"When I was young as you, my children, late one day in a party of five, after climbing down a five-thousand-foot cliff, on a ledge which was but one foot wide we found that an avalanche had blocked our chance to reach the bottom and that we must climb again to the top. All day we had climbed, we were weary men and, as I looked up at that great sheer cliff, the cold sweat of exhaustion and fear came upon me. I shut my eyes. Until then I had thought little of God but, with eyes still closed, I sent a call for help into the universe. Soon I felt such new strength inside, pouring from I knew not where, that I rose and took charge of our group and led them back slowly with picks and ropes from ledge to ledge and so to the top. And there I fell on my knees and vowed I would enter the Order of Saint Bernard. Forty years I have lived in our hospice at the top of this pass and, until a few years ago, it was I who came out in storms with the dogs to find travelers lost in the snow. I go no more, for I am old; but younger Brothers have taken my place and, in these last ten winters, not a single life have we lost; for now by a telephone from this inn, when a traveler passes, we get a call and go out and meet him before he is buried in the snow. Would you like to see the dogs?"

We would. He telephoned to the hospice to loose the pack and start them down. And on our two-hour walk with the old monk up to the top, they met us halfway, big glorious creatures pounding along through the whirling snow. The great stone hospice, gray and grim, looked utterly comfortless from outside, but within we found huge fires of logs and hundreds of laborers, Swiss and Italian, being sheltered and fed for the night in immense cavernous rooms below. Our own supper we had in a room above, the monks serving wooden platters of stew and big jugs of good red wine to some fifty trampers of our kind. Later a group of us joined the old monk to hear stories of rescues made with the dogs. Then he spoke of the telephone and said:

"For hundreds of years we have prayed to God for the safety of travelers; and now at last our prayer is heard. In ten years we have lost not a single life." A smart young American smiled and asked:

"Was it God or was it the telephone?" With a gracious smile the old monk replied:

"Both, my son, that is how God answered our prayers. For He lives inside of men and through us works His miracles."

From that old monk I began to feel the stirrings of a new religion, with a new God for the rest of my life. But I had little time for Him then, for all my thoughts and feelings went to Margaret Ann at my side. For many many mountain miles and later in Paris and all the way across the Atlantic and in New York, I argued and begged her to share my life. But it was not till just before she took train for her home in Chicago that at last I got her consent. I went with her, and I can still see the glad light in my father's eyes when I told him my good news, as he lay on a sofa one night.

"Ernest," he said, "you've got a grand girl. She'll make you happy."

And he was right.

Our wedding out there that winter belonged to the personal world I had known as a boy. It took place in her mother's lovely old-fashioned frame house. No stiff formalities, only friends. As we dressed to go away, we could hear them all downstairs singing to us Auld Lang Syne. Down we came through showers of rice and out to the old Poole carriage waiting to take us to our train. Our wedding trip, too, was of the old world. For we went to the Munich of long ago and, in my brother's tiny apartment, we lived for a month in the student quarter, where no thought of war or dictatorships entered our heads. We went often to the *Tonhalle* close by. I remember a great chorus there singing the Passion music of Bach, and a night when Ysaye with his violin was kept playing for five hours by excited young students who packed the house. We went to the *Hofbrau* on a night when that tremendous lofty hall was packed with Bavarians singing folk songs at long tables. At one we sat down. We firmly believed that we had concealed from the world our feelings at that time, but a Bavarian at the head of our table took one look at us, then rose smiling with stein in hand and called on the whole table to rise and drink to the health of the bride and groom! Fanny, my brother's one little servant, took care of us well and, when we left, she beamed upon us and he said that we had utterly spoiled her because, for her wages, heat and light and all food for our meals, we had paid her so much as three dollars a day! We spent April in Paris in the apartment of a *Beaux Arts* student we knew, in the old *Quartier Latin*, on the *Rue du Cherche-Midi*, the narrow curving street on which young d'Artagnan of The Three Musketeers was said to have once made his home.

Back in this country we spent the summer in the White Mountains, in a stone farmhouse close to the ridge where later we were to build the home in which I am writing these memories now, with a grand view of Mount Washington twenty miles to the northeast and another of Moosilauke in the south. All that summer I worked hard on stories for the magazines, but our afternoons were free for long tramps and buggy drives. We had no automobile in those days. Margaret's sister and her young brother kept their house across the road crowded with young visitors, and their mother made it a home where friends and relatives loved to come; and they all got a beaming welcome from Rose, an enormous old French woman, dear to the children because she had nursed them when they were small. My father came to visit us and was gay as a young lark, taking huge buckboard loads of people off to picnics in the hills at night. Long after our relatives had gone, late into October we stayed and, when we left one frosty morning at sunrise with our trunks, we were driven nine miles to the train by a sturdy old woman in man's clothes, who smoked a pipe on the high seat of her long mountain wagon and handled the reins of her four-horse team.

In New York we rented a small brick house on Grove Street, down in Greenwich Village, facing on a triangular park so tiny that it had room for three benches only and seven trees. No subway nor wide thoroughfare had crashed through the Village then, nor had that quarter yet been jammed with night clubs and studios, for this was in O. Henry's time and this was the Village he described. Oliver Herford lived near by. Paul Leicester Ford had laid the scene for The Honorable Peter Stirling in a house on our diminutive park, and William Dean Howells had set his novel, A Hazard of New Fortunes, down in that same neighborhood. On warm evenings boys trooped by singing in close harmony. At the back of our house was a wooden porch and I left there for a week two barrels of wedding gifts we disliked, in the vain hope that they might be taken from us by a notorious "fence," a receiver of stolen goods, whose place was just across the yard. Only a few blocks away lived our friend Paul Kennaday, who had tramped with us in the Alps. The Greenwich House Settlement was close by and, from there and from the A Club over on Fifth Avenue, friends came often to our house. Still better we loved the long quiet evenings we had to ourselves. My wife was already hard at work helping Mabel Kittredge install hot lunches in the public schools. She went on the district school board, too, and through her I came to know well a school with more than three thousand children and as principal old Mr. Doty, a veteran of the Civil War. Each day the children marched into school to the waving of the Stars and Stripes and the crash and blare of a boys' brass band. It was there I gathered material for my novel, His Family, which later took the Pulitzer Prize.

I was writing short stories still for the Post and others for Jack Cosgrave of Everybody's, the same magazine for which Tom Lawson wrote Frenzied Finance. More than once I met him there and, on another afternoon, I found in Cosgrave's office a stout quiet little man placidly smoking a cigar.

"This is O. Henry," Cosgrave said, "and you two fellows should be friends. I want you to dine with me some night."

"I'd love to, Jack," O. Henry said. Sydney Porter was his real name.

"And I want you to meet Poole's adorable wife."

"Oh, my God, Jack! Women there!" Then politely to me: "I'd love to, of course, but I'm not dining out much at parties these days."

Nor did he come to dinner that night. How did O. Henry

ever get his marvelous knowledge of womankind? For I never met a man so desperately shy of them!

My own work kept me digging hard, for most of my stories still came hot out of the teeming tenement life. But one evening to our house there came a quiet little man who had been a great bank robber in his time. After two terms in prison, he had decided the game didn't pay and had written a book for the Pinkertons, to be sent to all the banks they protected, to make them familiar with tricks of his trade. This book he hoped I would popularize in a series of magazine stories, splitting with him the receipts. I never wrote those stories, but two or three of them threw such light on the life in our cities when I was young that I shall try to give them here, just as they were told to me by our visitor that night.

"The way I got my first big chance was by not taking something," he said. "I was a boy of sixteen at the time, a young 'dip' [pickpocket] in New York. In the rush hour every night I worked the Forty-second Street cars from the Grand Central Station, where businessmen arriving in town would get on the trolleys with plenty of cash. In a crowded car one night, I squeezed through the straphangers to work on a prosperous-looking gent—but just as I started, my hand jerked back, for some queer feeling warned me to stop. His back was turned but I heard his low voice, as I moved away, say: 'Get off at Fifth Avenue.' And I did, for I thought he was a Bull and a Bull must be obeyed. But when I joined him on the street and he told me his name, I got a thrill like what some young boy singer would get if a stranger had said to him: 'I'm Caruso.' For this quiet-looking man was one of the biggest crooks of his time! 'You've got a good head, boy; you know when to stop. Now I'd like to see what hands you've got. Maybe I can use you,' he said. So on crowded trolley cars I worked for nearly an hour that night, to show him what my hands could do. Two watches and a pocketbook. When we got off at last, he said: 'O. K. Your hands are good

as your head. I'll look up your references.' He did—and it
ended in my joining his mob. In banks, offices and jewelry
shops we worked five years. Not one of us ever used a gun
and I have no use for the thugs of today. In my time the
game was a fine art. I learned with him and so got to the
top—and all from not taking something that night!

"Years later, with a mob of my own working cities East
and West, I was so well known to desk clerks that, when I
came to a hotel, they'd ask if I didn't want my old suite—for
our profession had class in those days. I was equally friendly
with chiefs of police, for they knew I'd be square in the split
that I gave 'em. On reaching Detroit one Saturday night, I
was told by my friend the chief to go slow, for a big newspaper owner, McCullough, had started an anticrime campaign. When warned by the chief that one of us might take
something off him for spoiling our game, McCullough had
laughed and answered: 'I'd like to see the crook who could
do it!' And when I heard this, I told the chief I thought I'd
like to try it myself. On the next day, Sunday, Nat Goodwin
hit town with his show, The American Citizen. One reason
why Nat was the greatest actor on the American stage at
that time was the warm human way in which he mixed with
Americans of all sorts and kinds and so learned his acting
from life. I knew him well. That Sunday night we met down
at the hotel bar with the chief of police and a tall thin crook
from New Orleans, and there we fixed up the following:

"Nat sent to McCullough a letter next day, asking him to
use a box at the theater that night. He put in three tickets
and explained that by a stupid box-office mistake the other
three seats had already been sold, but would McCullough
come all the same? McCullough did. With his daughter and
wife he took the three seats at the front of the box, leaving
the other three for me, the chief of police and our tall thin
friend from New Orleans, all of us in evening clothes. At the
end of the show, while McCullough put on his fur overcoat

in the narrow passage back of the box, my two companions did the same; they squeezed him close in that small place and Goodwin added to the squeeze by coming in just then from the stage and starting one of his funniest yarns. All this time I'd been working fast. McCullough was a big heavy man and was wearing a dress suit. I took first his wad and then his watch and after that his diamond shirt studs. Then I coughed. My three helpers quickly moved away and left me showing McCullough my two hands full of his property. So damned mad that he couldn't speak, he snatched them from me and started home, while Nat Goodwin laughed till he cried and took us for drinks back to the hotel. We celebrated late that night!

"If you were raised in Chicago," continued the quiet little man, "maybe you went to the World's Fair in 1893 as a boy." And as my thoughts went flying back to the stately White City, he said: "With a friend I had the only concession there to fellows of my kind. We got it from the police inspector in charge. He'd been told by the mayor that the lid was down, and he kept it so. I don't suppose any world's fair in any country was kept so safe. Two hundred a day was his limit for us and even from that he took his split. Poor pickings for men so high in the game, but he stuck to it all summer long. In the Tiffany show was a pearl necklace valued at eighty thousand or more, and we argued with him half one night, offering him half as his split. No, he said, he couldn't afford it. It would break him as a cop, and forty thousand was small return for the takings he'd lose all the rest of his life."

That was a busy year for me. From many varied angles of American city life, stories, real ones, crowded in. I worked hard, and so did my wife in the public schools—till Christmas. Then she had to stop, for only a few weeks later our first little son was born. She made a quick recovery and that summer we again went abroad. We took a slow boat and I managed to write a short story on the way across. I might well have written another one, called Paris with the Baby, for it was a city completely changed from any Paris I'd known before! We arrived at daybreak in the rain and went to my favorite little old hotel on the *Quai Voltaire*. But it wouldn't do. No fit place for our child! My wife set out to hunt for another while I explored the whole city in search of the special baby's milk we required. When after hours of desperate search, in some far corner of the town, I found a shop where they sold the stuff, I was told that the formula brought from our baby doctor in New York would have to be translated by me into the metric system of weights! At this I leaped into a cab and dashed back to our hotel, picked up wife, nurse and baby and took train for Switzerland and a cow!

We found an attractive clean hotel on a mountainside, looking down on Lucerne. There we stayed and the baby thrived and there I wrote all summer long, except for a few brief tramping trips with Bullard from Russia, my brother from Munich, my wife's young brother and other friends. On one such tramp, on a high ridge we got lost in a cloud, so left Margaret Ann and scattered out in search of the trail. It took us an hour. When we came back, we found her still sitting on a rock in the fog. From her rucksack she had taken out her knitting needles and was serenely working on a small sweater for our son.

Already she'd found that to share my life she must learn to take things easy like that. It was lucky for me that she learned so soon, for close ahead lurked hectic years of writing for the theater.

XVII

NEARLY EVERY FICTION WRITER I'VE KNOWN HAS SOONER OR later been attacked by a fever to write for the theater. It was the stock market of our lives—and it *was* a gamble, in the years when I buzzed in like a fly to honey. But first I shall tell a few little stories about the place where the fever took hold, a place which is still dear to me.

About this time I was taken into the Players Club, down on Gramercy Park, in the lovely old Tilden home done over by Stanford White with funds raised by Edwin Booth, "to provide a home where gentlemen of the stage may meet gentlemen of the other arts and professions." Booth had lived there in his last years and had stood, white-headed and slender, before the wide hospitable hearth to welcome each newly elected member into his family, his gracious manner shadowed by his big dark tragic eyes. The one black specter of his life was the memory of his brother's crime. Never was that brother's name spoken in the Players Club while Edwin Booth was still alive. But long before my coming he died and, among a few of his fellow players still to be seen in the Club, there was one old Virginia Reb who loved to talk about John Wilkes Booth. A little old man nearly eighty years old, he drew me into a corner one day and in his deep rich voice he said:

"Sir, I shall never forget the years of my youth with John Wilkes Booth. In those last years before the war, our company played Shakespeare from Richmond down to Charleston, through Atlanta to New Orleans and up the river to

Louisville and so back to our loved State. And never once, sir, did we play in a public theater—always in the ballroom on some Southern gentleman's great estate. Young Booth was our idol in those years, he was like a radiant young pagan god. Well I remember the day at lunch in our Richmond club, when he asked me:

" 'David, dear, will you be so kind as to take my part in Othello tonight? I have important business on hand and may be gone for nearly a week.' It was an arduous task for me to study so quickly a new part. But I could deny him nothing.

" 'John, I'll be glad to,' I replied. Well, sir, that afternoon in the Club, as I sat at a window to study my part, suddenly I heard a troop of gentlemen on horseback come clattering down the street outside. At their head was the Governor of Virginia and by his side rode John Wilkes Booth, talking and laughing as they came! Well, sir, I was keenly annoyed. I leaned far out and asked him:

" 'John, what is this important business of yours?' And, sir, I shall never forget the light in the eyes of that young god! He cried:

" 'David, we're off to Harper's Ferry, to help Lee capture old John Brown!' And by God, they did, sir!"

The effect of that little story on me was like an electric shock. For my mind flashed back to one of my own early idols, Jack Lincoln, making the Gettysburg Speech at our school when I was a little boy, and to the bronze figure of the gaunt lean man in Lincoln Park, and to a tragic incident there witnessed by a friend of mine.

"When I was a boy in Chicago," he said, "Edwin Booth came to play Hamlet and I saw his amazing performance one night. As a friend of my father's, he stayed at our house and, after the play, I was so thrilled by listening to him talk that night that I couldn't sleep. I rose at dawn and went for a walk in Lincoln Park. It was a lovely morning in May. As

I came to the Lincoln statue at sunrise, a two-horse carriage had just driven up and, when I saw the man who got out, I jumped back into the shrubs. It was Edwin Booth! Slowly he came walking toward the man his brother had killed. Then he stopped. As he stood looking up, I saw tears welling in his eyes and, because a good actor can speak with his hands, both of his were unconsciously raised as though pleading for forgiveness. Then he turned and went away. But my own hands were cold as ice! All alone, I had seen Edwin Booth in the real tragedy of his life!"

All this had happened long ago. When I came to the Players Club, our famous president was dead and the theater district of New York had already moved uptown. So there had come to us a time when funds dropped low and the house grew shabby for a while, the sort of place that could make its appeal only to the deeper-seeing eyes of a real connoisseur. And so I was surprised by what Al Smith said of it one night. As governor of New York, he had come down to speak to us and, while he sat drinking highballs at dinner, I watched him in that shabby room and wondered what he thought of it. When he rose red-faced to speak, he said, in that gruff husky voice of his:

"Gentlemen of the Players, I've come here to warn you to clean up the stage and head off censorship by law, a thing that my whole heart detests. But before I speak, I can't help an attempt to give you some faint little idea of what I've felt while sitting here. I was born in a tenement down on Cherry Street," he went on. My thoughts leaped back to the Lung Block there! "And, gentlemen, some of those rotten old buildings had once been fine private homes. Some of the most beautiful doorways were still there when I was a boy. I have never forgotten them, nor will I to my grave. And now, when I come from Albany on my many trips to New York, I find myself so God-damned sick of new hotels, new apartment buildings and new clubs wherever I go, that I can't help telling you what a joy it has been to me tonight to be in a lovely old room like this!"

The Players Club opened wide its arms! Did Al Smith know we would? He did. But would Coolidge or Hoover or Franklin Roosevelt ever have thought of saying that? Oh, great Al Smith, beloved of men, what a pity you could not have gone on as you were in the years when we loved you so!

But now to get back to my own career and my brief venture into plays. The Players Club in those early years became like a second home to me and, each time I came into the Club from digging stories out of real life, it seemed to ask with a gracious smile:

"Yes, young brother, but why not try to put them in form for the theater?"

So quietly the spell took hold. And yet it was from Russia that the final impulse came; for about this time Orleniev brought his Russian Players to New York for their first appearance here. They played at the old *Deutsches Theater* down on Irving Place near our Club. With my wife and our Russian furnaceman, who had been a schoolteacher at home, I went to their performances. Memories of Gorky stirred in me when they played his Night Lodging. Never had I seen such acting. Life, real life, before my eyes! For picturing the life of the masses, here was a far mightier brush than any I had used before. Now or never! I started in.

I wrote first a play about a steel mill—all big backgrounds and big ideas, with only a puny little plot. Nobody wanted it. Then I wrote another one. This had a story. It was about an engineer building a great steel bridge in the Rockies. Like the builder of Brooklyn Bridge, he had lost his eyesight and then, by a miraculous operation, had it restored. He came home to his wife in their mountain cabin; but his wife still thought him blind and, before he could tell her the wonderful news, her actions, so different from her

speech, stirred his suspicions; so he let her believe him still
blind, while he watched the love affair between her and
an old friend from New York, who had been visiting there
for weeks urging her to break away from this blind selfish
engineer and come back East to the life she loved still. A
good old-fashioned story modeled upon Ibsen lines. I wrote
it here in the White Mountains, finished it in August and
sent it down to my agent in New York. No news for weeks;
but then in September, late one day, riding hard before an
oncoming storm, as my horse galloped up to our little house,
a boy on another was riding away. He had come from the
village general store, where was our only telephone, to say
that New York was calling a man named Marges at our
house. With her quick intuition, Margaret Ann, who knew
that play of mine by heart and had helped me write so much
of it, said:

"By Marges they mean Roi Megrue, your agent, and he's
calling from New York! Get to the village quick as you
can!"

When I reached the store, I found she'd guessed right. The
place was filled with villagers and mountain farmers gathered around the old tall stove, for Bill Noyes with his stage
had just brought the evening mail from town. I wonder what
they thought of the talk I had that night with Roi Megrue?
They heard every word, for I had to shout! Royalties, five
per cent of the gross, sliding scale, four thousand, then six—
what did they make of those queer terms? But I had no time
to think of that. For Fiske and Shubert had taken my play
and would put it on that year in New York!

With Jack Mason in the leading role, we rehearsed for
six weeks, at first in a room and after that in a theater so cold
that Margaret Ann brought a steamer rug and utterly spoiled
the company, at least so our director said, by serving hot
coffee and lunch on the stage. We went to New Haven to
try it out. When later we opened in New York, I heard

wild applause and calls for the author and felt my play was a huge success. After a short fevered sleep, I rose early to read all the morning papers, ordered on the night before. The room was cold, for our Russian furnaceman had opened a window and was washing it, perched on a high ladder outside. I read the notices of my play, each and every one a roast! And just as I finished the last one, our furnaceman fell and broke his arm!

In the next three years I wrote nine more plays, two of them with Harriet Ford. Two were produced. One ran six weeks and the other about three months. What a gamble the theater was in those days! Success meant a long run in New York and two or three companies on the road, a fortune for the author and work for the players for several years. Failure meant just nothing at all. With no Actors Equity to protect them, the players, all except the stars, worked under directors who were czars. For weeks they rehearsed without any pay, and the strain increased to such a pitch that at one dress rehearsal, from nine in the morning till twelve at night, our leading woman fainted twice. She had good cause to. She'd had no pay for nearly six months, for she'd been in two failures before mine.

We took our plays out on the road to lick them into shape for New York. I remember one night in Philadelphia when, in our room at the Bellevue Hotel, I worked with our director until after three a.m., rewriting a troublesome third act. At last we finished.

"Now," he said, "we'll call the company at ten and put it in tomorrow night."

"We will not."

"Why not?" His word was law.

"Because I'm dead for a little sleep and I can't write a new fourth act between now and ten a.m."

"Oh, to hell with a new fourth act. We'll use the old one tomorrow night."

"But, my God!" I answered. "It has nothing to do with this new third!"

"Never mind, boy, never mind." We followed his plan and, on the next night, when our new third-act curtain brought loud applause, he said contentedly: "Now that's set."

So we went to our hotel beds and left a bewildered audience to try to make out what our old fourth act had to do with our new third. No wonder that cities on the road were slow to pay money to see plays until they had been done in New York!

That piece I entitled A Man's Friends. Centering on the struggle between a reform district attorney and an old-style Tammany boss, it tried to show the power of friends and of the gang in politics. To rehearsals I brought a Tammany man and, when he saw how George Fawcett was giving real life to his role as boss, he brought in other Tammany men who kept feeding Fawcett with wonderful lines. Bigger and bigger in my play loomed the power of human friendship and the humor of Tammany Hall. My poor district attorney did his best and on opening night in New York, when he thundered such lines as—"It isn't the man; it's the whole game that's wrong!"—the top gallery, packed with my radical friends, rocked and echoed with applause! All thought my play was a big success but I was too sick at my stomach to care. All I wanted was to get to bed, but this I found I could not do. For Theodore Roosevelt, who had kindly read my piece some months before and given me some good advice, was in a box with Bourke Cochran that night and, from that box in the last act, our press agent came to me with the news:

"The Colonel says he wants you to come out to supper after the show."

"Can't do it, Bill. I'm sick as a cat!"

"You'll have to! He has given us some grand publicity tonight!"

When the play was over, more dead than alive, I crept into a big limousine and there heard Bourke Cochran ask:

"Where are we going, Colonel?"

"To the Metropolitan Club."

"Oh, God. That place reminds me of a club in London, which always made me feel as if there were two dead dukes upstairs!"

I felt like one myself at first, but later in the empty club dry cognac and clear soup revived me so that I could listen to my two renowned companions. With my little play forgotten, they were deep in politics now, discussing the famous Roosevelt Square Deal. Bourke Cochran, that great orator who knew so well just how to praise, was speaking in his deep rich voice of other progressive movements and crusades for humanity. Back through history he went till he came to the movement launched by Christ. And then he said:

"Even there you find the same thing true. As in every other crusade, not the most perfect but the most human man became the leader. Which of Christ's disciples was the one who founded the Church? Saint John, the perfect man? Oh, no. It was Saint Peter, the most human of them all!"

And Roosevelt showed his teeth in a smile and answered:

"Cochran, you flatter me!"

When only a few months after this Roosevelt launched his Bull Moose Party, many friends of mine promptly joined; but the rest of us some years before had been drawn into the liberal wing of the Socialist Party of that time. My activities there had gone along with my work on plays. I'd been slow to join the Party at first, for it looked like a church to me still and I had kept free from churches so long. No creeds nor propaganda for me; the truth as I saw it was creed enough. But then I met Morris Hillquit, that able adroit successful lawyer who'd given his whole life to the Party and had slaved for it, day and night. His was the leading mind

of them all. Many disliked him. I did not. To me he became
a lovable friend. In a long talk with him one night, when I
voiced the scruples holding me back, he made the creed to
which I must subscribe so very broad and liberal that my
objections were swept away. So I made application and was
accepted by one of the "locals" in New York, and so got my
red card of membership, which was to prove such a help later
on, when I went as a correspondent to Russia in 1917.

Did my wife oppose it? No. She was not a Socialist herself nor did she know that she ever would be, but a man
had quite as much right as a woman to his politics, she said.
She herself marched up Fifth Avenue in one of the colorful
first parades of several thousand women and girls under banners demanding the right to vote, while her husband humbly
walked behind in a rear guard of husbands, fathers and
friends, to the tune of hoots and jeers from our fellow males
along the curbs.

And what did my father say to his son about becoming
a Socialist? Simply nothing, nothing at all. Once on a train
together from Chicago to New York, Hillquit joined us and
later I left him alone with my father for cigars and a long
talk. When it was over, Dad said to me:

"There's a mighty decent intelligent man. Fine mind—
smart—but he's on the wrong track." And Hillquit said to
me:

"Ernest, my boy, you ought to be ashamed of yourself.
When you've a father grand as that, why not have given him
some idea of modern economics?"

"Because I don't want to. We're fond of each other. He
leads his life and I lead mine."

But his life was nearly over now. It was only a little after
this that I was suddenly called to Chicago, where my grand
old father died.

Much as I liked and admired Hillquit, the Socialist who
appealed to me most was our candidate for President, Debs.

Lean, big-boned and towering high, with shining bald head and lovable smile, how different he was from the picture given me when I was a boy! For when in 1894 he had led the great railroad strike that came to a crisis at Pullman, where many cars were wrecked and burned, Grover Cleveland had sent the regulars and young Debs had been jailed for his crime and I'd heard him described as a devil with horns! But I saw the real man now. In the fall campaign of 1908, down on the crowded Lower East Side, I stood near him for hours one night on a truck that slowly plowed its way through a roaring ocean of people reaching far as eye could see all up and down dark tenement streets. No loud-speakers, no brass bands. The truck stopped and Debs leaned out with both arms raised, smiling over the roaring crowd. Stillness came. And then only his one voice was heard—a voice that could do with a crowd what it willed, not because of the mind behind it but because of the great warm heart which the crowd felt speaking there. How different from the raucous voice heard in Germany today!

I listened to him, tingling deep. What could I myself do for the cause? With some of our old Settlement group and Harry Laidler, I helped start the Intercollegiate Socialist Society; quickly we formed group after group in a score or more of colleges. But though I gave many nights to this work, I gave more to our Socialist daily newspaper, the New York Call. With Arthur Bullard, Leroy Scott and Charles Edward Russell, I slaved to build up that little sheet. But oh, ye gods of rigid creeds, what trouble we had with the old doctrinaires, who insisted on keeping their preachments still in the paper and had no use for our efforts to make it a popular sheet. I remember the friendly jibe that came from Walter Weyl one night.

"Keep it up, boys. Your circulation must be increasing by leaps and bounds. Only last night I heard one of your newsboys racing up Broadway with the Call and screaming at the top of his lungs: 'Extry! Extry! Extry! All about the materialistic conception of history and Karl Marx!' "

I had a little lesson in publicity work that year. Bill Haywood's organization, the Industrial Workers of the World, had spread from Colorado east and it took the lead in a big strike in the textile mills of Lowell and Lawrence. Its two young Italian leaders there, Ettore and Giovanitti, were jailed and, after they'd served their prison terms, our Intercollegiate Socialists organized in their honor a mass meeting in Carnegie Hall. Our expenses were heavy and, on the day before the meeting, with not half the seats yet sold, Walling and I racked our brains for some way to work up more feeling for our expensive show. New York's doughty sheriff at that time was noted for his hatred of Reds, so in the hope of stirring him up we sent to him a friend with the news that Ettore and Giovanitti might preach violence the next night. The sheriff quickly grabbed our bait. He called in the newspapermen and said:

"They'll do it over my dead body! Tomorrow night in Carnegie Hall with forty armed deputies I'll be there!"

Next morning that story made the front page and long before evening the hall was sold out. Jubilant over our success, Walling and I went to the hall—and there received a violent shock. Not from the sight of the sheriff and his forty huge men seated across the whole front of the platform —our trouble came in the speakers' room, where our two young Italian speakers were excitedly walking the floor!

"We've never yet spoken on a stage filled with American Cossacks," they cried, "and by God we won't do it tonight! We're going out there to call on the Comrades to rise and throw those bastards out of the hall!"

In vain we tried to quiet them down. Italian blood boiled hot and strong! It was lovable little Dolly Sloane, always proud of her Irish blood, who rescued our meeting that night. For with a score or more of girls she had charge of passing the collection; now she abruptly appeared on the stage and, with the friendliest smile in the world, she walked along that line of armed men with her collection basket, begging them to give to the cause! Never in my life have I seen more sheepish and embarrassed cops! The roar of laughter from the hall reached even into the speakers' room and abated Italy's fury there, and so no violence was preached and we thanked God for Ireland!

Soon after this Haywood came to New York to take charge of a big strike in the textile mills at Paterson. I was with him often there, in strike headquarters in a hall filled with Italians, Spaniards and Greeks, who gave me an abundance of life and color for the stories I wrote. And on a lovely spring afternoon at a meeting out of doors, from the porch roof of a small frame house, where I stood with Jack Reed and the strike leaders, I looked on a whole hillside massed with men and women and children, more than twenty thousand in all. Just below us stood an ominous line of armed deputies waiting for one word of violence in Haywood's speech. A born orator, he raised that crowd up and up and came to his climax, and then glared down at the armed men below.

"They say I'm here to preach to you violence! I do preach it!" he roared. He stopped and all through the multitude you could feel excitement go like some electric current just before a storm. Then slowly Haywood folded both huge arms across his chest. "But the only violence I preach is the violence of folded arms!"

He had known violence at first hand in many Colorado strikes. Only a short time before, he'd been tried for his life, wrongly accused of the murder of the governor of that state during the strike at Cripple Creek. Clarence Darrow had won an acquittal but, after nearly a year in jail with his life hanging by a thread, the strain had done things to Haywood's nerves. After a committee meeting, late one evening in New

York, as we walked away together up a dark empty East
Side street, sharply with a report like a shot a truck back-
fired just behind us. And Haywood startled me! For he
jumped! I could feel him taut in every limb! He was silent
a moment as we walked on and then he muttered:

"God damn that jail!"

Huge and burly, six feet two, with great blunt face all
pocked and seamed, there were yet in his manner, his deep
low voice and his quick warm brilliant smile, a power and
a magnetism that nobody could help but feel. I brought him
to our house one night for supper with my wife and me.
For a couple of hours she listened and watched and asked
him a question now and then. And when he went away she
said:

"That's the most magnetic and the most dangerous man
I've ever met!"

I remember I asked him this question that night:

"What would you do with the U. S. Senate?"

"The Senate?" He smiled. "I know damned well. We'll
change that hoary old body someday and make it what it
ought to be, with Senators elected by industries and not by
states."

The same idea that came later to life in Russia with the
Soviets. For Bill Haywood was a man with an imagination
that looked ahead. He could well have such dreams, those
days, for—like the Knights of Labor before his time and the
C.I.O. of John Lewis since—his organization was spreading
with amazing speed all over the land. He told me that, as
a climax to all he had done so far in the East, he planned
in the following spring to strike New York harbor and shut
it up tight.

"I know," I replied. "I've already been seeing one of your
men on the water front."

"Why?"

"I'm writing a book called The Harbor," I said.

XVIII

FOR ALL THESE YEARS SINCE I'D COME TO NEW YORK, OUT OF THE heat and rush and roar of the crowded city streets the harbor had kept calling me down to its big cool ships and the long sea roads opening there. The deep bellows of its steamers had reached me in bed on sleepless nights, and I had listened and sleep had come, as I pictured myself on the deck of a ship moving out to the open sea. Writing stories and sketches of harbor life, I had spent long afternoons on the last of the ships with sails, on huge modern liners, on grim old tramps. I had mixed with seamen and longshoremen, seen them drunk and seen them sober, felt rebellion on the docks. I had watched the tides of immigrants, fresh labor fuel for our national mill.

In the small log-cabin home of a Norwegian friend of mine, on a wooded ridge of Staten Island, I had supper with him one night; and from that high point you could see, from Coney Island and Sandy Hook all up the bays to the city behind us under the restful stars above, a vast shadowy region that twinkled back with stars of its own, restless, many-colored stars, yellow, green and red and white, moving, dancing, flaring, dying—a heaving changing world of life in this great gateway to the sea. "There's a big story here," I thought, and it was a story meant for me. For looking back over my life, I could see that this place had become for me like a symbol of this changing world that I had seen with my changing eyes.

And with all this behind me, on a spring evening in 1912,

my wife and I went to dine with some friends in their stately old house on Brooklyn Heights. After dinner we had coffee in their garden, looking down on the twinkling river below. Suddenly I noticed a thin blue column of smoke that rose between two flower beds close by. Then I saw that it came from a chimney, and our smiling hostess explained:

"You see, this garden is on the roof of an old warehouse down below."

Abruptly I drew into myself and heard nothing for a while. What a garden for a little boy, an imaginative little boy! My thoughts leaped back to those early years of my life in Chicago, when with my wild gang I'd explored the lumberyards and the river and lake front. How much grander this place here, upon the threshold of the sea! How would it be to try a story about just such a little boy in just such a place as this, with the harbor around him and even beneath, for his father would own that warehouse and pier and even the sailing ships that came. The boy would grow up and, as he grew—through good times, bad times, death, love, marriage, hope, despair, success and failure, pride, revolt—the harbor would keep changing, each time that he looked at it with his new eyes, changing like the boy himself, changing like this world I'd seen and through these forces I had seen; for wealth and poverty, labor, rebellion, and a whole world of trade and commerce, travel and adventure, were here! A harbor now wonderful, all romance, but again all grim and dull and flat; now friendly, now hostile! . . . My thoughts raced on, my excitement grew as I felt the possibilities. I have written many novels since then but never one that leaped together so quickly in my mind at the start. On our way home my wife asked me that night:

"What was it kept you so quiet out there—a story again? All evening you've scarcely opened your mouth."

"Yes, it was a story," I said. I told her about it and, with a glow, I caught the interest in her eyes.

I went back to Brooklyn Heights that week and for several afternoons sat upon doorsteps and garden walls, taking notes on the houses around me, chimneys, doorways, wide verandas looking on gardens and on the river life below. With friends who'd been boys there I had long talks about all they'd done when they were small. In one of their homes I was taken up to the nursery on the top floor. What a harbor a little boy would be able to see from its windows at night, before he was tucked into bed by his nurse!

Then I went down to the water front and, out upon the ends of piers, I sat and took notes on my memories of ships I'd seen ten years before but which were now forever gone, ships with great tall spreading sails, patched and dirty in the daytime but all ghostly white at night and making low mysterious sounds, flappings, spankings and deep boomings, as they moved out from their slips in the dark, swung around on the strong night tide and headed for the distant sea. Once again I heard their crews roaring out sea songs called "chanteys" as they heaved upon the ropes. Some of those "chanteys" I knew well. They made me think of "Frankie and Johnny," the song I'd known in Princeton days, for most of them were in weird minor key and were filled with verses that no little girl should see. But this was no book for little girls, so I jotted a few of the verses down.

And now for the cargoes of clipper days. I found them in big ledgers in a shadowy warehouse near by. Yellowed and dusty with age though they were, those books revivified for me that still odorous old warehouse until I saw it as it had been, a dim caravansary for the curious products of all the earth. Palm oil from Africa, coffee from Arabia, pepper from Sumatra, ivory from Zanzibar, tortoise shell from the Fiji Islands, India silks and rugs and shawls, indigo, spices! As I read I saw the sails speed out along those starlit ocean roads, stately East Indiamen bearing such names as Star of Empire, Daniel Webster, Ocean Monarch, Flying Cloud—

ships known all over the world for their speed. An old sea captain told me how a British vessel, her topsails reefed in a gale of wind, would see a white tower of swelling canvas come out of the spray behind her, come booming, staggering, plunging by—a Yankee clipper under royals!

But all that was long ago. Gone were the Yankee clippers now, crowded out by ships with steam and great foreign shipping companies combining in agreements with the American railroads to freeze out small shipowners and take to themselves the whole port of New York. Close to that old warehouse a German whaleback lay at dock. She had slipped in three days before and was already snorting to get away. She was black and stout and she wallowed deep. Hideous, she was practical, as practical as a factory. In her, romance of the sea was buried and choked in smoke and steam, in grime and noise and a regular haste. As the black sooty breath of her drifted into my face, I thought: "The damned sea hog!" And I wrote that down. Then I filled in the scene with all its details, the modern steamboats large and small, each one of them panting and spewing up smoke. I listened to their voices, too, hoots and shrieks from ferries and tugs, hoarse coughs from engines along the docks, the rattle of derricks, the clang of bells. I sat like a stenographer and took down the harbor's dictation, noting the rasping tones of its voice, recording eagerly all its smells. All this I focused on the "sea hog"—and then toward night I saw her "sail." She sailed in a nervous worrying haste to the grunts and shrieks of a lot of steam winches. Up rattled her anchor; out she waddled. There were no songs, no last good-bys, except from a man in his shirt sleeves who called from the deck to a man on the pier:

"So long, Mac, see you next month," and then went into the factory.

So I pictured the ugliness of this modern age of machines. But there was more than ugliness here. With a friend in his motorboat late one day I sped far out on the Upper Bay, a rushing black speck on a dim expanse, with dark empty fields of water around us, long luminous paths stretching off to the shores. On we went through the Narrows into a fog, and out there in the wide sea gate we drifted without a sign of a world around us—till in from the ocean there came a deep bellow, then another and another and, as our craft darted off to one side, a gigantic gray shadow loomed through the fog with four black towers of smoke overhead, lights gleaming from a thousand eyes!

We followed that liner in to her dock up on the North River, and I stayed in the dockshed half that night, till my mind was limp and battered from the impressions I wrote down. For in this long sea station, under the blue arc lights, in boxes, barrels, crates and bags, tumbling, banging, crashing, came the products of this modern land. You could feel the pulse of a continent here. From the factories, the mines and mills, the prairies and the forests, there flowed a mighty tide of things. The pulse beat fast and furious. In gangs at every hatchway you saw men heaving, sweating; you heard them swearing, panting. That night they worked straight through till dawn. For the pulse kept beating, beating, and the ship must sail on time! Quickly I could feel this place yielding up its inner self, its punch and bigness, endless rush, its feeling of a nation young and piling up prodigious wealth. From the customhouse I gathered tales of millionaires and their ravenous wives ransacking the world for rare old furniture, rugs and tapestries, paintings, jewels, gorgeous gowns and rich brocades. One day on a Mediterranean ship, in their immaculate "stalls de luxe," came two black Arab horses, glistening quivering creatures, valued at twenty thousand each. And into the same ship that week, as though in payment for these two, in dust and heavy smell of sweat I saw a thousand cattle driven, bellowing and lowing.

My work here rose to a climax one night when the Lusi-

tania—The Lucy we used to call her then—sailed on a voyage
on which she was to pull off a new world's record for speed.
She sailed at midnight. Out of taxis and automobiles the
passengers came pouring in. Many were in evening clothes,
and most of them went hurrying up into the gorgeous café
of the ship, which was run from a hotel in Paris. What had
all this to do with the sea?

"Come on," said the genial press agent. "You're the company's guest tonight." And while we ate and drank and
smoked, the tables around us filled with people whose rip-
ples and bursts of laughter rose over the orchestra's festive
throb, and corks kept popping everywhere. "Now come with
me," he said at last, and he took me along warm passage-
ways to the row of cabins de luxe.

First we looked into the Bridal Suite, to which one of the
Pittsburgh makers of steel, having just divorced a homely
old wife, was presently to bring his new bride, a ravishing
young creature of musical-comedy fame. They had been married that afternoon. A French maid was unpacking dainty
shimmering little gowns. The room was large, there were
other rooms and two big luxurious baths. There were tall
mirrors and dressing tables and capacious easy chairs. Low
subdued lights shone here and there and a thick rug was on
the floor. Over in one corner was a huge double bed of
cream-colored wood with rich soft quilts upon it. Beside the
bed in a pink satin cradle lay a tiny Pekinese dog.

"Next," he whispered. We peeped into the next state-
room, and there divided from her neighbors by only a thin
partition, a sober wrinkled little old lady in black velvet sat
reading her Bible. Soon she would be saying her prayers.

"Next," he whispered. And in the cabin on her other side
we caught a glimpse of two jovial men playing cards in
gay pajamas with a bottle of Scotch between them.

"Next." And as we went down the row, he gave me the
names of an English earl, a Jewish clothing merchant, a Min-

nesota ranchman, a banker's widow from Boston, a Tammany politician, a Catholic Bishop from Baltimore, a millionaire cheesemaker from Troy and a mining king from Montana.

"How about that," he asked at the end, "for an American row de luxe?"

"My God, it's great!" I whispered.

"There's only one big question here. Your long respectable pedigrees and your nice little Puritanical codes can all go to blazes—this big boat will throw 'em all overboard for you—if you can answer: 'I've got the price.'"

Soon after this I went one day up to the high tower in which a well-known engineer was drawing plans for a future port. From the narrow steel balcony outside, he made me see the ocean and both rivers and the railroad lines all pouring in their traffic, to be shifted and reloaded onto ocean vessels or trains in a colossal fever of confusion and delay. New York, he said, in true Yankee style had developed its water front pell-mell, until the port was now so clogged that it was able to grow no more. "And it's got to grow," he said. For within a few years the Big Ditch would open across Panama, and the commerce of South America, together with that of the Orient, would pour into the harbor here to meet the westbound commerce of Europe. Ships of all nations would steam through the Narrows and we must be ready to welcome them all, with an ample generous harbor worthy of the world's first port. He began to show me some of the plans. I saw tens of thousands of freight cars gathered in great central yards connected by long winding tunnels. I saw along the water fronts continuous lines of docksheds, with rows of warehouses behind; and along their heavy roofs of steel stretched wide ocean boulevards with trees and shrubs and flowers to shut out the clamorous life below.

Then back I came to the underworld of hard-driven labor

on the docks and saw it through the vigilant and bitterly rebellious eyes of Haywood's organizer, a lean lad of twenty-five who had left his Eastern college to work as a stoker on ships for two years and now had come here to prepare the way for a strike to tie up the whole port. Joe Kramer I called him in my book. I liked him and admired the way in which he kept driving himself for these men whose lives he had made his own. He asked if I'd like to see a stokehole; I said that I would, and he told me to meet him at dawn next day. The pier was cold that morning, for it was only five o'clock. The ship was not to sail till nine and the stokers had not yet gone aboard. A few wore seedy overcoats, but the greater part had none; they stood with their hands in ragged pockets, shivering and stamping, a dull-eyed wretched sodden lot.

"Hello," said Joe at my elbow. He looked more fagged than the night before. I noticed that his lips were blue and that his teeth were chattering.

"Joe," I said, "you're not fit to be here. Let's get out of this; you belong in bed." He glanced at me impatiently.

"I'm fit enough," he muttered. "We'll stay right here and see this show. What do you think of these friends of mine?"

"I think you're throwing your life away! Why not go to the steel mills where you have real men to work with? These are a lot of Bowery bums!"

"Yes, they're a lot of Bowery bums. And they feed all the fires at sea."

"And you think you can build a new world *with them?*"

"No, I think they can do it themselves."

"Do you know what I think they'll do themselves? If ever they do win a strike and get a raise in wages, they'll simply blow it in on drink!"

He gave me one of his bitter looks. "They'll do so much more than drink!" he said. "Come on," he added. "They're going aboard."

We followed them to their quarters down in the bottom of the ship. The low chamber was crowded with rows of steel skeleton bunks three tiers high. In some of these, men were already asleep, snoring and wheezing. Others were smoking; the air was blue. Some were almost naked and the smells of their bodies filled the place. Two stokers were bringing in a huge boilerful of a greasy watery soup with a thick yellow scum on the top and chunks of pork and potato.

"This is scouse," Joe told me. Men eagerly dipped tin cups in this and gulped it down. The chunks of meat they ate with their hands. They ate sitting on bunks or standing between them. Some were wedged around a bunk in which lay a sleeper dead to the world. His face was white.

"He reminds me," said Joe, "of a fellow whose bunk was once right next to mine. He was shipped at Buenos Aires. A crimp had carried him on board, dumped him, got ten dollars and left. The man was supposed to wake up at sea and shovel coal, but he lay like a log. The second day out I leaned over and touched him, found him stiff and cold. The crimp had sold us a dead one."

As Joe said this he stared down at the sleeper, a curious tensity in his eyes.

"Joe, how in hell did you stand this life?"

"I didn't," he said gruffly. "The two years almost got me. And that's what happens to most of 'em here. They can't take it long; it's a hell of a life! No day, no night, only steel walls and electric light. You hear a shout at midnight—that's you! So you jump down into the stokehole and work like hell till four a.m., when you crawl up all soaked in sweat and fall asleep till the next shout, and then you get four hours more. Feeding those white-hot furnace mouths, at each stroke of the gong you shovel in coal. You do this till you forget your name. Every time the boat pitches, the floor heaves you forward, the fire spurts at you out of the doors and the gong keeps on like a sledge hammer coming down on top of your mind! And all you think of is your bunk and the time when you're to tumble in!"

The voices around us swelled to a roar, for some of the men had brought liquor on board and half the crew were already well soused. Many had crowded close around a little red-faced cockney, who was the modern chanteyman. With sweat pouring down his face and the muscles of his neck drawn taut, he was jerking out verse after verse about whores. He sang to an old chantey tune, one that I remembered well. But he was not singing out under the stars; he was screaming at steel walls down here in the bottom of the ship. And though he kept speeding up his song, the crowd were too drunk to wait for the chorus; their voices kept tumbling in over his, and soon it was only a frenzy of sound, a roar with yells rising out of it! The singers kept pounding one another's backs or waving bottles over their heads!

"I'm tired!" Joe shouted. "Let's get out!" I caught a glimpse of his strained face. Again it came over me in a flash, the years he had spent in such holes in this hideous rotten world of his, while I had lived so happy in mine. And as though he had read my thought, he said: "Let's go up where *you* belong!"

I followed him up and away from his friends. As we climbed ladder after ladder, fainter and fainter on our ears rose that bedlam from below. Suddenly we came out on deck and slammed an iron door behind us. And I was where I belonged. I was in dazzling sunshine and in fresh and cool sea air. I was among gay throngs of people. Dainty women brushed me by. I felt the softness of their furs; I breathed the fragrant scent of them and of the flowers that they wore; I heard the joyous tumult of their talking and their laughing to the regular crash of the band—all the life of the ship I had known so well. And I walked through it all as though in a dream. For I knew that deep below all this the stokers were still singing.

With Joe Kramer then I turned from the stokers to stronger men, longshoremen and seamen of all races, from Irish and Norwegians to coolies and lascars, come ashore, and in meeting halls and in saloons talking of plans to strike the port. And though no strike came off that year, I got down there my settings for the strike scenes in my book. From the blind chaos at the start, I tried to picture to myself how in strike headquarters a crude new order began to appear, as the chaotic forces merged into that mass thought and passion which, in other strikes I'd seen, had given me such flashes of insight into the deep-buried power of the common herd. As I went along the water front picturing scene after scene in the unfolding drama, at times I made such notes as these:

"Show how great spirit of crowd is born—how you yourself have felt it grow. Give its blurred dream of a world set free by this awakening giant here and ask—do such upheavals as these mean an end to the rule of the world by the keen minds of the men at the top?"

So I tried to picture that strike as it would have looked and felt to me. And so in this harbor I'd known so well, from the days of the last ships with sails on through its swift chaotic growth to this era of steam and machinery—a gleaming, heaving, breathing thing filled deep with the rush and vigor of life—I tried to give my feeling of the ceaseless challenge of this fast-changing world of ours, which to you and me and all of us says:

"Keep changing with me, little man! If you don't, you might as well be dead!"

For weeks I went about taking notes, and with all this mass of material I came up to the White Mountains to write. I had little idea of the utter confusion and the long strain and agony of creation that lay ahead. My work on The Harbor took two solid years, and more than once in that long job I grew all but ready to quit in despair. And this I think

I might have done, had it not been for my wife. Unfailing in encouragement and fruitful suggestions, sound advice, Margaret Ann, in those two years and all the others later on, earned well the inscription—To M.A.—in every book I've written since.

All summer long I struggled to bring some order and coherency out of my material and marshal it as background to the personal story rapidly growing in my mind. By autumn, still deep in that jungle of notes, I went back with my family to New York. We had rented a house on Eleventh Street, over near Seventh Avenue. Our second son was born that fall, and in March he grew so ill that for days we feared he'd die. We saved him. He grew well again. But this infernal book of mine was still in the throes of being born. I grew sick myself and our doctor said:

"What you've got to do is to leave your desk and go off and get the rest you need, in good fresh air! Forget your book!"

I hadn't told him the name of my book nor did he know where its scenes were laid. In a meekly obedient tone I said:

"I can't leave New York just now, but how about going out on the harbor each morning for a couple of weeks and spending the whole day riding around on ferries, tugs and barges with old harbor men I know?"

"Splendid!" cried the doctor. "That ought to take your mind off your work."

So I spent two spring weeks like that. And though I never forgot my work, those days helped to clear my mind and gave me such a new perspective on the job I'd left behind that, when I returned, slowly at first but then faster and faster order came. My poor exhausted story struggled up through the jungle to life, its people all grew real like friends, and my backgrounds fell into line. Oh, the blessed relief of it all and the sheer joy of writing, writing—till like a stenographer I sat taking down the voices I heard!

XIX

When Macmillan's took The Harbor, in the spring of 1914, there came to me that dismal feeling which many novelists know so well. I felt utterly emptied, drained, restless, lost, my nerves on edge. Desperately I needed a change. Thank God for my wife and her kind mother. Her mother came East to look after the children and we took a flying trip to France. My book seemed all behind me now. Into it I had put my whole life and my feeling of those tides of change that were rushing us over the years into the maelstrom of today. But I had not the slightest conception then of the world-wide storm so soon to break or what a maelstrom we should see! Reaching Paris about May first, we joined our old friend Bullard there.

"What's the big news?" I asked him.

"Nothing much just now," he said, "but I've a hunch there'll be plenty soon."

"Russia again?"

"And then some!"

"What?" He gave me his old affectionate smile.

"Look here," he said, "you've worked like hell on that book of yours and you're all strung up. What you need is a rest. Forget you're a writer, forget you're a Red. Here's Paris in the month of May. Why don't you two just be gay?"

We had a lovely time at first. In the *Quartier Latin* we stayed with Bullard at Foyot's, the little old hotel café only a stone's throw away from the Café Odéon, where I'd once had that midnight talk with the Russian revolutionist. The

Luxembourg Gardens close by were lovelier than ever now and we went to the spots where I'd tried so hard to talk that girl into being my wife. We danced; we went to frivolous plays and to the *Opéra Comique*. We had such a good time, we got colds in our heads. Our only *bête noire* was a rat. At Foyot's there were a few bedrooms upstairs and we had the only quiet one, a large room on an inner court. But in its open fireplace thin steel shutters had been rolled down, and behind them every night a big rat stood on his hind legs and grabbed those shutters and rattled them hard! Sleepless, out of my bed I would leap and bang till he fled up the chimney, but in a few minutes back he'd come. We complained of him downstairs. Traps and poison were tried, but nothing could stop him. My wife said sternly:

"Very well. We shall go to the country, come back in a week and, if he isn't gone by then, we shall move to another hotel."

So down to the Pyrenees we went and spent not one but two grand weeks with a friend whom we both loved, George Twose, tramping in those gorgeous mountains and dreaming of some future time when we'd leave this turbulent modern world and spend a month in peaceful Spain. For Spain would always be like that. Returning to Paris, when our cab drew up at Foyot's, out rushed waiters, porter and maid, all radiant! A chorus of cries:

"*Monsieur et Madame, le rat est mort!*" When we asked what had killed him, we learned that the *chef*, knowing that this was a Foyot's rat and therefore a connoisseur in food, had at last enticed him to his death with *langouste empoisonnée!*

All Paris was dancing the tango that year and we watched and decided we'd like to learn. My teacher, an Argentine, was fat but miraculously light on his feet and he had a powerful arm.

"In dancing the tango," he told me in French, "you must

hold a woman so—like this—bend her far backward so she can feel that if you let go she will fall on the floor. That is how a woman should feel toward a man if she loves him, and in this dance she loves him but is also afraid. For the man is a tiger."

I tried to be one, with poor success.

"You will need many lessons."

"I'll take six."

"You will pay in advance."

Like a fool, I did. The first two lessons were all right. I began to feel pretty tigerish. But at the third, when he met me, he said:

"I cannot dance with you today. My poor father is so sick that he may not live. I feel very sad." But having seen him gaily flirting with a young Parisienne when I came on the dancing floor, I looked him square in his Argentine eyes.

"*Nous dansons!*" I said firmly. We did. When next I came for a lesson, his look was even more doleful still. In a low reproachful tone he said:

"*Maintenant mon père est mort.*" Why had I paid him in advance?

"*Nous dansons!*" I said firmly. We did. In a few minutes he stopped and groaned:

"*Je ne peux pas—je ne peux pas! Les vêtements noirs sont tout préparés!*"

"*Nous dansons!*" I implacably cried. And his memory then must have slipped a cog for, when next we met for a lesson, he said:

"*Je ne peux pas danser. Mon pauvre père est très malade.*"

"That's fine!" I answered cheerfully. "Last week you told me he was dead!"

He gave in then and went glumly on at this job of making me tigerish. I finished at last and danced with my wife.

"I am a tiger!" I breathed in her ear.

"Are you? You feel more to me like a rabbit. For Heaven's sake stop jumping and glide!"

The immense polished floor of The Magic City Café was a gay scene, those afternoons, crowded with dancers and all so French. If some implacable voice of fate had boomed through the music the news that in only six months this home of the dance would become a munitions factory, working at top speed day and night, what a burst of derisive French laughter would have risen in reply!

We ourselves would not have laughed so hard, for back at Foyot's our old friend Bullard had told us more than once of his fear that there'd be a big war in Europe soon. But Jean Longuet and other Socialist leaders, who came to dine with us there, were so strong in their belief that the Socialist workingmen everywhere would rise at once to prevent any war that our forebodings were soon at rest. In the evenings in student cafés, we sat among genial laughing crowds of young Frenchmen, Germans, Austrians, Poles, Russians and Italians. What chance of war between such friends? As we sat one night among them with a French painter whom we knew, I told him of the book I had written.

"That is a grand idea," he said. "The harbor as a symbol of change. For each one of our little lives the great secret of success is to change it also every few years, break it completely and make a fresh start. Only so can you keep yourself alive to this amazing world. Look at the boys in this café. I envy them. They have so long a time to live. They remind me of what Voltaire once said: 'Young men are lucky! They will see great things!' "

Our friend was only partly right. For those young men did see great things, but they were not lucky and neither was he. At Christmas time that very year, the top of his head was blown off one night by a jagged hunk of German steel!

Back at home in the White Mountains in June, I began

work on my next long novel. I loved this work, it absorbed
me so; and I drew even closer still to my wife and our two
small sons. My whole life seemed settled for years ahead. But
then the relentless world outside crashed in to challenge my
neat little plan and to swing me once again off onto a course
unknown. From Serbia, Austria, Germany, Russia, France,
Belgium and England came the news of men and boys by
millions marching. Into the roaring hell of death they plunged
and the whole world did change! Completely dazed and
stunned at first, my thoughts went back once more to The
Harbor; and although my novel now seemed suddenly a tiny
thing, I sent down to Macmillan's for the script and spent a
month on a new ending, showing the whole world in chaos.
What a climax for my theme!

Then I took long tramps with my dog through the hills
and tried to get back into my next book. But the news each
day kept crashing in. Once a correspondent abroad, it is hard
to stay home when all Europe flames. And although I looked
on war as the deadliest enemy of our race, I had no use for
the way in which my Socialist and Pacifist friends kept shouting against what they'd never seen. A blind attack. "Let's see
what it really is," I thought, "and try to describe it, just as
it is."

In New York that fall I applied to all the magazine editors
I knew. No luck. Too late. They already had men on British,
French and Belgian fronts. I went to Philadelphia then to the
Saturday Evening Post. And Lorimer said:

"If you want to go over, Germany is your only chance.
It isn't yet covered."

"All right," I said, and arranged with him for one big article on Berlin. In New York, from the American and Everybody's magazines, I got orders for others at the front. And
early in November I sailed, on a British ship convoyed by
destroyers. Its few passengers all were men and its decks were
black at night.

XX

So MUCH HAS BEEN WRITTEN ABOUT THE WORLD WAR BY FAR
abler and closer observers than I that here I shall give only
those memories that still come back as having significance for
us today.

Soon after I came to Berlin, late one afternoon I sat at a
window in a large café. Outside on the *Friedrichstrasse*, that
narrow crowded thoroughfare of sparkling shopwindows, a
November night had fallen, though it was not yet five o'clock.
The arc lights sputtered and flared in the rain. It was the
coffee hour and the café was packed with people, but my eyes
were on the street. Outside my window, on the curb, her
gray woolen dress and shawl sodden and dripping wet with
rain, stood a stout old woman with a bundle of newspapers
under one arm. The glare of light from an arc above fell on
the title, *Die Zukunft*—The Future. And as though it were
a message of ill omen, the old witch kept peering at the people
thronging past, and every few moments, darting out, she
would display this title and scream it in their faces:

"The Future! The Future!"

The life of Berlin swept endlessly by. Along the narrow
shopping street came wagons, drays and taxis, in one of which,
as it stopped in a jam, I caught a glimpse of a couple inside,
a most absorbed young officer with a slender young person
in brown in his arms. The old crone saw them, too, and thrust
her newspaper into their window: *"Die Zukunft! Die
Zukunft!"* A score of wounded soldiers passed, arms in slings,
heads bandaged, with a Red Cross nurse as guide. Soldiers not

yet wounded passed, in couples and in groups and crowds, heavy boots clopping over the pavement. And as all these youngsters, talking and laughing, hurried along, the old woman flourished her paper still. A girl of the street came gaily dressed, from under her small blue silk umbrella hungrily watching the faces of men. A woman with three small children came, and she did not look gay at all. She stopped before a window marked: "Christmas gifts for men in the field." Then anxiously watching the crowded street, she hurried her small brood across and, as they passed my window, I noticed how seedy and patched were their clothes. The old woman, as though she had noticed, too, called in a voice harsh and clear:

"The Future! The Future!"

What would it be? Twenty-five years have gone since then but I ask that question again today.

On *Unter den Linden* just after dark I heard the cry: "*Ein Luftschiff!*" And looking up, I saw an immense dark phantom, with spectral eyes of red and green, drift by under the stars above. How silently it sailed along! No mammoth fleet of enemy planes, no rain of bombs, no screaming death down in the quiet city below. Only a ghostly warning, cold and silent as the stars, that drifted off into the night.

At all hours I saw troops on their way to entrain for the front. I saw a whole regiment march along, an hour before daybreak, in a cold dense rain. They were in full field equipment. The street was empty except for one girl. Holding an umbrella over the baby in her arms, she hurried along beside one of the soldiers. I caught a glimpse of her face as she passed, and she looked terribly alone.

I remember one day when I, too, fell into line. I heard the approaching boom of drums, and down the street came a solid mass of men, women and children, filling the way from wall to wall. The music broke out with a crash, and now in the center of the throng I saw tall husky German boys swinging along in marching step. There were flowers in their helmets, flowers even in their guns. Some of these guns were carried by wives and others by young girls and boys. We passed a church, and out of the door came two women in black, one wiping her eyes with her handkerchief. But when she saw us she waved it instead. She waved as women always have and always will, in time of war, for war makes women feel like that, or at least pretend to feel like that. I felt it, too, that day in Berlin, for I had often marched to a band but never with men so soon to die. Despite all one's natural common sense, something seemed to swell and rise with the regular tramp, tramp of thick boots, and the steady looks in the faces of these simple men and boys. They were not the men who made treaties and broke them, but only the men from the fields and mines, the mills and shops and factories, simply the men who were going to die. By my side marched a little shaver not more than eight years old, taking prodigious strides to keep up. Every now and then he would look at those rows of faces and steady eyes and, as the music crashed and boomed, suddenly, eyes radiant, the little chap burst into tears!

On a Sunday night about one o'clock I went into a great hall where two thousand people sat sipping their beer. Sprinkled everywhere through the hall were men and boys in uniform, and I heard war talk on every hand. Suddenly on his high platform the orchestra leader turned off the lights and plunged the place in darkness. Then from down behind him a lurid reddish glow appeared, the drums made a sound like thunder, and now as he led the orchestra, with a rifle in his hands he fired blank cartridges over the crowd!

About Hindenburg, the national hero, I heard stories by the score. "Swampy Hindenburg," he was called, for he had studied swamps all his life with an eye to their use in warfare. And now his chance had come at last, and Swampy Hindenburg had made good, in the famous defeat of the Russians up in the Masurian Lakes. I was told of great wide roads leading out onto the marshes, where they still appeared like roads, with rows of trees on either side, trees planted many years before. Into these deathtraps fled the Russians, driven by fire from German big guns. But suddenly on every road the solid ground ended in ooze fathoms deep, and into it by thousands plunged men and horses headlong. Other thousands piled on top, and the night was filled with their frenzied cries. Some German officers went insane because of the horror of that night. I sat by the bed of one of them and I hear him rave about it still!

I heard atrocity tales by the hundred.

"In East Prussia up near Danzig," said an officer one night, "we entered a small village from which a troop of Cossacks had been driven out that day. They had left four women and young girls—all stripped naked, bleeding from rape, and nailed by their hands and feet to a barn! Crucified—dead—but their bodies still warm!"

"Six hundred of our stretcher bearers," said a German surgeon just returned from the western front, "have been shot by Belgian peasants as they bent over the wounded." And he went on to narrate in detail how the peasants had gouged out their eyes!

"In Belgium," said a soldier, "we found a wounded German inside a big brick oven that stood beside a farmhouse. We pulled him out but he was dead. His face was brown. He'd been baked to death. We found three peasants in the barn, and first we made them dig their graves. Then we shot the murderers and we threw them in the hole. One of them kept kicking still, even when he was covered with dirt, but we finished him off with our bayonets!"

So that flood of bloody folklore had poured over Germany as over France and England, and the effect was atrocious as though every story were true. For not only in Berlin but in every country at war, in every village, every hut, such tales were being passed around and being told to children, too, planting in their hearts and minds that fear and bitter hatred which is war's deadliest gift to men.

That hatred in all its intensity was brought vividly to my mind one evening in Beethoven Hall. The hall was crowded to the doors, and on the stage a famous actor was reciting poems of the war. He seemed to hold the crowd in his hand, rousing their worst passions, snapping every bond of restraint. Rising at last to his climax, he began The Chant of Hate, which millions of Germans knew so well. I give only parts of it here:

> In the captain's mess, in the banquet hall,
> Sat feasting the officers, one and all.
> Like a saber blow, like the swing of a sail,
> One seized his glass held high to hail.
> Spoke three words only: "To the Day!"
> They had all but a single hate!
> They had one foe and one alone—
>   ENGLAND!
>
> Take you the folk of the earth in pay,
> With bars of gold your ramparts lay,
> Bedeck the ocean with bow on bow,
> Ye reckon well, but not well enough now!
> You will we hate with lasting hate!
> We will never forego our hate!
> Hate by water and hate by land,
> Hate of the head and hate of the hand,
> Hate of the hammer and hate of the crown,
> Hate of seventy millions, choking down!
> We love as one, we hate as one!
> We have one foe and one alone—
>   ENGLAND!

His face red and distorted with passion, veins swollen and eyes blazing, his two clenched fists held high in air, the actor finished that hideous chant in a veritable scream of rage. And then those German men and women rose like one man from their seats; there burst forth a fury of cries which set the air to quivering! And looking on those faces, I wondered how many long years it would take for such a passion of hatred to die?

And the cost of it all, the life-shattering waste! It was already dark one afternoon when I came to a building of red brick, climbed the broad stone stairs inside and entered a lofty chamber, with lead-colored columns at either end and pictures of Prussian heroes upon the walls and ceiling. Although this hall was crowded, all was strangely hushed and still. Behind a long counter sat many clerks in black frock suits; and facing this counter in rows of chairs, several hundred men and women, tense and silent, sat watching a big red curtain, which was restless, never still. Every few moments it leaped apart as a messenger came quickly in. Then a name would be called out, and some man or woman would jump up and go to the counter, stand there rigid. So Germany learned of her dead. Forty-five hundred hospitals reported to this place each week, all pouring in the grim details, which in scores of busy rooms were neatly typed in little tales on post cards sent out every day to thousands of towns and villages.

There was a "prisoners' section," too, where another small army of men and girls were at work upon card catalogues, in which they entered records of enemies taken or killed. An official opened a heavy safe and lifted out an enormous steel ring on which were strung hundreds of medals of lead. As he tossed them into my hands, he said that each medal had come from the body of a Frenchman on the field. With a slight shiver I handed it back. He showed me, too, an amulet from the body of a Russian. It was a little block of wood, old and worn at the edges, bearing in faded blue and gold the picture of some Russian saint. Some simple peasant of the North had worn this faded holy thing to guard him from machine guns.

There were amulets from France with pictures of the Holy Mother. There had been hundreds of them here. And all these little safeguards were to be sent through Switzerland back to their homes, to come at last into the hands that had placed them once around the necks of many simple men now dead.

As I left that clearinghouse of death, a huge bright moon hung over the street; and by its light, on the wall outside, I saw a long narrow band of white made up of newspaper pages, where in columns of solid type, by army corps and regiment, were the names of the wounded, the missing, the dead. The line stretched clear to the corner and around down the other street. And almost imperceptibly moving along this band of white were dark figures, men and women, slowly searching page by page. For so they do in every war. *Die Zukunft.* What will it be?

On another evening, in one of the railroad stations there, I was made to feel again the uncanny care and precision of the German system of war, its precision not only in killing men but in conserving the lives of the killers. A long empty hospital train was about to start back for the front. There were about a score of cars with beds for some four hundred men. Each car was of white enamel inside and so fresh and clean you would never have guessed it had already carried thousands of wounded. The beds, in two tiers on either side, had wonderfully easy springs and about each bed were all kinds of contrivances, leather straps and shelves and trays, for the comfort of the patient. Bright-colored pictures hung on the walls. There was an operating car, an immaculate place of dazzling light, where a man could be laid on the table and put under the anesthetic while the train was still in motion. It stopped only while the surgeon worked. But on its last trip back from France it had stopped nearly every hour, they said.

I saw another kind of surgeon operate one afternoon, in

a church where they were about to hold a service of prayer for the men at the front. There was hardly a man to be seen in this church, but it was packed with women. A few of them in heavy crepe and most of the others dressed in black, in long sober rows they sat looking up at the chancel where, with a candle on either side, stood a small white figure of Christ. Close by stood a larger figure, tall and stern and robed in black, the pastor of the Kaiser. He was an old man, slightly stooped, his face was lean, powerful, deep-lined; and his voice, though low, had a deeply thrilling, magnetic note, as it cut like a knife into the faith these women had held in the small white figure by his side. And as he slowly explained to them how this was a war in the name of Christ, I thought of other church surgeons like this, in Russia, France and England, all preaching to rows of women in black. And I wondered what would be the effect upon the small white figure there? Would His power over the minds of men increase or diminish, after this war they had waged in His name?

There was another movement which had stood for the brotherhood of man. The Socialist parties of Europe for decades had been preaching peace. Their leaders had fought increased armaments and to the workingmen they had said:

"You are brothers with the workers of every other nation, and it is your world mission to stand together in one solid class against the class that exploits you all. All other wars are futile, will only drag humanity back."

But the war broke out, and in every land the Socialists by millions flocked to the colors with the rest. In Germany their leaders were so busy in war work that they were hard to interview, but I did have a talk at last with one of the best known of them.

"For years we have publicly declared that we wouldn't refuse to support a war in defense of the Fatherland," he said. "And that is what we have come to now. Encircled by enemies on all sides, we are fighting for our national life." How familiar again that sounds today! "It is foolish to talk of stopping this war and it is equally foolish to talk about disarmament. We Germans in the future must always hold ourselves ready for war. With open frontiers on every hand, we have no other way of defense; we must keep up our army. And, to be ready always against any sudden attack, we must have at the head of our government one man on whose shoulders rests full responsibility. I believe there will be other wars, and that war by increasing competition between the powerful nations will decrease it within each one—I mean that in each we shall see a swift spread of governmental control. We already have it here, and with it we have proved ourselves so strong against over half the world that other nations will be forced to copy our system to some extent. Each will build up its national strength by an increased control of its industries, for the profit of the whole people instead of for the gain of a few. For it is only by such means that all the men of the nation become good citizens, ready to serve, to give themselves both in war and peace."

What a jolt he gave to my Socialist faith! I little suspected how I myself would feel in only two years more, when the war came to America!

I heard the same kind of prophecy from Major von Herwaerts of the German General Staff, who dealt with foreign correspondents. A handsome charming friendly man who had spent ten years in Washington, in the War Office he sat at an immense table on which were spread scores of newspapers from other lands, all marked with colored pencils to show how public opinion, in countries not yet sucked into the war, was changing toward the Reich. On that same table, I have no doubt, American papers are spread this year. For so the War Office in Berlin keeps watching the world for enemies.

"This war is a great pity," he said. "There was no need for it at all. Germany, with England and France, if only they had listened to us, could have sat at one table and ordered all

Europe. The chance is gone. Now chaos will come. And order is what the world needs in these days. You Americans think we Germans have too much of it over here and too little freedom. You are wrong. For this modern civilization has become like a complicated machine and each little man must fit in as a cog. Someday you will see; you will have to choose. If you must keep your old independence of every citizen in your land, at least be logical. Leave this age and with Tolstoy go back to his peasant's hut. But you won't do that, nor will any nation. In the years of chaos that lie ahead, each nation will see and will choose our way. And then order will come in the world again. But not till then. Keep in mind what I say."

I look back and remember his words. Was he right? Was he wrong? Only time can tell. *Die Zukunft!* What will it be —democracy or dictatorship?

XXI

WHILE THE WAR OFFICE KEPT OUR GROUP of American correspondents impatiently waiting for a trip to the western front, to fill in my time I went to Silesia and spent a week with an American Red Cross unit stationed in Gleiwitz, a town so close to the Russian front that at night you could hear the boom of the guns.

In that big grimy mill town, three doctors and fourteen nurses had improvised a hospital out of an old theater. Gilt signs on either side the door, "*Parkett Rechts*" and "*Parkett Links*," directed spectators to their seats. But the seats were gone. Gone, too, were all the tawdry trimmings of that house of laughter and tears; the huge place was strangely still. Its walls were painted yellow and white, and through tall windows on one side the sun threw long soft bars of light. On the ceiling on billowy white clouds lay a great rosy Venus, with nude attendants all around and little cupids shooting darts. But in front, over the stage which had mirrored the life of a nation in peace, a gray steel curtain had come down. Just above it hung two flags, German and American, and between them a banner of white with a heavy cross of red. And above that cross two huge masks, one grotesque, one hideous—Comedy and Tragedy—looked down upon long lines of beds crowded close together. On small blackboards above them were the names of many battlefields, and men and boys with close-cropped heads lay motionless and silent there, looking up at that red cross and those enormous leering masks. Other men lay with eyes tight closed.

Men old and young, rich and poor, workingmen and peasants, doctors, lawyers, merchants, clerks, all hurled into the furnace of war, there to fight like animals with no time or wish to think—then struck down, and so brought here where every man had so much time. What dark silent dramas had been played here in the souls of men? What did they now think of this war? At first I got but little light. They seemed remote and strange to me—only "cases"—in such pain that I shrank from troubling them.

A score of new cases came in that night. "Slightly wounded," they were called. Most of them were Austrian Poles but a few were Russian prisoners. Just out of the trenches only some twenty miles away, they were a haggard filthy crew; with clothing in rags and encrusted with mud, they brought in a heavy sickening smell. Some had manure stuffed into their wounds in order to staunch the flow of blood, and already infection had set in. As the nurses removed the filth and dirty field dressings, I saw mangled hands and arms, already turning brown and red; and while the doctors went to work, some of these men gave shivering cries and low guttural groans of agony. One slim boy—he looked barely eighteen—held out his hand and smiled and smiled, till suddenly his face turned white and he pitched into the doctor's arms. He was soon brought to and he followed the rest, who trooped into the theater. There orderlies helped them undress and bathe. Soon they were all in clean cotton pajamas, each with a red cross over the heart. And a few minutes later, in a long row, these men who had so recently been peasants, factory hands and clerks, lay sleeping heavily side by side.

That evening I went to the stage box where one of the doctors slept each night, and we sat watching the scene below. There was but one soft light down there, on a table by the entrance door. The night nurse sat beside it. All the rest was indistinct and dim in heavy shadows. The beds looked like so many gray ghosts. Out of them, legs in slings pointed up into the dark. The only sounds were deep rough breathings, snores and groans. From a bed back under the gallery came a monotonous pleading voice, calling for the nurse to come. *"Schwester, Schwester, Schwester."* It sank into thick mumbling. Then suddenly out of the shadows there burst a savage beastlike scream!

"That's a brain case," said the doctor. "Partially paralyzed, shot through the head."

Again we heard that animal scream. I saw the dim white figure of the nurse as she went to the bed. Then morphine and then silence.

"This is a quiet evening," said the doctor presently. "There have been plenty of other nights when you lie here and can't sleep a wink. The lung-shot cases lie and cough blood. It's a long bubbling horrible cough. I remember one night there were six or eight all going at once, and they kept it up straight through till dawn. Others in the first sleep of exhaustion get nightmares, think they're in an attack and jump up with the God-damnedest shouts: *'Die Russen! . . . Kill the bastards! . . . Stretcher bearer! . . . Die Lazarett!'* One shout starts others and hell breaks loose! You hear the most infernal shrieks! A dozen men sit up at once and yell as though they'd all gone mad; while the orderlies try to hold them down! At last they all get quiet again and you lie here and listen. Every ten minutes you hear the nurse go up and down the lines of beds, for there's always the chance of a hemorrhage. I remember one case, a month ago: half the right thigh was torn away and the femoral artery was exposed. The night nurse stayed close by his bed. About midnight the artery burst and she called me. I ran down and got to work. I called for more light! She ran up on the stage behind the scenes and threw on every switch she could find! Up went the lights all over the house!"

"Like the end of an act," I ventured.

"Yes," he said. "The man was dead."

I watched him dressing wounds next day. At the head of

one line, close by the door, lay a tall gaunt man with a kindly face. By his bed sat a stolid young woman in a plain brown woolen dress. His lean right hand now sought for hers. She held it tight and looked down at the floor, and I saw her other hand grip the chair. The nurse was removing the wrappings from the man's enormous left arm. What I saw had little to do with an arm, it was only a swollen hideous mass, out of which the doctor slowly drew the dressing. The man on the bed gripped the woman's hand, the sweat came out on his forehead, he gasped and seemed to shiver. The woman beside him sat perfectly still.

Near by, on a bed which was raised at the head, lay a boy of nineteen shot through the brain. He it was whose howls we had heard from up in the box the night before. On his head was a long peaked bandage of cotton, from under which stared out glazed eyes. The boy's left side was paralyzed, but his right hand and arm kept pumping violently up and down, and he kept up a low regular moan, out of which from time to time came suddenly those beastlike yells. Again the nurse gave him morphine, and little by little he grew still. The bandage was removed from his head, the nurse lifted a mass of gory cotton—and I saw one of the horrors of war! Only a glimpse! I turned quickly away!

I returned to the man at the head of the line. He was lying back on the pillows now with an expression of deep relief. The woman still sat by his side, stroking his uninjured arm in a slow quiet soothing way, and from time to time these two would look at each other and smile.

"He is so much better," said his wife. "They say in a month we can go home. How good it is," she added, "that the wound was not on his right arm. He can write as well as ever, on paper or the blackboard."

"Do you teach school?" I asked him.

"Yes, in Hamburg," he replied, and we talked long about his school, for it seemed that he had loved his work. He

PICTURES TAKEN IN RUSSIA IN 1917

Soldiers Coming Home from the Front

A Bread Line   Starving Children

Babushka with Soldiers on Russian Front

reminded me of a teacher in a small Bavarian mountain town, who had carved these significant words over the door of his little house: "Dante, Molière and Goethe live here." This teacher was a man like that. He had felt very badly, he said, in August when the war broke out. "But what could you do," he asked me, "when your country's life was at stake?" So he had said good-by to his boys and had gone to the front in East Prussia.

"But I thought that your armies took only young men at the start," I said. He smiled.

"How old do you think I am?"

"Thirty-eight," I ventured.

"Twenty-six," he told me.

"How long have you lain on this bed?"

"Seven weeks," he answered. He had been wounded two months ago. From here he had telegraphed to his wife and a few days later she had arrived and had rented a small room near by. They were not thinking much about war. He wanted to get back to his school. Feeling how he loved the place, little by little I drew him out until that quiet schoolroom rose vividly before my eyes. I learned just where the windows were, and the door, his desk, the blackboard. I heard bits about some of his boys—boys he had quietly studied for months to draw out the best that was in each one. How different his method was from the steam-roller system used on the German boys of today! I questioned him until I thought I almost had him back in school. And then I asked abruptly:

"What will you say to your boys about war?"

He started just a little, then leaned back and closed his eyes. "I won't say much," he answered.

On a bed not far away lay a small thin man of middle age, with close-cropped head, sharp eager face, high cheekbones, eyes set wide apart. He lay there watching, watching and, each time that I came near, he quickly moaned or shook his head and jabbered Polish imploringly. No one of his neighbors could understand, but at last an Austrian peasant called from his bed up the line:

"I know his talk. I know what he says. He is from Galicia." They called Polish back and forth, and then the Austrian explained:

"He says he had a little farm—and he had a wife and two grown sons—and he says he had four cows. His sons they took for the army. He wants to know about his cows. If the cows are gone, he says, how can he plow his field next spring? He will have to harness in his old wife. I guess he'll never see those cows; the army took everything where he lived. I know, because I marched that way."

"How did he get wounded?"

"He says he drove a wagon in an ammunition train. One night both his feet froze hard, so he couldn't walk, and the next day they began to ache and grew as big as devils. So then, he says, he was sent here, and now they have cut off all his toes and his feet are good for nothing. He says that if his cows are lost it will be hard and very slow to go with such feet on plowed ground and hold his plow and drive his wife. He says his old woman is too weak—he does not want to make her pull. But what can he do? His sons are gone, and he thinks they are killed. He says war is bad for a peasant. He says he is feeling very bad. His feet are spoiled—he cannot walk. He says: 'How can I walk back to my farm?'"

"Tell him," one of the doctors said, "that when he is well he can ride home free on a railroad. We will get him a pass."

When this was translated, the Galician doubtfully shook his head. He lay there all day, thinking and planning, with anxious moans from time to time. The next morning the night nurse told me that he had barely slept all night. Again he seemed fairly bursting to talk, so I got the Austrian peasant to do some more translating.

"He thinks," explained the Austrian, "that they won't let him ride free on a train. He says on a train you must always pay. And he says that when he came here he had some boots, but they cut them off because his feet were swollen so big. He asks you will you get those boots? He thinks they are out in the beer garden where the Sisters pile our things. You take them to a shoemaker, he says, and fix them so they fit his club feet, so he can walk home and hunt up his cows. He says that if his cows are gone he and his old wife will die. There will be nothing for them to eat. He says they will sit in their hut and die."

I wonder what became of them?

That same week I had a glimpse of the famine which he dreaded so. I made brief excursions on foot toward the eastern front, through a flat bleak region of mills and mines, enormous heaps of coal and slag and tall chimneys belching smoke and flame from foundries working day and night to turn out more munitions of war. I saw long trains of wagons crawling over the landscape; I saw troops of cavalry and winding columns of marching men. I crossed into Russian Poland and heard the big guns booming there. So I came to a village of log huts and little sheds and hovels. And out of them, into a street knee-deep in stinking water and mud, came women and children and old men. Figures tall and figures tiny, figures thin like skeletons all, except a few little mites whose empty bellies were swollen with gas—they fell in the mud and grabbed my knees and begged for the food I could not give! The children screamed as I hurried away!

Back in the hospital next day, I talked with a tall smiling boy of sixteen who felt nothing of the horrors of war. He told me he had run away from a Prussian military school. Shot in the right arm in France, he had spent three weeks in a hospital there. Later transferred to the eastern front, he had fought in Russian Poland and was now here with a shattered jaw. His face was so tightly bandaged he had to talk between his teeth. He hoped soon to be back on the firing line.

"You see," he told me earnestly, "war is very good for me.

In war you can get promoted fast. In my military school they would have kept me working years, but as soon as the war broke out I ran away from school with my friend. He was only fifteen and three months. We heard troops marching by at night and all the boys got crazy. All sat up in bed and talked, yet all but us were afraid to go. We climbed from our windows and slid to the ground and ran to the road and hid in a bush. And when some more troops came by in the dark, we fell in and marched along, and so at last we got down into France. My friend is now an officer. He writes me he is very glad. You see, in peace promotion is slow; you must wait for officers to die. But in war they get killed by thousands!"

I used to notice him after that, hungrily reading war-propaganda newspapers and magazines. How many boys in Germany are reading such propaganda today?

But one evening toward the end of my stay, I sat for some time by the bed of a boy who would never fight again. The "brain case" was dying. A nurse sat holding his right hand. He had only a few hours left to live and, unless somebody gripped those clutching twitching fingers, he would begin his animal howls. I took his hand while the nurse went down to get his evening nourishment. The hand was hot and feverish. It kept opening and closing, eagerly and fiercely, as though sending back some message out of a strange wild world of pain. He was a Ruthenian, a goatherd from the mountains. Close by the bed there was a wall, and through this wall, from a café, I could hear an orchestra. They were playing the Barcarole. The nurse returned with a hot drink. He would not open his tight-set jaws, so she put a tube up one of his nostrils. He struggled hard and tried to shout. And so he had his last supper and died.

In a bed close by was a man who for ten weeks had lain on his back and stared at the flags and the Red Cross banner, and often he seemed to be thinking hard. But he gave not a sign of what he was thinking—until one day he spoke to a priest. It was on Sunday morning. At a table altar there the priest in his white surplice and vestments had been saying mass. The service had lasted nearly two hours, for he had preached to the wounded men, bitterly declaiming against Russians, French and English, as all men accursed of God. Then this wounded German, who for ten weeks had lain so still, raised on one elbow and shook his fist.

"Leave us alone! Stop your shouting!" he cried. "You are only making everyone worse! Stop talking of war! What do you know? We're all so tired! Leave us alone!"

I left the theater late one night. It was dim and cool and silent; it was full of tired men. I thought of the forty-five hundred war hospitals in Germany and of the men who lay on their backs and silently stared at bare ceilings and walls, at flags and the red cross of Christ. What would they say to their wives at home and what would they teach to their children? Would they say, like that tall smiling boy: "War is very good for us"? Or would they, like that silent man who had lain for ten weeks dying, shake their fists at the powers that be and cry: "We are tired! Leave us alone"? I asked myself that question then and I ask it still today. For all our lives depend on the answer. *Die Zukunft.* What will it be?

Back again in Berlin next week, when I found my correspondent friends still waiting for the passes that would take us to the western front, I planned another little trip. From Von Herwaerts in the War Office, I got a pass allowing me to go to the German frontier and come back on a hospital train loaded with wounded to Berlin. Though he had told me to go to Aachen on the Belgian border, the pass was made out "to the German frontier"; and on my war map, with a thrill, I discovered that at Mülhausen the frontier touched the western front! So I took a train for Mülhausen at dawn. All that day in a crowded compartment, I felt a long way from home; for not one German spoke to me and on the wall I read this warning:

"Beware of foreigners. They may be spies. One word may destroy a regiment."

Lonelier and lonelier, all day I faced suspicious eyes and, at Colmar late that night, when a squad of soldiers came through the train to examine all passes and looked at mine, they promptly put me under arrest. With two hysterical screaming women who were suspects like myself, I was taken off the train and, as we were marched in the rain to the local commandant's quarters, my little guard kept sneering up and pointing to his bayonet.

"*Es geht schlecht mit ihnen!*" he snarled.

In the guardhouse a tall thin lieutenant gave me a very dirty look.

"Why, with a pass for a hospital train, did you come here instead of to Aachen? All hospital trains now go that way." He had spoken in German. In the same language I tried to reply.

"All right, I will go to Aachen," I said. "I did not know. I'm a foreigner."

"Yes, you are a foreigner."

"An American correspondent."

"Yes?" I did not like that "Yes?" at all. "You had better wait till tomorrow here and see the commandant. He is asleep. If he gets permission from Berlin—"

But this was the last thing on earth that I wanted! If Von Herwaerts learned of this, he might drop me from his list for that big trip to the western front!

"No, thank you, I won't bother him. I came to see your wonderful modern hospital trains," I said. "If none are here, I'll take a train for Aachen tonight."

"No, you will sit in that chair and let the commandant decide on your case. Only last week we shot a spy. He is not fond of foreigners." I grew desperate.

"Look here! Would the English be so stupid as to send to your country as a spy a man who speaks German so badly as I?"

That fixed him! With a lovely broad derisive grin, he said: "That is true! You speak worse German than any I ever heard in my life!"

Worse but faster! I spoke on. For some time I pressed my point. He said he would see what he could do and he went into another room. He was gone for some time but came back at last and said with a smile:

"Very well, you may go." I caught a train for Aachen at dawn. The rain had cleared. Through light gray mist I could see the Vosges Mountains. Tiny white clouds kept rising there and I heard the reports of French seventy-fives. The western front—so near! It was tough! But I slept all day and I needed that sleep; for in Aachen (Aix-la-Chapelle) on the German-Belgian frontier, I spent most of the next night watching a big movement of troops from the Russian front to France.

Beneath the immense arched roof of the station, all along the concrete platforms were German Red Cross women and girls, with huge containers of steaming coffee and scores of wicker hampers and trunks packed with sandwiches, chocolate, cigarettes. It was Christmas Eve and, as a score of big gramophones blared out the old Christmas carol, *Heilige Nacht*, every few minutes a long troop train rolled into the station from the East. They had fought the Russians—now for the French! You could hear them singing as they came. *"Stille Nacht, Heilige Nacht"*—they sang it as only Germans can. All in harmony, rich and clear, that lovely old music of peace on earth and good will to men came rolling in. Then, barely before the train came to a stop, out tumbled by hundreds big German boys in a rush pell-mell for the coffee and food. Laughing and talking, they had their ten-minute Christmas there. As their train moved out, they sang again; and their voices had scarcely died away when from the East came another train, with fresh voices singing that grand old hymn. They, too, had ten minutes of Christmas and were then rushed on for some big bloody push in France. In the midst of all this Christmas cheer, back from France came a trainload of wounded. They did not sing. From those dark crowded stifling cars all I could hear were harsh deep groans. Two men were taken out. They were dead.

Far into the night I stood watching those trains. Suddenly I felt both my arms gripped from behind by tense quivering hands; and my captor, a gray-haired old man with a white set face, cried:

"English spy!"

Arrested again. In vain I explained. Between two soldiers I was marched to the commandant's quarters close by. But there, thank God, at a big desk sat an elderly kind-looking officer quietly smoking a cigar. After reading my pass and credentials, he looked up and smiled and said in English:

"How you do keep moving about."

"What do you mean, sir?" I asked in alarm.

"Oh, just that you American correspondents are so restless," he said. "I see you were in Silesia last week. Have you been yet to the western front?"

"No, but I hope to go very soon. All that I came here for was to see your wounded."

"Where did you come from?"

"Berlin."

"But you hope to go to the western front. Well, try not be so restless and soon perhaps you'll have your chance. I'm so sorry for this little trouble tonight, but you see that old man who treated you rough had both of his sons killed in France and he is insane on the subject of spies. The rest of us all welcome you here. We like to be friends with Americans."

"Then can I go back to the station?" I asked. He still kept smiling.

"Don't you think you've seen enough of our troop movements for one night? You know what I would do in your place? There is a drugstore across the street with a fine little druggist, who cured a bad cold for me last week by rubbing goose grease on my chest. You need it. You can scarcely speak. Your cold is even worse than mine."

So I went and had my chest rubbed, then took a train back to Berlin. There I went to Von Herwaerts to report. With a friendly smile he said:

"Hello, Poole. Did you go to Aachen?"

"Yes, and it was wonderful!" I went on to thank him for what I had seen.

"I'm so glad you found it so interesting in Aachen. How about the western front?"

"What do you mean, sir?"

"You still want to go there?"

"Yes, sir!"

"Then get over your cold and we'll arrange it very soon."

But at the Adlon that afternoon, Jack Reed came to my room and said:

"Well, Ernest my boy, you're in bad with Von Herwaerts."

"My God, Jack! What have I done? What's wrong?"

"Oh, I don't believe he's very sore. But I was in stirring him up again about that trip to the western front, and he told me: 'Look here, Reed, kicking won't do you one damned bit of good. We'll send you chaps to the western front when we are ready and not before. Poole tried to get there the night before last but we had him stopped and sent to Aachen. Remember this German army has eyes!' "

XXII

Only a few days after that, our group of correspondents, led by a doughty little man with great bristling whiskers, Captain Kleaver of the General Staff, started off for France by train. In Belgium we took to automobiles driven by German army chauffeurs, speeding at seventy miles an hour over roads so narrow that Belgian peasants had to jump off into the ditches as we passed. They mistook us for Germans, for we were in field suits of army gray. The men stood silent, but the women spat at us, and in one wrecked village a stout old man with shaggy white hair stood all alone and shook his fist and shouted as our cars roared by. In France we made our headquarters at Lille, where nearly half the buildings were in ruins from German guns. As a way of meeting the French in the town with no Prussian officer at my side, I told Captain Kleaver that I was hungry for French cigarettes and, with a little street gamin as guide, I spent a long winter afternoon visiting small tobacco shops, where in low tense voices I heard how these French people hated *les Boches!*

Day after day for a couple of weeks we motored along the German lines, but here I shall write only of one long typical day and night and the feelings and thoughts they stirred.

It was still dark and the stars were out, for we had made an early start. In three open automobiles, we were speeding down a long straight road about three miles behind the front. In dark deserted hamlets one hut would always show a light, and here at the cry of "Halt!" we would stop while a sentry examined our papers. These sentries seemed to be everywhere. We met one on a lonely railroad bridge, a stolid silent German boy who came with his flashlight from car to car, carefully checking us off on a list. And while he kept us waiting, suddenly a great meteor rushed half across the heavens. It gave me a sharp tingling shock, for it was like a fiery sign of this war which had torn a blazing path across all I had believed in. In an old Greek play that I once read, a man is fighting in the dark and he cries: "Give me light that I may see the face of my enemy!" All peace lovers, it seemed to me, would do well to see the face of war. And so I had come to look at this monster and paint him hideous as he was.

Our motors abruptly started on. From the East came a stronger glow of light and rumbling heavy crashes of guns. A cold dawn wind had brought low clouds, and now the rain was falling. We sped through ruined villages, empty and silent, bleak as death, and stopped in one where we could hear the crackle of rifleshots close by. Walking around a barn we came to a trench half full of yellow water; and in it, with our heads bent down, splashing through water and mud knee-deep, we came at last into the frontline trench, with a brick-paved bottom in which cesspools here and there had drained most of the water away. But where was war? Here was only a line of big German boys standing with their rifles stuck through holes in the wall of mud, firing every now and then, but most of the time just watching. Watching what? I looked over the top, and across a wide sloping watery field I saw a long crooked yellow line from which kept coming sharp little cracks. "*Achtung!*" A hand jerked me down, as a bullet hissed just over my head. But none of these stolid German boys were taking any fool chances like that. For weeks they had stood in a drizzling rain shooting at the upper rim of that long crooked line of mud. And you can't hate mud: it's impersonal. The men here before them had grown so bored they had made little truces with the French to trade food and cigarettes; and for this they had been moved to another sector of the line.

"They got too damned friendly," an officer said.

We lunched that day in an old château which was headquarters for the staff of a Bavarian army corps. It stood on a slight rise of ground, and from the low French windows we looked out on a spacious park. On the walls were soft old tapestries and here and there a painting, but the chairs had all been shrouded in gray and the rugs had been taken up from the floors. For this was now a nerve center of war. Through these leisurely old rooms thin copper wires were strung here and there for telephones and the green-shaded lights that hung above small wooden tables; and upon the grand piano war maps and German books were mingled with music portfolios, in which one officer showed me with pride that the French people here had loved German music more than their own. But they did not love the Germans. The old *comtesse* had not fled away; she lived upstairs and she never came down. When you wished for anything, he said, you were solemnly ushered by one of her servants up to her room and there you found her seated in state. Looking at you with a frigid politeness, this old *grande dame* would inquire:

"What is it that you wish, *monsieur?*" You told her as briefly as possible and then the interview was at an end.

"*Madame la Comtesse,*" he had said to her once, "please believe me that I deeply regret these troubles with which we annoy you. Please do not be angry, *madame.*" She had answered with a mocking smile: "Why should one be angry, *monsieur*, knowing that you gentlemen will be for so short a time in France?"

But war is full of sharp contrasts. We visited hospitals that afternoon. In one, which had been a village school, I found a young French prisoner. With big beads of sweat on his face, he lay staring up at the ceiling. Both his legs on the night before had been amputated above the knees. He looked at me,

gave a quick stern frown, then went on staring as before. On
the wall above his bed was a large school map of France, and
near it hung "The Rights of Man" writ large in French for
children. Across the street was an old stone church. I had
a little talk with the priest and he told me how the village
mayor and other civilians had been lined up against his churchyard wall and shot down. He had buried them in two rows,
one on either side of the path leading up to the church door,
so that his people and their children and their children's
children would remember the Germans, he said. His low
voice was hard like steel. That lean old priest had terrible
eyes.

We sped on to a larger town and, in one room of a hospital
there, Jack Reed and I found a German lad just coming out of
ether. They had cut off his right arm. Into the room came a
brigadier general with his staff. He stopped by the boy, made
a brief little speech and laid on his chest an Iron Cross. We
lingered after they had gone. For a moment this boy who'd
been crippled for life lay staring up at the ceiling. Then
slowly up came his left hand to the Cross. Reed whispered:
"Throw the damned thing on the floor!" But slowly and very
carefully he placed it on the table beside him. Then he licked
his hot dry lips and went on staring as before.

"In this war," said the surgeon in charge, "in the trenches,
we find scarcely any disease. This is partly due to our system,
for war is like the traditional pig: it need not be so filthy;
you can often keep it clean of death. We keep experts on
cholera, typhoid and lockjaw traveling up and down our
lines. But there is a force still deeper here, something I never
found in peace, a mysterious vitality. It seems as though men
could not die. They stand to their knees in ice-water and mud
and get no pneumonia. A hundred men are shot through the
lungs and all but one or two get well. It's a strange new ally
we surgeons have here, a power we can count on in every
operation performed. I have known it now for months, but

I never get over being surprised. And let me repeat, it belongs to war."

Here, too, we saw the German system, sure, methodical, tireless, working upon soldiers just come back from the trenches to rest. In an old foundry building, at tubs under pipes from which spouted hot water, scores of men stood naked, scrubbing. In a big loft overhead tea and coffee were being served and, at the *Kantine* down the street, for a few pfennigs could be bought huge glasses of beer and light red wine, and tobacco and chocolate, to top off the rations of soup and sausage and bread. Thousands of peasant soldiers had worked in the fields in the last few months, and in Belgium and North France the fields that fall had been green with crops almost up to the firing line. Again the German system, for they knew well that they couldn't afford to lose a single crop of grain. Here in France they had gathered the sugar-beet crop and turned it into alcohol to be used in driving their automobiles. And on the road that afternoon we met a steam roller, rolling crushed stone into the mud, ponderous, solemn, grinding along as though in a suburban town, though shells were exploding across the fields only a hundred yards away.

"These rollers," said an officer, "have saved thousands of our wounded from being jolted in ambulance cars and bled to death, as they are on the French and British fronts."

We saw now war and nothing but war. Everywhere to the horizon crawled dark sluggish masses made up of trucks and carts and men. There was deep intensity in it all and an elemental bleakness. Everything that men had made in ages in this peaceful land was now stripped naked, jagged, rough. Our party entered a village church and climbed by rickety ladders a hundred feet to the bells above. Church towers in flat country made good observation points, and so they were used and so they were shelled. The French guns had shelled this one only the afternoon before. From the bell tower overhead I looked down and off to the West. The sun had just set. Outlined against the afterglow, over a small village rose lovely little clouds of white which went wreathing up to the heavens. Each cloud was a bursting shrapnel shell, the afternoon fire of the French. The Germans called it The Evening Prayer. These little prayers hung lovingly around a church tower over there. From each came a dull sullen boom.

I slid down the ladders to an organ loft below. On the organ the music was scattered and half the keys and stops were out. There was other music in the church, a rattling din that echoed against the old stone walls, in which were gaping shell holes. Looking down, I saw hundreds of young recruits being drilled in pumping cartridges out of their rifles and in shoving fresh ones in, while officers walked up and down urging them to hit up the pace. Even the chancel was filled with these youngsters; above them a white image of Christ stretched forth a hand as in benediction, but nobody seemed to notice Him there, for every man was so absorbed in acquiring speed in killing. I heard an impatient shout from below, for our automobiles were ready to start. Just before I left the church, the young officer who had called me out pointed to a shell-torn image of the Virgin on the floor.

"Jack the Ripper," he said with a smile.

In a muddy hollow some miles away we found a German battery. By each one of the four guns stood shrapnel shells in tall wicker cases. The fire was being directed by an officer in a distant church tower, whose orders came over a telephone to an officer in a dugout close by. He called out the range and time and, while one soldier fixed the range, another timed the shell's explosion. Every few moments someone called *"Fertig!"* There was a roar and a leap of a gun and then a deep long swishing sigh as the big shell went rushing off. It took on a weird savage animal sound, and in a few seconds we heard the crash as it burst in the midst of the enemy. What had happened? Had men been killed? Only the man in the tower knew. These chaps might go through the whole war and never see one of their victims. Murderers? No—machinists. As I stood in the yellow mud, they glanced at me from time to time with that same superior smile I've had from other men in skilled trades. We stood watching for some time. Then French skilled killers somewhere must have gone to work, for now in a meadow close by us there was a flare and the crash of a shell. In a moment another burst closer still, whereupon these German mechanics quit work and crawled into their bombproof. As we ran back to our automobiles, the shells tore holes in the field behind. They alone seemed to feel like killing.

The twilight deepened rapidly, and it was dark when we stopped next between a farmhouse and a barn. Here we left our cars for the night and started off on foot in the dusk, splashing heavily through the mire of a narrow country lane which led up to the front line. A light rain was falling now and the night grew rapidly warm. The heavy sleeping-bag under my arm grew heavier and soggier. After about a mile of this, I heard a sharp hiss close by.

"That's a bullet," said my companion.

"It is," I replied. Another hiss. Soon there were quite a few of them. "Well," I remarked, rather pleased with myself, "if this is being under fire, I think I'm getting used to it." The top wire of the fence by my side cried "Bing" and hummed a little.

"Don't jump like that!" my companion growled.

Suddenly from the trenches ahead a rocket shot up. In the flare that it made, I saw a small house half a mile away, the place where we were to spend the night. Over it with long weird sighs the enemy shells were flying. A bullet with the voice of a wasp struck the mud just under my heels, and the man at my side pitched forward. He was not hit, and I helped him up, and we told each other earnestly that this was quite a story. From here to the house was a long long walk. But when at last we did arrive, we found not only a farmhouse but near it a big comforting barn, which rose between us and those steel wasps like a motherly Rock of Gibraltar. A steep flight of steps led under the barn to a bombproof hole beneath. And it was wet, that hole in the mud, but it felt dry to me that night, dry and deep and cozy!

It was shaped like the cabin of a small yacht, with a long bench on either side. At one end was a little table and above it a white mirror stuck full of colored Christmas cards. This hole and the house and barn above were headquarters of a regiment, on a sector close to Ypres. The colonel, a strong middle-aged Bavarian with a kindly face, told us that a big French shell had burst in the barn three days before, killed five of his men and wounded four.

"Now, gentlemen, let us go up and dine."

We went up to the farmhouse kitchen, a snug low-ceilinged room with a lofty fireplace of brick, an old French clock on the mantel, and three enormous holes in the walls. More shells, I thought, and began my soup. It was hot and comforting. After that came a good meat stew, then bread and cheese and Munich beer. From outside came the crackle of rifles and the shriek and whine of shells flying over the roof of the house.

"No shells," the colonel assured us, "are likely to call on you here tonight."

"Why not?" I asked imperturbably. All war correspondents talk like that.

"Because this house was not hit today, and the French as a rule use the same range at night."

After supper I went outside. The house and barn were perfectly dark. Not a glimmer of light through the windows to attract shellfire, but from French rifles and machine guns bullets smacked like hail on the barn. I jumped over behind it. Peering out, at first I saw nothing but dense dark rain. Then suddenly up went a rocket, which threw a wild uncanny light on a bleak expanse of watery mud; and roused afresh by this sight of their world, the men in the hollow just below fiercely redoubled their fire now. Here the French and German lines were less than a hundred yards apart. The men in those trenches just below were standing in water up to their knees. Every few minutes they sent a rocket flaring up into the rain, to make sure that No Man's Land was still clear of the enemy. Plenty of blood had been spilled in that mud and there were still dead bodies out there. But in all this time, by attacks that cost them heavy in lives, the Germans had pushed forward only two hundred and fifty yards. And as I watched, a picture came of this broad brown band of mud, reaching for nearly three hundred miles, winding like some monstrous snake, which as the line swayed back and forth was always slowly writhing.

I went back into the farmhouse kitchen. There was a telephone by the wall. Its ring was a thin treble purr, and it kept a man busy most of the night, for its long delicate copper nerves spread all along the winding snake and back into the Reich. More than war came over this wire. Late that evening the brigadier general in a farmhouse three miles back gave a little telephone concert to our sector of the line. The piano at which he sat was rather an old and battered affair, but that Bavarian knew how to play! With the receiver pressed to my ear, I heard first a gay little waltz and later the Love Song from Tristan—while from the night the crash and jar of shellfire came as accompaniment. This concert, I learned, was a nightly affair and the audience was scattered wide. Men in other lonely kitchens and in holes down under barns, and even in trench dugouts, heard Tristan with me that night.

Later I heard soldiers singing, faintly, as though far away. I asked the colonel where they were.

"Not far," he said. "Just underground. Would you like to go and hear them?"

"Yes."

And going outdoors we followed him down a steep flight

of steps into the *"Villa Sorgenfrei,"* a bombproof chamber they had dug deep under the manure pile. It was small, with walls of logs and a ceiling so low we could not stand. A little stove made it stifling hot; the only fresh air came through cracks in the door. But here we stayed for nearly an hour with eight or ten Bavarian boys. A drum, a mouth organ and a flute, an old iron gong and a clumsy guitar with telephone wires for the strings, made up their soldier orchestra. Leading them was a lad who in Munich had played the piano in a café. With spectacles on the end of his nose and a drumstick for a baton, he sternly rapped for order and then carried his small band through *Puppchen* for our benefit. After that came folk songs—*Röslein auf der Heiden, Morgenrot* and many more. The colonel was singing with them now and they seemed to have forgotten us. Out in the trenches that afternoon two of their comrades had been killed, but they had grown so used to death it didn't stop their singing. Stolid smiling German boys, so many to be killed so soon! And the others, I felt as I watched their eyes, would go home proud of having fought and would tell proud stories of war later to other boys, their sons. Already their little leader had written a song they sang that night, to the glory of that bombproof hole and the courage of men "in the iron rain." The refrain was to the machine gun. Another folk song for Germany.

A little after midnight we went into the bombproof under the barn, and there I lay for hours listening to the gunfire which never for one moment stopped. Half waking and half sleeping, the images of what I had seen kept rising vividly in my dreams, and confusedly I grappled for some meaning in it all. But things looked black to me that night. If war were hell and only that, one might have hoped that in sheer disgust men would learn their lesson and that this war would be the last. But I saw little hope of such disgust. For I had seen my enemy's face and it was not hideous as I had hoped. I had seen deep gleaming flashing eyes and heard a voice that thrilled even me. For listening to those roars outside, I thought of young men by millions, Germans, French and English, all along this winding snake, each one offering up his life, with no inspiring blare of bands, but standing deep in water and mud week after week and month after month and still keeping the looks I had seen in their faces!

"And who are you," a voice seemed to ask, "to talk to these men of my ugliness? Have *you* ever offered to give your life for the things that you believed in? And all your countrymen over the sea, are they so honest, generous, kind and noble in their works of peace? Or is it only the fever of the Yankee dollar-chase that makes them so reluctant now to stop getting rich and think of me? What have you in your little life ever known that can call to men as I call, pulling them out of their creeds and greeds to give up their lives by millions, to shake the entire civilized world and put all institutions on trial? There are many shams, many idols of peace, that will come down before I am through. For things are going to crash, these days, and the world is going to be reborn!"

So spoke this grim old pagan god, come back to build a pagan world. And groping long for an answer, at last I saw a ray of light.

War was youth, I told myself, and it was youth that had thrilled me here. War had made the glory of youth its own and so had clothed its ugliness. For what was this strange vitality that doctors did not find in peace? In peace youth was scattered; here it was massed and, gathering strength in being massed, took on this mysterious vital strength. Fill all the armies with middle age and then where would be war's vitality? And to youth, too, of right belonged this grand spirit of comradeship, this readiness to offer up one's life for the sake of an idea. Youth, youth and only youth, I thought. Strip war of that and what had you left? You had broken treaties and well-greased guns and dead bodies, already more than a million, rotting above or in the ground. And you had atrocity tales, and homes of desolation and bitterness and hatred. Here was a ghastly price being paid to settle a mean and sordid dispute over the markets of the world, as Germany tried to grab her share. Nor were these deaths the only price; there would be others for ages to come. I remembered what a German, deeper-thinking than the rest, had told me only a week ago. He was an economist.

"The world is bound together by the commerce of mass production in this age of machines," he had said. "Tear it apart by the hatreds of war and God only knows how long it will take to bind it all together again, so that civilized life can go on."

Thinking of such things as these, half waking and half dreaming, I lay in the bombproof hole that night. Long before daylight I got up and climbed the steep stairs to the ground above. A bright moon was shining now. Bullets still rained on the barn. Down there in the trenches, men were still firing thick and fast as they had been doing all night long. Up here by the barn and the farmhouse a sentry, a tall German boy, was walking slowly to and fro. I walked with him for some time. Later I woke my companions. We breakfasted, said good-by to our hosts and started back along the dark lane. Again the hiss of bullets came, but the long night had changed me and I did not mind them now. At the brigade headquarters our three cars started off at once, to be well out of the firing zone before the day should break. The moon had set and the stars grew faint. The pools of water on the fields slowly turned to silver. Masses of wagons, horses and men were still crawling over the landscape. As we sped on, the light grew stronger. Uglier and drearier grew all the world around us. It was Sunday morning. A little after sunrise, we met two French peasant women in black veils of mourning picking their way toward a village church. They stepped into the ditch and glared at us as we spattered mud upon them. I remembered the millions of women all over Europe in empty homes, and once again I wondered what they were going to teach to their sons.

XXIII

WHEN OUR TWO WEEKS AT THE FRONT WERE OVER, I LEFT OUR group—they were going to Belgium—and started for Berlin alone, there to get my passport cleared, for I was ready to go home. Although I had a special pass, in Belgium I was put off the train in a dismal little town in the rain, to make room for German soldiers. In vain I tried on the station guard my pass, my passport and other credentials. All no use. He shook his head. But just as the train was about to start, in desperation I jerked from my pocket a menu card, a souvenir of a dinner given to our group by General von Falkenhayn, chief of staff on the western front. On the back of the card was a plan of the table, with the names of American correspondents sandwiched in between those of German generals. And when he saw my humble name in that exalted company, it worked on that old station guard like magic! Blowing his whistle to hold the train, he rushed me to a first-class compartment. It was empty, except for an officer with a monocle and a Heidelberg scarf wound around his neck and shoulders, who sat reading and smoking a cigarette. When the guard asked if I might come in, he curtly nodded. The door was locked and the train pulled out, I leaned back in my corner and fell asleep. When I awoke we were still alone. The young officer was sitting directly opposite to me now, smoking and quietly watching my face. He spoke English:

"You are an American?"

"Yes."

"War correspondent?"

"Yes."

"What do you think of this war?" he asked.

"Well, there are two sides to it." But he cut me short with a wave of his hand.

"Oh, you need not be so careful. I'm no chauvinist. Let's be men. And first, tell me what kind of a man you are. What were you doing a year ago?" I thought for a moment. A year ago, I'd been taken from my work on The Harbor to help in the belated production of an old play of mine in New York.

"Rehearsing a play on Broadway," I said.

"Ha! Perfectly splendid! And I was a dramatic critic in Frankfurt! So we are enemies!" he cried. He fairly beamed upon me. "Now let us talk honestly. And to prove to you how I trust you—look." He unwound the big scarf from about his neck and, by revealing the absence of all insignia on his shoulders, let me see that he was no officer but only a humble private! At my look of astonishment he laughed and chuckled like a boy. "It is a little joke I play on this big war," he told me. "I grooft a first-class compartment so!"

"Grooft?" At my puzzled expression he looked disappointed and asked:

"Do not I speak your American slang correctly?"

"Oh, I've got it now—you mean graft!" I answered.

"Graft! That's it! I graft a first-class compartment here!"

"Aren't you taking big chances?" I liked this man. His eyes darkened.

"Chances? Ah, my friend, I care so very little now whether I am alive or dead. But do not let us talk of that; let us gossip of the theater!"

For two hours we did as he wished, and his hungry eagerness gave me a sense of how terribly alone he'd felt in all this mud and stink and blood. Poor devil, in the theater world he'd been a highbrow of the highbrows; and now, plunged into the ocean of war, he felt, as he said, like a man being drowned.

"All Europe is now a prize fighter's world and so it will be all the rest of our lives—ruled by prize fighters!" he said.

When at a dreary shell-wrecked town he left me and got off in the rain, in his place into the compartment climbed a mob of muddy tired soldiers on furlough going home. Crowded tight into my corner, once again I fell asleep. When I woke up later, I saw the others all sleeping but one, a lean dark lad with quick bright eyes, who sat intently watching the faces of those opposite, studying them one by one. After a stop for free coffee and food had roused them all out of their sleep, he began to talk to them; and though he spoke in a careless tone, I caught the vigilance still in his eyes. He spoke first of how good it would be to get home. But then he said:

"In my village, though, they write me that life is getting devilish hard."

"How is that?" somebody asked.

"Oh, there's almost nothing to eat, and they say fuel's so hard to get that their houses are freezing," he replied. "And the worst of it is that half the best men in our village are killed, so the old people have to do all the work. God knows what they'll do after the war, if all the rest of us get killed and none are left to plow the fields. For they write that these war taxes keep getting heavier all the time."

The young peasants around him grew gloomy now.

"Yes, it is hard," one of them sighed. "But this is war. It has to be."

"You think so, do you? So do I. But what you say reminds me of a funny thing I heard from a queer fellow at the front. He said in his sector the boys begin to feel that this war can soon be stopped."

"How?" asked a peasant. The lean dark lad's expression grew even more cautious still.

"Well," he replied in a casual tone, "he told me that in his sector they found the enemy were all good fellows, just plain people like themselves. They often called jokes across to our line. They even ran out and traded such things as sausages, matches and cigarettes. At Christmas they sang and the others sang back. They made quite a night of it, he said; and if their officers hadn't been there, they'd all have quit fighting and started for home."

"But their officers!" several voices cried. "They'd never allow it! They'd shoot them down!"

"Just what I told him," the speaker agreed. "But then he said a funny thing. He said their officers might be got rid of and then they could soon stop the war."

"Heigh!" a huge young peasant growled, and his broad face took on a look of suspicion and alarm. So did the other faces now. "I don't like this talk," muttered one. "It is bad to talk like this of our war." The lean lad smiled.

"Just as I told him, *Kamerad;* I feel like you do. This is war. I was only telling you what that other fellow said. He said if all the officers, both in the enemy trenches and ours, were gone, we'd all jump out and shake hands and call it a day and all go home."

He yawned and leaned back to go to sleep. The others had lost their jollity and sat glum and silent, thinking new thoughts from the seeds he had so cleverly planted in their minds. Now I saw that his eyes were open again. He was sitting opposite to me. I yawned and wearily stretched both arms. My left arm dropped but I crooked the other just for an instant over my head, while my right hand clinched into a fist. It was the Communist salute. And he got it all right—I could tell by the little leap in his eyes! But quickly they hardened into a stare. He was taking no chances with strangers like me. Once more he leaned back as though to sleep. I wonder what became of him? If he lived, he must be nearly fifty now. Is he still talking to simple men in Hitler's Germany today?

Only a few days after that, I reached England and from Liverpool boarded a big ship to come home. On our first night out, running fast through a fog without any foghorn or any lights—for we were in a submarine zone—I sat in the smoking room with three men, and one of them, a Canadian, said:

"I don't like running through fog like this. I hope to God we hit nothing tonight." Somebody smiled and answered:

"If we do, it will be just too bad for the ship we hit. We're the biggest thing on this ocean, friend."

"That's funny," the Canadian said. "I heard somebody make the same remark on a ship about as big as this. Have you ever heard of the Rule of Three?"

"The what?" I asked.

"The Rule of Three—old sailor superstition that two accidents bring a third."

"What is this? A story?"

"Yes, if you want it."

"Sure we want it. Go ahead."

"Well, men," the Canadian said, "on that ship—we'll call her Ship Number Two—I sat at a table just like this. The talk turned to accidents, just like this, and somebody said we were safe enough because we were the biggest thing on the sea. But a man across the table from me smiled as I'm smiling at you men now, and told us he'd been on another ship— we'll call her Ship Number One—and she'd been just as big as our Ship Number Two—but her name was the Titanic and she hit an iceberg and went down! He told of the hell of a night he had spent, on the ship, in the water and then in a lifeboat. After he'd finished, he smiled again and asked us: 'Now how safe do you feel?' We told him our bets were still on our ship—get it clear, gentlemen, Ship Number Two. But her name was the Empress of Ireland and she went down that very night! I jumped overboard and climbed on a raft and spent eighteen hours there—damned near frozen, damned near dead! So much for Ship Number Two!" The Canadian looked at us, smiling still. "And now? Are your bets still on Ship Number Three?"

The American next to him raised his glass.

"Are you with me, men?"

"We are!"

"Then here's to the Lucy!" he cried. We were on the Lusitania! "And to hell with the Rule of Three!"

It didn't work till three months later. Meanwhile we had a smooth crossing and landed safely in New York.

XXIV

IT WAS GOOD TO BE BACK IN MY HOME—BACK WITH THE WIFE
and children I loved, back in this free country so safe from
all that slaughter across the sea. To do my bit to keep it safe,
I began to write for the magazines about the horrors I had
seen. But I had been working for less than a month when a
most amazing thing happened to me. For my novel, The Harbor, was published in that early spring of 1915; and its theme,
the challenge of change, found a world so receptive, because
of the war, that my book had an almost instant success. After
the first grand reviews, Macmillan's swung into action on a
publicity campaign. Twenty-two editions were printed in the
next few months, and meanwhile letters came pouring in
from Theodore Roosevelt, William Allen White, William
Dean Howells and Hamlin Garland, Lillian Wald and Walter
Lippmann, Jack Reed and so many more! One came from
the Australian Bush, for the book appeared in England soon.
Three hundred copies were sent across on the fated Lusitania
and lie in her now deep in the sea.

Then came translations. In those next years the book was
done in Germany, Holland, Norway and Denmark, Sweden
and even in Soviet Russia, where for the new government
Gorky put it on his list of books significant to our times. I
have that Russian edition still. For the German edition, done
after the war in the days of inflation over there, and run first
as a serial, then in book form, my London agent sent me a
check for several hundred millions of marks—which in American money came to two dollars and eighty-three cents! May

such a flood of inflation never roll over us here! But though in foreign countries The Harbor brought little money reward, it brought such thousands of new reader friends that they changed the whole color of the world to my grateful writer eyes.

In the spring of 1915, I finished my war articles and turned to the new novel which I had planned the summer before. For when the war was over, I thought—as it must be in another year, for the nations couldn't stand such waste—the world would want books about fresh new life, as a relief from what it had seen. New life. I had always been fond of children and my feeling had deepened in these last years, as my interest grew in our two small boys. But my writing in the tenements and my wife's work in the schools had planted in me the idea that each man with a home of his own has two families, a little one inside his home and a boundless one outside. And to put this in novel form, I built up a story about a father watching the lives of two grown daughters, one of them married and all wrapped up in her own small family; the other one mothering three thousand children, as principal of a New York public school. I called the book His Family, and later it took the first Pulitzer prize.

I began it in the White Mountains in June. Several years before that time, we had built a summer cottage up here and, toward the end of winter, had come from New York to see it begun. I remember how, in a mountain world all dazzling white, we stood on skis and, as the men touched off the first blast of dynamite to start the foundations of our home, we watched a glorious cloud of snow rear up into the clean blue sky! I had a workroom in that house, with two kitchen tables as desks, one for myself and the other for our old friend Arthur Bullard, who from his many trips abroad came to us often in summer to write. As in my work later on, so then, I wrote in riding clothes. Each morning about eight o'clock I got to work, with my big dog Max waiting patiently on the floor by my table. What did he think of me sitting there, making thousands of marks on sheet after sheet of paper with a small piece of wood, so often stopping to light my pipe or stare or scowl or walk the floor, and suddenly laugh and sit down as before? Little or nothing! But Max was my friend. At noon with a triumphant bark he would greet the horse being led up outside, and then off we would go together for an hour before lunch. More writing in the afternoon and then two horses, one of them for Margaret Ann; and those long rides we took together, often two hours and even three, now cantering on small dirt roads, now walking our horses on mountain trails, were the very greatest joys of our days.

My book moved well, almost from the start; and thriving, too, was the big world of American public schools and children that I lived in at the time. Our small son Nick was three years old and had long since learned to walk, but what he loved still better was to ride on the shoulders of his Dad. Long after he had gone to bed, I told him stories every night. Our older boy Billy was seven now and, right on from his toddling age, he'd been up to so much mischief that, to shield himself from blame, he'd invented a mythical brother Johnny whom he loudly scolded for the misdeeds of Billy Poole. For our two boys about this time we bought an old Welsh pony, whom they rode till they ached in every limb from the tumbles she had given them. We had two horses for ourselves, and Margaret Ann's young brother and sister, John and Katharine, had two more. All summer friends and relatives came to their household and to our own, for riding, mountain climbing, vociferous tennis and at night charades or picnic suppers with guitars and much close harmony. My brother-in-law had finished Yale but still brought his college friends up to us in vacation time. At New Haven some of them had belonged to the famed and ribald group known there as The Whiffenpoofs, and I can still hear the ominous growls and cries of the mob scenes that they staged as they drew near to our cottage at night, led by Monty Woolley, who has since won such a place in dramatic circles in New York.

So passed two happy summers here. In the second autumn in New York, where we lived in an uptown apartment now, I finished my book, His Family, and began at once another novel I had in mind. Not even the newspaper headlines each day, with all their tidings of bloody waste, could alter my conviction that the world would soon come back to peace, that Wilson would keep us out of the war and that, even without our aid, the Allies were bound to win. So blindly thinking and blindly forgetting the warning challenge in the theme of my own book, The Harbor, I worked on in my orderly life—till once again the world of change came crashing in and tore my thoughts from little books to that vast fury across the sea.

All through the late winter and early spring, I read the ominous messages that kept flying back and forth between Washington and Berlin. Oh, the darkening tension of those last weeks! But step by step inexorably those messages and the events behind them swept us on. When war was declared on April 6, through excited crowds in New York on that wild chaotic night, with my own thinking, too, in a whirl, I went down to Luchow's restaurant to learn how the German-Americans felt. I found the big place nearly empty but I met a German I knew, a scholarly man, a psychologist. His face was haggard, set and white. When I asked him what his compatriots in New York were doing, he said:

"They're all running to cover—scared to death!"

"And what about you?"

"I'm standing pat. I'm for Germany," he said, "and for anything that can end this war before it pulls the whole world down!"

And what about me, I asked myself. As a Socialist I had

been against war, and what I had seen in Germany had set me more against it still. Could I stick to that attitude now? In vain that week my wife and I went to meetings large and small of Socialist and Pacifist friends. We found many German patriots there, patriots in Pacifist clothes, and among the real Americans a dogged unreasoning sticking to creed that seemed to me blind to the suddenly changed situation overseas. For with Russia in revolution now and her armies already crumbling, that powerful German army I'd seen could soon throw its entire force on the weakening French and British lines. If we held back, the Junkers would win, and then what kind of a world would it be? So went my thinking at that time. I reread Wilson's messages. His influence on me had been strong, ever since my Princeton days. How hard he had tried to keep us from war! Could a man do more? But now I read, in that last message on April 6:

"The world must be made safe for democracy. . . . It is a fearful thing to lead this great peaceful people into war. . . . But the right is more precious than peace and we shall fight for the things which we have always carried nearest our hearts—for democracy, for the right of those who submit to authority to have a voice in their own governments, for the rights and liberties of small nations, for a universal dominion of right by such a concert of free peoples as shall bring peace and safety to all nations and make the world itself at last free!"

More and more strongly those words beat into my confused thinking at that time. As I read them, how clear and plain they seemed! I had little suspicion of the job waiting for me close ahead. I went out to Governor's Island and on the big drill field joined hundreds of clumsy raw recruits being formed into squads by drill sergeants and marched around. Next to me in our squad one day was an intensely serious lad who'd just begun practice as a dentist.

"There's nothing like jumping in right at the start, if you

want to get a commission," he said. "I've already got my name in for Plattsburg. You see, I've been reading up on this war and I find it helps a lot if you can go as an officer."

"How?"

"You eat better, have better clothes and get treated like a gentleman." I grinned at him as we marched along.

"I've seen it, brother. This war is no place for a gentleman."

"Yah! No talk in the ranks!" our red-faced drill sergeant snarled.

But only a few days after this, I had a telephone call one night from Washington from my friend, George Creel, whom the President had put in charge of our war publicity.

"The chief wants you," he told me. "Take the next train."

I went at once to Washington and was there till early in June. Creel gave me a typescript by Arthur Bullard, called: How the War Came to America.

"Bullard has here put into shape the story of how this country has been forced into the war," said Creel. "Now he is busy with other work, so the President wants you to take this and make it all so plain and clear that every enlisted man or boy can read it and know what he's fighting for."

I did not like that job at all, but I started in and worked five weeks. From the plain strong clarity of Wilson's declaration of war, I plunged into a jungle of all the many varied events and forces that lay back of it. Bullard had cleared that jungle in a way I never could have done, but now for the enlisted man and how to make him understand! Each time I got it simple enough, it went to the White House for revision. My main trouble was not there, for the President was a writer himself and knew what I was up against and so he was merciful. But from him it went to the State Department to two hard-hearted experts upon international law and, every time I got a sentence clear enough and simple enough for the Rookies and the Gobs, those two would revise it into a tangle of legal complexities once more. How I grew to hate the job! It was finished at last and never again will I help in the writing of anything so widely spread around the earth. Translated into twelve languages, some 26,000,000 copies were printed. I wonder how many were ever read?

Oh, the grandiose projects and dreams that were started in Washington, those days! I remember one night at the Cosmos Club a well-known scholar drew me aside and confided that he had been asked by a great encyclopedia to edit a history of the war and all the forces behind it. He wanted me to do the chapter on American shipping and the freedom of the seas. How long a chapter, I asked, would it be?

"Oh, about the length of your book, The Harbor."

"Good God! How long will your history be?" With a strained anxious look he replied:

"Oh, it will run to more millions of words than I care to think about!"

Millions of words and millions of men, millions of guns and billions of bullets, millions of tons of food for the Allies. From his relief work over there, Hoover came to launch his campaign to conserve and increase our food supplies. The day he arrived, I saw him with Creel to help start his publicity work; and I wrote a brief story of his life for the Saturday Evening Post. All bone and muscle at that time, tall and rugged but tense with strain, all afternoon in his hotel room he walked the floor, in a low dynamic voice pouring out his story of starving Europe's need of food and his plans to gather it here.

Creel was kept busy day and night, and so were his fast-increasing recruits, rushing about from one big project to the next. As the glare of war publicity spread, only one event in Washington escaped the searchlights that we threw. Out at Mount Vernon the small group of ladies of extremely blue blood, who had charge of Washington's home, vowed that this one place at least should be saved from our vulgarity. Quietly they met one day in the narrow front hall of that lovely old house, while from its glass case on the wall Washington's sword was drawn from its scabbard and the two were hung side by side, so fulfilling the request in his will, when he bequeathed to his country his sword, with the one condition that it be drawn when the country was in danger. Oh, ladies, ladies! And Creel never knew! With hordes of reporters and cameramen giving that picture to the world, ye Gods, what couldn't we have made of that simple little ceremony?

Hotter and hotter Washington grew, hot with weather, hot with war, hot with burning dreams and plans for America and the whole world. To escape from it all, I went down the Potomac one night with a group of correspondents, to write up the Fleet at Hampton Roads. Ever since in my early years I'd been told, whether truly I do not know, that one of our ancestors was the redoubtable John Paul Jones, a feeling for the Navy had been planted in me deep. And now I found at Hampton Roads, reaching far as eye could see—with the sea roads and lanes between filled with little launches and speedboats dashing here and there—a great ocean city of armored ships, which sparkled and flashed and twinkled at night and winked countless messages. Down through the center on Sunday morning came the Mayflower, the President's yacht. At her bow a bugler blew a call to each pair of battleships it passed, and in answer came the crash of bands playing The Star Spangled Banner!

What had all this glory to do with the mud and blood of war I had seen? But these vessels meant business, I soon learned. The Utah, on which I lived for a week, was training some two thousand young Gobs from all over the country, East and West. From dawn until midnight the big ship hummed with numberless activities, in rigging, in turrets, on gun decks, in blacksmith, rope and carpentry shops. On her I went out to sea to watch her target practice. I took my meals in the junior ward and, late for breakfast one fine day when I'd lazily slept till seven o'clock, I had a noisy meal alone, with a battery on each side of me firing through the open ports. A few hours later, high above in the turret of a monstrous gun, I perched on a narrow ledge of steel, with the gun crew close around me, deafened by the crash and roar of ponderous machinery. Each time that a projectile was launched upon its twelve-mile flight, the great breach opened and with a shriek sent out a blast of ether that filled the turret, sickened me and made me suddenly aware that not only on land was the foulness of war, and that the grim business of death, destruction and defense stood foremost in the purpose of this glorious ship at sea.

So passed six or seven weeks of work for me in Washington. But I grew impatient to go "over there," and a plan began to take shape in my head. In Washington I sat one night on a bench in Lafayette Square, looking at the lovely old White House. With motorcars constantly coming and going, it was a busy place that night. I knew how anxious the man inside was to prove to the new Russian Republic, through substantial aid from us, that America was its friend, and to encourage by such aid its leader Kerensky to keep what was left of the Russian army still upon the eastern front. And I knew Russia. I had been there and had kept in constant touch with its movement for freedom since, both by letter and through talks with Russians who came to New York, and with my friend Bullard, who knew Russia far better than I. Only a few months ago, while that country was floundering down to defeat through the stupidity and graft and pro-German intrigue in the Old Regime, a letter had come from Babushka, Katherine Breshkovsky. Exiled for a second time to a hamlet in Siberia, from her snowbound little hut the heroic old woman had written me:

"My very dear friend Ernest Poole! It was such joyful surprise to me—your dear letter with picture of your wife and little sons. I put them on my table quite near to my eyes, and I greet her first because she is a woman and second because she is your wife. I am so happy to have such friends as your America gave me for the end of my hard spent life. I am healthy and strong enough and I feel quiet for myself, knowing that my children will never forget their grandmother who loves them so sincerely. But oh, my boy, I wonder how long the humanity in my country will suffer all the wrongs this war is crowding so heavy over its heads! The pro-German cabal in the Czar's regime slaughters our poor boys at the front by millions through lack of the bullets and guns. Starvation and taxes spread over our land and the torturings of our peasants are over all descriptions now! Only the hope of better future gives forces to support them!"

So she had written six months before. And now that better future seemed about to be realized. Back came my thoughts to the man in the White House, his wish to prove to the new free Russia that America was their friend. But back of that friendship he must have public opinion over here, and most Americans knew so little of Russia's long struggle to be free. So why should I not go over at once and write a series of articles describing the Russia of today? I knocked the ashes from my pipe and went to the stifling office room where Arthur Bullard was still at work.

"How about our going to Russia?" I asked.

"The sooner the better," he replied. "I've already had it in mind."

I went that week to Philadelphia, saw Lorimer and arranged for some Russian articles for the Post. Next, in New York I got a job as ambulance driver in a British hospital unit still active on the Russian front. Then I had my life insured for the trip and, in those days when the challenge of war was working deep in most of us, it was some satisfaction to learn that the insurance company rated my risk as high as though I had gone in our army to France. I had just time left for a hasty trip to my family in the mountains. From here my wife went down with me to New York to see me off. We slept in our apartment that night and next morning were awakened by a special-delivery letter from my publishers, Macmillan's, inclosing one sent to me in their care from my old friend Tarasov in Russia! We had not written to each other for something over eleven years; but a copy of my book, The Harbor, had been given to him over there, so he had my publisher's address.

"Come to Russia," he wrote. "What happens now here will deeply shake all the rest of the world when smoke of this war has cleared away."

XXV

How make the new free Russia feel that America was her friend? What aid did she want from us? Could she hold the Germans on her front until our armies got to France? On our small Norwegian boat, well above the torpedo zone, one evening far North where the midnight sun flooded the ocean still with light, I stood with Bullard by the rail. He pulled out a letter and asked:

"Have you got all the points in this?"

"I have."

"So have I." He tore it up and threw the pieces overboard. One didn't keep such letters, those days, not letters like this one from Colonel House, the man so close to our President.

Through Norway and Sweden by train we went up to the head of the Baltic Sea, and around the Gulf of Bothnia came down into Russia from the North. What an ironical change since then! For the forests through which we came have since been filled with masses of troops, launched by a Red dictatorship and rolling in on Finland, there to be slaughtered by the guns of men fighting to stay free! On the frontier we were delayed five hours by a railroad strike, and out of our train to talk with the strikers poured hundreds of Russians from New York, revolutionists coming home. As they argued the pros and cons of the strike, the place became a bedlam. And when to escape from the uproar I walked into the cool pine forest near by, back there under the huge dark trees, reaching far as I could see, were enormous stacks of barrels and crates—war munitions and food supplies bought in our own and other countries at exorbitant prices by corrupt agents of the Czar and, through Russian railroad mismanagement and German intrigue, left still up on the frontier, while the Russian armies had been starved and slaughtered for lack of food and shells and guns! Twenty-three years have gone since then but again those forests have been scenes of death by confusion and delay.

Our train, at last allowed to start, was slowly hauled by a war-weary panting locomotive, with showers of sparks from her wood fuel, on the trip south to Petrograd, which had been St. Petersburg and which is Leningrad today. How different from my train ride into Russia that winter years before, when I'd dreamed of revolution clean as the spotless sparkling snow! Arriving after midnight, we drove to the *Hôtel de France* and found that whole immense old building in the throes of another strike—of waiters, cooks and chambermaids. Supperless and tired out, we were led by a proprietor even more weary than ourselves up broad winding stairways and through long carpeted corridors, with only a dim light here and there to show the refuse, dirt and dust. In my room the bed had not been made. Pulling together the dirty sheets, I undressed and tumbled in. I was roused next day by a knock on my door and in came my good friend, Bill Shepherd of the United Press, who had been in Russia three months. Under his leadership our small group of American correspondents, including Dosch-Fleurot just come from France, went down to a huge pantry, where from floor to ceiling were piled dirty cups and plates and coffeepots. We picked some out and rinsed them well, then went to the kitchen, where one old cook, who had not gone on strike with the rest, gave us vile black coffee and big chunks of soggy rye bread. Each with his breakfast on a tray, we followed Bill Shepherd back to our rooms. As he led us in slow procession up the broad grand stairway, he said solemnly:

"War correspondents."

We laughed at that. But we found very little else to laugh

about in the next few days. Where was the new free Russia?
Heavy gloom was all around us and beneath it we could feel
a tension of nerves as before a storm. In our immense hotel
one night, in one of its long dark corridors, a woman came
quickly around a corner and bumped into me. Then she
screamed and fell on her knees and huddled close against the
wall! I shall never forget the Nevsky in those hot and sultry
days and through those long White Nights of the North,
filled with dense processions of traffic—military automobiles,
motorcycles, ambulance cars, enormous army trucks and lorries, countless little droshkies and peasant carts with wooden
yokes over the sweating necks of the horses. Gone was all the
brilliancy and sparkle and pomp of former days. With a harsh
clamor of voices, soldiers and civilians passed, most of the
soldiers tramping along in dirty boots and uniforms, with an
air of derisive indifference for the officers who came by.
Bread, tea, sugar and cigarettes were so scarce that, to buy
them, people stood waiting for hours in line. I saw crowds in
front of war bulletins. At midnight they would still be there,
with the yellow glare from the newspaper-office windows
striking down on their upturned faces and their anxious
gleaming eyes. Meetings, meetings everywhere—on the streets,
in halls and theaters and in stifling little rooms—where by the
hour people discussed the problems of revolution and war.

I went to the small office of the British ambulance unit, in
which I had intended to serve and so get a look at the Russian
front.

"No use," they told me. "Under the preaching of Bolsheviki in German pay, the Russian armies are crumbling fast, so
we're going to France for service there."

"I'm staying in Russia," I replied. With Bullard I talked to
various members of Kerensky's government, Social Revolutionists and liberals, old friends of ours. They were making
desperate efforts still to keep Russia in the war and so insure
her freedom against invasion later on by a victorious Ger-

many. But in every effort they were balked by a new organization, the first All Russian Soviet; for though the majority there, the Social Revolutionists, were friendly to Kerensky still, they too were blocked by an aggressive noisy group of Bolsheviki, who kept shouting:

"Peace for the people! Land for the peasants! Bread for the workers! End the war!"

To get to the heart of the trouble I chose a Bolshevik as interpreter. He was a strong-looking man with quiet clever confident eyes. Having spent half his life in Siberia for his ideas, he felt sure now his time had come.

"There's nothing that can stop us," he said. "Workingmen and peasants, army and navy, all are ours or will be soon. Peace, land and bread, that's what they want, and they know we can give it and we alone. For this we work from the bottom up, organizing everywhere. This isn't just a Russian affair. We mean to see the Junkers in Germany and Austria and France and England and everywhere else put out of business! A year from now the fellows who have been shouting: 'Go on with the war!' will be saying: 'We've had enough!' But the rest of us won't be Pacifists then—we'll go right on all over the world until the one big job is done!"

He took me to the old Tauride Palace, headquarters of the Soviet. Out on the edge of the city, surrounded by a spacious park, it had been built for one of her lovers long ago by Catherine the Great. An immense low rambling building of white and yellow stucco, it ran around three sides of a court; and from three porticoes in there, in strained excited voices, speakers shouted down to crowds of workingmen, half of them armed. With my Bolshevist interpreter, I wedged through the entrance door and came into a lofty hall crowded with hot sweating men, most of them talking. What a din! In the middle, a speaker shouted hoarsely but nobody seemed to hear. The air was thick and humid and filled with body odors. All around lay scores of soldiers asleep, with their rifles stacked close by, while others sat about buckets of soup and ate big chunks of black bread, or drank tea from their tin cups. On every hand were dirty papers, heaps of garbage. At tables along the walls sat men and women writing.

We walked through and up a low flight of stairs to a gallery, from which I looked down into a huge square chamber with a large skylight overhead that threw a soft light on the men below, at desks in semicircular rows—the All Russian Soviet of Workmen's and Soldiers' Deputies. About a hundred of them were labor representatives. There were a hundred soldiers, too, and half as many sailors. I saw some fifty officers and about as many more who wore on their breasts the white cross of the university graduate. My eye ran up and down the rows of suits and blouses, black and brown. The broad white sailor collars and the officers' gold epaulets gave touches of color here and there but the main effect was sober enough. Some leaned back with cigarettes, others bent forward on their elbows listening intently. The speeches were short, about five minutes each, and were made from a high speakers' box which stood in front of the president's seat. From outside came a hum of voices and the rhythmic tramp of feet. As the afternoon wore on, many delegations came to plead before this parliament; and the soldier guards at the door, with their rifles and fixed bayonets, gave a grim aspect to it all. For several hours the debate was orderly and quiet. Then abruptly from the Bolsheviki, who numbered only twenty per cent of the four hundred delegates, came an outburst of angry cries and, in the uproar that ensued, again and again I caught the words:

"Peace for the people! Land for the peasants! Bread for the workers! End the war!"

With this slogan rapidly gaining recruits, the Bolsheviki grew impatient and, only a few days after I came, they made in the city their first attempt to seize control of the government.

On a sultry July evening, in the gray light of a Northern night, with Bill Shepherd I made my way through crowded streets to the lower Nevsky. We found it wholly black with people, massed across from wall to wall. A bareheaded speaker, who stood on the seat of an automobile, was shouting to them in a voice that was high-pitched and quivering. The feeling of panic was in the air. All up the great dim thoroughfare extended that dark human mass; while through narrow lanes at the sides armed motorcars sped up and down. And yet through it all, it seemed to me, the people around me did not respond; they looked only uneasy and alarmed. Now the dusk grew deeper and from the motors headlights flashed. Nearly every car had a machine gun and was packed with workingmen, students and soldiers armed with rifles and revolvers. I heard a low incessant roar and the trampling of countless feet, piercing whistles, the honk of horns; speakers shouting on all sides. But still the crowds did not respond. They did not cheer the speakers and I felt no mass power there. The people began moving off to their homes.

But then, I think, some German agent, who felt that all chance of a riot was now rapidly slipping by, decided to act while there was time. From a big truck up the street came the long sharp ugly rattle of a machine gun and the buzz of bullets close above our heads. At once there was panic everywhere. In the rush I was carried off my feet; I threw up my arms, as I'd learned to do in the Princeton Cannon Rush years ago, and riding on shoulders was borne with the mob through an open gateway into a court. Behind, the fusillade increased, but I heard no shouts or screams. I looked back upon the street and saw it dense with people lying on their faces. Bullets were flying thick and fast, and I could hear the crash of shop-windows as men dived through to get indoors!

In the crowded courtyard where I stood, a hysterical boy with a Browning began to shoot haphazard. Again there was a rush for cover, into the barracks that faced on the court.

Through a window at the back I climbed and came out on a side street which ran along the Fontanka Canal. Four or five soldiers, dripping wet, were climbing up out of the canal, into which they had dived for safety. Two workmen near the corner were binding up a comrade's arm, and I saw a slender youngster pass holding his wrist with a queer dazed look. Blood was dripping from it.

I worked my way back to the Nevsky, and found the big street nearly empty. What a change from a few minutes before! I met an ambulance coming away but saw no bodies anywhere. It was fearfully hot, and the soldiers there drank greedily from the water hydrants, while others sat in long lines on the curbs, talking in low voices, most of them smoking cigarettes.

Again the excitement seemed at an end, and I turned to go back to my hotel. But all at once the street ahead grew dark with another surging mass of people. They drew quickly near. In front came lines of armed workingmen, the first of the world-famous Red Guard. By thousands they came streaming by—the same people who, at the very start of the revolution the spring before, had come marching out for Liberty, Equality, Fraternity. Five months had passed, and they had found little change in their war-weary lives; and so from their dark tenements they had come marching out again, looking for a strange new land where they should be the equals of all. Most of the men carried rifles, and here and there I saw a girl with a pistol in her hand. Some bore huge banners and red flags. A few sang the *Internationale,* but more were singing Russian songs. Many women had brought their children on this midnight people's march. I remember one who wore a white kerchief and walked with her arm around her small son. Her head was thrown a little back, and the strange dawn light fell on her face. She was singing softly, with glad eyes. A line of young girls passed me, smiling straight ahead of them. An old man came by, his hat back on his head; and he, too, sang loud and clear. Here was a group of laughing boys, but close behind them came a file of silent frowning workingmen, armed. And as that marching multitude swept on down the Nevsky, I could feel the turgid hungry soul of the whole vast dark country there. I watched till they had all gone by. I heard no shots nor any screams. The night's turmoil was over at last, and so I went back to my hotel and for a time sat making notes. Dead tired, I soon gave it up and from my bedroom window looked down into the street below. Now it was broad daylight. The street was absolutely still. Only a lean hungry dog was slowly and carefully sniffing about in the refuse for his breakfast.

XXVI

As the desperate goverment gathered what few troops in the city it could muster in its defense, street fighting broke out next morning and continued for three days and nights. With food scarce at our hotel, we gathered provisions in our rooms for hasty snacks between trips about town. The old *Hôtel de France* itself was on the edge of a fighting zone. Every few hours armored cars roared through the narrow street outside to pour machine-gun fire into the tremendous square of the Winter Palace close by, scene of the Gapon Massacre that had brought me to Russia twelve years before. Late one night I came back to my room and found my old friend Tarasov there. His letter had given his Moscow address and I had telegraphed to him to come and join me if he could. But how he had changed since last we met! He was in his early forties now. Huge of limb, he still looked strong, but his face was haggard, pale and drawn.

"What has happened to you?" I asked. Plainly the revolution, I thought, had played the devil with my friend. As I looked at him, there came to our ears the rattle of a machine gun outside. But Tarasov was not thinking of that.

"When she left me last week," he replied, "I lay on the floor like a man who is dead!"

Then he told me all about the girl. What dark beautiful features she had, and a form that would have driven the old Greek sculptors to despair! In short, a goddess! How he had labored with the wench, to educate her and give her a soul! They had lived together for two years—and then last week she had left him for an empty-headed young cavalry officer home from the front! What a young animal! Well, she was gone, and he was ready to go where I liked, anywhere in his country, he said. But Tarasov was gloomy about Russia now.

"We are sliding down into the hell," he declared. "From now comes chaos everywhere—with these damned followers of creeds trying to force their wild ideas on all our war-torn Russian life. Here you will find many men like me who are bitter because of the chance that was lost. We are bitter because of the happiness, the immense and amazing happiness, of those first weeks of the revolution, revealing what powers for brotherhood lie buried underneath the men. I am no dreamer; I am a chemist, smiling at all social dreams. But in those days I was quite changed, for I could feel beneath my feet this brotherhood like solid ground. People no more religious than me, and quite strangers, would embrace on the streets and say: 'Christ is risen! Russia is free!' There was no end to what we could have done, if only we had been shown the way by practical men of action here!

"I came one night into the square in front of the Winter Palace and found it black with swarming thousands. I made my way deep into the crowd. Thousands were singing, and all my thoughts and feelings were gripped by a force gigantic —like the world! But a new world! It was like a dream! Then suddenly I heard the word go 'round to burn the Palace, and soon that word grew into a roar! At once I thought of the Hermitage, which stood so close to the Palace that one could not burn without the other—the Hermitage with its Rembrandts and all its other treasures of art. I had often been there with my father, the painter; the place had been like a holy cathedral, my only religion as a child. So now I shouted to two men to lift me on their shoulders. This they did and I started to speak. My voice was strong. People listened and said: 'Hear this man.' I could feel the roaring stop. Hundreds and then thousands grew still.

" 'If you burn the Palace,' I cried, 'the Hermitage must burn as well! So I beg you to stop and ask yourselves: Shall our new republic be marked in black by history because it destroyed the loveliest pictures by men of all countries all over the earth? I beg of you, brothers, no, no, no!'

"I do not know what more I said, for like some fellow in a trance I felt myself rise high as I spoke until I was speaking down to them from somewhere in the cloudy sky. When I regained my senses I was lying on the pavement. There was dirty snow on my face and a soldier on his knees beside me was unbuttoning my shirt. The Winter Palace was not burned. I do not mean in the least to say that the Hermitage was saved by my speech—it was saved by the good will in those crowds. My speech played but one little part in the thoughts and passions deep and obscure that go surging through such a multitude. I was simply a molecule in a storm."

The light died out of his weary eyes.

"But now all that is gone," he said, "and with these damned squabblers—Bolsheviki, Mensheviki, Social Revolutionists, Kadets, Kerensky and the rest—Great Russia's life is in a swamp of black muddy schemes and lies that will lead to murder and robbery and last long after I am dead. Even tonight the slaughter starts."

The street fighting continued all next day, but late that evening from my room I heard singing in the street below and looking down I saw a Cossack regiment riding into town, with some field guns drawn by mules. With these they were able to clear the Nevsky. The government rallied its forces next day and the insurrection was put down. Eleven Cossacks had been killed, and Kerensky now proclaimed that these men who had given their lives to save the new republic should be buried in the graveyard where the Russian grand dukes lay. Into St. Isaac's Cathedral that night poured endlessly a colorful throng of Cossacks, soldiers, sailors, Red Cross nurses, priests and Tartars, Georgians and Circassians, in costumes

and in uniforms of a hundred kinds and hues. With Tarasov
I followed them inside. The great cathedral was so dark, you
could see only human shadows pressing close around you, but
on the stone-paved floor you heard the slow shuffle of thousands of feet. Borne along in that living tide, we came under the
cathedral dome, where the eleven dead Cossacks lay on cata-
falques raised high, with the tall candles at their sides revealing gleaming bayonets of their Cossack guard of honor. Then
I heard the crooning of a dirge from the Don plains, and
turned and saw behind me a boy in Cossack uniform. No, not
a boy, it was a girl—I could tell it by her voice and her eyes!
Tarasov spoke with her and learned how she had followed her
lover to war and fought by his side in his regiment. And now
he was dead. We learned no more, for the crowd pressed in
and swept us on. But we heard from her again next day, when
from the cathedral, watched by tens of thousands, came a gorgeous procession of priests and army and navy officers, with a
Cossack band that played a shrill soul-piercing funeral march.
Behind them in khaki uniform, bareheaded, walked Kerensky.
After him came eleven horses, with stirrups crossed over
empty saddles. Behind each horse a woman marched—and one
was the girl we'd seen last night, still in her Cossack uniform,
worn and patched from long service at the front. When at
last we came to the graves and Kerensky in his burial speech
turned to the Cossack widows and asked:

"What can our republic ever give you to repay your
losses?"— suddenly, sharp and vibrant, the girl widow's voice
rang out:

"Give me his horse!"

It was given her; and she leaped in the saddle and rode
away.

We talked with another young Cossack woman in a war
hospital that same week. Having fought, as so many of them
did, in her husband's regiment through the war, she had organized the Black Battalion of women and girls a few months

before and had been wounded with them at the front. Her left arm in plaster and her head all swathed in bandages, she lay on a hospital bed, smiling up with eyes like a hawk's, and told us what she thought of the battalion she had formed. It was all very well for women trained to fighting like herself, in regiments of men, she said; but all together in one battalion, women and girls, all raw recruits, were useless, for they lost their heads. She told how going over the top she had lost control of them and they had screamed and fought like wildcats, blindly, madly, all for nothing—for the Germans mowed them down!

"When I get well, I shall go back to my old regiment," she said.

Tarasov returned to Moscow next day, for he had some work to do; but he offered to give up his job and act as my interpreter, if only I would come with him out once more to the villages.

"I say to you what I said long ago—the real Russia is in the country," he said. "Beneath all these political squabbles and street riots in the towns, deep beneath and well outside, eighty per cent of all Russians are peasants and country people still. They are slow; they are quiet. It may be years, many long years before they will act—but in the end inevitably they will make Russia what they like."

"That's all very well for the future," I said, "but I was sent by my magazine to find whether Russia will stay in the war, and the answer to that is in cities and towns. Later I will gladly go with you to the villages, but first I must learn how the cities feel."

So Tarasov went to Moscow and I turned back to my Bolshevist guide. In those next days upon the streets, as we watched many trucks go by filled with Bolshevist prisoners, men active in the recent revolt, my guide was scornful and amused.

"Why only lock them up?" he asked. "Why not shoot

every one of them down? That is how a strong government acts in an emergency like this. But Kerensky is a bourgeois still. His new republic must be kind and not kill men for their ideas. Free speech and democracy—what twaddle and what sentiment! And who are these that go to jail? Only little leaders all. Our big men, Lenin and the rest, have got away and are in hiding, waiting till time comes to act."

He took me to cellars and tenement rooms and empty factories at night, where we talked with groups of men and boys and watched them being drilled to fight. They already had thousands of rifles and machine guns and were getting control of half the big munitions plants. Where were Kerensky's spies and police? More and more I was made to feel the weakness of his government, compared with the forces pent up beneath —the same forces I had felt before on that first Russian trip of mine. But my sympathies were not with them now, for most of my friends from years gone by, the Social Revolutionists, were working desperately still to save the new republic and help the Allies win the war. They felt as I did at the time, that, if Germany won, it would not be long till she sent her veteran armies East to steam-roller Russia's freedom and make all Europe a Junker land. I heard this feeling strongly confirmed one day by Babushka, my old friend. With Bullard I went to the Winter Palace, for we had heard that she was there. Nobody stopped us. Through empty halls and up stairways and through more halls, we wandered in search of our friend. At last we found an old palace official. His weary wrinkled face was grim.

"I am tired of this place," he said. "It is not what it used to be. And these six hundred cooks, they bother me so!"

"Cooks?"

"Yes, cooks," he answered. "When the family of the Czar moved years ago out to Tzarskoe Selo, six hundred cooks were left behind. For years they have slept and eaten here—and what a dirt they make all around! And now they say they will organize into a little soviet!" When we asked for Babushka, he answered:

"She does not often sleep here now, for most of her time she spends at the front. But I think she came back last night. We shall see."

We followed him down a long corridor into a handsome billiard room, where he drew himself up and announced in low reverential tones:

"Nicholas the Second deigned to play billiards here when he was young."

We found Babushka in her room close by. In her seventies now, with hair snowy-white, her great powerful wrinkled face showed even more vitality than when I'd seen her last in New York.

"Bullard, my boy! Poole, my boy!" In a moment she had us in her arms, and she told me with her wonderful smile: "From Siberia I brought back the picture of your dear wife and your little sons!"

From her second exile, freed by the new republic, she had been brought by sledge and sleigh and then by automobile back home, with welcoming crowds to greet her in every village and town she came through.

"I traveled day and night," she said, "for I was so eager to work for Free Russia! Ah, boys, it was good to be back in my home! But what a home!" With a quick deep chuckle she turned to the window and pointed across the river to the grim fortress prison of St. Peter and St. Paul, where in solitary confinement for years she had talked with comrades in cells all around her, by rapping code signals on a pipe. "That was my old home," she said, "and this is my new one! How funny is life!"

But she did not care to stay here, she said; her real home now was a sleeping car in which she traveled along the front, speaking to enormous crowds of war-weary soldiers, her boys, begging them to stay in the war and keep the revolution safe.

" 'Boys, dear boys!' I cry to them. 'If you let Germany win this war, their armies will come marching into our beloved land and back you will go to slavery!' That is how I speak to them—nor do I speak any longer alone—for I have nearly two hundred brave lads, wounded and crippled in the war and for acts of courage wearing still the Cross of St. George, who keep going like me along the lines, telling the troops why we must fight on until the war is over and our hard-won freedom is safe from the Kaiser and the Czar! The boys all listen and mutinies die. But after us come Bolsheviki agitators in German pay, preaching peace and shouting: 'Go home!' And back here in the cities they talk in the factories day and night, stopping all work and stirring up strikes. They are bold in the cities, for there they are strong. But the cities are still only a tiny part of this mighty land, and out in the villages we Social Revolutionists are strong as we have always been. There a new free Russia will rise! For we shall give the land to the peasants and build thousands of country schools and agricultural colleges to teach how best to till the soil! Land and bread and freedom—and peace as soon as peace is safe from danger of old slavery!" At the end of our talk she said: "Poole, go to the villages, my boy!"

I wanted to see Moscow first, so I went there with Bullard and joined Tarasov and, in the huge dirty building that housed the Moscow Soviet, listening, watching, we made our way through arguing and shouting crowds outside of the committee rooms. The Bolshevist leaders whom we met were all of them even more confident there; but as they planned behind closed doors, we talked with the people massed outside, workingmen and deserting soldiers; and among them we could find only deep confusion still.

We listened to a deserter one night, in a stifling basement teahouse packed with others like himself, who filled the place with smoke and din. No liquor was sold in Russia then, but in the Russian army the belief had spread that, if you strained wood alcohol through your gas mask, it would do you no harm. A group of them now were doing just that and already they were very drunk. All the others drank only tea, but their minds were drunk with the excitement of that slogan—Peace, land, bread! Close by us a young peasant soldier, with a look of angry grievance in his big bewildered eyes, was telling two companions of a talk he'd had at the front with his young captain the week before:

"He was a gay young devil, that *barin*. All my life I'd known him well. We'd fished and hunted when we were boys, for his father owned the big estate and mine worked in the stables there. So the young *barin* took me off to the war, and I shined his boots and looked after his horse and cleaned his clothes like a regular slave. But now we were free and we fellows had talked and said: 'All Holy Russia is ours.' And so we grabbed our officers and told them we would run things. Then my young *barin* sent for me and, when I came into his tent, he sat smiling in such a devil's way as he smoked his cigarette. Up he jumps and salutes me and says:

" 'Now you will rule all Russia, my boy, so you must tell what you will command. How will you get food for the army and shells for the guns?'

" 'We need no guns,' I said to him. 'We're sick of this war; we're going home!'

" 'Ah, home to Holy Russia!' he cried. 'And there, please tell me, what will you do? For you must rule all Russia now. How will you manage our big estate? To get new plows and all that you need, you must manage the towns and factories, too. How will you run them; what will your wise orders be? Please—I am interested, my boy. I am your servant. What shall I do? Humbly I will take my place, but now you must plan for me and for us all. So what are the plans in your wise head for tilling the land and selling the grain and running the railroads and the mills and all the government?'

"So many questions so quickly he asked that he got my whole head spinning around! Then he laughed, the young devil, and quick as a flash with a pistol he blew a big hole in his head—and there he lay in front of me, dead! It made me so mad I wanted to kick him! What right had he to treat me like that?"

Up in the Kremlin one afternoon Tarasov and I sat watching groups of other peasant soldiers, who came and stood silently scowling up at the great bronze statue of one of the Czars. Suddenly I heard a voice speak in English, close at my side:

"It is interesting, isn't it so?" I turned to a smiling little Russian in a soft shirt and flowing tie, who shared the bench on which we sat. " 'What will we build in place of this Czar? How will we manage Russia?' they ask. They do not know how. They will manage so badly that soon there will be ruin here. Only this week I have closed my office, and I have rubles for food for two months. After that, God only knows what this revolution will do to my life." He still smiled. "But I have no good right to complain, because I myself as an architect have conducted a little revolution of my own in Moscow for years, tearing down such lovely old homes and in their place building modern apartments with plumbing, steam heating and all the rest. Would you like me to show you the few lovely old houses still left, before they are all swept away?"

I said that we would; and for hours that evening, in the long gray twilight, he took us through regions of the town where upon tree-shaded streets were long low stucco houses in the French style of Louis the Fifteenth. And he took us into large courtyards behind them, lined with stables and workshops and huts, the living and working quarters of the family serfs of old days, when each autumn from their country estates, in long caravans of coaches and wagons, the great families drove to town, bringing not only household serfs but their own carpenters, cobblers and blacksmiths. In one such yard stood a little chapel and, with a tingling glow of surprise, I heard our companion say:

"In this chapel two people were married one day about a hundred years ago. Count Leo Tolstoy knew them well, so he put them into his book, War and Peace. He called them Natasha and Pierre."

Toward midnight our guide left us in a dreary little park filled with deserters from the front, who sat on benches or on curbstones, eating thousands of sunflower seeds to ease the craving for cigarettes. Tarasov said:

"It is late, we are tired and your hotel is far away from us over the town. I shall take you to a place near by and there you shall sleep in such a room as never in your life have you known. It is the very little home of an enormous friend of mine; and when she is out of the city, she asks me to sleep there when I like."

In a building a short distance away, we came up a flight of stairs to the door of a small apartment. The old servant who opened it bowed and smiled and led us into a tiny salon.

"I shall sleep here," Tarasov said, "but you shall have the bedroom. Come."

When we entered the low-ceilinged room close by, I stopped short and felt like rubbing my eyes. On all four walls from ceiling to floor hung a dizzying mass of broad satin ribbons of many hues, all swaying gently back and forth in the light hot breeze through the open window.

"Who is she?" I demanded.

"Our Russian Schumann-Heink," he smiled. "In opera houses all over the world, she has saved the large ribbons from her bouquets and brought them home, for she holds them dear. And this old woman is so loved by people of all classes here that not even revolution can very greatly change her life. For still she will sing under any regime. Come now to her piano and look in her photographs, how she has grown!" He showed me one of a slim young girl and another of a woman

enormous. From her immensity I turned to the small rose-
wood bed by the wall, with cupids carved upon its head. And
in that bed I slept that night!

"If you would look far ahead into the future of Russia,"
Tarasov said to me one day, "do not look at the storm on the
surface but into the waters underneath—not so many fathoms
deep. You will find the real soul of Russia there—not what all
these planners would make us to be but what we Russians
have really been and what we are and shall be again, when all
the storm has blown away."

And he gave me a revealing glimpse into such deep waters
that day, in a monastery not far out of town, where we talked
with an amazing old man, head of the Old Believer sect. Long
ago, when the Russian Church was brought under the power
of the Czar, the Old Believers had held out for freedom to
worship as they pleased and to live according to the commands not of their Czar but of their God. They had refused
to change their ways. Even to many minor rites they had held
with grim fanatic zeal. For this they'd been tortured and
burned at the stake and massacred by thousands. But retreat-
ing to lonely regions down along the southeastern frontiers,
through centuries they had kept alive and made converts
among the Cossacks there. The name Cossack comes from an
old Russian word that meant bachelor or single man, and
Peter the Great had placed such men by thousands down there
to hold back the Tartars. Like our early cowboys, those Cossacks were a wild rough crowd, trained to violence from birth.
But the independent ways of the Old Believer sect appealed
to some so strongly that many of their leaders joined. And as
owners of great cattle ranches and of millions of acres of
wheat became members of the sect, their power grew at last
to a point where government persecution ceased.

But though his church was wealthy, the Archbishop himself lived in a cabin of four small rooms. In the one where he

received us, the log walls were unplastered and the floor was of bare planks. This old man, reared on the plains and still strong as a bull at sixty-five, had broad shoulders, a square face of hard solid muscle and keen gray eyes. He wore a black gown and on his head was a high purple hat. But how different from other priests! When he learned I was an American, he pounced on me with questions about our tractors, gang plows, reapers and binders—all with a close knowledge that soon had me floundering! When he saw my confusion and surprise, he smiled grimly and he said:

"We are old believers in new things. Long ago, when the Czar emancipated the serfs, one of our bishops said to him: 'This new thing that you have done is only part of our old belief—in liberty and brotherhood.' And it has been so ever since. For the deepest part of our belief is our faith in the progress of mankind, through liberty and mutual aid, and hard work and education—always learning what is new—up the great long road to God. The God that we believe in commands that we better the lives of the people. More than half our people are peasants who live by the land, so we teach them better methods of tillage, stockbreeding and all the work on a farm. But in that, to compete with the rest of the world, we need the machines of these modern times. In them your great republic stands first and, if she would prove her friendship now, let her send us such machines by thousands. Our credit is good, if she will wait, for the resources of Russia are boundless, once we can get them out of the earth.

"I have been for the war from the start," he declared. "To drive it through to victory, this is in my Cossack blood. There can be no peace between Free Russia and the man who rules from Berlin. When we heard that your country would stand by our side, our hearts grew warm. Let us win the war and, when it is won, let us bind your country and ours together both in trade and industry. For no real freedom can come to our land except through the practical knowledge that has made your country what it is. To be free we must be strong. Broad moral education and practical instruction, these must be bound together tight. Our plan for building a nation is first to gather its citizens into small congregations like ours—which are not only religious concerns but manage education, too, and all the vital business of life—and then very slowly, one by one, to weld all these cooperative groups into a solid body, in such a way that, while each one is largely independent, still it is bound to all the rest. So we shall build a democracy of liberty and brotherhood. Cooperation is our cry. Our works of irrigation are only another form of it, and they have met with huge success. So we shall spread the plan through our life —to work together as brothers and then divide the produce in shares. Nothing hasty, nothing wild. In a steady practical way we shall form joint-stock concerns for farming and for industry. Only so can Russia be free from the ignorance and misery here.

"In the cities the revolutionists talk. They laugh and blaspheme about our God and promise the people a heaven on earth. But what do they know about tilling the soil? Nothing, I tell you, nothing at all! So, if by all their promises they blind the people and seize control, millions will die of famine and in the cities blood will flow. And if by armed force they keep their power, often and often the world will hear of bloody deaths by execution of those like us who refuse to bow down. To win back the freedom we love took us long centuries before. It may take centuries once more. But never forget us and men of our kind—for in forests, in villages, out on the plains, we shall be working everywhere still, working for freedom to work and live and worship the Great God as we will!"

XXVII

From the fire and vitality of that powerful old priest, we came next to some one of paler hue, an appealing mild old man, who made me feel how the life of Old Russia was sinking inevitably to its doom. Near Moscow we visited on the estate of a liberal prince who, as president of the local *zemstvo*, had spent all his active years in work to better the lives of the peasants. For this he had been exiled twice to Siberia by the Old Regime. But now all his labors had come to an end. We found his small provincial town filled with soldier deserters rapidly being organized by Bolshevist agitators. Already the *zemstvo* had been closed. From the building he came out to meet us with huge books of record under his arm.

"These are the records of my life's work. Today it is all ended," he said. Tall and stoop-shouldered, with hair and beard already gray, looking like some old professor in his shabby linen duster, with spectacles over kindly eyes, he read the letter I had brought from his brother in America and at once invited us to come and stay on his estate. On that drive of twenty miles in his little droshky, he pointed out along the road the schoolhouses, dispensaries and cooperative stores built by the *zemstvo* under his lead.

"Our progress has been slow," he said, "for we were balked at every turn, not only by the Czar's regime but by those of our neighbors who wasted their land and oppressed their peasants. Look at that, for example," he said, and he pointed to a massive stone Egyptian pyramid close by. "That is an icehouse. To build it took the hard labor of countless serfs and even the deaths of some of them—and all for one rich landowner's whim. So now we must suffer for their sins. For on top of all this oppression and waste the government plunged us into a war where millions of our best young men and our horses and cattle have been killed. So the peasants have grown desperate and the Bolsheviki here will soon set them to seizing our estates. Already some have been pillaged and burned."

"Will you come to America?" I asked.

"No, I love Russia. This is my home."

His home was a friendly hospitable place. Upon a high river bluff, with a river winding past below, a pine wood on either side and great fields spreading out behind, it looked like some Virginia homes I'd visited in my Princeton days— a white frame house with wings at the sides, slender wood columns at the front and behind it a little village of huts where had lived the workers of the estate. Of seventy in former times, only two men and a boy were left; and of a score of house servants, only one old cook remained. While his wife and two grown daughters attended to the housework, the old prince and his two small sons (the two older boys had been killed at the front) helped the men in the gardens and in the stables; and with garden produce, chickens and eggs, milk and butter, and fish from the river, they were able to live still. Three rifles standing in the hall were the only grim re-minders of the menace of attack. Meanwhile each day they swam in the river, talked and laughed, told stories and sang folk songs, with friends who came from estates near by. Gath-ered around a long table about nine o'clock each night for cold supper, tea and cigarettes, their discussions and stories flowed easily on. When it came their bedtime, the two little princes, dressed in threadbare blouses and shorts, at a signal from their mother, rose and came around the table, lifting the hand of each woman or girl to their lips. And so good night.

Good night to Old Russia, I thought, and to the liberal movement I'd known; good night to its most appealing and friendly and most lovable traits. We prolonged our visit to a week. I remember still how, when we left, they smiled and waved to me good-by. What became of them all? I never knew.

Returning to Moscow, we journeyed by train up to the province of Yaroslav and, passing by the landowners, we went straight to the peasants there. Driving when we could find a cart, more often tramping through the mud of winding little roads, and sleeping at night in huts and barns, we visited scores of villages surrounded by forests of birch and pine. And we found only gloom and despair. Not only had three years of war robbed them of their strongest men and most of their horses, cattle and pigs. They told of the dearth of plows and spades and all other tools for tilling the soil. Already in their tiny fields the weeds grew thick and rank and high. The summer's harvest they had hidden deep in the forests, to keep it safe from government agents. They looked at us with suspicion and asked:

"What in Christ's name do you want here? Why are you spying on us like this?"

All the more vivid by contrast was the story that we heard from a young peasant woman one night. At the end of a day's tramp in the rain, reaching a village long after nightfall, we found the huts all dark but one, in which from the window shone a light. Tarasov knocked, and a little woman with bright black eyes appeared with a candle and let us in. The air inside was heavy and hot, and the log walls literally crawled with flies. A little girl lay sleeping on a mattress on the floor, and on a long chest by the wall an old woman with dirty feet lay on her side, wheezing painfully. We asked if we might sleep in the barn. The little woman said we could, but insisted on giving us supper first. Tired and hungry, we sat

down, while she bustled about on bare feet. In the tall brass
samovar she soon had water boiling, and into it she dropped
six eggs—three for each of us, she laughed, because that was
a holy number. She made tea and brought out an earthenware
jar of rich cool milk, a pat of fresh butter and a loaf of dark
rye bread. In her corner the old woman snored. Our hostess
poured our tea for us and sat down while we had our supper.
When we asked her to join us, she said with a smile that she
was too tired. She had been mowing in her small field from
early morning till nine that night.

"My bones all ache in such a way that I don't want to eat,"
she said. Her low sweet voice was husky, and from time to
time she coughed. Her breast was flat and her shoulders
stooped, she had big overdeveloped arms, and the nails were
worn half off her stubby little fingers. But she was not too
tired to talk. When she heard that I was an American, her
small black eyes grew doubly bright. She threw out rapid
questions about my country and what I had seen in Russia.
Her excitement increased. On her narrow face, with its sharp
little nose, the color heightened; and she was soon talking
eagerly of the revolution and what it had meant in the village
life. She leaned forward in the candlelight, and talked on so
rapidly it was hard to get our questions in. At midnight the
old woman woke up. Again and again she muttered and
wheezed, and at last she shouted:

"Take those *barins* out to the barn!"

Her daughter jumped up and led the way in her bare feet
out to a little log barn. And there until nearly daylight, we
sat on the log sill in the doorway, while in true Russian fashion
she poured out her very soul.

"I have been all alone!" she said. "I have never had a
chance in my life to talk like this to anyone—and I may never
have it again! I want to tell you all I can!"

She went far back of the revolution into the life of the great
"dark people," the peasants, and her own life as a child. The

rain had stopped and a big pale moon hung over the trees on the river bottom. She coughed and coughed, then hurried on.

She was thirty-one years old. Born in the squalor and ignorance of this hut where she lived now, she had not found it so bad at first, for her father had loved her and he had taken her with him out to the fields or the forest, where he worked from dawn to dark. But he died and her uncle took his place; her mother often got drunk with him, and for the daughter life in the hut became at last unbearable. At fourteen she went to Moscow and worked in a dressmaking shop for two years. Then her mother grew sick and she came home and here her family forced her to marry a teamster who hauled goods from the town. He, too, was often drunk. He kicked her one night when she was pregnant, and so she lost her first baby, she said. But the village priest and all the women told her: "He is your husband. You must obey." Just before her second child came, he deserted her and she came home and here another child was born dead. She started a little shop in the village. He came back and drank all she earned. But again the priest and the women told her: "He is your husband. You must obey." At nineteen she escaped to Moscow, worked in the same shop as before, went to night school and studied half the night. But her teamster now had a job as a brakeman on a Moscow train; he often came and pestered her and took her wages. To get quite free, she moved to Warsaw, found work and saved money and went to night school as before. Then her husband got himself transferred to a Mos-cow—Warsaw train and, on his nights in Warsaw, made her live with him once more. She bore a third baby. It did not die. She slaved and scrimped for her little girl and, to give her a decent start in life, put her into a kindergarten run by some Swiss people she knew. She was happy there, she said. But then came the war and the German armies and, with her small girl in her arms, she walked all night among great crowds of Russian refugees like herself, until they could get on a train to Moscow. There she could find no work, so came home and took charge of this tiny farm. In the army her husband was killed at the front, and so now she was free to work for her child, the heart and center of her whole life.

"This village is a wretched place for my child to grow up in," she said. "A little girl should keep her soul just as clean as a dress that is new. But the whole village is dark with scandals of the very dirtiest kind, for here girls only ten years old run out with the boys at night. I am trying to think what to do with her. My mother is so old and sick I cannot leave the village, and the school here is so poor! All our village schools are poor, and the new Russian government has done nothing to make them better. How many millions of children are growing up to be savages! And this darkness of the people may last for generations still, for Russia may settle down as before. Now is the chance, and they let it go by!

"These political men have talked so much of what they are going to do for us, and they never see that our deepest hope is to be taught to do things ourselves. The only miracle in the world is one that comes with new wishes that grow up in people from inside. This miracle is in us all. I take my crop to the market and speak to men and women there, and hear little that is wrong; for I turn the talk to clean sensible things, and then their dirty chatter stops, and out of their mouths come words at times so wise that it is wonderful! I tell you we do not need to be dark! All we need is schools—*real* schools— to teach us how to work in such ways that all our lives will be better here! They wave red flags and tell us to work and raise food for the towns. But how can we work without any good tools? To till my little field of rye takes me weeks, for I have only a spade; and to mow it I have only a hand scythe and must go down on my knees to cut the grain by handfuls. With a horse and a mowing machine and a plow I could do all my work in half the time, and so I could be more with my child and not leave her alone in the hut with her granny, who scares her by the things she says! I could keep the hut clean, and raise vegetables and even a few flowers there! I have talked to so many peasant women, and so often I have found that they had the same idea in their heads. The things we would do if we had more time!

"But what a terrible waste there has been! What a start the revolution had, and how they have disappointed us! When it came, I joined the village committee that was to manage our affairs. Every minute I could spare from the fields I was writing for the committee. We wrote down all the peasants' names, we looked into the books of the church, we chose a gendarme of our own and we elected delegates. We worked often half the night but I never felt tired. I was glad! I thought that the new government would soon tell us all we should do. But instead of that, their political parties quarreled and fought. And that was wrong! They should have told us: 'Now work hard for the revolution! And this is just how you must do it!' If they had, how we would have worked! For what a spirit was here at the start! But fine words were not enough. We wanted real work, and it did not come—and all the great spirit went out in the dark! That was wrong, I tell you; it was wrong! And we must get that spirit back! God is not a great man in the clouds; He is a strange bright miracle that lives deep down in the spirit of every man and woman on earth! We must let this deeper spirit rise in the black darkness of our souls! As it is, I have to hunt in my mind for my thoughts as though they were lost in the night! I work in the field and I know I am thinking, but nothing seems to grow clear to me! But then, like a flash of lightning at night which shows you every house in the village, so my whole mind is lighted up! It is strange what we all have in us and what we would be if we had the chance! That is the one big miracle!"

As her low clear passionate voice rose loud in her excitement, at daybreak suddenly from the hut the old woman came hobbling out to the barn and, when she found us sitting there, she yelled at her daughter:

"You sleep with strange men! The priest shall know of this —he shall know!"

And then she dragged her back to the hut. An hour later we went on our way. I wonder what became of her?

Another story I'll never forget we heard from an old fisherman one evening in the following week. Down the Volga we had gone and in several river towns had seen the same picture of war weariness and gloom and Bolsheviki everywhere forming local soviets. We went to an open-air meeting one night, where from a torchlighted truck speakers shouted down at the crowd and answering shouts came from below. Soon the whole crowd was in little groups disputing and arguing. Fists were shaken; the uproar rose.

"Let's get out of this," I said. It was nearly midnight now.

"Very well," Tarasov agreed, "I shall take you to a quiet old man who thinks deeper than any of these. All his life he has fished on the Volga and I used to know him well, for my father painted a picture of him one summer when I was still a boy. Since then I have been here many times. I shall ask him to take us fishing tonight."

So we went to his hut by the riverside and found him sitting at the door, a stocky old man, white-headed now, but with shoulders broad and vigorous still. After a little talk with my friend, he rose and took us down to his boat and, as with slow and powerful strokes he rowed us far out on the great broad stream, the hubbub of angry little voices died behind us in the town. Out here the night was cold and still.

"It is too cold to fish," he said, and he rested his oars and looked up at the stars. Tarasov talked to him. He shook his head but, as my friend persisted, at last he sighed and answered:

"Very well, I will tell you once more the story they told."

He looked up again into the starry sky. "In the Holy Book it says the world was made in seven days—but old men here, when I was a boy and we fished together in the night, told me it took a mighty time. And this is the story that I heard." Again he was silent. Then he began: "So long ago that no little man can ever know how long it was, on a night as cold and still as this, through the wilderness of the sky the Mighty First One made His way. It was hard to go—and deep He breathed—and so cold it was that every breath became like a little white cloud behind him. In one of His moments that little cloud melted away in the cold still night. But only one of those little clouds became the whole Milky Way in our sky. For us that cloud is up there still and so it has been for a million years—a million years of our little time. But in His great time it was only a moment till the cloud melted and was gone. For one moment of His time is like a million years to men. So great He is. And little men, who shout and talk their little plans until the eyes of their souls go blind, would do well to stop their babbling, look up at the heavens and bow down."

He stared up in silence. We, too, were still. Then slowly he picked up his oars.

"I must go back to my hut," he said, "before they steal my nets back there. Thank God, I have my son's rifle still."

And he rowed with long strokes back to the shore.

XXVIII

FROM THE SOUTH WE WENT BACK TO PETROGRAD AND THENCE
by train and river boat we traveled north, to spend two weeks
upon Tarasov's little farm. From the station where we left
the train, we carried our bags down a high river bank to a
small steamer waiting below. It was night and she would not
start till dawn, so I lay down on the upper deck. Just a short
way up the river loomed the massive span of a bridge, and
every few minutes a long train would go thundering across,
leaving behind a white tail of wood smoke rising into the
dark of the sky. Soon I, too, would be crossing that bridge,
homeward bound across Siberia. I thought of the crowds
in those hot cars, arguing about the war; and then of the numberless rivers like this, upon which these same silent stars
were throwing their mysterious light, and of the countless
villages all over this war-ridden world. Into each the war had
come. How times had changed since my first trip to Russia
in her war with Japan! Then I'd been able to go home to an
America safe from war; but over the bridge of years we'd
been hurled since then into this other world, in which no
country was safe any more from the upheavals in the rest. I
thought of my own village back in the mountains of New
Hampshire. Some of its boys were already in camp, and their
parents were buying maps of Europe and the danger zones.
Soon every day and every night their thoughts would go out
over the sea to villages with foreign names. These villages all
over the world, would they come to know each other better
after all this gory waste, stop hating each other, realize how

all alike they dreaded war, and so impel their governments to
some great plan for a lasting peace? Well, at least I could do
my bit by picturing for our neighbors at home those Russian
villages I had seen and these I was now to see with my friend.
All next day our boat bore us north till at last we reached
our landing place and climbed the bank to a small log house.
There Tarasov drew a quiet breath and said:

"This is the place where I was born."

The house stood on a wooded bluff. Behind it were two
little barns and a hut for the peasant who worked the land for
him on shares. We entered through the kitchen and found a
stout Finnish woman, Tarasov's only servant, there. And
thence we came to what had been the studio of Tarasov's
father, a large square room with brown log walls, a studio window at one end and an easel with an unfinished canvas. Others
stood against the walls, pictures of peasants here in the North
and of others down in the Ukraine. In one corner was a narrow bed. But what a curious bedroom! For Tarasov had a
passion for farming and he had lived with his hobby here. A
mud-encrusted American plow leaned against the foot of the
bed, and a harrow lay close by. Spades and shovels and other
tools, and skis and snowshoes and a rifle, hung on wooden
pegs on the walls. Near me was a grindstone. I stumbled over
a rake on the floor.

"Tarasov," I said earnestly, "I hope to God you don't walk
in your sleep!"

"This will be your bedroom," he replied.

After a swim in the river, as we waited for supper in the
neglected garden near his house, in the high rank weeds I spied
the frame of a huge sledge, some twelve feet long by eight
feet wide. Stout oak posts rose at the sides, with tattered
shreds of blue velvet and satin dangling upon them still.

"What sledge was this?" I asked him.

"It belonged to my grandmother," he said. "And the whole
story of Russia is there." Tarasov lit a cigarette and then began

PICTURES TAKEN IN 1917 OF THE SCHOOLTEACHER AND THE COUNTRY-
SIDE NEAR TARASOV'S HOME

this narrative: "Though my father was a peasant's son, my mother's mother had been born in a family of high title and enormous wealth. She was brought up on a large estate, where there were over a thousand serfs and household servants by the score. She had French and German governesses. When in winter they went to Petrograd or to balls at other estates, there would be three or four great sledges with eight horses hitched to each, and they would travel day and night. When I was a little boy, often here my grandmother would sit with me in this old sledge, which was not so ruined then; and she would tell me stories of the long long rides they took, the singing and the sleigh bells and the wild music of the horns.

"Educated down in France, she was a girl of such character force that, when she came home at nineteen, she soon tired of the balls and soirees in the court life of the Czar; and she saw how her father, absorbed in his work as a high official there, was letting all his wealth be wasted by the thieving managers and stewards on his many estates. So she begged him to let her do what she might to save their wealth before it was gone. He agreed and he built for her this sledge. All covered it was, with arched roof and walls nearly a foot in thickness and heavy steel plates on the outside for protection against robber bands; but inside it was padded with satin and velvet. Four wide cushioned seats were there, and were made into sleeping berths at night. She had a silver washstand, too, and a small table and shelves for the books, for my young grandmother loved to read. So she traveled with her maids by day and the long winter nights over thousands of versts of little roads. Eight horses pulled her sledge along and twenty Cossacks rode as guard. More than once they drove off robber attacks.

"So she went from estate to estate and dealt with the thieving managers; but in spite of all that she could do, their fortune melted soon away. Then she married a professor of medicine in Petrograd; but later she left him and with her

baby, my mother, she came up to the North and built a cabin
on this spot, and here she lived all the rest of her life. Hard
she tried to show the peasants how they could improve their
land. In this my grandmother utterly failed, because she used
books on tillage sent from France, the country she loved, and
the needs of that mild climate were not the needs of the Russian North. But in spite of her failure, she was a woman of
such power of mind and heart in helping the peasants in their
homes that, when I was a little boy, all their disputings they
brought to her here. Like a judge she sat and gave decisions
with such a sound deep human sense that the peasants admired
and obeyed.

"Often when she had saved a bit, she would take her daughter to Petrograd. On one such trip, my mother grew acquainted with my father, who was a student in the Fine Arts
Academy. He was the son of a prosperous peasant in this
neighborhood. He married my mother and I was born. They
brought me here in the summer months and later it became
our home. And here from my grandmother I heard this story
I have told to you—of how a great family came down until its
daughter married a man risen from the peasant class. My
father was proud of his peasant blood, and later he reached to
his fame by painting pictures of village life. It is this life that
you shall see and describe for American villages, so that they
may know us better and at last become our friends."

All that next week we tramped about the countryside, visiting the huts of peasants in the little hamlets scattered along
both river banks. No regular hours; no regular meals. Just a
snack now and then in some peasant's hut. Through that rolling country of fields and woods and orchards, narrow dirt
roads wound like paths, and over them came tiny hayracks
drawn by ponies. Peasant men and women and children passed
Tarasov's cabin at all hours, day and night. A few wore boots
of leather or bark, but most of them went barefoot, and at

night in the darkness they would flit by without a sound. Whole families worked from dawn till dark in fields strange to American eyes. The land was divided in long thin strips of light green, yellow and silver gray, of oats and barley, flax and rye. For the village held the land in common, and about once in twenty years it was reapportioned according to the number of males in each family. Each would get a few thin strips, some of them barely ten feet wide, in different parts of the neighborhood.

In the huts we visited, we stirred great excitement soon. From our embassy in Petrograd, urged by Tarasov, I had procured a huge old tattered copy of an American catalogue, filled with pictures of tractors and plows and other machines and implements used upon American farms. This we showed to the peasants now and, slow at first to understand, as the pages were turned and they began to see the mechanical treasures there, their dull eyes gleamed and they bent close. With the excitement of starving men who see food, their questions came. The peasants were cattle, I'd heard in the towns; but here were keen shrewd farming men, firing questions that soon had me floundering! I remember one man of middle age, broad-shouldered and grizzled. As we sat on a bench in front of his hut, with the catalogue on his knees and his shaggy head bent down, slowly hundreds of pages he turned and, with his many questions, he kept us there straight through until night. I remember his bright scowling eyes straining to see in the deepening dusk. Again and again he muttered:

"Oh, if only we could have such things!" Once he looked up at Tarasov and said: "For Christ's sake, *barin*, beg your friend to send from his country such tractors here!"

"If your government would do as he asks," Tarasov told me on our way home, "and send a thousand tractor plows to plow land for our peasants everywhere, how every village would crowd around to watch the American miracle! No agitators from the towns could stir them up against you then;

they would say: 'America is our friend!' And that friendship would mean much to the peace of Europe in years ahead!' "

We developed his idea that night; and later, on my return to this country, I tried hard to put it through. But Russia had gone Bolshevist then and had made peace with Germany, leaving us with the Allies to win the war without her aid. And so all my efforts failed.

"Now you shall see what a store we have," said Tarasov, one day later that week. "It is a cooperative. The steadier peasants all belong. Each paid five rubles to buy a share, and we have already joined the Union of Cooperatives. With thirteen million members now, we are a power in Russia today and will be even stronger soon, if only the cities will let us grow!"

He took me to three small brick buildings owned by the Cooperative, on the edge of the river town; and we entered first the general store. Though its shelves and counters had been nearly emptied by the war, several peasant women and girls were gossiping there and looking over the last of the calico prints and ribbons, babies' caps and blankets. Behind the store was a log shed where once had been small harrows and plows, and in a larger building close by was a little farmers' bank where, if a peasant's assets were good, he could get cash at five per cent. On the walls of a room at the rear were crude and vivid chromos, showing fields of wheat and rye, first under the old-style cultivation with the resulting meager crops, and then with modern methods producing double or treble the yield. The largest chromo of them all displayed a peasant family before and after joining the Cooperative. They were shown at first in squalor and filth in front of a tumble-down old hut; the women and children, the horse, the cow and even the pig, puny and half starved to death. But then behold a miracle! A clean new house, a stable and barn, two stout horses and two cows and a pig fairly beaming with content—while the peasant, his wife and children, all ruddy with health and in brand-new clothes, smiled on their new environment. Over this picture was draped a red flag.

The third house was a little hospital. In the war the government had taken it for wounded soldiers, but the wounded had all left and, having thoroughly cleaned the place, the Co-operative was looking about for another doctor and a nurse. Meanwhile, on the upper floor, the local midwife was installed. She used two rooms for herself and the other two for maternity cases. She charged four rubles for each case. She was a genial bright little woman with quick vigorous movements and a humorous turned-up nose. In her small sunny room there were plants in the windows, gay curtains and pictures all about. After serving us tea, preserved cherries and bread, she brought out her cigarettes, and with a contented sigh she settled down for a good Russian talk.

"Just think! A real American here!"

She talked frankly of her twenty years of work with peasant women. She had never lost a mother, she claimed. The baby? That was different. One could not expect to save every child in such homes as these women had.

"Sometimes I meet a patient later. 'Well, what of the child?' I ask her. She answers, 'It lived,' or else, 'It died.'" The midwife shrugged her shoulders. "But there are wonderful women here; they are great breeders," she went on. "They will live and thrive where a horse would die." She smiled as she lit a fresh cigarette. "Well, since the revolution has come, the main difference I see is that the women have been quite changed, because now they have the right to vote. Their husbands used to thrash them—once a week when sober, and more often when they were drunk—but now each one on Saturday night shouts at her man when he comes with his stick: 'Just you try to beat me, and watch how I will spit in your face!' Besides, they come crowding to all the new meetings and say: 'We must all have our share! In this new land that we take from the *barins*, women and men must share alike!'"

I shall long remember something I saw in a hamlet on our way home that night. We found a peasant there, alone, scowling at two proclamations nailed to the log wall of a barn. One had been sent from Petrograd, urging the peasants everywhere to help in nationalizing the land. The other proclamation, laboriously written in ink, was more recent and was a local affair. Awkwardly inscribed were the names of some three hundred peasants, not only men but women, too, who lived in the neighboring villages. Here were the new voters of the Russian Republic. No local election had yet been held, but on the other half of the sheet was a list of a dozen candidates, and it was announced that the first election would take place the following month.

"You must think over carefully all these candidates," read the announcement, "so that when you come together, each one of you will have decided which are the ones he wants to elect."

At all this the peasant beside us was scowling in a puzzled way. We asked him what he thought of it.

"Well," he answered slowly, "we must have this meeting. We must have it because we need more land. But how we are to do it, God knows."

We left him standing in the dusk. And as we walked home I had a feeling that in numberless hamlets like this, mere specks in that boundless land of the North, other lonely figures were standing in the dusk that night, uncouth and silent, puzzling, trying to read the signs of the times, straining their eyes for a glimpse of the dawn. But the dawn was not yet. The dusk slowly deepened. Night was settling over the land.

As we tramped about the countryside, I came to notice what a part the river played in the lives of the people. It was their main highway still. Many came to the landing where the steamer stopped morning and night. Here they got their news of the world. And besides, with fishing and logging, the river helped them to eke out their hard living on the land. There were always peasants fishing, patient stolid figures kneeling in dugouts, working in pairs with a long coarse fishing net between. Often they caught the sturgeon so prized for its roe, which is caviar. On our walks we would stop to watch the stout women, girls and boys, loading wood and heavy blocks of limestone onto barges. And at all hours day and night great rafts of logs came floating by. At night I would see their slow-moving red lights and would listen to the voices coming up out of the hazy dark, and to the mysterious voice of the stream as it swirled along on its way to the distant capital.

It carried my thoughts to Petrograd. There in those feverish days of July when the Bolsheviki had tried to seize the government, one morning I'd seen a riderless horse come tearing around a corner, snorting blood, shot through the neck; and as it galloped along a canal, a big black-bearded peasant on a barge piled high with wood had risen up from a pit in the logs and scowled about in a puzzled way. I had wondered what he was thinking of this city revolution, the shouting crowds, the volleys of shots, the armored cars that were racing by with shrill screams of warning. For so much depended on what he thought, this man who had come from the boundless fields and forests where the great masses of the Russians dwell.

In the fast-deepening dusk one night, as we tramped along the high river bank, we heard a hubbub of voices below, with roars of laughter now and then; and going down, we found a score of men and boys, their faces lighted in the dark by a large bonfire, with a couple of black iron pots swinging slowly over the flames. They were raft men, we soon learned, who had put in to camp for the night. They sat on logs around the fire, drinking strong tea from rusty cups and devouring chunks of rye bread and pork. Near by lay half the carcass of a pig they had stolen from some farm. They were a noisy rollicking crowd.

"Where are you from?" Tarasov asked.

"Most of us from Novgorod!" cried a short towheaded chap, with a bullethead and wide square jaws. "Where the devil else could we come from? See what hooligans we are! Only in Novgorod, brother, does God make such specimens!"

"That's a lie!" said a tough redheaded boy. His mouth was full at the moment; with an effort he gulped down his food. "We come from all over," he declared. "I come myself from down the river—but Christ knows where I shall end! Before I get through I will make every river in Holy Russia give me a ride!"

"Those Bolsheviki," growled a man with a short heavy beard already half gray. "How they shout about being free men! What in hell do they know about being free? They know nothing but books, they sit indoors and scribble and read and talk like clerks! Let 'em come and find what freedom is! We'll show 'em!"

There was a chorus of cries. One of the youngsters started a song, and the rest came in on the refrain, to the glory of their wandering life. There were about a million such men on the long winding rivers of Russia; their ranks were recruited constantly from villages along the way; for the river called, and the peasant boys strolled into the bivouacs at night, and soon they joined the wanderers. Tarasov, in his house that night, told of other wanderers—of the armies of labor that roamed about from one big job to another, on railroads, bridges, dams and canals. And I thought of the thousands of bivouacs along the rivers of the land. They would soon be multiplied tenfold; for as the armies disbanded, numberless recruits would come to join these wandering hooligans. I wondered what part they would play in the tumultuous months ahead.

Tarasov had talked till long after midnight. Several times he had stopped to listen to shots that came from the river below and, remembering accounts we'd heard of raids on his neighbors before we came, he had taken his rifle down from the wall. Now we heard quite a fusillade and a chorus of angry cries.

"It's those hooligans," he said. "I think it means nothing but, in case it should, I shall let you have my Browning tonight, while I keep the rifle."

"No, thanks." In various little mix-ups, I have learned it is better to be unarmed. I was tired and drowsy now and, when Tarasov left me, I threw off my clothes and got into bed. I was nearly asleep when suddenly from the river came a deep bellowing voice. The cry was taken up at once from across the stream, then farther down, and I heard it caught up again and again, repeated far off in the distance. Silence for perhaps ten minutes. Then the same bellowing voice again, and again the answering calls.

"What's he trying to do?" I asked, with the peevish irritation of a man half dead for sleep. "Get together a crowd for another raid?" Again the bellow. "Damn him, why can't we *all* go to sleep tonight?"

Then with a little rush of relief, I remembered what Tarasov had told me in his descriptions of river life. The man below was a watchman, guarding the logs on the river bank; and as had been done for centuries, so now at intervals all through the night he would call to the watchman across the river, who in turn would call to the man on this side a mile farther down. So the voices would zigzag back and forth, and travel off into the distance. A queer old custom. I had read of Chinese cities where you heard such watchmen's calls. What a strange country Russia was, midway between East and West! Tarasov could talk all he liked about his shrewd practical peasants and his sensible little plan for cooperative farms. They were deeper than that, these Russians, mysterious as the Far East. Now the bellow came again. It was taken up from the opposite bank; it was echoed by a voice downstream, then by another still farther down, and so traveled away in the heavy night.

XXIX

On Sunday morning I met a man who took me so much farther back into the vast deeps of Russia's life that for the moment I forgot all the chaos of our modern age.

We had come to a little white church, with a green roof and a gilded dome, between the river and the forest. The bells were already jangling, and the narrow dirt road on the river bank was dotted by hurrying figures. In a long open shed near by stood a row of carts and horses. The church was already packed to the doors, so we joined the men who sat in the yard, smoking pipes or cigarettes. They were dressed in sober black or gray, with trousers tucked into high boots. A few wore colored blouses. From a peasant choir of boys and girls, through the open windows the music poured in waves of sound, with a crude sweet yearning, pleading for Holy Russia with God. Then Tarasov touched my arm.

"Look," he said to me softly. "You asked for something very deep. It is standing by the gate."

I saw a short gnarled figure there, an old man leaning on a stick. Upon his shock of thick gray hair a soft brown hat was pushed far back. His face was tanned and wrinkled, his eyes so sharp that I noticed them even from across the yard.

"His name," said Tarasov, "is Kraychok, which in English means Wild Duck. He is one of the very last of his kind. He is the village sorcerer."

As we drew near and he saw my companion, his grim brown face relaxed in a smile. A vigorous handshake, a few gruff words, and then abruptly he led the way out of the little churchyard and off along the river bank.

"We are going to his hut," said my friend. "And I shall tell you about him first. My father made many portraits of him; in his studio they had long talks; and I used to listen, a scared little boy, for it was a fearful thing to be listening to a sorcerer. Kraychok was a hunter, too. He would be in the forest for weeks at a time; and there, the peasants used to say, he communed with the powers of darkness; but all that he learned of such forces he used only for the people's good. At a sickbed in some peasant's hut, I have seen him cause a high fever to drop by the slow hypnotic words he spoke and the strange power in his eyes. As I grew older, Kraychok took me often into the forest to hunt; and there one day, after telling me some stories of enchantment, he stopped short and said to me:

" 'Now put your rifle on the ground and I will show you something.' I put down my gun; and in a voice with a gathering power in it, he said: 'Walk across this clearing, and be sure you don't look back!' So I walked along. The ground was quite smooth, yet suddenly, as though my feet had struck upon some obstacle, I stumbled and pitched forward! I rose quickly and looked back; and there, ten steps behind me, stood my companion laughing, in such a way that he made no sound. There was sweat upon his forehead and an exhausted look in his eyes. I stared at him, then begged him to tell me how he had made me fall.

" 'First,' he explained, 'by telling you those stories of enchantment, I got you into the right mood. Then I told you to walk along, and I came softly close behind. I put my whole soul into yours. And all at once I made myself feel as though I had stumbled and fallen down. If I do this so hard that I feel myself fall, then nothing can stop you from doing so, too.'

"I have studied hypnotism since, but never have I come

on a case where the power of it was shown so sharply as it was that day by this old man in front of us."

Presently we came to his home, on the edge of a wood of birch and fir. The small hut of old brown logs was lined with bear and wolf skins inside; dried herbs hung from the low rafters, and before the fireplace was a black iron pot in which he brewed his medicines. At a word from my friend, the old hunter took down from the wall a long flintlock gun, carefully wrapped in red cloths. These he removed, and without speaking handed the weapon over to me. The barrel was inlaid with silver, and faintly engraved upon it were words in some Far Eastern tongue. It had belonged to his father once, and to his grandfather before that. Tarasov talked to him for a while. Then we left the hut and took a path that led into the cool dim forest.

"I have tried to persuade him," Tarasov said, "to take us to his favorite haunt. Perhaps he will. I am not sure. The best chance is to leave him to walk ahead, and let him take us or not, as he wills."

"Tell me some more about him," I begged, "and this hypnotic power of his."

"As I told you, it was amazingly strong. For something over thirty years he attended peasant women in childbirth. Often with my mother he would come to a woman confined, and would stand by her bed and look into her eyes; and slowly stroking her head, he would say: 'All is still well. You don't feel any pain.' He would repeat these words many times, in a voice so kind and soothing, no one could have imagined that such a dirty uncouth man could speak in such a gentle way. And my mother told me that even up to the moment of birth the faces of those women gave no evidence of pain. I asked him once where he got his power. He said that in his family it had been handed down from father to son, and it came from a secret place in the forest. To that place he would go and lie like a dead man, and into his spirit would

pour the strength of the living soul of this old Russian land,
a soul made up of the spirits of many strange dark peoples
who used to live here long ago. They may have been Finns,
for we are almost on the edge of Finland here, but he told me
he thought those people belonged to some even older time.
Only in that one spot in the forest has he been able to feel
that soul. I think now he is taking us there."

We walked through the forest for nearly an hour and at
last came into a clearing surrounded by tall silent pines. In
the center was what I took to be a high mound about eighty
feet long, all tufted over with grass and weeds. But in order
to get a better look, we climbed a huge hummock not far
away—and there for some time we stood perfectly still. For
from this point the mound appeared as a prodigious granite
figure, hewn with a crude terrific art to depict a woman in
childbirth. After the silence, Tarasov said:

"Very few peasants will come to this spot. Kraychok heard
of it from his father, who told him this figure had been here
for many thousand silent years. It reveals its secrets only
to those who go into a trance, he says, and dare for a time
to join the dead. He first brought me here when I was a boy.
Young and sensitive at that time, I had an experience that
could not come in later age. I felt great steps that shook
the ground and I heard an enormous laugh that echoed
against the forest walls! I heard old Kraychok muttering
prayers, and the whole world grew suddenly dark! When I
regained my consciousness, I was lying on the ground. He
was slowly stroking my head and repeating: 'All is well, little brother.' There was still a stern wild light in his eyes, but
his voice was only kind as he said: 'You are too little to lie
with the dead.'"

Again we were silent for a time, then slowly old Kraychok began to speak.

"In old times, here strange people came, and they made
human sacrifice. This woman's great womb was a flaming

cave, and back to this mighty Mother of Life they gave the children she had borne. In this there was a fearful meaning. If a man lives, so too he must die. Do not think that what you see is only a granite figure, for here many hundreds of mortals have shrieked and given their souls to God, and their spirits have never gone away, and all the powers of living and dying are still to be felt in this spot."

He stopped. He was standing rigid now. He went on in a voice intense and low:

"Any fool from the city coming here will feel his knees grow weak with fear, for there is something here that cries: 'Stop, you fool, and look into the depths of life and death beneath you!' Here this is plainly to be seen. But they do not know, those fools, that in all the cities, too, there are such ancient figures. Only there they cannot be seen—for greedy men, who rush about after money and other little things, have trampled such great figures down and buried them beneath the dust. But the souls of the figures still are there. They only sleep. At times they rise. Then hellish passions are let loose. Now once more these city men, by their little greed and rage, have stirred the great figures. War has come. The earth is black with armies; the winds are filled with voices—screaming, roaring. Guns, they say. But they are not guns. They are the voices of great spirits, gods and devils, still alive in the hearts of men. So it is. And what will be the future nobody in the world can tell. For the future is a mystic thing, bound with iron to the past. And the past we do not understand."

Abruptly he turned and led us away. Bound with iron to the past—and Russia's dream of empire. I wonder if old Kraychok lived to see those forests drenched in blood, as Finland's little army held the Slav steam roller back? And in all that human sacrifice up there in the Arctic night, I wonder just how close they came to that great granite Mother of Life?

Toward the end of my stay with Tarasov, I came to know another old man whose rugged force and vision made an impression nearly as strong—not of the depths of Russia's life but of the hope and power there. He was a school-teacher. The weather-beaten frame house where he lived stood on the high river bluff very close to the home of my friend, and often he was to be seen mowing the hay in his small field or sharpening his shining scythe. He wore a loose white cotton blouse. There were sandals on his feet, and a round cap of brown leather fitted close to the back of his head. He had small ears, a long powerful face with receding chin and gray mustache, a high forehead, a long straight nose and two little blue eyes that were still amazingly young. His voice, though harsh and guttural, was almost always very low.

"When I came here long ago," he said, "the peasants were a lousy lot and the little schoolhouse stunk like a pigsty in August. They said the school could teach their children nothing of real use to the farm. But I thought: 'I will show how a school can help the lives of children and parents, too. I will make my school the very heart and center of the neighborhood.'" His little blue eyes twinkled. "I had big thoughts when I was young. But I worked hard in those next years and started orchards and produce gardens on the land around the school. The boys and girls all helped me and in time we had such success that we sold at a profit all that we grew. In the winter I taught the children from books; in the spring and summer we worked out of doors. And after some years of practical work, the attitude of the peasants changed, for the older boys showed a knowledge of gardens that brought them all good wages from the landowners near by.

"Meanwhile there had grown in my mind the dream of building a larger school, where in addition to classrooms there should be workshops of all kinds. I began to make drawings for the new school, and for eight years I went through the

district begging the landowners and the merchants to subscribe. Some gave cash, and others promised building materials free of charge. Picnics we gave and dramatic shows,
all to raise money for the school. Many peasants gave me
trees. Tree by tree was promised me and the owner of the
sawmill sawed the timber as his gift. The blacksmith, too,
worked free at his forge; and carpenters and peasants worked
by my side with no kopeck of pay; and so did the big boys
in my school. At last the building was completed. It had
taken eleven years. But then a joke was played on me. For I
had built a school so large that the Petrograd authorities decided the head teacher here must be a very intelligent man
with full university training. They got such a fellow, and
all the years since I have worked under him. For it is good
to live with your dream.

"But we know that our schools must be poor and small,
compared to those in America, and we hope your great
country will help us soon. If I were an American I would say:
'By the love of Christ and Liberty, those Russians shall be
made our friends!' The German agents tell us here: 'The
Americans are money hogs. They have joined with England
in this war to build a world power that shall grab all the
richest lands of the earth.' Such lies are being believed by our
peasants, who are blind and weary of war. We want better
lives. You can help us there. You must tell us how you live
and work—all your latest tricks in farming, all your latest
tricks in schools. We must see each other closely as friends.
Not by a whirlpool of chatter like that going on in Petrograd,
but by hard slow work and learning, we must climb the
long road to a better world."

We went to his schoolhouse one evening that week. Down
at one edge of the small river town, a great square building
of logs, three floors high, it rose above all the houses around.
Although this was vacation time and the place was empty
by day, the peasants' dramatic society was giving a play

there that night. Before the entertainment began, Tarasov
showed me the classrooms and workshops. Enormous beams
ran overhead, supporting the high ceilings. There were huge
tile stoves, and the rooms were immense, with generous windows. We went up the crowded stairs to the main hall on
the third floor, where a rough stage had been improvised.
The benches were already filling and we hurried to get a
place, for a stout old peasant on the stage was loudly ringing
a big bell. Then he placed a row of kerosene lamps as foot-
lights and stood a plank on edge between them and the audience. As the crowd grew denser down in front, I watched
the stolid faces around me, the expectant gleaming eyes.
Again the big bell jangled. Slowly the curtain rose, with
jerks, and revealed a living room in the house of a small-town
merchant. The play was a classic by Ostrovsky, one of comedy satire on the petty bourgeois life. I had read it long ago
in the years when I wrote for the theater. In deepening surprise I watched these village players now and the spell that
they were casting. Like most amateurs, they dragged their
lines; but it was just this leisurely art, this lack of all impatience for having anything happen, this complete and delighted absorption in the characters themselves, that held
this peasant audience, stirred them to quick bursts of laughter, followed by silences tense and deep.

I thought of my mountain village at home, and of a performance of Uncle Tom's Cabin I had seen. What a difference here! No little Eva, no Legree, no Eliza crossing the
ice. These Russian peasant players were giving us a picture
of life simple and profoundly real. And because I was leaving next day to go home, I thought of these villages and of
our own and of all that we might give to each other. I fell
to dreaming for a while of some tremendous friendship which
might come out of this bloodstained land.

The next morning we rose early, breakfasted and packed
our bags. We had arranged with a peasant to bring his dory

and take us out to the small steamer when it came by. As we carried our bags down the steep bank to a raft of logs below, I spied the teacher coming down from his cabin with a towel on his arm. When he caught sight of us, he called out:

"You're just in time for a last swim!"

We proceeded quickly to undress. I remember the teacher's long lean body, muscular, brown, as he poised on the raft. Then he dove, and with long overhead strokes swam out into the river, where he turned over on his back and blew like a porpoise. In a few moments, all aglow, we were dressing in the crisp cool air. A dory put out from the opposite bank, and the steamer came puffing around the bend. The dory reached us just in time. We threw in our luggage. The teacher warmly grasped my hand.

"Remember that you are to come again! And in your country, tell them—no matter what happens, remember us—the people in the villages!"

XXX

BACK IN PETROGRAD I FOUND CONFUSION DEEPER THAN BEFORE, with faction against faction and most people of property crowding the trains to get away. For the power of the Bolsheviki kept increasing day and night. But even if they were able to seize the government, I thought, America by sending food supplies and other aid might keep them still from making peace with Germany for one winter more, and so give our country time to bring support to the Allies. As I look back, I can see now how my whole picture of Russia then was colored by my only half-conscious straining to believe just that. With little sleep, my nerves keyed up by the constant rush of impressions and work late at night to jot them down, my thoughts kept turning to Belgium and France and the relentless power of the German army as I'd seen it in 1914. And I felt that if Russia failed us now Germany would win the war, and would then turn on Russia, too, and there and all over Europe would spread her rigid Junker order, crushing all democracy down.

Bullard's view was like my own and he put it in a report for me to take back to Washington. No matter what government Russia had, America must keep friendly still. Already our Red Cross mission there had been making a survey of hospital needs and of the dearth of food supplies and was planning to bring from America a million cans of milk for the children already starving in cities and towns. They had completed their survey and half of them were about to go home; and through the kindness of their chief, Dr. Billings of Chicago, an old family friend of ours, I was able to buy a berth in their car on the Trans-Siberian Express. With me I took Bullard's report. He was to go to Moscow and organize our publicity to tell Russia of our government's purpose and plans to send them aid. I should have liked to stay with him, but back in Philadelphia the Post was waiting for my articles, which I hoped would help to keep our public friendly to Russia still. Tarasov had come to say good-by the day that I left Petrograd. All through our lunch together, I poured into him my hope in our plan, but he listened in weary Russian despair.

"It will be useless. We shall have such years of bloody confusion as the world has not seen in ages," he said.

So many Russians were of his mind that, when our Red Cross group of thirty left the city that night, it took a guard of mounted Cossacks to open a pathway for our cars through the frantic thousands in front of the station struggling for places on trains. When at last we reached the sleeping car assigned to us on the Express, exhausted I tumbled into my berth and slept for hours. But at dawn I woke up as we rumbled across a bridge and, from the window looking down on the same small river steamer which had taken Tarasov and me up to his home a month before, I thought of the village sorcerer and remembered how he had said:

"Now once more these city men, by their little greed and rage, have stirred the great figures. War is here."

But then came memory pictures of the great deep peace of forest and field and riverside. And so again I fell asleep.

From my tension it was good to relax, on that long trip of eleven days and nights across Siberia. The Red Cross men were fine companions. I remember how at one station an old Boston sanitary engineer chuckled as he figured that, if you bored a hole from there straight through the earth, it would come out in the Boston Common. Home was right down there, he told us, pointing into the ground; and the sooner we got

there the better he'd like it. So said they all and so said I.
Along the track we caught glimpses of the narrow winding
road, over which so many Russians had gone into exile long
ago; but I was in no mood for them now; and from such
dark memories I turned to the children along the way and
among them made many silent friends; for I had brought from
Petrograd an enormous bag of candy and, from the rear platform at the many stops we made, I distributed all-day suckers
to wild shy little goatherds in the Ural Mountains, to children
in the dirty snow high up on the Lake Baikal range and to
strange small creatures in the valleys far beyond. And as we
neared the Orient I looked forward to a few days more of
forgetting war's confusion in the eternal peace of the East.

But at first I did not find it there. When we came into
Manchuria, already controlled by the Japanese, our Red Cross
group was blandly welcomed by a little official in the name
of the Emperor of Japan. From our shabby old Russian sleeping car, he took us out for supper to a brand-new Japanese
hotel of gray stucco, in the Spanish Hollywood style; and
while waiting for supper he seated us, with American magazines to read, in an inner court around a fountain. When
presently supper was announced and we trailed into the dining room, he rubbed his hands and smiled and said:
"Knowing how you gentlemens have been starved by ex-
cessive bad food under Russian government, we try hard to
please you now with food to make you feel at home. And so
for supper—ham and eggs!"
Cheers from the Americans. Good advertising for Japan.
After supper he led us back to the station and there we found
our luggage all moved into a spick-and-span Pullman sleeper.
In this he rode with us that night and next day, talking of all
Japan had done for the country through which we passed.
It was early fall. All along the line Chinese peasants and their
families were busily gathering their crops.

"See how happy they live," said our guide, "under new influence of Japan."

But when we came to Mukden that night and our train stopped long outside the city, he said he had an interesting monument to show us there. Some of us went with him and, after walking a mile across fields, we came to a low rounded hill. Up a long flight of marble steps, he led us to the inclosure above; and there, encircled by cypress trees with a half-moon rising over their tops, stood the loveliest and the deadliest monument I've ever seen. Gleaming in the moonlight rose a slender tapering column of bronze—so simple and pure in outline, so grim! For it was a replica of a shell for a big gun. As we faced it in silence, the little man said:

"Here in Russian-Japanese war was fought great battle of Mukden, by which Russian armies were forced back from Asia and driven to defeat. It cost two hundred thousand Japanese lives. But we are realists in Japan and, because like Napoleon we know that not by men but by force of big guns are all such battles lost or won, we have built such a monument." He was silent a moment, and then once more, low, clear and precise, came his voice at our side: "Here Yellow Race turned White Race back from effort to invade the East. Better let East manage own affairs. So Japan and America remain friends."

It was good to escape from that little man. In China, where our Red Cross doctors stopped to buy opium to be made into morphine for Russian hospitals, we spent an unforgettable week in the disorderly, lovely and human old city of Pekin. I had been impatient of the delay, but the ancient town reached out kind hands and, with war and revolution soon quite driven out of my head, for seven days and evenings I wandered through its maze of streets, drinking in its loveliness, sinking into its timeless peace. Here at least was one country safe from the chaos of these modern times. I little suspected how Japan meant to "manage own affairs" or what red death she was to launch on China in the years to come!

The American colony nearly killed us with kindness and cocktails at first, but the second evening at a dance I met a lad from our legation, who took me away to the Chinese house where he lived with two other young diplomats. All three of them spoke Chinese and through them I came deeper under the spell of the old city's charm. By day, on a small polo pony lent to me by one of them, I jogged through winding colorful streets lined with little booths and shops; I rode up along the broad gardened top of the ancient city wall and visited spacious temple gardens in the country just outside. And by night with my new companions I went to crowded theaters and to a dark old temple for a weird midnight service there. From my rich jumble of memories of those enchanting days and nights, one that stands out clear and strong is of a warm evening when, from an upper window of a restaurant, we looked down into a region of little low houses, courts and gardens, in the soft glow from Chinese lanterns; and we heard the tinkle of music coming faintly through the night.

"That is the red-light district, and I want you to meet a girl down there and hear the story she has to tell," said my companion. In two rickshaws, to the clear melodious notes from silver gongs and shouts of "Hoy—hoy!" from our runners, we made our way through a crowded street. In front of each house on either side hung three or four huge ribbons of white satin with inscriptions in gold, each one indicating a girl inside. Into one such house we went and back through tiny garden courts. In one I stopped abruptly, listening to incongruous sounds that came from the small house just ahead.

"Isn't that a cabinet organ?" I whispered to my companion. He smiled.

"It is—and that's the story," he said. A few moments later we entered a room where, at a small organ on which her inexperienced hands were groping for Seeing Nellie Home, sat a slender Chinese girl in a clinging gown of black silk. She

was dark and had big clever eyes. As she welcomed us with
a quick smile, my companion pointed to a huge crude portrait
of her hanging on the wall and said:

"She's only twenty-four years old but she's already president of the oldest labor union on earth, the Prostitutes' Guild
of Pekin. Now let's get her story."

He began to talk with her and, through his translations, I
heard the strange narrative of her life. Born on a farm in the
great valley of the Yellow River, when she was only ten
years old she'd been carried away in a river flood on the roof
of her house and taken off by a man in boat, who sold her to
a house in Shanghai. It was a house, she told us, for rough
dirty Christian sailormen and, by the time she was sixteen,
those men had made her so sick and old that she was useless
at her trade, so they did not lock her in any more. On a walk
one day, as she came by the open door of an American medical mission, she heard music and looked in and saw a big
Christian with a beard, smoking a pipe and playing a small
cabinet organ. She had no use for Christians, for they had
made her so sick and old; but as she turned to go, he saw
her and called out in Chinese:

"Wait! Come in! Let me look at you!" She stopped and he
came and looked at her and said: "You are a very sick little
girl and I am a doctor." Then he took her into his room and
gave her some medicine and said: "Now you must come every
day for two months and I will make you well again."

She came back, and soon she began to feel better, and so
she liked this big kind man. At first he tried to talk to her
about a young God named Jesus Christ, but she had heard
sailors, drunk like beasts, shout that name so many nights that
she had no use for such a God. What kept her coming still
every day was a scrapbook filled with photographs of the
doctor man's young sister back in a country called Kansas,
she said. He told her girls wanted to vote back there and his
sister was a suffragette. The Chinese girl was spellbound by

the pictures in that book! Her life had taught her that all girls were slaves, but here was an American girl standing up in an automobile and speaking to a crowd of men. And the men all listened! What a country!

So she kept coming to this man's house for medicine and many talks about what Chinese girls could be. At last he induced her to promise to run away from the house where she lived; but he'd made her look so much better now that again she was useful at her trade and so they locked her in as before. Two months went by before she could escape and come back to the doctor man, and then she found his house locked up and a cholera sign above the door. When she could not find him anywhere, she kept to the promise she had made and started on foot to go home to her farm. She walked for many many days; when she got there she found all her family gone. So on she walked all the way to Pekin, sore, tired, in rags, and went back to her trade.

But one night on the street a Chinese girl, who saw how tired and ragged she was, took her home and gave her good food and a bath and clean clothes, and told her: "This is how we treat girls in our guild." So she joined the guild, eight years ago. Since then she'd become its president. But still she remembered what the doctor man had said of how girls could better their lives if they tried. So she bought this organ and, when she played it, she thought about him and tried to make the lives of all the girls in her guild more like that of his sister, the young Kansas suffragette!

"She has made already such headway in reforming her guild," said my young diplomatist, "that in this house, as I know well from Chinese friends who come here, when a man on his first visit chooses the girl he likes best, he must just sit and talk with her. At the end of an hour or so, if she likes him, she says: 'Good night. Come again.' If she doesn't say this, he can't come. If she does, he often comes many times before at last he's received as a lover. She herself has only three lovers now. Soon she hopes to have only one and then perhaps she will have a child. All this I know, not only from her but from men who have come here. Yet still they come. And this is true of quite a few houses in which the girls belong to the guild. Where else in the world could girls make men treat them with such humanity? But China is a human land. Before you sail from Japan next week, go to the Yoshiwara in Tokyo, and there you will feel the unbridgeable difference between China and Japan."

In Tokyo, one night next week, with a doctor companion I did go to the district known as the Yoshawara. And what I found in that immense and rigidly ordered region of lust —with its immaculate houses and strict inspection of women and girls, its spotlessly clean little narrow streets with a policeman in a booth at every crossway, its ravenous men, its naked women smiling from windows, and the chuckles and panting breaths that came to my ears through paper walls in the one house we visited—still looms like some foul nightmare in my memories of pretty Japan.

At last we were ready to sail for home. Our long trip from Russia had been arranged in Petrograd by one of the Red Cross mission, Major Swift, the Chicago packer; and he had surely managed it well. Though all summer I'd sent a cable each week through our embassy home to my wife, only two of them ever reached her; but through some mysterious means known best to Swift Brothers of Chicago, the major's cable to his firm went through so well that, when now we took ship for the voyage home and, after months of vile Russian food, came down to dinner the first night on board, we were served with great juicy four-inch steaks! And these tasted better to our group than the propaganda ham and eggs served by the government of Japan!

From Pekin the week before, I had cabled to my wife that I was out of Russia, well and safe, and would soon be home.

But walking the decks of the ship that night—with memories of the vast Russian upheaval crowding back into my mind for the articles I had still to write—I remembered that word in my cable, safe, and wondered what all this revolution and war would mean in years ahead to the homes of every one of us. Would we ever be safe again, as we were in the world I'd known as a boy? More than twenty years have passed since then and today as I write I am wondering still.

XXXI

ON THAT TWELVE-DAY VOYAGE I WROTE TWO MORE OF MY
Russian articles. On landing I came East at once, but in Chicago stopped overnight with one of my sisters; and my
brother Abram, who had a captain's commission now, came
from his cantonment to meet me there. Adjutant of his regiment of four thousand men and boys, for months he'd been
working day and night. Would Russia stay in the war, he
asked. I told him something of what I had heard. When we
went up to the bedroom we shared, his thoughts turned back
to his years as a painter and he asked, as he got into bed:

"How about those paintings in the Hermitage over there?
Are they safe?"

"They are," I said, "and I knew a man who helped to save
them." Then I glanced at my brother and stopped. For the
moment his head hit the pillow he'd fallen into a deep sleep!

After a brief happy visit with my family in New York,
I went to Philadelphia to see Lorimer of the Post, and from
there to Washington with Arthur Bullard's Russian report.
And there George Creel got hold of me. He had already
started men to Russia to join Bullard in Moscow.

"We want you at this end," he said, "to help feed news
material not only to him but to agents we're sending all over
the world. We haven't got a day to lose. The defeatist spirit
you found in Russia is spreading all over Europe now. Fed
by German propaganda, not only the neutral countries but
even some of our Allies are beginning to feel that, with

Russia out, Germany by a last big push in France will win this war—because we won't be there in time! All the gathering force and speed of our war activities get barely a mention in papers abroad. We've got to make 'em print the truth! We've got to get the whole American booming war picture into the news in foreign papers all over the world!"

For this Woodrow Wilson had asked him to form the Foreign Press Bureau. Already Creel was sending abroad men, most of whom had been correspondents and had a wide acquaintance with foreign journalists and their ways, so very different from our own. In cooperation with our embassies and consulates, these agents were setting up news bureaus employing both American and foreign translators to rush the work, including in most countries a moving-picture expert, to show and distribute our war films. To feed them with material, Creel planned to send them a running news picture of America in the war. This was to be done by three divisions—Cable News, Moving Picture and Mail Feature Service. This last he wished me to organize. I told him I'd be glad to try, if we did not have to go in for the kind of propaganda the governments were using abroad, and attempt to picture ourselves as a hundred per cent Sir Galahads. They would like us better if we did not try to pose as saints. The truth about us was good enough, so I urged that we stick to that and give a true news picture of a great democracy, in spite of blunders and mistakes, crashing through all obstacles to do its part in winning the war and a safer and more decent civilization for us all. It was a tall order for those days, but Creel agreed, and in months ahead he stood back of us so well that the censors gave us the freedom we asked for.

I got to work the following day. Spending all my mornings for weeks on my last articles for the Post, and my afternoons and nights on this new job for the government, beginning in one room in New York with my able colleague, Paul Kennaday, and two experienced newspaper friends—to meet the demands soon pouring in from our agents overseas, our work grew so fast that we had to move to larger quarters late that fall; and by spring, with a staff of nearly a hundred and hundreds of volunteer helpers besides, we needed two floors of a skyscraper. New York was so crowded with war work and with business of all kinds, it was hard to get space anywhere; but we had to have it now. Still, I don't like to think of the day when with our office manager I walked through the halls of the building he'd chosen, knocking on doors and announcing to defenseless businessmen:

"Sorry. The government needs this space. You'll have to move out of here next week."

We had to grow to meet the need. So fast did the demands increase that very soon our weekly "pouch," consisting of dozens of huge sacks, included not only what we wrote but photographs and cuts and mats to illustrate our articles, and posters and news pictorials to be shown in thousands of windows abroad. We sent millions of picture post cards, too. Our news articles went out in hundreds of sets on multigraphed sheets, amounting to from seventy to eighty thousand words each week. Most of them were very brief and they were mainly rewrites from newspapers and magazines, war bulletins, trade and professional journals and foreign-language papers here—covering activities not only of the army and navy, work in our shipyards and cantonments, the going of our troops to France, but also of all the forces behind our armies day and night, in mills and factories and mines, in homes, post offices, country stores, on ranches and plantations and farms, in schools and colleges, churches, hospitals, research laboratories, banks. Brief articles, too, by well-known writers and leaders in all parts of the land, supporting and interpreting America's purpose in the war. Among the writers were William Dean Howells, Booth Tarkington, Ida Tarbell, Edna Ferber, Fannie Hurst, Owen Wister, Robert Herrick, Walter Eaton and William Allen White. One article by Tarkington was reprinted in pamphlet form by the British government, and 850,000 copies were distributed over there.

In thousands of Russian villages, peasants who could not read were attracted by our photographs of American tractors and plows at work on fields where millions of bushels of grain were raised for our Allies. For the Russian newspapers and for labor and radical journals in Europe supporting the Allies, some of our contributors here included labor leaders and other progressives and liberals, willing to back our government but not to whitewash our whole life. And certain private citizens, who made it their business as patriots to hunt down all radicals, no matter how loyal they might be, grew so disturbed that one of them wrote a long letter to the President, denouncing us as a lot of pro-German traitors and Bolsheviki. The President sent it to Will Irwin, chief of our Foreign Press Bureau then. On the margin of the letter the President had written just this:

"Dear Mr. Irwin—How dreadful—Woodrow Wilson."

It was good to feel a man like that behind you and to be left free to meet the demands that came piling in from our agents overseas. As the interest of the whole world turned to America's part in the war, foreign countries wished to learn more and more about our resources and the one great urgent question:—Can America turn the tide? And in that year when days counted like weeks, to learn without any waste of time just what they wanted to know in each land, every article that we sent had a serial number—like 2B1 or 3X82—and each agent was asked to cable a list of those articles he had been able to get printed in papers abroad. We sent to each agent questions, too, with a serial number for each. And the answers came in cables that were strings of these code symbols and kept one man in our office constantly busy at his desk, decoding and making long lists of articles actually printed in foreign newspapers the week before. One day I heard our cable editor chuckle as I passed his desk.

"What's funny?" I asked.

"This answer to twenty-seven," he said, "just come from Buenos Aires."

Twenty-seven was this question: "What American personalities shall we feature for your press?" And the answer from the Argentine was: "Carlito Chaplin and Elihu Root." Both those gentlemen in the next week gave us interviews to send down to Buenos Aires, explaining why we were in the war and how soon we'd have millions of men in France; and those interviews translated in Spanish were printed in scores of newspapers.

This country was sending to our Allies prodigious quantities of meat and wheat and other food supplies, and we featured that in our weekly pouch—until our foreign agents began to report:

"We can't get it printed. The Allies are sick and tired of being told how Generous America feeds them."

To meet this point, I telephoned to Dr. David Fairchild, the scientist so noted for his able research work in our Department of Agriculture, and asked him:

"Dr. Fairchild, is it true that nearly all of our grains and meats came originally from seeds and stock brought here long ago from abroad?"

"It is, in a large measure," he said.

"Then could you please write for us a series of little articles to show how the seeds of our grains and the ancestors of our cattle and hogs came to us at the start from abroad, and we're only giving Europe back, with interest, what they once gave us? Put into it the feeling of Pershing's 'Lafayette, we are here!' "

A queer angle, you may say. But this twist made all the difference. His articles had such effect that the European press printed hundreds of others soon about American food conservation in the cause of our Allies. Rival government propagandists asked our agents hungrily:

"How do you Yanks get so much space? Are you buying the press over here?"

And this was not an insult, for it was reputed to be common practice in those days. Anxious to keep neutral nations in line or to win them over, we were told, not only Germany but even some of our Allies spent millions to buy foreign newspapers or their support. This country spent not a dollar that way. But we did get effective help from American exporters here, an aid that cost us nothing at all. To Latin-American countries, where they were rapidly building up trade, our exporters sent agents with large sums of money to place in the Latin-American press to advertise their wares. These agents before sailing came to us to see our list of the newspapers in those countries that had proved to be our friends. Those newspapers generally got the "ads." I may add that our list soon doubled in size. The exporters helped us in other ways. Under the guidance of Edward Bernays, one of the ablest and most devoted younger workers on our staff, from our articles they printed inserts in their export journals and catalogues and in thousands of business letters sent to foreign lands each week.

By the last month of the war, the material we sent abroad got a wider press than did that of any other government. Even in China, now an Ally, we were given space in an average of some sixty Chinese papers a week. We sent torrents of appeals to the German people, too, to be dropped by airplanes and to be distributed by our Military Intelligence secret agents over there. And meanwhile our Cable Division had tripled the number of readers of President Wilson's messages, seen that they were correctly translated in a score of languages and flashed to every part of the globe.

In spite of our efforts to put the whole truth into the picture that we gave, many of us found it hard, for the war fervor everywhere colored all our thoughts and feelings. From the rush and strain of work in our office, often I went down to the harbor, my old hunting ground for stories of this rapidly changing world. And how it had changed from years gone by! With a pass that admitted me to all piers, I watched huge ships, grotesquely streaked and daubed with camouflage against German submarines, slip silently down the river and out toward the dangerous sea. On their decks I saw tens of thousands of boys from North and South and East and West, all grimly silent. So they went. The sight of them always humbled me. When my brother's regiment sailed, as he stood with brother officers on the bridge of their British ship, I raised my hat and kept it raised as they swiftly moved away. Later my brother told me how at sunrise on the coast of France, as adjutant last to leave their ship, he had watched the regiment file up a winding road into the hills with their band playing:

"Mine eyes have seen the glory of the coming of the Lord."

In those strange days we felt like that. On Armistice Day, when the air was filled with whirling bits of paper outside my office window and a thunderous victory roar rose from the crowded streets below, I dictated a message to Creel and begged him to relay it to the White House. My letter ran about like this:

"The one great thing for us to do now is to announce to our Allies that we give them all that money we lent, as our contribution to the cause of world-wide democracy. It will cost us nothing in the end; we shall get it all back in good will and increased foreign trade resulting from that. And just now such a statement would immensely strengthen our influence at Versailles for a just and lasting peace."

Rank presumption on my part. For what did I know about finance? And yet now I look back and wonder if after all I was not right.

XXXII

IN THE EPIDEMIC OF FLU AND PNEUMONIA IN THOSE LAST weeks of the war, we had some forty cases among members of our staff, and in our apartment Margaret Ann and both our children were laid low. We got through as best we could; but when, soon after Armistice Day, orders came to close our office, suddenly I found myself on the verge of a little smash. My wife, too, had been under heavy strain, not only from illness but from a year of hard work as president of the New York Women's City Club. On the night when she took office, a federal judge had come to me and, contentedly smiling, had said he was glad to bequeath to me his place as husband of the president; and I soon learned why he was glad, for mine had been a busy wife! Now we both needed a little rest, so went down to Virginia for two weeks of riding and golf.

But back in New York in those next months, oh, what a dismal letdown from Woodrow Wilson's great world dream! The world made safe for democracy. As I saw the vision fade and our Allies, gone victory mad, plant the seeds of bitterness and of future wars at Versailles, slowly there came into my mind a long war novel. I called it Blind, and the opening page gives a feeling of my own outlook at the time:

"Late on a warm cloudy night in April, 1919, upon a hill in Connecticut a few miles inland from the Sound, a large capacious spreading old house of brick and frame loomed like a great squat shadow. Upstairs were many people asleep.

337

Below there was not a light nor a sound—except in one room, where in the darkness the click of a typewriter was heard." So this narrative was begun:

"I am blind—but no blinder than is the mind of the world, these days. The long thin splinter of German steel which struck in behind my eyes did no more to me than the war has done to the vision of humanity. In this year of deep confusion —clutching, grabbing, spending, wasting, and in Europe plague and famine, desperation and revolt—mankind is reeling in the dark. And in these long queer crowded nights, half waking and half sleeping, it has seemed to me at times as though the bedlam of it all were pounding, seething into me. I was once a playwright—and vividly there comes to me a memory of the Broadway crowds on a big rush Saturday night. A sightless beggar stood by the curb, and in a harsh shrill piercing voice he kept repeating: 'Help the blind!' The Soul of Man is like him now."

With this dark theme, late that spring I came from New York with our family up here to the White Mountains to write. But I shall not dwell on that novel now, for after all the memories of war and revolution that I have already set down, it will be a relief, I feel, both to the reader and my-self, to turn for a while to this life in the hills that has come to mean so much to me.

More and more time in those next years we spent in our mountain home. We still had our winters in New York, in a small house on Turtle Bay, where on Christmas Eves the big garden behind was lovely with hundreds of candles in all the windows of houses like ours, and inside we had parties of sixty or more of all ages, for carol singing there. Our two small boys went to New York schools and we led busy city lives and made many more warm friends. And between the novels I wrote, I made trips for magazines, not only in this country but to London and Paris, Geneva and Rome. Later we shall come to them. But from the chaos and disillusion in such cities over there, it was good to get home to this place in the hills, where life was still in so many ways like that I'd known long ago as a boy, in the old world of security.

From Chicago my wife's family still came in the summers with their friends, and our own household was enlarged by our children's friends and our own. We had a little daughter now. On warm June evenings long after her bedtime I'd steal up to the nursery, giving a secret whistle first, and would take her to the window to watch from my arms the fairy dance of fireflies on the field outside. In that nursery her brother Nick and she grew close as twins, and he took her for many rides with old Beauty in the pony wagon. Nick and Bill rode Beauty still, but she was nearly thirty now and her occasional gallops would end abruptly when she came to roadside grass or to an old-style water trough. When Bill brought me a school composition he had written on Sheridan's Ride, and I told him it wasn't real and advised him to describe that ride from what he knew about horses himself, Bill pondered long upon the rides he'd taken on Beauty and then composed this narrative:

"Off dashed the General on his horse! And Sheridan twenty miles away! The horse then saw some grass she liked and stopped and ate a lot of it—so Sheridan was still away. He struck her savage whacks with his sword and on she rushed along the road toward the distant cannon roar! And Sheridan nineteen miles away! But then she came to a watering trough and the General had to hit her hard and nearly yank her head off to get her to go on again. But she got going pretty soon and Sheridan eighteen miles away! And they kept at it most all night long but they got there at last and the battle was won!"

As our boys grew, we taught them to swim in the little river below, we fished the trout streams, climbed the hills, built a log cabin in our woods and often went there to sleep at night. In the meantime our daughter was growing fast and busy with her own affairs. She organized a club of three girls and wrote a constitution which had only this one article:

"The caption of this girls club will be Betsy Ann Poole."

More and more our children joined with us in the lives of our summer neighbors here, who had small children of their own. My old college roommate, Mallery, built a house not far from ours, and our friendship grew deeper than ever before. His children and ours played together and on Saturday afternoons we had exciting hockey games with players of all ages on the field beside his house.

Long before this I'd begun to make friends on the farms and in the villages. Bob Frost, the poet, lived down in the valley and, knowing these mountain people well, he gave me more insight into their lives. As he did, I liked best the fall when, with the city people gone, our North Country grew so still.

"I like it this way," Frost said one day, at the end of a long autumn tramp we had made. "I don't like cities; I don't like noise." Just then a cow lowed on a neighboring farm. He smiled. "Even that's too much," he said.

It was good to feel myself sinking roots here, after all those trips I had made. Though my father had died long since, his influence was with me yet and, as he had loved the wheat fields and the rolling prairies, so I loved the hills. Good for living, good for writing. I once asked old William Dean Howells why the Russian fiction was so much more real and strong, and struck so much deeper, than our own.

"Because so many Russians," he said, "in their country homes from the time they were born, fed by peasant nurses with folk songs and peasant tales, sank roots deep into the life of the people—while in America, these days, only the children in the South have their colored mammies still, and even they will soon be gone. We live in cities. Our country

ERNEST POOLE'S WINTER HOME
SUMMER COTTAGE

homes are mere summer places, with no real part in the life of the soil."

Up here in the White Mountains we drew closer to it now. We built a house for wintertime of our own granite and our own pine, on a ledge looking down across the valley to the mountain range close by, with Moosilauke twelve miles to the south and Washington twenty to the north, their peaks in autumn white with snow. One year when we planned going abroad and Billy was in boarding school, we stayed up here till Christmas time and sent Nick to the school in the valley below. Early each morning he'd harness old Beauty and hitch her to a small sledge we had made, and off he'd go over the sparkling snow down to the village for the day, giving Beauty her oats in a barn by the school. He felt a bit awkward there at first in a class of twenty boys and girls and, when he got up to recite, his stammering in the first few days brought chuckles from all over the room. But later, from out of his depths of gloom, he heard more chuckles and looked up and saw that the new mirth was caused by a farmer's little son, who was reciting in shirt and suspenders and a pair of his father's old pants. Although cut short, they were still so vast that the boys at desks near by would often lean over with wastepaper and quickly cram it into them. But united by their two afflictions, Nick and that boy became such chums that soon they could face the world together with the stammer and the pants and get away with both of them. And in the months that followed, Nick made so many friends at school that, when later we sailed from New York, his classmates sent a long round-robin letter to him at the boat. He liked those kids and so did I. I became a trustee of the school and through it I drew closer still to the life of the community.

Deep people—hard to know at first. Dhan Mukerji, who in India had belonged to the Brahmin caste, spent one summer here and he said:

"Now for the first time since I came to your country, I feel at home—for these people, poor but proud and deep, are the Brahmins of America."

Deep people, with points good and bad. Gossip and back-biting are here and jealousies that rankle long. Yet when desperate illness is in a home, always neighbors come to nurse and help. Deep people, with a rugged force. When Wilson declared war and called for a first draft of a million men, our old storekeeper of that time went into his office and figured our quota as eleven. From long and close acquaintance with every village home and farm, he knew well which ones could best afford to send their sons. Soon he let their names be known, quietly in personal talks; and without waiting for the draft, those eleven all volunteered. Two were boys whom I had helped by small loans to go to college. One was killed at Château-Thierry. The other, a young army surgeon, died of pneumonia in France. His widow promptly wrote to me, offering his life insurance in repayment of my loan. I refused it and she complied at the time, for she was ill and in desperate straits. But fifteen years later she wrote again, from the school where she was teaching in Maine:

"Ever since my husband's death I have been teaching and at last have saved money with which to repay that loan. I write to be sure of your present address, so that my check will not be lost."

In vain I wrote to her in reply, begging her to keep the money and to use it, if she liked, on sick people such as her husband would have doctored free if he had lived.

"Do that yourself, if you want to," she answered. "My part is to clear that debt. The money is yours. I inclose my check." What a contrast to this age of inflation, when unpaid debts all over the world keep mounting toward catastrophe!

One of my best friends up here was the old Baptist minister, who lived in a little frame house on the edge of a village a mile from our home. He was six feet five, with shoulders broad and a white beard like a prophet's. Coming home from a hike or a ride, I would meet him bringing his cow from the field or see him at work in the garden, where he hoed out his sermons, he said. In our first years we hired a horse and buggy for long afternoon drives, and often I took a spade along to dig up wayside plants or shrubs that Margaret wanted for our home. One night we came back with a gorgeous big thistle and, when he caught sight of it, the minister came out on the road and smiling, with both hands uplifted, in a thundering voice he cried:

"In the name of the Lord I command you to stop! All our lives we've been burning these pests of our farms, and now you bring back the enemy!"

We promised to burn it and we did. In one of my many talks with him, he told me how at the age of nineteen, just after the Civil War, he'd been sent to his first mission down South. On his arrival, for a church he found only a dark little log barn. He chopped windows in the walls and then, with a team of mules, drove out and collected powder boxes on the battlefield near by. Of these he built his pulpit and pews and preached his first sermons in the smell of gunpowder, he said. Coming North later, he joined the Free Baptists, who stood for free will and free communion, and founded the little church up here, where he had preached ever since. The village was much larger then, and his church had grown so fast, in those years of flourishing farms, that all one day in a grove near by hundreds of people had gathered to hear sermons by many exhorters and, when worked up to the needed pitch, had given two thousand dollars to send a missionary to China. But since then, with the rush of young people to towns or to homesteads in the West, as the old folks died and left empty farms, his church membership had decreased till it was only twenty-eight; and to eke out his small salary, with an old-fashioned camera in his buggy he had driven about, taking pictures of these mountains he loved, to be sold to two picture-post-card firms, one in Detroit and one in Berlin. But the World War closed his German market, and a little later he faced the great tragedy of his life. For in his seventies, year by year, this man who took pictures of mountains went blind.

Did he let it beat him? Not at all. After losing not only his eyesight but his church and home and going to live with his married daughter on a farm not far away, in his eighties he learned to read print for the blind. In his bedroom his New Testament, printed in Braille in a score of huge volumes, was stacked on the floor by the wall. He found it easy to read, he said, for he knew most of the chapters by heart. Then someone gave him a radio and this became the joy of his life. When he was ninety, I asked him one day how it felt to look back on all he had seen. Was it like looking through a long tunnel to that world of vision behind? With a radiant smile he answered:

"No, no, brother—no, no, no! I was in a tunnel—now I'm outside! For all my life preaching up here in these hills, with never a chance to go away, I grew hungry to see the outside world; and now I do see, for my ears are my eyes!" He pointed to his radio. "Nearly all last night I sat getting reports of those two lads making their flight over Siberia to Japan on their big dash around the globe! I was right with them; I saw with their eyes—on the wings of the morning I saw the dawn break on the uttermost parts of the sea—I mean the Pacific! I traveled last night!"

But from such trips he still liked to come home. When I took him in my car for little drives through the hills that he loved, he knew the contour of the road so well that often he'd say:

"Drive slower now—still slower—now stop." Then he would point to some mountaintop bathed in the afterglow from the sun, and in a low voice he would add: "From here you get the best view of it—and just at this hour how grand it is!"

Often he would urge me to live in this country the year around and write stories of its life. And another clergyman friend up here urged upon me the same thing. "You've no idea how rich this life is in material for your pen," he said. "It's deep, it needs digging, but it's here—not only in the valleys but up in far corners of these hills. Just to show you what surprises you find, here's one that I got some years ago." And then he told this strange little tale: "I was preaching over in Vermont, in the prohibition days, and one Sunday on my way to church I met Home Brew Lizzie, a friend of mine.

" 'Mary's in trouble,' she told me.

" 'Do you know who the man is?'

" 'Yes.'

" 'Will he marry her?'

" 'Sure he will. They want you out there this afternoon.'

"I went there. It was back up in the hills, a farmhouse over a century old. In one room in a huge double bed lay Mary. Her baby was three days old. Her mother and grandmother sat close by. The young groom came from his neighboring farm and we waited till father and grandfather came in with the evening milk from the barn. Then I married Mary to her young man. By that time I knew, from the talk we'd had, that in this same room in this same bed, both the mother and grandmother had been married in this same way—after the baby had been born. I don't give this as typical—for most of these mountain people of course get married in the usual way. I give it only as one of the many surprises you will find in this life, if only you dig deep enough."

In those same prohibition years, a ragged man, who lived with his wife and ten children in a shack up in the hills, was the local bootlegger for our summer colony. Each Thursday night he ran his old car eighty miles to the Canadian line. He could go only on Thursdays, he said, because he'd fixed a federal man to let him cross on Thursday nights. Coming back with his load of Scotch, rum and gin, he drove around quite openly to the summer cottages. And this he did in spite of the fact that the native citizens here were nearly all teetotalers. Why was it they didn't put him in jail? Deep people. It took me months to find out. But at last I learned the reason from our justice of the peace.

"You know our summer group," I began. "We don't get drunk but we do like a cocktail or highball now and then."

"Yes, and you've a right to it."

"But what I want to know is, why don't you put this bird in jail?"

"Because if we do, his wife and ten children will all have to go to the county farm, where to feed 'em will cost the community eleven dollars a month per head. We figure expense to the taxpayers will come to fourteen hundred and fifty-two dollars every year he's behind the bars. And it ain't wuth it. We don't drink. Don't believe in it and never will. You do. That's your business and not mine."

The rumrunning rapidly increased, nor was it just a local trade. Down at Dartmouth sixty miles to the south, two young men, so I was told, entered college in the freshmen class— neat quiet respectable-looking lads, who made no trouble and did their work well. So they got through to senior year. Then the president called them in one day and said:

"Gentlemen, you're both expelled. We've learned of your activities here."

"O.K., sir, that's all right with us. We're lucky to have stayed so long."

"I'm interested," the president said. "I understand that all these years you've kept half a dozen liquor trucks coming through here late each night. Just why did you choose this town to live in?"

"Because, sir, it's a halfway point between Canada and New York—a good place where we could watch our men and check up on every load."

"Just for my own interest and that of my professors, whose salaries are not very high—while here, about how much have you made?"

"Oh, about half a million or so."

Up in our country the growing traffic soon developed a tragic side. For on many lonely farms between here and the Canadian line, old farmers were tempted by huge bribes to let the rumrunners use their barns as hiding places for trucks from the raids of flying squads of federal men. Some were discovered, gun battles took place, and not a few farmers landed in jail. Only in low voices did the natives talk of such affairs, and only once did they break out against this deepening disgrace and curse to the community. But when they did, they broke out hard and showed the force pent up inside!

In a town some twenty miles from our home, one winter when we were living here, a young schoolteacher—who in the war had gone to France and on his return had found the old life much too tame, and had gone into the rumrunning game and had landed in a federal prison—having now escaped from jail, stopped on his way to Canada to see his young wife and their baby, just born. When the old policeman in the town recognized and tried to arrest him, he shot the old cop and ran into the hills. The Boston papers ran the story—Schoolteacher Turns Bandit—on the front page. And then our silent mountain friends, who had been eager enough to read of bandits in Chicago, were so outraged at this disgrace to their own home community and the effect that it might have on the morals of the young that, in the sheriff's posses from half a dozen neighboring towns, through a zero snow blizzard for nearly a week, hundreds of grim farmers with rifles and shotguns joined in the man hunt. Forcing lonely farmhouses to give him food and shelter each night, the young teacher steadily worked his way by forest trails up toward the border. Bloodhounds were sent for, to track him down. But this, too, was featured in the news, and the outlaw must have learned of it in some place where he had spent the night. For he took some black fly dope, left there from the summer before, and rubbed it on the soles of his boots before continuing his flight, just before the hounds arrived. And that saved him—for when they sniffed that pungent odor, the bloodhounds sneezed and refused to follow his trail. So he escaped to Canada.

"Thank God, he's gone. Good riddance," growled one grim old neighbor of ours. "It's 'bout time this scandal stopped."

And so we all grew quiet again. Deep people—poor but proud and strong. A picture of them at their best I had at the local town meeting in March, when, in a long narrow hall up over the village general store, the town clerk and three selectmen sat at a table at one end, and some three or four hundred men, women and children from the village and the farms sat in rows or stood against the walls, leaving a long open space in the center, across which every now and then some child would run or some baby would crawl. For three days the meeting went on; and as the problems of mountain roads, schools, health, sanitation and water supply and protection against forest fires, one by one, were taken up, not only the men but women, too, stood up and had each his say. A picture from an age nearly gone. Old American democracy.

All small potatoes, you may say, for a writer in a world in which democracy is assailed by such gigantic forces in this country and abroad. Yes, but we shall come to them again, as we did in the World War; and meanwhile, from the trips I took to watch the deepening bitterness and chaos made by those same forces, what a relief to get back here to this North Country home of mine! I felt like a Dartmouth lad I had known, who came about the time that we did, more than thirty years ago. His people had raised quite a storm because, with a diploma from Dartmouth which opened the way for a city career, he had chosen instead an outdoor job at a famous inn near our house, one of the earliest of its kind to develop winter sports and so keep open the year around.

"Why shouldn't I come here?" he asked me then. "I love this North Country and life out of doors."

So well did he work that in time he became leader of sports and right-hand man to the owner of the inn. In summer and winter I knew him well. With rod and with rifle and ax in the woods, in sugar camps, in mountain huts or cooking suppers out of doors, and again on snow shoes or on skis, he made so many friends from all over this country and even from across the sea that, when at last some years ago he was killed by a live-wire shock, many helped the owner of the inn build a library in his memory. It is a restful little room with a splendid view of our mountain range. Its log walls are lined with books, and over the stone fireplace is a copper tablet, with a depiction of him on skis and under it these lines from a well-known Dartmouth song:

> The Still North remembers him.
> The hill winds know his name.
> And the granite of New Hampshire
> Bears a record of his fame.

There was another man of his kind, who in summer stayed here for months at a time, but he had chosen to spend his life in the world of big cities, with tenement boys—Fred King, my old friend of the Settlement days. Since then his day and night work for such boys, in street gangs, reformatories and jails, had broken at last his rugged health; and though he had found a grand girl for a wife, a social worker like himself, and she had courageously tried and tried doctors, hospitals, operations, all her efforts had been in vain. With only a few years left to live, still he kept on at his work for boys, worked till he had to take to his bed, then came up to us to gain strength enough so that he could get back to his job. Like other boys, our two small sons adored this lean tall quiet man, with the slow kind understanding smile of relish that he had for them. As his strength returned, we took him on tramps; and Beauty, the pony, came along, so that, when Fred grew tired, he could sit in her little wagon with his long legs trailing behind. When fever forced him back to bed, still he wanted our kids at his bedside for games of cards and long long talks. And often then I would catch in his eyes his memories of those other boys, in tenements, hobo camps and jails. At last, when he could no longer come up, in midsummer I went down to New York and sat by his bed nearly all of one night.

"Nothing can save him," the doctor had told me. "Give him anything he wants."

And he wanted cigarettes. I gave him several that night and he inhaled them long and deep. Toward dawn he whispered to me:

"Good night, fellah."

Then he was gone. He went like men I'd seen die in the war, but his war had been on poverty and all the evils it can bring, and the record of his fame was written in the memories of those for whom he had given his life. In tenements, hobo camps and jails, when the news spread as such news will, I could almost hear them say:

"Our old pal, Fred King, is dead."

In the memories of our own small boys, he left a place so deep and warm that years later one of our twin grandsons was named after him, Fred King Poole.

As our two boys grew older, first one and then the other went to Exeter Academy, here in New Hampshire down near the coast; and I went often to see them at the Big School,

as it is called, and to dig into its rich life. I liked the Latin
inscription which for a hundred and fifty years had been over
the entrance of the main academy hall:
   Hic Venite Pueri Ut Viri Sitis—Boys, Come Here That
You May Be Men.
   There are seven hundred of them now, for since the American Revolution the school has grown to be a place with
splendid equipment for work and play and a teaching staff so
large that every boy can be studied and helped. And yet it
is no rich boys' school. Though a few come from wealthy
homes, more are there on scholarships and eke them out by
work they do. In the campus grillroom at supper one night,
my small son Billy nudged me to notice our waiter, and said
in a low fervent tone:
   "He's one of the biggest men in school!"
   With the old democracy goes still the old spirit of liberty.
They have few rules and the customs hold little threat of
tyranny. One of the teachers said to me:
   "One reason why I like this place is that, though school
spirit and athletics count so strongly here, if any boy doesn't
care to go to the Andover football game and, as one of them
did last fall, reads a novel by Anatole France with his friend
the French teacher instead, it doesn't hurt him in this school.
It's nobody's business but his own."
   In his opening-day address, I once heard the Headmaster
say to the seven hundred before him in the great assembly
hall:
   "I wish I could come close at once to every new boy here
today, for I have so much that I want you to feel about this
life in front of you. You feel lonely at first. It's a big school.
But I want you to understand that right from the start you're
as much an Exeter man as the rest. Nobody will haze you
here and you will find we have few rules. Keep these rules and
stay here and we'll help you all we can. But to do your work
and make your place will be mainly up to you."

To watch those seven hundred respond and develop, under that system of freedom and democracy, took a hold on me so strong that I could write a whole volume of stories about the boys and the ways of the school—in such strong contrast to what later on I was to find in Fascist Rome. I saw the life of Exeter first through the eyes of our two sons. Each time the view was different, for Bill found schoolwork easy and succeeded in winning a place on the staff of the school paper, while Nick cared more for friends and athletics than he did for the printed word. One autumn night he wrote me:

"I played against Andover today and won my E and came back feeling swell. But tonight I've just seen my monthly report and out of five subjects I got three Es, so now I'm feeling kind of low." Quickly I wired him in reply: "Loud proud cheers for that E in athletics but in all other subjects for God's sake work back up the alphabet!"

This he did and won even more credits than he needed for his diploma next year. Long after our two boys had left school, I kept going there, as I do still, to spend a night or two with the Dean and learn how he handled the needs and problems pouring in upon him. His experience was rich and deep. One autumn evening, I remember, he had a lad of sixteen "on the mat." And this is the gist of what I heard, as I listened from a room close by:

"B——, you have been here six weeks. Your work has been good and you have already begun to make a real place for yourself in the athletics and life of the school. You like it, don't you?"

"Yes, sir, I do."

"Then why have you cut Sunday chapel every week since you arrived?"

"Because, sir, I don't believe in any religion. I think it's all bunk." There was just a moment's silence. Then I heard the Dean reply:

"That's mighty interesting. There's a whole lot to be said

about that. Though I myself don't feel as you do, nobody living knows for sure but what possibly you may not be right. But I'm trying to put myself in your place. If you won't go to chapel you can't stay in school—and I think, if I were you, before I gave up Exeter and all that it can mean in my life, I'd try going to chapel this Sunday. Nobody will bother you there. You needn't sing or pray or listen to anything the preacher says. If I were you I'd just sit there and think of all the reasons why you feel you shouldn't be there. You may be right and you may be wrong. Think it out as you never did before and then decide if you'll stay in school. How about it? Will you give it a try?"

"By golly, I will, sir!"

And he did. He thought it out and decided to stay and comply with this rule of the place, for the grip of the Big School's life was already upon him strong. And though often in chapel, I've no doubt, he was bored by what he heard, he would have felt a real jolt of surprise if he could have been there once with me, in the years of postwar disillusion, when a lean old bishop of the Episcopal Church looked down from the high pulpit and said:

"Young men, I shall spend my time today talking to you about four men who have loomed large in this world of our time—Woodrow Wilson of America, Cardinal Mercier of Belgium, Nikolai Lenin of Russia and Mahatma Gandhi of India. For although I myself agree but little with any one of them, I do believe in tolerance toward other points of view than my own. And they all four, each in his way, had the qualities this war-weary world needs so terribly, these days—purpose, passion, vision!"

And he preached his sermon on those men and those qualities. For Exeter is a liberal school which gives welcome and free platform to men of the old bishop's kind.

But what draws me most to the school is the ever-changing river of new life pouring through. It's grand to be young.

If you can't be young, it's good to feel youth close by and borrow of its vitality. One morning I did not get up for chapel at a quarter to eight. Weary and lazy, I lay in bed, listening to the hundreds of footsteps underneath my open window and to the chapel bell. It stopped. The footsteps had passed by. I yawned and thought, now for a little more sleep. But soon I heard the sauntering carefree footsteps of just one boy—then three last clangs from the chapel bell, and then from just below my window burst a whisper:

"Jesus!"

And as he raced for the chapel door, I jumped out of bed. No more sleep for me! That's what Exeter does to me.

I have space for but one more story here. In the Dean's room on a Saturday night stood a boy of eighteen with face set and white. I could see him through the open doorway of the room in which I sat. A young alumnus of the school, who was a Harvard freshman now, had come back that afternoon and taken this boy and his roommate out for a long ride in his car. The young fool had a quart of whisky. They had finished it and this boy had been caught. Abruptly sobered by the shock, for he knew well that it meant expulsion, he stood there and lied and lied and lied in the vain effort to save his friend. When he'd gone and the Dean came back to me, his face was lined and tired. In a low feeling voice, he said:

"Oh, God! How many times I've wished I could act as their lawyer instead of their judge! When it comes to the test, they're so damned fine! And that goes deep as it ever did. You heard how he lied to save his friend. Old-fashioned stuff, all out of date—so say your modern novelists; and so they fill their books these days with postwar disillusionment. It may be true of the war generation but not of this one. They're starting new! I don't mean they're like we were at their age—they have a different world to face. Last year most of them believed that they would not be drawn into war. This year they feel they may have to fight. Next year again their feeling may change. But that's just it. Their lives are uncertain, not only in war but even in a world at peace, where they don't even know what jobs there'll be. But they don't let it worry them. As realists who have no use for anything they believe to be bunk, they're facing the world of tomorrow in their own new way, with their own new eyes!"

XXXIII

THE WORLD OF TOMORROW, WHAT WOULD IT BE? IN ATTEMPTS to get some clues, between the novels that I wrote, I had made trips for magazines about this country and overseas. And at home I had checked my ideas with those of our old friend, Arthur Bullard, who often came to us here with his wife. Since I left him in Russia years before, he had come back and married a girl who soon became one of our dearest friends. With her he had gone to Russia again. In a Siberian winter he'd been desperately ill with mastoid and, although an emergency operation saved him then, it had left a trouble which later was to cost him his life.

About Russia he felt as I did at that time. Though we had no use for the Old Regime or the attempts of reactionaries to regain power through foreign aid, we couldn't forget that the Bolsheviki had killed so many of our old friends, the Social Revolutionists, because of their refusal to subscribe to the rigid Bolshevist creed. In the first All Russian elections in the fall of 1917, by an overwhelming majority of votes of the peasants, still eighty per cent of the people of Russia, the Social Revolutionists had been given control of the government. But the peasants were scattered far and wide, in villages like those I had seen; and in cities and factory towns the Bolsheviki by force of arms had seized the power denied them by vote. So even in Russia our old ideals of political democracy, freedom of speech and press had been lost. And when later in Italy, too, we saw force crush down democracy, and all over the Continent the bitterness planted at Versailles begin to put the entire world in danger of more disastrous wars and an end to human liberties, we pinned our hopes in those next years to the League of Nations, then so strong.

Nearly all the last part of his life Arthur Bullard spent at Geneva. During the time when he was at work in the Secretariat, often Margaret and I went to visit him and Ethel, his wife, in their lovely old apartment there, while our little daughter Betsy Ann was in a small Swiss school near by. And had I space I could tell countless stories, heard as I watched the League in those years gather power until it became a great clearing house for all forces of peace and developed a new technique of settling quarrels through mediation and publicity and delay, in the effort to hold off war until it could grow strong enough at last to make all Europe safe.

But already it had been assailed by ominous emergencies, as in the Corfu crisis, when it was defied by Rome. One of my clearest memories is of the sardonic smile with which Italy's representative on the Council of the League listened to proceedings there. A still more ominous crisis developed in March, 1926, when both Council and Assembly met in a first attempt to bring Germany into the League. And though so much has been written about all the work at Geneva that I shan't try to cover it here, I shall at least give a few little pictures of that disastrous effort in March; for it helped plant the seeds of the dark world crisis with which we are all confronted today. And who knows but what this crisis and these surging forces now at work all over the earth, by the dangers that they bring, may not in the end impel the nations back again to Geneva and an agreement to give the League the armed support that it lacked before, to build a new order and prevent such wars and economic chaos as the world has never seen?

The League had power even then. In that crisis of 1926, on the day before the sessions began, the hotels on the *Quai Wilson* were bright with many-colored flags, as the delegates from forty-eight of the fifty-four nations in the League, including four heads of governments and sixteen foreign ministers, came pouring in by every train. With them came some three hundred newspaper correspondents, hungry journalists on the scent of a big story. But many of them had come before and gone disappointed away, for a "story" was exactly what the League had always tried to avoid. One veteran war correspondent exclaimed in disgust at the height of the row:

"Oh, nothing will happen. They'll fix this up. I can't tell you the number of grand news stories I've seen start here and fizzle out."

But the story this time proved an exception to a calamitous degree. It revealed the old spirit of national jealousies and of secret bargainings, the same spirit that is rampant today. For Germany had demanded a permanent seat on the Council and, though England and France had agreed, Poland had secretly rebelled and refused her support unless she, too, were given a seat. The old Balance of Power idea; and it had appealed to Briand of France, who had privately favored Poland's demand. But England had promised long ago to use her influence to get Spain a permanent Council seat someday, and Brazil for years had claimed one, too; and both countries at this time were holding temporary seats and so could block not only Poland but Germany also if they liked; for the vote must be unanimous. All this had been kept secret but, only in the last few days, the news about Poland had leaked out, the claims of Spain and Brazil had been heard, Germany had felt insulted, enraged, and the end of it was that the delegates had come to Geneva in a state of suspicion and tension which led to a carnival of intrigue!

I attended the first public session of the Council at that time. They held it in a room of glass. Ironical setting at such a moment, as though inviting all the world to look in at them, if it liked. But in the days and nights that followed, the real story was not there. It was in the private "tea parties" of the

Council members up in Sir Eric Drummond's room, or in still smaller meetings in the rooms of hotels close by. What would these wise diplomats do to get out of the snarl they had made for themselves? At dinner one evening my wife sat next to Lord Robert Cecil, that fervently honest worker for peace, and with a weary smile he said:

"With Brazil claiming a Council seat on account of her glorious future, and Spain a seat for her glorious past, it's not so easy to deal with the present."

So the secret discussions went on. The days and nights lengthened out to ten, and the delegates from the little nations all grew angry or depressed. From far over across Lake Leman, the majestic Mont Blanc range, its mighty peaks and snow fields gleaming in the evening sun, looked with a grand and radiant indifference upon it all. Out of the Secretariat would come tired figures, alone or in groups. One worried glance at those distant peaks, that vision of eternal peace, and off they would hurry to some hotel, or in pairs they would anxiously pace up and down, discussing, discussing. The *Quai Wilson* was a grim parade for all the quarrels in Europe, it seemed!

They gathered, too, in the great main lobby in the Secretariat. I never grew tired of watching it, for the scene kept changing all the time. Now it would be almost empty, then suddenly filled again with crowds and a harsh clamor in many tongues; and as the discussions went on and on, the brown carpet on the floor grew speckled with little dots of black, from lighted cigarettes thrown down. Every hour or so, some one of the main protagonists would appear, and eyes would quickly turn his way. One night the members of the Council came down from a secret session upstairs. Up charged the correspondents by scores, all pushing and clamoring:

"What will you do? For God's sake, gentlemen, tell the world!" But the answer was still: "We have nothing to say."

"At the meeting this afternoon," Sir Eric Drummond told

me that night, "I put on the table a box of two hundred cigarettes. Each of the eleven men on the Council had brought his
own. They smoked them all, then turned to mine. At the
end there were less than a dozen left. And that," he added
smiling, "is everything I have to say."

What numberless plans they considered up there the little
nations never knew. But the one that emerged at last was
this: Sweden and Czechoslovakia would resign their temporary seats to Holland and Poland, the former known then as
rather pro-German and the latter as pro-French. The Germans had agreed to that. Theirs would be the only new seat;
for Spain and Brazil would have to wait. A breath of relief
went through the lobby. Thank God, they had fixed it up at
last! But after the Council meeting that day, a dark thin little
man with a lean face and feverish eyes came quickly out of
the room of glass. He was Melho-Franco of Brazil. And later,
as the setting sun cast long serene soft streams of light into
the big rotunda, the news spread swiftly through the crowd
that Brazil still held to her old threat to veto a seat for
Germany!

"So the Council has decided to call it all off!" somebody
cried. "We're going home! The League is dead!"

So swiftly did that rumor spread, and so astounding was
its effect, that in a moment the whole aspect of the big lobby
had utterly changed. From the stairway I looked down upon
a surging mass of men, swirling and eddying like the sea!
Unconsciously in their excitement they reverted to their
mother tongues, in a roaring babel of sound, with gesticulat-
ing hands and furious shrugs and sparkling eyes! Both the
friends and the enemies of the League could now be seen—
the enemies all exultant, the friends distractedly rushing about
and refusing to believe!

I dived into it behind Edgar Mowrer of the Chicago Daily
News. As he elbowed his way about the great room, sharply
questioning men that he knew, in the next few minutes I

heard him speak in English, German, Italian and French. Other excited journalists swarmed about like so many bees, and I heard one of them ask: "Who's behind Brazil in this, Germany or Italy?" A little Jap pushed smiling by, steady and cool and unconcerned. The huge handsome delegate from Ethiopia stalked past. "Oh, Black Man," one frantic journalist cried, "go on back home and thank God you're not white! I've got to cable a story tonight!"

For the journalists, what a night! It ended at dawn. The news was no fake. They wired long stories all over the earth, and then limped wearily to their hotels for a little snatch of sleep, before the Assembly met at ten.

"Now comes the love feast, the great show," my neighbor in the press gallery said. "Will they get up now and tell the world the whole truth about this? They will not. We'll get fine speeches."

And we did. Chamberlain, Briand and many more did their best to counteract the bitter oration in which Melho-Franco of Brazil declared his nation's policy. But early that evening I went to the station where a train was waiting to take the German delegation home. I asked one of them: "When will you come back?" And he glanced at me with hostile eyes. "We will never come back," he said.

From the station I walked with Bullard up into the silent crooked streets of an old quarter of the town and there entered an old church, where a chorus of two hundred was rehearsing Bach's great cantata called Peace. The chorus was not perfectly trained, but the music was grand to me that night. In tumultuous rivers of sound, like irresistible torrents of life, all the yearnings and rejoicings of the earth rose to the skies. Always changing, wild and free, yet all those many torrents of sound kept rolling and thundering into one! In my mood that evening, there was something tragic in its joy. For I could not help but wonder, when will the nations sing like that?

I left Geneva that same week, but Bullard stayed on at his

work. Though I never quoted him by name, he had given me more than anyone else of what I wrote for the New York Times. And so he did with numberless others. In the Section of Information his French chief told me one day:

"Bullard has been invaluable with many hostile journalists here, for he shows himself so ready to hear their different points of view that they like him, and so he is able to bring them closer to our own." When I told him this, he smiled and said:

"That Frenchman is an optimist."

Just a few years after that, at Geneva, Arthur Bullard died. Like our mutual friend Fred King, from our old group at the Settlement, on the last evening of his life he lay smoking cigarettes. But he talked to a friend of Briand's that night and gave him ideas, which the great French orator used before the Assembly next day, in one of the most powerful speeches that he ever made for peace. And that was Arthur Bullard's good-by. The news of his death took my thoughts far back to the summer when in our early twenties we had tramped in Switzerland and dreamed dreams of what we might do with our lives. In the service of those dreams, he'd been untiring ever since. The world of tomorrow, what will it be? Peace, progress and democracy, or wars of the dictatorships plunging the whole civilized world into a welter of chaos and blood? Arthur Bullard had given his life for democracy, progress and peace.

XXXIV

COMPARED TO ALL THE DARK CONFUSION LEFT IN EUROPE BY the war, how safe and strong and sure of herself our country seemed in those next years! Woodrow Wilson? Never again! With "good old Cal" Coolidge keeping us free from all entanglements abroad, and with prosperity surging up in cities and towns all over the land, high wages, movies, automobiles, low costs through mass production, efficiency and new machines, Yankee genius everywhere was building a New Era here, with no depressions ever again to be allowed to jerk us down from this Hollywood Heaven we had made.

But from this new prosperity one great class had been left out, the millions on our plantations and farms. And now from the network of forces world-wide which, with my own existence secure, I had watched as a writer for twenty years, this poverty of the farmers reached in and made me feel the ominous grip of the outside world on the life of my home. For my father had left to his seven children money invested mainly in farm mortgages in the West; and as the prices of wheat and corn came down from the heights they had reached in the war and brought poverty to our farms, in a few years I found myself faced with heavy losses. In vain my agent gave farmers years to pay the interest due on my loans. As conditions grew worse and worse, they moved with their families into towns and left farms on my hands, with unpaid taxes and houses and barns so out of repair that renting them was impossible.

But from this first little scare the outside world had given me, I made a quick recovery. For half of my income had come from my pen and, with the popular magazines rolling in prosperity, I found it so amazingly easy to earn all the money I needed, those days. I remember one short story which I sold at a dollar a word. And still more clearly I recall an offer I had one afternoon in the immense Park Avenue office of a high-power publicity firm, a place divided in cubicles with low glass walls that shut out sound. How quiet it was! And yet it hummed! A modern Yankee dynamo—and yet quiet as a church. Advertising was a religion there. In a row upon one wall, richly framed and reverently lighted by soft glows from above, were those great masterpiece picture "ads" that had sold millions of dollars' worth of lustrous corsets, chewing gum and cigarettes. But now to business! In his glass stall, the spruce young man who had sent for me said:

"To advertise the Badmington watch, we're running a series of double spreads in Collier's and the Post. It's costing thirty thousand a week and we'll pay you a thousand for six hundred words on a midnight sailing from New York of the *Île de France*. If you'll do it, we'll run your text in a box in the middle of the ad."

"And all around it pictures of the watch factory?"

"Not at all. Only pictures of the *Île de France*. And your text will be all about that and the importance of accuracy in time when you are traveling. You might mention your book, The Harbor, too. Only once need you mention the watch. We like to be subtle nowadays."

Subtly and quickly we went to work and planned a description of the great ship, her fabulous cost and the fabulous wealth in her first-class cabins and in her freight, including stacks of gold bricks sent from one land to another to meet the shifts in foreign exchange. With such a load and such a ship, thousands of dollars were involved in every minute of delay. So we reached our climax up on the bridge, where an able quiet officer, who controlled the whole big show, shot a look at the Badmington on his wrist, said—"Midnight"—and pressed a button that loosed above us a bellowing roar, as the great ship moved out to sea.

As it happened, I did not write that "ad," for I found so much of the real stuff of life that I could work on at that time. With the postwar disillusion rapidly being swept aside in the rush of our prosperity, the business of the common good, pushed wholesale in the Yankee way with a speed that brought much flubdub and waste, still could show an immense amount of real constructive work of all kinds. In our factories many plans of profit sharing were being tried. At a Princeton reunion I met an old friend who was working as an engineer on safety devices to head off disasters in mines; and this movement for Safety First, in our work and life and play, was rapidly spreading all over the land. Already some effort was being made to decrease the slaughter on our big new motor roads, where every year we lost more lives than we had in the World War. Meanwhile, in the dark and crowded tenement regions of our cities, wide new boulevards and small parks and playgrounds let in sun and air; and towns and cities made great drives to weed out fake philanthropies and for the efficient kind raise funds in one municipal purse. For public schools and colleges new buildings by the thousand appeared, and the rush into education all over the country was so great that, even up here in our White Mountains, half the farmer boys and girls began to plan to go to college. As a decorator, my wife had already worked with the architect of the new Spence School in New York, and now with two able women friends she was furnishing the rooms of Bennington College in Vermont.

With the same rapidity spread public-health work of all kinds. Up here our small railroad town built a bigger and better hospital, and soon we had a district nurse motoring out to the loneliest farms. Even down in the Old South, Mary Breckenridge, to combat the awful waste of life through disease in

the mountains of Kentucky, had organized the Frontier
Nurses and had so ably pushed the work that eight years
later, when I went down, I found some thirty trained nurse-
midwives in nine stations far apart, lonely little houses and
barns connected with the outside world only by narrow
mountain trails, over which they rode day and night to still
lonelier mountain cabins, where children with diphtheria,
pneumonia or snakebite lay at the point of death, or babies
were about to be born. Dramatic crusaders, these women on
horseback, often swimming their horses over flooded rivers
and creeks, or through blizzards riding icy trails with flash-
lights on black winter nights. Still more dramatic, the people
down there. Descendants of the pioneers in the days of Daniel
Boone, they spoke in slow soft voices and were hospitable
and kind; yet most of the men and half-grown boys carried
rifles or pistols still, and several little gun fights took place
in the two weeks I was there. But the men kept quiet about
such affairs, and the women were quiet as the men—quiet in
living, quiet in dying, quiet in giving new life to the world.

"Nearly every one of them," said a nurse, "goes through
childbirth without a cry. She smokes a clay pipe almost till
the last and then clamps her teeth on her agony."

And from another nurse came this:

"I was called to a case away up in the hills, where I had
never been before. Alone in a cabin I found a young wife
only eighteen years of age, who told me this was her first confinement. Already near the crisis, she lay there silent all alone,
under a lovely old homemade quilt. When I tried to examine
her, she refused, for these women are modest about such
things. I insisted, however, and threw off the quilt—and saw
two pistols on her breast! When I asked her why they were
there, she answered:

" 'Well, I told my husband to go on up an' hoe the corn an'
let me handle myself till you came. But he's had a few gun

fights with folks up this way, so I reckoned I wouldn't take no chances. This baby is a go'n' to be born.'"

Although these people were so poor that money was scarcely ever seen, few of them had any use for it, for in its place the age-old custom of barter still prevailed in the hills, and the nurses were paid for their services in chickens and eggs, ducks, squirrels and possums, fruits and vegetables, hay and corn. One day at a station I saw a young woman drive in with a small load of hay. With a pitchfork she put it up into the barn.

"That's to pay for my baby," she said.

I found such a wealth of stories and scenes that my magazine could use only a part, so I gathered them all in a little book called Nurses on Horseback. I loved that job. It was such a relief to be writing about people who cared so little for money and whose lives were still so close to the very elementals of things.

But meanwhile, back in those years of the boom, in a long series of articles for the Saturday Evening Post, I had followed the trail of a lean old man, who from frugal poverty had risen to enormous wealth, and had then ranged around the globe and become a familiar figure in ports of all the Seven Seas. He was one of the last of our pioneers, Captain Dollar of the Dollar Line.

From a rigidly religious home in a fishing village on the Scotch coast, he had come to Canada as a boy and, in the next forty years, had made a great fortune in timber, first in Wisconsin and later on in California and Oregon. To carry his timber down the coast, he bought small steamers and little ships. And so, at an age when most rich men are ready to sit back with their gains, he went into the shipping business. Ships with sails and ships with steam, all along the coast they went, taking thousands of gold diggers North in the wild rush of the

Klondike days. But the coast trade could not hold him long. Off to China and Japan and later to India he sailed, with still bigger and bigger ships. With his staunch old wife at his side, in their sixties and seventies voyaging hundreds of thousands of miles, making friends and getting trade, as Captain Dollar he was known in many crowded Eastern ports. And finally, over eighty years old, with his two sons he embarked on the greatest venture of his life, a line of ships around the world.

All this he gave me in graphic tales and vivid scenes, before he died. But the ones that rise most clearly now, in my memory as I look back, are the pictures he drew of the life in China, where he had numberless Chinese friends, and his dreams of a glorious future time when, from American shops and mills, on American ships like his own, millions of hats and pairs of shoes and radios and automobiles would pour in on the Chinese to wake them at last from their long deep sleep to the bustle and roar of modern life, and in this country would bring a boom beyond our dreams in foreign trade.

But with those memories comes another of a talk I had one day with a dark little man in the San Francisco office of a Japanese line. For though very careful in all that he said, the meaning he conveyed that day reminded me of what I had heard from that other little man from Japan, who at Mukden had told me:

"Here Yellow Race turned White Race back from effort to invade the East. Better let East manage own affairs. So Japan and America remain friends."

On our way back from the Coast in that autumn of 1928, my wife and I stopped for a few days in Chicago with our families. In our home city what a change! From a chain of parkways and lagoons reaching for some twenty miles or more along the lake, wide boulevards and avenues plowed through the city that had been, to give space for the city that was to be. But meanwhile what a chaos of growth! In the neighborhood I'd known so well as an eager exploring little boy, our street was a broad avenue now, with huge office and apartment buildings rearing up on every hand, crowding out the homes I'd known and making the few houses left look like grim lonely little dwarfs. Our own house, now a gaunt old shell, had just been sold, and in the recorded deed it appeared that, since the Indian grant, my grandfather and my father had been the only white men owners of our lot, which was now to become the site of a skyscraper of today!

And so it was all over the land. With America booming on to big things, as the passion and energy of it all converged on Chicago in the West, back in the East in that next year I could feel it center more and more upon New York and the Stock Exchange.

Often in those last few years, with money of my own to invest, I had talked with various banker friends and so had learned of a man described as "one of the wisest heads downtown," and had put nearly half my funds into his new investment trust. For who was I to manage such things? And so amazingly well did he do that I can still remember an afternoon at the Players Club, when I read an evening paper and learned I had many thousands of dollars in paper profits in three months!

But investment was by no means all that had taken me downtown—for there were two of me down there; one, the would-be money-maker, hungry for profits as the rest; the other, the writer watching it all. Toward the end of a big day, from the gallery of the Stock Exchange I had looked down on mobs of men around the many trading posts, their voices pulsing up in waves to a shrill high vibrant scream, that tore the nerves with the age-old passion in this grand new gambling game. From all over the country the orders poured in, to be put through with such speed that an order given in San Francisco, telephoned to a New York office and from there to one of the booths lining the walls of the Exchange, was executed on the floor and the news was telephoned back to the Coast—all in less than two minutes' time!

So many people all over the land were tempted by easy money, those days. Up here in our New Hampshire mountains, the village telephone operator told me one day that a well-known banker was staying at our local inn, under doctor's orders to rest his nerves.

"And the way he's a restin'," said my friend, "is to get New York every day on the 'phone. He's a buyin' thousands and thousands of shares of a certain stock down there, an' every day the price of that stock keeps goin' higher. Seems like a chance to make some money. I've got a little saved myself and I'm wonderin' if you could put me in touch with some stockbroker in New York."

Although I argued against it, he insisted and took a broker's address. Two weeks later he called me up and said:

"Seems like that investment ain't turnin' out so bad after all. The stock's way up and keeps a goin'."

"Sell it! Sell it!" I replied. And I cursed the power of this game that could reach even up to the heart of New England and make a victim of my friend. When later the stock dropped in a week to less than what I thought he had paid, anxiously I asked him whether he had sold in time. And then New England answered me.

"Oh, hell," he drawled, "I couldn't sell, because I never bought the stuff. I was just a figurin' how it would feel to be a fool gambler like that."

Another lucky friend of mine was a Swede down in New York, who ran a delicatessen shop. Hearing from friends on every hand of the wonderful profits they had made, at last he couldn't stand the strain of missing such chances for easy gain, so in 1929 he went to a big broker's office on a frenzied market day. There he produced two thousand dollars, named a well-known stock and said:

"I want you to sell me a hundred shares."

When the transaction had been made, he went home and could not sleep that night. Later, when the crash came and his stock dropped from twenty to only two dollars a share, he went back to get what was left of his money and to his amazement learned that, on the day he'd first been there, a terribly busy broker had interpreted his order, "to sell me" as meaning "to sell for me"; and by selling the stock short had brought him not a loss but a profit of eighteen hundred dollars!

"Vere is it? Vere is it?" Sweden cried.

"Oh, it's all on paper yet. You haven't told us to cover you."

"Then cover me! Damn! I don't know what you mean—but do it, do it—get me my money!"

An hour later in a daze, he walked out with thirty-eight hundred in cash!

But few of us were so lucky as he. Most of us held on and on, in those grand safe New Era days. And to bring still more of us into the market, in the publicity room adjoining the gallery of the Stock Exchange, I was shown upon one wall a large map of the whole country, with many pegs that were moved each day. For every peg represented a speaker moving about from town to town, advertising the great boom.

Such was the body and soul of our country in the years leading up to 1929. And contrasting all this prosperity and safety of ours to the black depths of poverty and deepening tension I felt upon my trips abroad, I wrote a novel called Silent Storms—little suspecting at the time how those deep and silent forces of impending storm, gathering not only there but right here in our country, too, would soon reach in on me again and tighten their grip on my own small life.

XXXV

WHEN THE NATIONAL MAGIC BUBBLE BURST AND THE STOCK Exchange went panic mad, when the stock of my investment trust dropped abysmally overnight, and as time went on the magazines bought fewer stories and articles—with my income down to a point where I could give but little money to the fast-increasing hordes of people thrown out of their jobs, I gave some of my time to them instead and wrote appeals to the public for aid.

One was for a mammoth bread line down close to the Bowery. Grim and stark in my memory still is the picture that I had of it one darkening afternoon in March. In double line stood the shadowy forms of seven thousand men and boys, reaching off around the block. These were no hobos, I soon learned, but steel workers, bridge builders, railroad men and factory workers of all kinds. Their faces wore dull hopeless looks. But as in drizzle, slush and mud they stood in the cold gathering dusk, suddenly one of them jerked his head up toward the darkening sky; and a moment later, faint but clear, came a sound like a bugle call, dropping down from a flock of wild geese flying north—the call which meant that winter was gone and the season for jobs out of doors had begun. And now I saw scores of faces of men and boys along the line all staring up into the sky. But the bugle call soon died away in the distance, and the heads went down, and eyes that had gleamed grew dull as before, and slowly the great line shuffled on.

I saw many bread lines, that first year, and shivering crowds that gathered around bonfires in vacant lots. No warm bright barrooms took them in, for these were prohibition days; but the Bowery had speak-easies in plenty, where for a nickel you could take a "flop" for the night. I went down into some such basement holes, hot and stifling, with the sleepers lying thick on the foul wet floors. In one of them a white-faced boy sat up and vomited, then fell back. And my guide said:

"He ain't used to Smoke. That's the hootch down here, these days; you'll find it all along the line. You bring an empty milk bottle here and you can get it half filled for a quarter. Then pour in water to fill up the bottle and a sort of steam comes out. That's how it got its name of Smoke. It's wood alcohol, that's what it is, with the biggest part of the poison took out. But it has a hell of a kick in it still. Your first drunk makes you sick for a week."

Around us several sleepers woke up and yelled: "Shut up, for Christ's sake!"—to the boy groaning on the floor.

As the hordes of homeless men increased, some of them were sheltered in a vacant factory building run by the Salvation Army, which was known as Gold Dust Lodge. I went often to describe in appeals the good work that the Army was doing down there. Into that old building came two or three thousand every night, men from every walk of life. I saw scores with shabby bags and old brief cases in their hands. In the entrance hall one afternoon I stood for a time with a doctor, who was picking out the sick from those crowding through the door; and as they came in from slush and mud with shoes from which the soles were half gone, the doctor told of pneumonia cases that kept coming by the score.

"For God's sake, tell the public that what we need is shoes!" he cried. "These men are no bums—all winter long they've tramped the whole city in search of jobs—in shoes like these—and so they come to me like this!"

In one of the tremendous shadowy sleeping halls above,

kept clean by a miracle of hard unceasing work each day, were hundreds of double-decker bunks. And the night watchman said to me:

"Only a few nights ago a little guy in here went nuts. I heard him yelling and ran in and pretty soon got him quieted down, but then he lay and shook all over. The kid had a God-awful cough, so I took him to the doctor's room, where the nurse got his story out of him. He was a white-collar boy and he'd felt like a lost soul till he met another boy of his kind, who told him that the guards in the subway let fellahs ride for a nickel all night, so they could sleep in the empty cars after the evening crowds were gone. So this kid went there with his new friend. But along about a month ago he was waked up late one night by the jar of the train as it made a quick stop. He heard some track men shouting and he saw that the boy beside him was gone. The train had stopped just after it had started to leave a station—see—so the kid got out— and they backed the train—and when he saw what it had done to the face and guts of his suicide pal, he got crazy and ran up to the street and wandered around all the rest of the night. It was damned near zero, too. That's how he had got the cough and that's what had made him yell like he did. He said every time he fell asleep a subway train ran over him."

I had no chance to talk with him; he died of pneumonia that week. But I'll never forget the bitterness in the eyes of another boy, who sat with hundreds of others on benches in the great assembly room, where to help them forget their troubles the Salvation Army ran entertainments every night. The soloist that evening was a well-known baritone from uptown. He had brought along his gorgeous young wife and her equally gorgeous friend. The young fools had come in full evening dress, and the bitterness of the boy I was watching had been sharply stirred by the sight. The lad next to him had caught his look and had shoved a small leaflet into his hand. He read it and dropped it, they whispered a while and then he went out with his new friend. I picked up the leaflet and read:

"If you've had enough of this rich man's country come to our headquarters."

The address was that of a Communist "cell" (district organization) close by. But with such propaganda, though they were active day and night, the Communists won few recruits compared with the numbers of unemployed. In the bread lines of that first year, I watched them slip thousands of leaflets into the hands of those in line; but in most cases, after a glance, the paper was dropped into the mud.

"To hell with it," I heard one giant mutter, as he shuffled on; and he was typical of the whole line. From an old Salvation Army colonel, a veteran of some forty years' service, I heard what later was confirmed by many relief workers I knew:

"In all the big depressions I've seen, the average man goes through three stages. First, he's fired and feels lost, gets scared and hunts hard for a job. Second, when he can find no job, he gets bitter and joins the Communists or some other brand of Reds. This isn't so bad, this second stage, for when hard times end and he gets a good job, he'll lose his bitterness and tone down. But if he goes on to the third stage, he's hopeless, for then he sinks so low he can't even be bitter any more; he no longer wants a job and wouldn't be any good if he did; he's a pauper for the rest of his life. And the thing that worries me most about this present depression is that most of these lads are jumping through the second stage right into the third, where they get so used to being fed just enough to keep 'em alive that they'll go on like that till they're dead."

Nor need it be such poor living at that, when once a man has learned the game. As I sat one night in the reading room of the Bowery Y.M.C.A., my attention was caught by the utterly lost and desperate look of a boy in a chair close by, a typical white-collar boy, with his threadbare coat brushed

clean and his celluloid collar washed by himself in the basement laundry below. Next him sat another lad who had
bright shrewd clever eyes. As he talked to the first one, his
voice was low; but they sat so close that I could hear.

"I felt like you do once," he said, "only about a year ago.
I'd come down the line alone and didn't know my way
around. Hell while it lasted—it sure was. But a wise bo got
hold of me then and showed me the easy money he made
workin' a few street corners uptown. You gotta pick your
corners and the time of day or night, and pick the guys you
talk to—see—and even that ain't all of it. You gotta talk and
dress the part of a nice respectable little boy. You learn a
half a dozen lines and choose the line to fit your guy—and
you gotta be quick about it, too. But once you've learned to
play the game, it's so easy, it's a laugh. I've took five dollars
in one night. Keep at it and you can save enough by spring so
you can hit the road, like I did last year with a pal of mine.
Christ, what a hitchhike—clear to the Coast! Ridin' on trucks
and in storage vans and on freight trains in empties full of us
guys, I've heard the God-damnedest songs of the road—real
smutty ones like back in the war. You can sleep in camps in
the open—see—you find 'em all along the line—old hobo camps
hid back in the woods. When you get in, you pool your cash
and send guys out to get the chow. I've seen hunks of meat
as big as your head and a damn sight bigger, go into the pot!
And that ain't all—the towns are gettin' so scared of us guys,
they give us free camps and even free chow, just to keep us
out of town. That's livin', bo, that's livin'! Jobs? To hell with
'em! That's the life!"

So hundreds of thousands of men and boys moved over the
country in ceaseless tides. Some of them still hunted for jobs
in the old American way. But times had changed. From
"Young man, go West" we had come to this—"Christ, what
a hitchhike—clear to the Coast!"

And so, not only out on the road but in cities and mill

towns all over the land, four million American paupers were made.

All through those years of deepening chaos, ominous misery and despair, what was being done by our leaders, the great heads of industries and the famous financiers? Far be it from me, a mere writer of stories, to try to sit in judgment here. I am neither an expert economist nor any kind of businessman. My business all my writing life has been with social forces and the tides of feeling back of them. And so here my main concern is not so much with our leaders themselves as with what most people thought of them. And what they thought was plain enough. For here were leaders to whom for years had come incomes fabulous to most men, in payment for the genius they were all supposed to possess in the management of our affairs. Surely we had a right to expect to find at least one Moses there to lead us out of our wilderness. But when the country turned to them, no such powerful figure appeared. No big clear vision, no great plan or program for recovery. Having begun by assuring us all that this would be no long depression and would be over in a few months, when times instead grew worse and worse and they'd proved to be as blind as ourselves, they acted like men paralyzed, and from them a defeatist spirit spread to smaller men of their kind. Not all of them did; I knew a few to whom my humble hat is off for the grim courage that they showed. But exceptions prove the rule, and even I heard enough to be sure of the stories I could tell of the rest if I had been close enough. I remember a talk I heard among three Wall Street men one night. One, who was the president of an immense trust company, said:

"The Bank of United States"—which had crashed some time before—"is going to pay fifty cents on the dollar to depositors." And when his remark produced no stir, he went on with a grim little smile: "But my God, men, just think what it means! Where are the stocks we recommended to customers two years ago? Is there one worth half the price they paid? They'd all be better off today if they'd taken their money out of our hands and put it into this bank that crashed, for then they'd at least have got half of it back!"

The second banker frowned in a way that showed his displeasure at such talk; but the third one, with a sense of humor, chuckled and said:

"I know one young dame who got more than *all* her money back." And then he gave us this little yarn: "She was a gay young broker's wife and riding on the crest of the wave. When she'd so often overdrawn that first one bank and then another asked her to take away her account, her husband sternly warned her that if she overdrew again he would stop her credit at every luxury shop in town. He then opened a new account for her in an uptown branch of the Bank of United States. His warning slowed her up for some time, but at last she was so tempted by a necklace in a Fifth Avenue shop that she drew a check for the price they asked, two thousand dollars, and brought it home. But at home on coming out of her trance, she rushed for her checkbook and there found she was nearly a thousand overdrawn! How about her credit now, as soon as Jimmy learned of this? Then the telephone rang—and when she heard her master's voice, she shrank with terror! She heard him say:

" 'Amy! There's a run down here on the Bank of United States! Go at once to your uptown branch and draw out every dollar you've got!'

" 'But why?' she stammered. 'What do you mean?'

" 'I mean the bank has crashed!' he cried. 'And if you don't reach your branch in time you'll lose all your money! Grab your hat!'

"As Amy stood there petrified, into her fluffy little head came a wonderful bright idea that would make her life happy for years to come. In a reproachful tone, she asked:

" 'But Jimmy, darling—really—wasn't it pretty foolish of you to put all my money into a bank as bad as that?'

" 'Never mind that now! Run! Grab your hat!'

" 'And if I get the money out—will you promise never, never again to make a fuss if I'm overdrawn?'

" 'Sure I will! For God's sake run!'

" 'Oh, Jimmy, there's no need of that,' drawled the placid little dame. 'For as near as I can tell from my book, I've already taken out a thousand more than I put in!' ' "

A most diverting little tale. I laughed with the rest of them. But I had other banker friends and, when I found among them so little hope of remedy for the misery I'd seen in bread lines, I grew bitter on such nights. Yet now as I look back on those men, there come other memories that bring some realization of the difficulties they faced. For they were not the gods we'd thought them—only men—and the forces raging then were as vast as the war that had loosed them into this close-knit modern world. Moreover, all were by no means defeatists but fought on to the end. I knew one of that kind, a big man downtown, who kept working day and night to save great banks and factories and mills from closing shop and throwing more workers out of jobs. When the strain on him grew too hard, he went South for a week or two of golf. I went with him. But so did his work. At all hours of the day and night came those desperate calls for help. New York was calling. Then he would go to the telephone and I would hear his low quiet voice, friendly, reassuring and kind. But when he came back from such long talks, behind his smile I would catch in his eyes a look like that of a captain up on the bridge of some rudderless ship, trying to ride out an ocean storm.

And I have another memory of a smaller man of that kind. In the gloom of the Bank Holiday, when every bank in the country was closed, over the entrance to our own, in the mountain town not far from our home, the anxious farmer depositors read a notice to this effect, put up by the bank president:

"This bank is closed by order of the Governor of this State. But we have money with which to pay every depositor in full. In the meantime go ahead as before, using our checks. They're good as cash."

Later these words proved to be true. But the same could not be said of hundreds of little country banks. So millions of farmers all over the land lost what scant savings they had left, and their poverty deepened that of those in our cities and factory towns. For farmers had no money to spend on factory goods, so the factories closed; and the starving unemployed had no money for bread or meat or milk, so prices went lower still on the farms. As never before since I started to write, I realized how our whole country had grown to be like a tremendous machine, each part dependent on all the rest. Blame any one man or group of men for the misery of that last collapse? How futile and blind to these modern times! For it wasn't only the men but the whole system we had to blame. Our great machine had broken down.

XXXVI

INTO ALL THAT BITTERNESS, THAT MISERY AND DEFEATIST gloom, over the air came the voice of a man who once by sheer force of his will had raised himself from a cripple's bed, and now called on a whole nation paralyzed to get up and walk. Politics? Yes, politics, in nearly every speech he made. But what a political genius was here!

"I don't agree with a word of it, but it's the best political speech I ever heard," said a judge I knew, at the end of one of those "fireside talks." Their effect was like a miracle. And as with the first magic of inflation, prices soared, and into the factories, mills and mines, department stores and offices, men and women, boys and girls went pouring back to work, the old familiar name of "Roosevelt!" was heard like a slogan all over the land, leading us back to prosperity. Businessmen have forgotten how enthusiastic they were in those days. I remember a dinner my wife and I went to in New York one night. We were going on to the Opera, so dinner was early, but we had to wait for a brilliant young man of the new Brain Trust, who was on his way from Washington. When he arrived and we sat down, all through dinner he was kept talking by admiring men from downtown. And smilingly he played his part. But later at the Opera, he came with me out of the box of our hostess and, as we walked in the foyer, he said:

"These people won't like us so much later on, for they're going to see such government interference with business as they never saw before. These rugged individualists will now find their day is gone and their whole show is out of date.

Any fool knows how the whole world is moving straight toward Moscow. We don't like it and so we mean to block that movement here if we can. When a smart young hussy the other day, who'd known the Big Chief all her life, came and asked: 'Will you be our greatest or our lousiest President?'—he smiled back at her and said: 'Not your lousiest, my dear; I'll be your greatest or your last.' The Communists know that damned well; and as they see us spoiling the grandest chance they've ever had, they're going to be mighty sore. But while they call us bourgeois trimmers, these gentlemen here will call us Reds. For in this last drive of ours to hold up Moscow's little game, we mean to go right into the factories, mills and mines these gentlemen own, and even right into their sacred banks to the altar where they bow down to gold." When I asked him what he meant, he said:

"We'll try government interference first, and we think the plan we're ready to spring will bring a big recovery. But if it doesn't, we'll make it come—by consumer credit."

"What is that?"

With a cheerful grin he answered: "Well, to put it short and plain, we'll hand you money and tell you to go buy yourself a new suit of clothes."

With these two arrows to its bow, the great New Deal set blithely out to hunt all our troubles down. Often in the next few years I went to Washington with my wife to visit two old friends of ours, Frances Perkins and Ethel Bullard; and from their different points of view and those of others whom I knew, I saw from many angles the activities surging into life. The new bureaus springing up on all sides gave welcome to all sorts and kinds of new and "liberal" ideas, so long as they could be hammered onto our wrecked American machine in this new national garage. But all done carefully, "all as we planned." And the plan, as rapidly it grew, in numberless pages of documents and bewildering blueprint maps, into an immense patchwork affair, all centered on the man in the

White House. As he issued his orders and Congress obeyed, the magic of his first success was poured into my ears from every side. In the home of Frances Perkins we met many appealing young college lads, who with the fervor of a religion were planning government careers; and they slaved literally day and night to make the New Deal a success. But elsewhere in Washington I found other boys of a different kind, who were there to rock the boat, and did. A big industrial leader from Chicago, my home town, who had worked for months in Washington, told me one night that first winter:

"I'm through. I've tried my damnedest to help this show, for God knows this country needs something new. So I've tried to play ball, but it can't be done. Every practical plan that I offered was stopped. I traced my trouble all to one desk and there I found a quiet young lad, with one of the most brilliant minds I've ever known in any kid. But that whole mind was set like rock against me and all of my kind."

When I learned the boy's name, I had to smile, for I happened to know him well. After an amazing record in one of our great universities, he had turned Communist and was here, as he frankly admitted, to block the show.

"My three-thousand-dollar salary is ridiculous," he said. "In Moscow I'd work for food and board, and so would I here if I could see any use at all in this last attempt to save the system of private profits. But I don't—and so I'm here, by God, to throw in a wrench wherever I can."

Having finished off the man from Chicago, he was now working hard to squeeze the profit out of the making of cigarettes.

"But I'm getting sick and tired of this whole bourgeois game," he said. "The President is a political trimmer. Already he's moving to the Right. I mean to throw up my job soon."

He did, and so did others of his kind. I met few Communists later there, and much of the work of the New Deal made a strong appeal to me; but in the old American way too much was done and done with a rush. When the N.R.A. came cracking down on American business that first year, into the factories, mills and mines, offices, stores and little shops, rushed government interference in the persons of thousands of men, too many of whom had got their jobs through some local political pull and knew even less than I do about any business large or small. And the result, in countless cases, very soon began to appear in such tyranny and budding graft as made harassed Americans think of our prohibition days.

About the plan that appealed to me most, for old-age pensions and social insurance, I talked with a Supreme Court Justice, a liberal whom I had known for years.

"I think it's a grand idea," he said. "But just because it is so fine, it worries me to see it now being attempted on such a scale for the whole nation all at once. In Wisconsin a similar plan has been made a real success. Why? Because trained, careful experts there have devoted years and years of work to plan it out, put it through and adapt it to realities."

I heard very little talk of this kind. In place of it on every side, brilliant young men told how they meant to make over the nation in a few years. Moreover, their work was in a stage of theories, plans and figures that gave no chance whatever to my humble writer's pen. I've always liked more human stuff.

John Lewis down there had the stuff. His whole life had been full of it. I had heard him once in a great hall filled with several thousand United Mine Workers. Rebel factions had raised a rumpus that ended in a storm of shouts and boos and yells, all over the hall. But over all that ocean of sound, from the platform came a bellowing voice with a power that made all others still. John Lewis knew how to handle men.

In Washington he looked different now. In his well-cut dinner coat, I met him at several dinners there. I remember one large one. I was late. As I entered, I was given a card with the name of the woman I was to take in. Not knowing

her, as the fifty guests moved toward the dining room, I spied
John Lewis and asked for help. He glanced at the card.

"Don't know her," he said. "We'll ask my wife."

Mrs. Lewis, a quiet little woman, who had been a doctor's
daughter and a schoolteacher in the West, was sitting on a
sofa waiting for her partner. She glanced at my card and
promptly said:

"One of the oldest families in Washington. She's standing
just across the room."

"Thank you, Mrs. Lewis," I said. When I had taken my
lady in, at table she turned to me with a smile and asked:

"Who's this big man on my left?"

"John Lewis," I whispered.

"Merciful God!"

She seemed to get on splendidly. But after dinner her remark reminded me of what my wife had said of Bill Haywood
years before:

"That's the most dangerous man I've met."

Dangerous with the force that comes to a man who has
only a few big aims and plugs at them day and night. In one
of several talks we had, as he told me what he aimed to get
for workingmen all over the land, I asked:

"But what if Europe crashes in?"

"To get us into war again?"

"Yes."

"They can't do it. We won't go."

"Not now we won't, but you never know. And I was just
wondering," I said. "A major war means railroad trains with
locomotives that burn coal. Haven't you an international
federation of coal miners?"

"Yes, we have. I've been over there twice."

"Then how would it be, the next time Europe gets right
up to the brink of war, if you asked all the miners over there
to join with you in refusing to mine any coal for war use?"
With a quick smile he answered:

"Not for me! I've been over twice and seen enough! It's a fast game, brother, leave it alone! For once you're in, you're never out!"

So he stuck to his own field. And as his new industrial unions rapidly spread over the land, they were given a more friendly reception by many big employers than ever appeared in the news at that time. Typical was what I heard from the manager of a big paper mill.

"For years our three thousand employees have been organized in twenty-nine different trade unions," he said, "for we need a good many skilled trades in our plant. Twenty-nine different labor leaders coming in here from outside, each one to get all he can, not only from me but from the other twenty-eight unions in the plant. Over half the strikes we've had have come from their interunion disputes. We'd welcome one big union, with one responsible leader to deal with."

So at first felt many employers. But then Europe did come in. Not with a crash—it was quietly done, by my brilliant Communist friends, who felt about John Lewis much as they did about the New Deal, and so, in the effort to steal his show, imported from France their new idea, with such success that it was soon in front-page headlines—the sit-down strike. It failed in Detroit. The public reaction was too hot, so it dropped underground. But I can't help feeling it won't be long until it is tried again over here; for although it has no place in organized labor democracy, it's grand as a starter of revolution, and the Communists know that well.

Though I could not go to the strike in Detroit, I did try hard to get out to the farms, to hear at first hand from the farmers themselves what they thought of the New Deal's plan for them. I mapped out a three months' motor trip all over the country. What a chance for a series of articles! But to my keen disappointment no magazine would agree to send me.

"Three months?" one old editor smiled. "Why, brother, in this New Deal rush three months is like a thousand years!

By the time we got ready to print your stuff, God knows *where* the country will be!"

So it is of this chapter I'm writing now. For already the voters have had their say and in Washington changes are being made, and the increasing danger of our being drawn again into war across the sea has started the cry of preparedness here. So by the time my book is in print, God knows where the country will be. But meanwhile I can write only of what I have seen in these last years. For this is a book of memories.

As the New Deal rushed on its way, it grew more complicated and bewildering all the time. But in spite of all the good in it that I could see, and that was a lot, two things stood out more clearly each year. First, the fact that sooner or later we would all have to pay for this. Already, up here in my mountain home, I could feel once more the outside world tighten its grip on my own little life. For my taxes took an appalling jump. Not important, you may say. Even if I were forced out of my home to a smaller house and smaller living, what great difference to the country would it make? Very little, I agree. But not so with my mountain neighbors; their homes were already small enough. Farms taxed fifty dollars ten years ago were now paying a hundred, or even more. And the farmers did not like it. I knew one who had cheered for the New Deal, when a generous bonus was given to his young war-veteran son, but since then his taxes had made him grim.

The other point that stood out clear was the manner in which, from the very start, all power had centered in the White House and the whole plan from month to month depended on one man's mood and will. And this I did not like at all, no matter who the man might be or how he stood for the common good. For I liked not even this much approach to the growing dictatorships overseas.

XXXVII

But any dictatorship we've had here has been democracy, when compared with those in Moscow and Berlin, and to what I have seen in Rome since 1924. I went over there first with my wife in the early spring of that year. I had always wanted to go, ever since my Princeton days, when that lovable scholar, Andy West, had taken us through devious byways of ancient scandal and intrigue into the savage and glittering brilliant world of Imperial Rome. But from the evening when we came, the modern world began to break in and shut out all such memories.

The first interruption, strangely enough, came to me not from Italy but from Russia, far to the north. It came silently, in only one weird curious little incident. My old friend Tarasov had sent me in the last two years many little stories revealing the resources deep hidden in the spirits of men, those powers known in the Far East but strange to our Western world. While writing a novel on this theme, I had often stopped to put into shape some of the stories Tarasov sent and I'd published them in magazines, and the proceeds I had shared with him. He had needed any help I could give, for he was a penniless exile now. He had at last found a job in Vienna and, fearing he might give it up and come down to see me if he knew I was in Rome, I had written him not a word about this little trip with my wife. But learning that Rome was crowded, from Monte Carlo I sent a wire reserving a room at the *Hôtel de Russie;* and now, arriving there early one night and asking for the room reserved, I was told by the clerk at the desk:

"Yes, we have a room for you, and here also is a book that came for you from Vienna today."

I tore open the package and in the book I found my friend Tarasov's card! Then, as I stood for a moment transfixed, a memory came of one night in his small log home in the North. For that evening he had told me:

"In my family for centuries there has been some power of television which I do not understand. All I can tell you about it is this, that when you go back to America, though I have no other friend there but yourself, at times I shall be ably dimly to follow and see where you are."

Resources buried deep in men! As I stared at the book he had sent me on that theme we had so often discussed, back leaped my thoughts to his sorcerer friend, to that image of the Mother of Life and the powers that the old hunter believed poured from her into him in his trance.

But then, discordant, loud and shrill, came a roar of singing from the Roman street outside and, going to a doorway, abruptly I was jerked from thoughts of any mystery in life by the sight of a few hundred young Black Shirts, with rifles on their shoulders, shouting a propaganda song to the glory of new Imperial Rome. And wherever I went in the next two weeks about that wonderful old town, every effort that I made to revive memories of its past was spoiled by enthusiasts young and old, who eagerly tried to make me feel how with the *Duce* the grandeur that had once been there was rearing up at last again to startle the world by the force of its arms. To me there was something so grandiose about it all. Watching the self-conscious dignity of the Fascist salute, more than once I was tempted to tell the little story I had heard in police headquarters in New York. As to its truth, I do not know.

About two years after the war, the Italian detective on the bomb squad, who had ferreted out activities of Italian anarchists and the *Mafia* in New York, had been shot and killed one night. To take his place, an old police official said, they needed an Italian, a man of unlimited physical courage and one who knew the Italian Reds, and yet was unknown to those in New York. So they sent word to Italy, inquiring for such a man. An answer came suggesting one who before the war had been editor of a Red newspaper, had proved great courage in the war and had never been in New York. They cabled promptly to the man and offered him three thousand dollars a year. He thought it over, then turned it down. His name was Mussolini. What a detective he would have made for the bomb squad in New York!

But how I would have been mobbed in Rome for repeating such a blasphemous little story about their new god! And yet to call the Fascisti mere fanatics and reactionaries is to miss the essential nature and power of their creed. For as I shook off my first annoyance and tried to see with an open mind, more and more I was forced to admit that these Black Shirts had a system which, with the vitality of some new religion, took hold on this nation and gave it new life. Though Fascism had just made its start, we found a clean Naples and a clean Rome, the filthy beggars gone from the streets, everyone working, everyone eating; and people of all sorts and kinds already had plain evidence to show of such a swift success of system over chaos, that I was reminded of the ironclad efficiency I'd seen in Berlin in the World War. But where was any freedom here of press or assembly or private speech? When our Ambassador asked my advice about a plan of the *Duce*'s to invite a whole shipload of American journalists to come over at his expense and write of his new Italy, I answered:

"This writer's humble advice is that all we ask of him is freedom to look and see for ourselves, at our expense, see everything, without any government propaganda or guidance or hindrance of any kind."

This freedom we were all denied. Edgar Mowrer was then

CHILDREN'S DORMITORIES IN SEASHORE CAMPS, SMALL ITALIAN BOYS
WITH FIELD GUNS, SONS OF THE WOLF, AND THE MUSSOLINI FORUM
SEEN IN ITALY IN 1937

in Rome and, like other journalists, he had many stories to tell of such interference on every side, such a heavy clamping down on all rebellious forces left, and such a strict close censorship of cable and mail news sent out, that he was ready to give up his job. But he didn't have to—for only a little after this he was expelled from Italy and went for his paper to Berlin, there later to meet like treatment by Hitler's new dictatorship.

I saw the *Duce* three times in Rome—once about seven o'clock in the morning, trotting by on horseback, quite unprotected, all alone; and again in a car that plowed its way through roaring crowds of enthusiasts after some speech he had made. But what impressed me more than that was a little war sermon I heard him preach to some three thousand blackshirted boys, many only six years old, up in the Borghese Gardens, where they were drilling one afternoon. As I watched, I thought of our sons at home and of Exeter Academy. The world of tomorrow, what would it be? For Italy the answer stood in those ranks of rigid little boys with their toy guns at Present Arms.

But to make them into soldiers, the *Duce* was taking them out of the hands of another power, old and strong. What did the Church think of this? In New York, at a committee dinner on the night before I sailed, the banker who sat next to me had asked if there was nothing that he could do for me in Rome. Suddenly remembering that he was a Catholic, I had said:

"Thank you, yes, there is one thing. I know nothing about the Catholic Church. Could you send me a book to read on the boat?"

He had agreed and next day in my cabin I'd found a book about the Church. In it was a scribbled note from the Paulist Father to whom he must have telephoned.

"On such short notice," the Paulist had written, "this is

the best that I can do. But remember what I have told you before. A mind like this should be personally handled."

What message was sent I do not know, but I was well handled by three Paulist Fathers while in Rome. Three more delightful, friendly, courteous churchmen I have never known. But when I tried them on Fascism, I was given only smiles and quite noncommittal replies.

"That is quite out of our sphere," said one. "Ask us about something we know."

So I spoke of my novel, The Avalanche, which I was still writing at that time, concerned with the theme of how to tap the inner resources of us all. I had read some books on the technique of psychiatry, I said, and I hoped to compare it with some book instructing young Catholic priests how in the confessional to learn a man's real secret sins before giving him advice. They were interested in that and promptly searched the Vatican library for such a book, but found none. Priests were expected to learn such technique through human experience, they said. Then I turned the subject to the controversy at that time, in the Episcopal Church in New York, between Bishop Manning and my old friend Percy Grant, on the doctrine of the Virgin Birth.

"From what little we have read about that," one of the Paulists answered, "this question they are discussing is how a little physical body was born in a woman's womb. But that lies in the province of the doctor and biologist. The more interesting question is this. At what moment into that physical body entered the spirit of our Lord?"

Admiring the adroit sagacity of that reply, I asked next about the doctrine of the Infallibility of the Pope. Their answer came in this series of questions:

"As an American like ourselves, what do you think of the Prohibition Amendment back at home?"

"A most damnable mistake, which is breeding crime wholesale."

"We agree. And yet it will be hard to change, because it is now in the Constitution. What do you think of our Constitution, rigid, because all written down, compared with the much more easily changed unwritten Constitution of England?"

"I like the British form better than ours."

"But have you ever stopped to think that this doctrine in the Church of the Infallibility of the Pope is essentially like the idea behind the unwritten Constitution of England?"

"How?"

"Because if each Pope is infallible, then he can undo when he likes any doctrine grown lifeless and cold. And so the Church, never cold and dead but a living body of religion, keeps herself forever alive in her power over men, by always meeting new needs that arise."

My admiration was increased. Oh, wonderful Paulist Fathers, friendly, intelligent, courteous, kind! But what answers would some village priest in Italy, Ireland or Spain have given to such questions from some peasant in his flock?

Once more I tried my Paulist friends on Mussolini, but their reply was like the one they'd given to my question on the Virgin Birth:

"Fascism is concerned with the bodies and the citizen duties of men, while the great concern of the Church is with their immortal souls."

After the Ethiopian conquest, I made a second trip to Rome with my wife and our daughter, Betsy Ann; and while for a month they reveled in galleries, churches and museums filled with treasures from the past, I hired an interpreter and spent my time in the Rome of today. I was struck by its amazing growth since my visit of twelve years before. The city was nearly doubled in size, and all classes of its populace were apparently prosperous and content—for into my ears were poured accounts of mills and factories running full blast, of new roads and railroads, immense malarial marshes drained and up in the mountains reservoirs and dams for the development of electric power, "white coal." I was told of an army and navy renewed and of the need of speeding up all work to be ready for more wars. But I'd come to learn not of this great machine, with its grip on forty-three million lives, but of its effect on the minds of its boys, from the time when at the age of six they enlisted in the *Sons of the Wolf*, to be passed on through the *Balilla, Avanguardisti* and *Junior Fascisti* organizations until at last, "with body, mind and conscience formed," they entered the army at twenty-one.

They did not look like soldiers at first. In a lovely old garden one day at noon, some two hundred little boys and girls were taking a deep-breathing drill. Up through the grass and gravel rose bits of ruins from the Baths of Titus and Nero's Golden House. Close behind reared the grim gray walls and arches of the Colosseum, and the children looked tiny against that background of ancient Rome. In open formation they went through their breathing and their exercise, and then they were marched off to lunch in the *Balilla* clubhouse close by. When we entered, an order rang out and up they leaped in the Fascist salute. Before luncheon a slim little girl came shyly to the head of the room and, as all the children rose, she clasped her hands and recited this prayer:

"Our Father, we thank you for the bread and all the kind care you give us each day. Our Father, protect our dear Italy and the glorious soldiers that guard on land, on sea, in the air, the reborn Empire of Rome. Bless our King, his Royal family, protect the *Duce* and grant him a long life for the sake of our beloved Italy."

She finished. All made the sign of the cross and sat down silently to their lunch. But then I was made to feel the presence of another deity there. The director called up a six-year-old boy and made him slip off his white smock. Beneath

it he wore a black shirt and shorts with broad white belt
and shoulder straps, his uniform as a *Son of the Wolf*.
"It's hard to make him take it off," the director said with
a smile. "He loves to wear it always, ever since the day when
he was kissed by the *Duce*. He can tell you not only the day
but the hour. Now he will show you the photograph."
Eagerly he ran off and brought back a large picture of himself
with Mussolini kissing him. I glanced at it, then looked up
and saw all the children watching breathless, as though this
were a boy once kissed by God! As I left the room, up they
leaped and gave again the Fascist salute. And I left them that
way, silent—citizen soldiers in the bud.

That afternoon, on a dirt field along the yellow Tiber, I
watched fifty little *Sons of the Wolf* being drilled by an old
navy noncom. All in tiny navy suits, the six in front beating
loudly on drums, with big high steps they came down the
field, stamping at intervals to keep time. Meanwhile some
thirty older boys were being put through the manual with
short marine rifles. They finished and at a sharp command
they swarmed up the rigging of a mast about eighty feet high,
while others in the field below were busy cleaning and oiling
two large field guns. In the gun room of the clubhouse, I was
shown two Colt machine guns and a section of a torpedo—
weapons fascinating to boys. Some of them there had already
had machine-gun target practice in summer camps, they told
me.

Next Sunday morning we motored out to a small town in
the hills. Winding up through crooked streets, we came to a
Balilla clubhouse, built in modernistic style, all tile and plaster,
spick and span. On a field at the rear, sixty boys from eight
to twelve in *Balilla* uniforms were being put through the
manual with rifles just sent up from Rome. The drill was
snappy, for the boys were greatly excited about the new
guns. After the manual they marched, singing in shrill voices.
When they broke ranks and were told they could play, some

of them started aimlessly kicking a couple of footballs about, but soon came again to the guns, discussing and admiring.

I talked with one of them that day, a peasant's son with a blunt face and deep-set serious blue eyes, who lived in a dark lonely cluster of huts upon a neighboring hill. After working there in the fields from dawn, he came over here late each day and stayed into the evening, at special drills for a sergeant's commission. Already a fine skier, he hoped to serve later in an Alpine regiment, he said. I looked across at his distant home. What chance had it to hold a boy, when over here he had this clubhouse, sports and games, drill, songs and movies, radio broadcasts, in winter ski trips to the Apennines and in summer two weeks in a camp by the sea? And as though all this were not enough, he had heard last year in Rome the *Duce* make a stirring address to some fifty thousand boys. Patriotism dramatized.

In the next two weeks I saw thousands of boys, in schoolyards and gardens and out on the streets, drilling and drilling, all over Rome. I remember about four hundred *Avanguardisti*, from twelve to sixteen, marching down a broad shady street, with an infantry barracks along one side. Some of them were in uniforms, others had come in their school clothes and some wore only jerseys and pants, and marched bareheaded. Fat boys, thin boys, well to do, poor. Many looked tired. They had drilled for nearly three hours and were by no means finished yet. We followed them till they came to a halt and then talked with one of the officers. Field work and target practice came in camp in the summer, he said. Drill now was not compulsory except at week ends; these boys were here because they had the Fascist ideal. Tired? Perhaps, but they didn't mind. A shrill whistle. Ranks were formed. Attention! Hands all stiff at sides, bodies rigid and eyes fixed. The drums beat and off they went with long straining mannish strides. It was nearly six-thirty now but I met still others marching on the way back to my hotel.

They learned more than drilling, for the government had them all week in school. In a large elementary school which I visited one day, in the first classroom we entered upstairs the teacher snapped out a command and twenty small boys from nine to eleven instantly rose in the Fascist salute. The teacher was a captain in the Black Shirt Militia. Each morning he read from a newspaper bits interpreting the world news, and in that and in all lessons he tried to give them the Fascist point of view, he said. While he talked, my eyes were on one wall half filled by a huge lurid picture of steel-helmeted soldiers with rifles and fixed bayonets advancing on barbed wire. To make the picture more real to the boys, real barbed wire was strung on the wall! In other classrooms of the school, men and women teachers alike told me they brought the Fascist culture into all courses wherever they could. And on a wall in one of the halls was this message from the *Duce:*

"Youth is beautiful. It has clear eyes with which it looks out on the vast and tumultuous panorama of the world. It is beautiful because it has a courageous heart that does not fear death."

In a high school which I visited I found more mottoes from the same source. "Live dangerously," was one of them, and another: "Believe, obey, fight!" And this message for a history class: "Parliamentarianism has never fallen so low as it is today and, where it has not been abolished, it is dying." Poor England, poor France, poor America!

I went with an army colonel to an immense trade school one night, and there, in lofty shadowy halls, to the clank and din of hammers on anvils, the whir of lathes and the roar of propellers of airplanes, hundreds of older Italian boys were at work on the motors of planes and on broken-down lorries and cars. Though most of them, the colonel said, had been working all day on their feet in shops where they earned their living, they were glad to come here six nights a week

for two hours more of hard work like this, for the chance
in the army to become drivers of lorries, tanks or cars, or air-
plane mechanics or pilots. As though to increase their zeal,
in the halls I found on the walls these mottoes from the
Duce:

"In the shop of the Fascist Regime there is place, work and
glory for each one." And again: "Without effort, sacrifice
and blood nothing can be achieved in history."

These are but a few of my memories of all that I saw and
heard of the training given Italian boys, rich and poor, from
the time they are small.

"It is all like a net," the colonel said. "At six a boy joins
the *Sons of the Wolf*, not because he has to, he wants to, he's
a volunteer. Of the *Balilla* the same is true. But the net tight-
ens every year and it is hard for a boy to drop out. His
friends would call him a coward and traitor. Parents objecting are summoned to court."

So at last the *Duce's* ideal of citizen soldiers was achieved.
But ever since my first visit to Rome and my talks with the
Paulist Fathers there, the Church had watched with jealous
eyes this government encroachment on her power over her
sons. The *Duce* had stolen her technique. As the Church had
dramatized religion, he dramatized patriotism instead. He set
up Fascist martyrs, too, and *Balilla* leaders as father confessors.
He closed the Catholic clubs for boys and took over the
Catholic Boy Scouts. The Church did not like it and, at intervals ever since, dissension has waxed hot between the Vatican and the government. There is truce between them today
as I write—but which will prevail in years to come?

New priests are training in Rome today, priests of the new
Fascist faith, training to be *Balilla* leaders and mold the boys
of Italy. I went many times to watch them in the Fascist
Academy out upon the edge of the town, in a lovely little
valley between the Tiber and the hills. The three hundred
and fifty students, from nineteen to twenty-four, were kept

busy summer and winter from five-thirty in the morning until night, when they slept like logs in their double-decker steel bunks. They had only ten days of vacation a year. No liquor, wine or beer was allowed them, and each day only three cigarettes. From October to April they worked in classrooms and spent the rest of the year in camp, or at athletic sports and drill in the Mussolini Forum there, a great sunken field arena with marble tiers of seats and huge statues all around. There in those lovely days of spring, students in squads, in white shirts and shorts, played soccer, hurdled, threw the discus, drilled in the manual and marched. Splendid physical specimens all. Even at sports, I noticed, most of them kept their rifles close by. Watching them were people from Rome, while younger boys of all ages marched and drilled and exercised. At the end of the afternoon, both Academy students and young boys took up their rifles large or small and marched singing off the field. All around the great Forum their voices were heard. All ordered, drilled and disciplined. Suddenly one such afternoon, in a sloping pasture in the Farnese hills above, I saw a young colt who had broken loose and was kicking and tearing about, mad with the joy of just being young! He was a relief to me!

I had a good long talk one day with an Academy student who had been ordered to take us around. He gave me a detailed account of his work.

"There are two great things about it," he ended. "First, that here and in camp you get such military training, both from books and in the field; and second, all the classroom work makes you so clearly understand why Fascism is better than Communism or Democracy."

A new priest for Italy, a maker of soldier citizens strong in this new Fascist faith. He would spend his life molding boys from the time when they started to think. My thoughts ran back to the six-year-old high-stepping little *Sons of the Wolf*, marching to the beat of drums, and on over the whole teaching, training, drilling process I had seen. What kind of nation will it build? Like the rigid systems in Russia and in Germany, Fascism has made a strong start—that no fair-minded man can deny. But how strong will all three dictatorships prove in the years that lie ahead? All through our talk the crackle of rifles came from a target field near by.

XXXVIII

FROM ROME WE WENT TO LONDON. IT WAS CORONATION WEEK. We had been invited to stay with friends; and at a small dinner which they gave for our daughter and another girl before the Coronation Ball, I found myself at table with four Oxford graduates. One was a Conservative, one belonged to the Labor Party, one was a Communist and the fourth said he belonged to no party at all. Each one thinking for himself. What a change from the manufactured minds of the youngsters I had found in Rome!

London big with Empire. Nobody had to tell you so, you could feel it on every side. On the night of our arrival we drove through sparkling crowded streets, glamorous with uniforms and costumes of countries all over the world. I remember a little Indian princess wrapped in chiffon embroidered in gold, smiling out of a taxi at a huge red-coated sergeant of the Canadian Mountain Police. On the night before the procession, I watched crowds of countless thousands gather to camp on street curbs and so get places for next day. Two nervous old women came up to a Bobby and I heard one of them say:

"Oh, officer, thank Heaven for you! We shall feel safer with you here!" From under his helmet he smiled down.

"Oh, madam, there'll be no trouble," he said.

Their easy managing of the crowds reminded me of how after the war I'd seen a small procession of Irish Revolutionists come roaring down the Strand to Trafalgar on a drizzling afternoon. At their head walked a very drunken old woman

with a Union Jack in her hand, which she kept pitching
ahead of her so that she might stamp it into the mud. Along
both curbs stood helmeted Bobbies smiling at her. Not one
of them stirred to make her a martyr, and so that absurd and
pathetic old hag went stamping and screeching down the
street. Strong to me that afternoon had seemed the British
government, and so it did again to me now in its handling
of this gathering throng. Men, women and children from city
and country and outlying parts of the Empire came, workingmen, farmers, middle-class clerks, all kinds, of all shades of
political view, but all good-tempered, out for a lark. With
rugs and oilskins, overcoats and boxes and parcels of food
they came, ready for a night and a day of sitting and standing, cheering and singing. Soldiers and sailors and marines,
with their little swagger sticks, passed; and tearing up and
down the street came cars of all sizes, packed with people,
boys and girls perched on the backs of the seats, rending the
night with their hoots and war whoops, piercing whistles and
horns. White-suited peddlers called their wares, sandwiches,
roasted peanuts, ice-cream cones and cigarettes. Two young
girls lay on their stomachs, eagerly holding a small flashlight
on the Funnies in the newspaper beneath them, chuckling
over the pictures and jokes. People around them lay asleep
on rugs and newspapers, old fur coats. How could they sleep,
in a din like this? Not far off sat a family group with an enormous bag of food and a jew's-harp going like mad. I caught
these snatches of their chatter:

"Easy on them san'wiches, Madge; we've got a whole night
of it and a day. Not till near four in the arfternoon will the
procession come by this way."

"But then what a show! Oh, what a show! The whole
bloody Empire as it were!"

"There'll be an orfficer an' three men from every regiment, they say, not to mention the boys from the fleet and

all them rajahs an' the like!" Then a woman's voice came loud and shrill:

"It's the royal coach I'm here to see! All gold it is, an' six gray hosses!"

From that unthinking eagerness for the glitter and pomp of tomorrow's show, I went on up the street and sat down on a curbstone to rest. Next to me sat a young mother with two children, both fast asleep, the little boy on a raincoat, the girl with her head in her mother's lap. From under a soft brown felt hat the young woman smiled, as her eyes met mine, and soon we were talking.

"Aren't these kids of yours rather small for a strain as long as this?" I asked. "The head of the parade tomorrow won't be here until afternoon."

"Silly of me. Yes, I know." Her smile was steady and quiet and strong. "But I'd no idea it would be like this and I couldn't bear that they should miss this chance to see something they'll remember all over the world, wherever we'll be."

"All over the world?"

"Colonial Service." I looked at her with interest.

"Colonial Service? Then why are you here?"

"We're only in London for this one week. My husband is in the parade."

"Army?"

"Yes, an engineer. Wherever some great mountain road or reservoir or dam is built, or an old one breaks and brings a flood, there we go and make our home. We've seen some rather awful floods, whole cities filled with refugees."

"And you take little children there?"

"Oh, most of the time it isn't like that. It's life in the open, it's quiet, it's strong. We've lived in tents and cabins in dear little towns far up in the hills. We were in the Punjab for two years. Our girl was born near the Khyber Pass—the boy in the Canadian Rockies."

"But isn't it hard to live like that?"

"No—strange at first, but then you find you're still in England wherever you go, with English people, English ways. That's why I did want the children here to see the whole Empire come by!" She smiled up at me and asked: "You're an American, aren't you?"

"Yes."

"Then perhaps you think this is all for our King. But what has brought most of us here tonight is something far greater and deeper than that. It's the old human wanting to belong to something bigger than one's little self—something on which the sun never sets—something that's keeping off war from our sons. For the Empire is the strongest power in the whole world for peace today."

Long after midnight I left her there. Early next day, from a Piccadilly office window I looked down on a roaring mass of men, women and children, who stood packed solid, ten rows deep. From down the street to bursts of cheers came a khaki-clad regiment with their band—Territorials, I was told—and soon they were ranged along the curbs to help the police hold back the throng. It grew harder as the day wore on; for as more regiments came by with blare of bands and boom of drums to reach their places in the parade, the human mass came surging forward. In the pressure screams were heard and every few moments some fainting child or woman was lifted out of the squeeze, placed on a litter and carried away. One of them shrieked with hysterical laughter but nobody seemed to hear or care; for at that moment, in high white gaiters, with their kilted officers, the Gordon Highlanders came by, and the pushing roaring mass closed in even denser than before! There was something terrible in its force, blindly unthinking, not even aware of the depths of this passion in itself that kept it so hungrily waiting here, never heeding its victims, the weak and the fainting, waiting till a king and a queen in a golden carriage should come by!

But all this time beneath the roar small acts of kindness had been done, and I began to notice them now. In one awful surging squeeze, I saw a slim young mother with a small boy in her arms suddenly drop him and sink down. At once a burly gray-haired man beside her bent and lifted first the woman and then the boy to another man close by, to be passed on to other men and so to the stretchers waiting outside. Soon I spied others doing the same. They kept calling back and forth, as limp forms were lifted and passed from one to another out of the throng. Acts of kindness under the roar, by little groups of twos and threes, self-appointed Red Cross helpers: I could see them everywhere, working constantly, tooth and nail. For me they so humanized the crowd that it took on a new aspect soon. I remembered the mother with two small children whom I'd met the night before, and recalled bits of what she had said:

"The Canadian Rockies. . . . The Khyber Pass. . . . English people wherever you go. . . . The old human wanting to belong to something bigger than one's little self. . . . The Empire is the strongest force for peace in the whole world today!"

I began to realize how many like her were down in the crowd, people from all over the earth, from lonely little hill towns and from fever-stricken ports, not only soldiers but civil servants, doctors, schoolteachers, engineers, people of all sorts and kinds, all gathered here for something greater than any king.

The crowd knew nothing of what I saw, knew only it was here for a show. But by its rough kindness it was drawing me into itself and so into the deep instinctive passion that had brought it here. It had done with me what crowds can, and at last I was ready for the parade. And when to a louder roar of cheers than any we had heard before, led by a scarlet-coated band with its drummers lifting drumsticks high, men in varied uniforms and civilian costumes of countries reaching 'round the globe, to blare of bands and boom of drums, began to march by in that ocean of din, I felt myself swept out on a tide of elemental forces stronger than any I'd known since the war. When at last, in a teetering coach of gold, a king and a queen came slowly by, it seemed a trumpery affair, compared with the sense I'd had that day of something far deeper than any king, the feeling planted in this crowd that they were part of a great chain of democratic countries reaching all over the face of the earth. I liked this English democracy. Its liberty-loving tolerance may seem slow-moving in these dangerous days, compared with the swift centered force of Berlin. Faults and blunders and mistakes? Yes, in plenty. So have we. But I remember the London I saw in the dark days of the World War. They had power then and they have it still: resources of money and credit vast; and greater, the power of free men, when once stirred and organized, to act together in a crisis.

XXXIX

From England we crossed over to France, and in Paris I found a city harassed and haunted by uncertainties. In a railroad terminal there, over one of the train gates hung still a large dramatic picture given by an American artist whose son had been killed in the World War. It showed a troop train starting off, with women sobbing, children shouting, soldiers cheering from the windows, flowers tied to bayonets. But the picture was many years old like the war, and the suburbanites rushing for trains didn't even look up at it that night. For they'd grown so used to this specter of war always hanging over them. And one must work and one must live, and the people of Paris had grown so used to living in anxieties that they had time for none but those pounding right into their lives. The whole spirit has been transformed since then, and France like England has courageously pulled herself together to meet the menace from Berlin. But at the time when I was there, back in the days of the *Front Populaire*, with the cost of living rising fast and the whole country torn by strikes and fights between political factions, from people rich and poor I heard stories of such troubles as made our own in this country look small. I shall picture a few of them here. For though conditions have changed since then, the very crisis that has changed them may in the end bring them back to us all. In this tumultuous surging world it is so hard to see ahead!

Not only in Paris but all over France, the small employers and tradesmen faced such troubles in their shops that hundreds of thousands had organized to try to save the businesses

407

on which their very lives depended. I went to their headquarters late one day and found a burly dark-haired man still in a rush of work at his desk. In his eyes was an angry glare of light.

"What lies ahead no man can tell!" he said to me between telephone calls. "At these inflation prices already our sales have dropped so low, we've nothing to live on any more! It's not only that we must pay more for our goods, the Reds have come right into our shops and made us pay more to our employees for less work than they ever did before! We're against this forty-hour week; it means absolute ruin to most of us! What does your American President mean by preaching such a ruinous week? The Reds use that against us here. 'Even a bourgeois American thinks forty hours are enough!' That is what they tell us now! The whole world today is small as this!" He made a small circle with his hands. "What one country does affects all the rest—and with these everlasting threats of strikes and Communists and war, we're none of us safe! What lies ahead, God only knows!"

To enforce the shorter week, I saw a little riot one day in a square in front of a milliner's shop. It was Monday and her shop was open, when by the new law it should have been closed. Gathering from side streets, a crowd of several hundred young Reds made a sudden rush for her door. They smashed two of the lower windows, then threw rocks at those above, and all this time they yelled themselves hoarse. I saw some of them smiling. What was the joke? Were they staging all this fury to frighten the customers inside and so ruin the milliner's trade? Soon sirens were heard and the *flics* (Paris police) came pouring in, on motorcycles and in lorries. Quickly the crowd was cleared away. Then one by one the badly scared women customers came out and hurried from that dangerous spot. They would not soon return to buy hats! One excited old lady had to be helped, half fainting, to a taxi, to go home weak and shivering with fears of Red Revolution in France.

The landlords were in trouble, too. Late one day I sat in the office of a municipal counselor (alderman) listening to complaints from his voters. A thin tired-looking woman came in and said she ran a rooming house. Her big trouble was this new law that people who were out of work need no longer pay any rent.

"What can I do? Half the people in my house are out of work and will not pay. They like my house. I keep it clean. But I have let my girl helper go, and alone I have to scrub the halls, for these free tenants even refuse to help me there! So all day I trot up and down stairs and work till I'm all tired out! And my taxes are now so high, I can't see how it all will end!" As she faced the months ahead, her face and eyes grew tight with strain, as though her nerves were ready to snap. "What can you do for me? Nothing, *Monsieur?*"

"I can't make your tenants leave," he said, "but I promise to do all I can to lower the taxes on your house." Sharply at that the woman sat down and buried her face in her hands. Then she rose.

"Thank you, *Monsieur!*" She went quickly away.

Next I heard this story from the night manager in a garage. Three years ago he had left that job and started a small garage of his own, but times were hard and each month he lost money. Then in the strikes of a year ago all four of his young employees, his sister, her husband, and two boys, demanded higher wages and shorter hours. He brought out his books and showed them his losses. No use. His obstinate brother-in-law promptly declared a sit-down strike. So they stayed there and the boss went home. He thought over his business—two years in the red and worse to come. He came back to his former employer and succeeded in getting back his old job. Then he saw a lawyer and turned over his own little business to his sister and his brother-in-law. Let them do the worrying!

"With this government running France, it is better to be an employee than an employer!" he declared.

I went one day to the office of a lean trim man with dark hair and straight-looking friendly eyes, who employed about sixty women and girls and ten men, and made cheap traveling bags, in a little factory on both sides of a narrow paved court.

"What I can't get used to," he said, "is the changed spirit in my shop. Like my father before me, I've always been good friends with my workers. There was no union here. In the sit-down strikes last year they did not strike till one girl cried: 'Hurry, or we'll be the last shop not on strike in the whole town!' So they struck. It was like a holiday. I played ball with the men in the court. But in the sit-down strike this spring, everything was different. There was no playing ball with them now. They shut up and stared when I came in. There was a hard rain and I had to move some tons of wood fiber in from the court. Did anyone offer to help? Not at all. They treat me like an enemy."

At the stroke of the five-o'clock gong, the girls came quickly out of the shop. In the court as they passed him, not one said good night, and I heard some snicker when they went by.

"I don't like this; I hate it!" he said. "The main advantage of a small factory over a big one has always been that personal friendly spirit we had. Now it is gone—and for me and for them its loss will do more harm in the end than any forty-hour week!"

The only employer that I found who had no worries on his mind was one who ran two small factories and was making good profits still. I asked him what he made, and he said:

"Parts for airplanes and bombs. My customer is the government."

As I left him, I thought of the billion dollars voted for armament that year, plunging the government into debt even deeper than it was before, and so doubling the danger of just that wild inflation panic which other employers so sharply feared. For if prices went soaring, that meant more strikes, more power for the Communists. All through the labor unions of France the Communist power had fast increased. In Paris, in the last city election, they had polled nearly a third of the vote. And from big and little business I heard such fear of their rapid growth and the wonderful organization which could almost instantly mobilize half a million men for the revolution they hoped to start from the desperate chaos in France, those days, that, wanting to see them at first hand, I went early one evening to one of their district centers up in Saint-Antoine.

I walked up a steep narrow street teeming with humanity. Between small shops and open booths and pushcarts filled with shoddy clothes, slabs of horse meat and of pork, fruits and vegetables looking decayed, moved a chattering, laughing, shouting, scowling mass of men, women and kids, an appealing but highly inflammable crowd. For this was one of the quarters where ever since the French Revolution other rebellions had been born and gone roaring down into the town. But as the wild and picturesque old stagecoach of our cowboy days compared with the modern motor bus, so did those colorful past rebellions compare with the tightly mechanized modern revolution I felt being organized, as I listened to the routine work of the Communists of today.

I came into a long dingy room packed with young workingmen moving about. The air was blue from their cigarettes and filled with din of voices. I pushed through to the man in charge, showed him my headquarters' pass and was allowed to squeeze in beside him on a narrow bench by the wall. To the table in front of us, quickly elbowing through the crowd, came a constant stream of young men and boys, leaning over the table to get their orders from city headquarters, then hurrying off. He showed me the orders, quite a list, and a pile of printed questionnaires filled in to make detailed reports;

for his big district was organized in eighty subcenters called cells, he explained, and every week he had to check up on the work of each cell, see that none slowed down. I asked if I might visit a cell. He agreed and gave me a card, and I went to a routine meeting of one of them one night that week.

At the back of a tiny café—where the tall thin proprietor in his shirt sleeves, with a drooping mustache, brought beer from the bar, while his huge fat wife sat knitting and listening to the talk—around two tables were fourteen men, most of them young, and two or three girls, and a big woman of middle age with clear steady capable eyes. No red shirts or flowing ties—they'd come from their jobs in their working clothes, some in old jerseys, others in shirt sleeves, two or three with caps still on their heads, half of them smoking cigarettes.

"Come in and sit down and stay long as you like," said the lad to whom I showed my pass. And as I did so, they started in to question me about the New Deal, John Lewis and our sit-down strikes. Then they began their evening's work. Here at least, I thought, I should find no doubts, no worries or uncertainties; I should find men living by a creed more rigid than that of any church. But once more, in this city of change, I found the same yeast working still. For hoping before very long to run the whole government of France, the Communists did not propose to be caught unprepared and so make a mess of things, as their Russian comrades had at the start. Already taking an active part in the city government, they'd begun to learn their job ahead and already they were finding it tough, bristling with emergencies. The discussion that evening to my surprise was about soup kitchens, public works, help for labor unions, strikes, wages, prices, profits, taxes, old-age pensions, social insurance. I might have been listening to the New Deal! Then came collection of food and clothing for their comrades down in Spain. Two from this group had gone there to fight. One had been wounded and had come home but later had gone to Spain again and they read his last letter from the front.

"One of Mussolini's planes," he wrote, "dropped a bomb on us this week. It did not burst—broke open instead—and inside was a message from one of our crowd. He said: 'Hold out; boys, we are here. In Franco's headquarters I've got a job loading his Italian bombs and I'm loading them with Red proclamations—a new kind of dynamite!' "

After this letter, they planned how to gather more people in the district to see free movie films about Soviet Russia and Spain, and to hear the Communist radio broadcast given from headquarters two nights a week. Next came newspapers, and how to sell more copies of *L'Humanité*, the Communist daily, which had nearly doubled its circulation in Paris that year. In this one district the eighty cells had brought it to more than twenty-five thousand. The figures were sent them every week, with urgent orders to speed up the work. Who was lying in bed Sunday morning, district headquarters wanted to know? Sell 'em, sell 'em, boost those figures! Report all crimes in the neighborhood, too, featuring murders by jealous lovers —good hot human-interest stuff! The paper was broadening out, these days! Then came a discussion of how to make friends with every little shopkeeper and make him feel their cause was his own—because higher wages meant better trade; and if he would only give them his vote, they would soon pass laws to keep manufacturers' profits and wholesale prices down. For the Communists were vote getters now, right out for the votes of the middle class.

"We want them with us or at least not against us," they said. "They could block our whole show."

Very greatly to my surprise they took a somewhat similar stand toward the Catholic Church.

"We must show the people here that we have no wish to

abolish the Church," said the big middle-aged woman in black, "that religion is none of our business and that we mean to leave it alone."

Sharply a red-haired girl broke in: "There's not a girl I know in Paris who has any use for the Church!" But the older woman smiled and said:

"You don't know *all* the girls in France. Not only in the cities but still more in the villages, millions of them are Catholics still. I've been a Communist half my life, I've been all over France and seen us grow, but that doesn't make me lose my head. The peasants, the middle class and the Church are still so powerful today that if we're to take the government we must be mighty careful there."

The discussions went on till long after midnight. A gray old comrade at the table kept objecting or shaking his head. For him the Bible of Karl Marx had come into strange uncertain times!

But as against this picture of difficulties in their way, here is another to give an idea of the power they had in Paris then and may have again someday.

On a stifling Sunday afternoon from the lower edge of *Père Lachaise*, the tremendous old graveyard on a hill where in 1871 the last of the Communards were killed, I looked down a broad boulevard filled as far as the eye could see by a monster Red parade, bearing red flags and great white banners reaching half across the street. For this was the Red Memorial Day. On they came and, singing and cheering, poured up into that vast hillside of graves; and as I climbed paths by their line of march, looking close down on them through the trees, I watched an endless human tide winding through narrow lanes between tombs—men, women and children, all ages, all kinds, some of them clean and others dirty, all of them drenched in sweat from the heat, bearing not only big banners and flags but huge heavy wreaths of flowers, too; yet in spite of their burdens singing their songs and responding with roars of cheers to those of the comrades on either side, who stood on the graves and clung to the tombs, boosting their children up on the roofs. Strange music for those homes of the dead! In dense ranks six or eight abreast, on up the hillside moved the throng to the wall where the Communards were shot down, there to pile hundreds of huge wreaths. From two o'clock until nine in the evening they came and they came—there seemed no end; for up through the trees from far down the hill could be heard still the Communist song:

"The *Internationale* tomorrow will lead the whole human race!"

They believe that it will. I doubt if they're right. But at least in France, when I was there, numberless thousands lived in constant dread of that; for such demonstrations, not only parades but monster mass meetings, riots and strikes, kept coming so often, they never let die the fears of little businessmen. Nor did such disturbances come only from the Communists; for employers of labor, large and small, were banding together all over France, and they, too, had their extremists and hotheads, young men itching for a fight. With the slogan: *"Vive la France!"* thousands had taken active part in bloody street battles against the Reds by those ardent patriots belonging to the *Croix de Feu*, or Cross of Fire. I saw them in action one hot day.

On the *Champs Elysées*, where immense crowds had gathered to see an army parade, the moment the last troops had gone by, into the great boulevard poured several thousand silent young men. Up went their hands in what looked to me exactly like the Fascist salute; and as other thousands moved quickly in, they started singing the "Marseillaise," once the revolutionist but now the patriotic song. No riot so far, only that song and that surging ominous mass of men. But the government of that time was taking no chances with these boys. As though by magic, on foot and in lorries came rushing hundreds of *flics;* and from behind them, with shining brass helmets and sabers drawn, the famous mounted *garde mobile* rode straight into the dense throng, driving it off to either side. Then in two divisions the mounted men came riding down the sidewalks, while panicky thousands of women and children rushed pellmell into side streets. In fifteen minutes it was all over and normal traffic was restored. For they are fast workers, these Paris police. Yet in view of their past history in dealing with the Communists, there was irony in the sight of them now working for a Red government and sternly clamping down the lid on aristocrats and bourgeoisie!

But just because of the tension caused by these opposing extremes, the greater part of the people in France, who wanted peace and liberty and political democracy still, were already looking for some less radical government, which would steer a middle course and pull together the nation against the danger from Berlin. All factions were so well aware of this that each political party declared it was working for all France. All were patriotic. It had even its funny side, as when many Communists claimed Joan of Arc as a Red! From every group in Paris I heard:

"We don't want war but, if it comes, we are Frenchmen and will fight!"

The Communists even cheered the names of generals in the High Command—because if France were forced into war, they believed that Soviet Russia would be one of its allies, against the Fascisti and Nazis, in a struggle for the Continent.

"And how about the High Command?" I asked a young aristocrat whose father was a general. He smiled.

"You see," he answered, "even though the High Command have natural leanings to the Right, they are professsional soldiers first. If there must be war, they mean to win; and by long experience they know that the *poilu* fights his best only when he feels he defends liberty and democracy. So now the army High Command quite fervently and honestly makes love to those two great ideals."

But it was no smiling business, this deepening patriotism in France. Up the *Champs Elysées* one day came a small procession led by an army band in trench hats. Behind were several hundred middle-aged men in civilian clothes, many with crutches and heavy canes, winners of the *Croix de Guerre* in the war of twenty years ago. That was their only decoration —yet men round me all took off their hats as the little parade went by. Here and there marched a widow or a son.

"Look at that woman," said my companion. Gaunt and lean in a plain black suit, she came along with a slender boy of eighteen or twenty at her side. With a rigid smile, she looked straight ahead; there was something tragic in her eyes.

"I know her. I rented one of her rooms when I was a student," my friend went on. "The tragedy of her whole life is the war."

"But that was a long time ago."

"Not for her; it has stayed in her home. Her husband was gassed. He developed t.b. She fought for his life till a year ago. Then he died. This is the first time she has marched. That boy you saw is her only son. He begins his two years' service in the army early next month. There are thousands of mothers like her in France. They say nothing but they are afraid."

Now I understood that look in her eyes. Still that dark uncertainty.

I sat that night at a little table in front of a *Champs Elysées* café. I was dog-tired from a long day. The noisy torrent of automobiles on the great boulevard got on my nerves, and so did the loud blaring jazz band and the chatter and shrill laughter around me upon every hand. Pepped up, jazzed up, sexed up! Step on the gas and let her ride! There is something terrific in the blind speed of this modern mechanized world, I thought, that doesn't know or care where it goes. But it is hard to worry long in the glamour of a Paris night. From theaters and dinners to night clubs or double beds, that great river of city life on street and sidewalk came pouring by. At the small table next to mine was a pretty young *demi-mondaine*. In a close-fitting dress of heavy black silk, white jacket and a little white hat, she sat with a small black dog at her side. There was confidence in her gay young eyes. We talked for a while and then I asked:

"If all Europe goes to war, will it make any difference in your life?" She looked at me and I looked back. When she got my meaning, she said:

"Oh, I suppose not."

"Or a Communist revolution here—any difference?"

She kept smiling.

"I know several Communists. I suppose it will still be the same," she replied.

"You mean he will still come."

"I suppose so." Suddenly her smile grew bright. "Don't you think, Monsieur, that I am right?"

XL

I CALLED MY PARIS ARTICLE THE CITY OF UNCERTAINTIES.
That was some three years ago, and France has a strong government now. But back here in my home in New Hampshire,
as I think of the many cities I've seen in this country and
overseas, all facing swift and radical change, I realize that all
my life as a writer has been in cities of uncertainties, watching the great forces rise that have brought us over the bridge
of years into this world crisis today.

For when I was young I began to write about the mass life
of the common people and their attempts to lift that life out
of the sweated labor, the long hours and low pay, of an iron
age that ground them down. Slowly but surely I saw them
rise. But meanwhile this same iron age, in its grab for the
markets of the world, had planted the seeds of the war that
came. I saw it stop progress everywhere and slaughter and
starve the people by millions. A war to end war and make the
world safe for democracy. How did it end? In the fatal
Treaty of Versailles. Then I pinned my hopes to the League
of Nations, saw it build and crumble, the Fascisti and the
Nazis rise, and even the new free Russia come under a Red
dictatorship. And now I see these forces bringing the entire
world to the red brink of war again.

With wars and strikes and revolutions looming all around
us, what will it mean to our own little lives? Will we ever
be safe again? Never as we were before. But who were safe
in the old days? The masses? Yes, they were safe from war,
but they were not safe from poverty. Now they want what

we had, and blindly or with open eyes they are following all
over the world new leaders, who have risen to tell them how
to get what they want, either through war or through chaotic
peace. But can they get it? What lies ahead? World happiness
or world collapse? The answer just now seems to lie with
such gods as Hitler, Mussolini, Stalin, riding on great tides of
change. But even such dictators loom small in the long slow
mighty story of the life of our humankind. From vast dark
beginnings up through countless ages, with blunders and de-
lusions and many long disastrous halts, slowly, slowly, surely,
democracy has forged ahead. And so I believe it will do still,
with its horses and chariots of fire ever and again appearing
up on the high hills of life to lead the struggling masses on.

The plain people of the world, who always bear the brunt
of wars, will turn from the great dark roads to death and join
with all the rest of us who stand for progress by the roads of
peace and liberty and fair play. And so these constant threats
of wars and revolutions will force us all to come together,
work out ways to keep peace between nations through fair
dealing with each one, and in each land to achieve by degrees
the political and industrial democracy we so urgently need.
For the people will never again turn back to the poverty they
had before. So at least I see the road that stretches out in front
of us. It will not be an easy road. I see such problems bristling
there that any prophecies today of their solutions would be
blind.

And yet these years that loom ahead, shadowed by problems though they be, will be flooded, too, with dazzling lights.
For the laboratories of the world are already dreaming dreams
of such life in abundance for all men that our children in the
future years will soar by air around a world whose civilization
will compare with that of this present age as ours with the
horse-and-buggy days. Through hell and chaos our sons may
go—but ye Gods of the Pioneers!—the chances they'll have at
new frontiers, not only in the physical world but in that

region of the spirit whose mysterious fruitful depths of power in each one of us we have barely started to plumb! For the grand work of real education has now only just begun. And so, as I think of those years to come, I hold to the prophecy of Voltaire:

"Young men are lucky! They will see great things!"

What things? Must you know in detail? Then turn to some dictator or other fanatic and swallow his creed. You will get no clear definite answers from me nor from any men of my kind, for by hard experience we know that life does not follow these plans we make. Life keeps changing all the time. Long ago in my novel, The Harbor, I wrote, at the outbreak of the World War:

"I was nearly asleep when I was roused by a thick voice from the harbor. Low in the distance, deep but now rising blast on blast, its waves of sound beat into the city—into millions of ears of sleepers and watchers, the well, the sick and the dying, the dead, the lovers, the schemers, the dreamers, the toilers, the spenders and wasters. I shut my eyes and saw the huge liner moving slowly out of its slip. . . . Bellowing impatiently as it swept out into the stream, it seemed to be saying:

" 'Make way for me! Make way, all you little men! Make way, all you habits and all you institutions, all you little creeds and gods! For I am the start of the voyage—over the ocean to heathen lands! And I am always starting out and always bearing you along! For I am your molder; I am strong—I am a surprise; I am a shock—I am a dazzling passion of hope—I am a grim executioner! I am reality—I am life! I am the book that has no end!' "

As at that time, so now once more I am planning to go abroad. War again! Will we never be free from this curse of all the centuries? How long will it last? How wide will it reach? What kind of world will it leave to us all? I wonder if, before it ends, I shall sit once more some night at a window in that Berlin café, watching an old woman with a bundle of newspapers scream at the people passing by:

"The Future! The Future!"

What will it be—democracy or dictatorship?